PATERNOSTER BIBLICAL M

# Old Testament Story and Christian Ethics

## The Rape of Dinah as a Case Study

PATERNOSTER BIBLICAL MONOGRAPHS

Series Editors

| | |
|---|---|
| I. Howard Marshall | King's College, University of Aberdeen |
| Richard Bauckham | University of St Andrews |
| Craig Blomberg | Denver Theological Seminary |
| Robert P. Gordon | University of Cambridge |
| Tremper Longman III | Westmont College, Santa Barbara |

A full listing of titles in both this series and
Paternoster Theological Monographs
appears at the end of this book

PATERNOSTER BIBLICAL MONOGRAPHS

# Old Testament Story and Christian Ethics

## The Rape of Dinah as a Case Study

Robin Allinson Parry

Foreword by Craig Bartholomew

**PATERNOSTER PRESS**

First published 2004 by Paternoster

Paternoster is an imprint of Authentic Media
9 Holdom Avenue, Bletchley, Milton Keynes, MK1 1QR, UK
and
P.O. Box 1047, Waynesboro, GA 30830–2047, USA

10 09 08 07 06 05 04   7 6 5 4 3 2 1

**British Library Cataloguing in Publication Data**
A catalogue record for this book is available from the British Library

ISBN 1-84227-210-1

Typeset by Robin Parry
Printed and bound in Great Britain
for Paternoster
by Nottingham Alpha Graphics

# Series Preface

One of the major objectives of Paternoster is to serve biblical scholarship by providing a channel for the publication of theses and other monographs of high quality at affordable prices. Paternoster stands within the broad evangelical tradition of Christianity. Our authors would describe themselves as Christians who recognise the authority of the Bible, maintain the centrality of the gospel message and assent to the classical credal statements of Christian belief. There is diversity within this constituency; advances in scholarship are possible only if there is freedom for frank debate on controversial issues and for the publication of new and sometimes provocative proposals. What is offered in this series is the best of writing by committed Christians who are concerned to develop well-founded biblical scholarship in a spirit of loyalty to the historic faith.

*To my three girls*

# Contents

# FOREWORD

As a Christian scholar it is not always easy to be optimistic about biblical studies. Neither the dominance of historical criticism nor the smorgasbord of postmodernism is the most helpful context for reading the Bible as Scripture. However it is the kind of scholarship that Robin Parry has produced in this book that gives me real hope.

Dr. Parry wants to read the Bible to hear God's address, but he never does this simplistically. He is prepared - and exceptionally well equipped - to attend to the many aspects such a theological interpretation of the Bible requires, and he executes these with authority, all the while keeping his attention firmly on the biblical text, in this case the difficult story of the rape of Dinah.

In my opinion Robin is quite right in looking to a narrative or story approach to help get at the Old Testament's ethics. This type of biblical theology is fertile for such analysis, as James Barr has argued. Robin recognises that a narrative approach to Old Testament ethics must draw on insights from philosophical work in this area and he thus casts his net wide and deep. His work is exemplary in its concern for philosophical hermeneutics without getting stuck there – his work on hermeneutics moves him back more strongly to the biblical text, as indeed it should.

Robin combines hermeneutical insight with an examination of the history of interpretation of Genesis 34 and detailed exegesis of this text. The focus on this specific text is a test case for the whole, and it works very well in this regard. Feminist and ideological critique are unavoidable elements of biblical ethics nowadays, and Genesis 34 enables Robin to address these issues in the light of this particular text rather than vague generalities. For biblical ethics the individual text must be related to the canon as a whole and Robin explores this as well.

The range and depth of this book is a tour de force. It is precisely the sort of scholarship so badly needed in biblical studies today. Robin himself notes that his work is of the nature of a prolegomena. My hope is that he will continue to pursue this kind of work for years to come.

*Rev Professor Craig Bartholomew*
*Redeemer University College, Ancaster, Canada.*

# Acknowledgements

I would like to acknowledge with gratitude my debt to those who helped me, in one way or another, in the completion of the thesis. My thanks go to the Bible Society for making the whole project possible by the provision of a very generous grant.

I am especially grateful to Professor Gordon Wenham for teaching me Hebrew from scratch and for his meticulous and wise supervision, and Professor Craig Bartholomew whose constant advice and encouragements meant more than words can say. These two men embody Christian virtues in their lives and scholarship.

Thanks must go also to Janet Tayler for her *painstaking* proof reading of the original PhD. Thanks are due to Anthony Cross for his hard work on the indices and rooted out an unnerving number of little errors in the text. I would also like to acknowledge the time that various busy academics made to talk with me (or reply to my emails) about the content of the thesis. In particular mention must be made of the helpful feedback Melissa Raphael gave me on Chapter Six.

Thanks to Jeremy Mudditt and his noble monograph committee for agreeing to publish the thesis. I know that they take great pains to ensure high academic standards for the series so I count it an honour to have the work accepted. Jeremy Mudditt is a publishing phenomenon who seems to know just about everything one could possibly know about publishing - but then he has literally lived every day of his life under the shadow of the company his Father founded back in 1935, the good ship Paternoster.

I thank Hannah and Jessica for patiently allowing their daddy to be a boring old toad on regular occasions. Words cannot express just how sweet my girls (usually) are. In particular, I honour my wife, Carol, for her constant support for me, and belief in this project. This book is dedicated to the three wonderful girls in my life (though I doubt that any of them will ever be foolish enough to try and read it).

# INTRODUCTION

Until relatively recently Old Testament narrative ethics was a subject rarely
commented on in anything other than the most superficial ways. Given the
sheer number of stories in the Hebrew Bible this is a serious oversight and,
happily, the situation is gradually changing.[1] It is still true, however, that
narrative ethics plays second fiddle to law and wisdom ethics in both the
academy and the church. This book is an attempt to defend the centrality of Old
Testament narratives in the Christian moral life, and to indicate how their
ethical potential can be opened up within Christian Bible-reading communities.

It is crucial for the reader to understand, right at the start, that what I offer
here is *prolegomena* to the Christian ethical reappropriations of Genesis 34
rather than an attempt to offer such a reappropriation. I am concerned with the
*limits within which* Christian ethical readings must live and move and have
their being. There is no such thing as '*the definitive* Christian ethical
interpretation of the story' but it is the case, or so I shall argue, that the
multiplicity of *Christian* interpretations will be located within something close
to the parameters set out in the pages which follow. Obviously, the setting out
of such parameters will require me to make certain claims about appropriate
and inappropriate ethical uses of the story, but the life-changing impact of the
text on the reader is what ethical appropriation is all about and I cannot
prescribe how all readers should respond. All I offer here are guidelines for
Christian readers.

It is also important that the reader appreciates that what I offer is
hermeneutical guidance to *Christian* readers. Anybody can read Old Testament
narratives and make some ethical use of them but precisely how the stories
ethically impact readers will vary enormously depending on the worldviews
through which they are interpreted. This is not to suggest that *all* Christian
readers will take away the same lessons but it is to suggest that a biblically
shaped worldview will set boundaries for Christian ethical interpretation. My
guidelines for Christian readers are to be taken as *prescriptive for, and not
descriptive of, Christian practice*, although one would hope that practice is not

---

[1] See, Wenham, 2000; Mills, 2001; Friedman, 2002. See also my review of Mills in
Parry, 2003b

too far removed from theory.

    One cannot simply read off general conclusions from a single narrative so I have divided the study into two parts. Part One deals with general philosophical and theological issues in the hope of setting up a broadly plausible model for reappropriating Old Testament stories for Christian ethics. These considerations are provisional and subject to refinement and correction in the light of actual ethical interaction with particular texts, but it represents my thinking after several circuits of the hermeneutical spiral. Part Two is an attempt to apply the model to a specific text. Genesis 34 may seem an odd choice in that it is one of the least known stories in the Bible and is in several respects atypical. The reasons behind my choice of it are many and varied but I think that it serves to illustrate quite well how the model I propose could work in practice. At very least, I hope to show the ethical potential of one of the obscure stories of Scripture, hoping that more mainstream plot lines will be at least as fruitful, if not more so.

    Chapter One seeks to achieve two goals. Firstly, it aims to set out the philosophical justifications and foundations for the claim that stories in general are fundamental for the good life. Paul Ricoeur's hermeneutical philosophy is taken as a framework for these reflections and it is argued that our sense of selfhood is narrative in nature and that stories actually shape our self-identity and values. The chapter moves on to consider different ways in which stories can ethically shape readers. It is argued that they exemplify general models of good or bad characters and actions, that they teach attention to particularity, that they train readers in emotional perception, and that they can even contribute to the very grammar of what virtues and moral rules are. What is true of narrative in general is, I maintain, no less true of *biblical* narrative. The second goal is to provide some contours for the hermeneutical strategy to be employed in the book. This is achieved by means of the exploration of Ricoeur mentioned above. The reader may feel that I spend too long on Ricoeur for the *ethical* cash value of his thinking. My justification for dwelling so long on his work is that he also provides some contours for my hermeneutical approach and I judge that to have two sections on him (one for ethics and one for more general interpretation) would lead to unnecessary repetition.

Chapter Two is an exercise in Old Testament theology. Here also the chapter engages in two Herculean tasks. Firstly, I attempt to demonstrate that narratives are central to the ethics of the Old Testament and that their neglect leads to a serious distortion of those ethics. John Barton has identified three models for ethics in the Old Testament: the imitation of God, divine commands and natural law. I explore the links between narrative and these models in an attempt to show that narrative is crucial to all of them. Thus the centrality of biblical stories to Christian ethics is put on solid philosophical grounds as well as solid biblical grounds. The second task is to defend a theological hermeneutic proposed by N.T. Wright. Wright argued that Christian readers of the Bible should read it first and foremost as a single super-story in which all the parts of the plot are interpreted *in the light of the whole*. My concern is to explain and defend this claim with an eye to demonstrating its impact on ethics in Chapter Five.

Part Two moves on to examine the case study. Ricoeur, among others, argues that all readers stand within a reading tradition both in terms of methodology (Chapter Two) and interpretations of particular texts (Chapter Three). Interpretation is better served if the reader is aware of their tradition and the insights of previous readers. Chapter Three takes samples of Jewish and Christian ethical appropriations of Genesis 34 from *Jubilees* to Sternberg and from Tertullian to David Gunn. It becomes clear that there is considerable disagreement over the moral evaluations of *all* the different characters in the story and that significantly different moral lessons have been drawn out. These reflections raise some of the key questions that the following chapters investigate.

Ricoeur, following Gadamer, sees the importance of distancing a text before attempting to appropriate it. Chapter Four attempts to do just this. First of all, the literary structure of the chapter is considered and then its place within the structure of the book of Genesis. These structural insights guide the following interpretation. The rest of the chapter proceeds by taking each Scene and doing a careful exegesis of it. My work on that chapter was also guided by the detailed discourse analysis provided in Appendix One. I have kept it separate from the main chapter so as not to drown readers in a mass of detail. Those who like such detail may refer to the Appendix. The text is allowed to set its own agenda, as far is as possible, in an attempt to set up limits for interpretations. I maintain that Christian interpretations need to respect the integrity of the text in its literary context. It is argued that the narrator will not allow his readers to give unqualified approval or disapproval to any of the characters in the story. The difficulty of the situation is accentuated, and complexity of the characters makes evaluating their choices difficult. It is also argued that the massacre is disapproved of by the narrator, but that the readers are left to ponder how the sons *should* have acted. No answers are given other than those a reader may care to provide.

Chapter Five puts Genesis 34 into the context of the whole biblical canon. Firstly, our story is related to several Old Testament intertexts (Gen 49:5-7, Ex 32-34, Num 25, 31) in order to demonstrate that the Old Testament generally does not reverse our conclusions about the narratorial disapproval of the massacre at Shechem. I argue that Genesis 49:5-7 indicates *divine* disapproval of Simeon and Levi and that God backs up the curse Jacob places upon them. This curse, in the case of Simeon, is never reversed, but in the case of Levi, we can trace a plot line whereby God transforms the curse into a blessing in response to Levitical zeal for him. Secondly, Genesis 34 is shown to be a story about the patriarchal age that has been read from the perspective of the Mosaic age. I suggest that the narrator exploits the similarities and differences between the two dispensations by giving the massacre a double function: it is a model of a *wrong* response to a terrible situation but it is also an antitype of the quite *legitimate* (from his perspective) conquest of Canaan. This dual function is what has led to some of the confusions in the history of reading the text over the years. Finally, Genesis 34 is read from the perspective of the New Testament. It is argued that this shift in plot from Moses to Jesus leads to significant changes in the way Genesis 34 should be appropriated. Christian readers cannot apply the text to themselves in the same ways that the original readers could have, nor in totally different ways.

By this point I hope to have set out the exegetical and theological fences which mark out the territory of Christian ethical readings. As stressed at the start, I have not actually produced an ethical appropriation but leave that to each reading community in the diverse situations they face. Much remains to be said about how the context of readers and their reading communities affects appropriation, but there are limits to what one can achieve in one book and thus I leave that important task for another.

It has been assumed throughout chapters One to Five that a Christian can approach the Bible in an attitude of trust in seeking divine guidance for the moral life. This has been the practice of the Christian community for two millennia but it is a practice that has been subjected to serious and sustained critique in recent years. Feminist readers, for instance, often approach the Bible with suspicion, seeing it as a tool for the oppression of women, and this claim serves as a potential defeater to the trusting approach advocated in the previous chapters.[2] I explore the feminist challenge, asking how far a traditional Christian can take on board the suspicions of the critic. It is argued in Chapter Six that feminist hermeneutics opens up important ways of re-reading old stories and that, within certain limits, these do not undermine the authority of the biblical canon for Christian ethics. I propose that imaginative, *midrashic* retellings of stories such as Genesis 34 from the perspective of the silent women are ethically beneficial and complement the approach discussed in the previous chapters.

The argument of this book has required me to range over philosophy, theology, history of interpretation, linguistics, exegesis, feminism, not to mention attempting to give an account that claims to apply potentially to *any* story in the Bible. To become relatively well read on all these topics is too big a task for a mere mortal as the secondary literature on any one of them is vast. Arguably, one would also wish to take sociological studies and reader-response studies into account but lines have to be drawn. What I hope I have achieved is a contribution towards a plausible hermeneutical model which can guide Christian readers towards legitimate Christian embodiments of Old Testament stories in their communal and individual lives.

---

[2] On the notion of a defeater see Plantinga, 2000, pp. 357-366.

**Part One**

# A Hermeneutic

# Chapter One

# Philosophical Reflections on Narrative Ethics

*We are part human, part stories* - Ben Okri[1]

*I can only answer the question, "What am I to do?" if I can answer the prior question, "Of what story or stories do I find myself a part?"* - Alasdair MacIntyre[2]

*Stories are the secret reservoir of values: change the stories individuals or nations live by and tell themselves, and you change the individuals and nations* - Ben Okri[3]

This book is an attempt to argue that Old Testament stories are ethically valuable and to set up some guidelines for *Christian* ethical *re*appropriation of such OT narratives. To demonstrate the importance of biblical narratives, we must first seek to clarify why narratives in general are important for moral education. This chapter seeks to accomplish that goal. Once it is clear why narratives have such life-shaping potential, it should also be clear how the *biblical* stories can ethically shape readers. So our first task is a philosophical one, akin to laying foundations which will be built upon in later chapters.

The chapter will progress in two phases: First I shall to set up a framework within which the diverse contributions of narrative to ethics can be located. Using the work of Paul Ricoeur, I shall argue that narratives play a major role in shaping individual and community identity, and that ethics finds its home within such narrative identity. In the course of our analysis of Ricoeur we shall establish some hermeneutical strategies for the task ahead.

Secondly, having established the framework, I shall set out some of the central contributions of narrative to ethics. Here the work of philosophers such as Robert C. Roberts and Martha Nussbaum can find a fruitful home. I shall

---

1 Okri, 1996, p. 24.
2 MacIntyre, 1996, p. 216.
3 Okri, 1996, p. 21.

argue that:

- narrative can exemplify virtues or general principles of action.
- narrative can raise the particularity of specific situations to new heights.
- narrative can train us in the emotional perception essential to ethical wisdom.
- within a particular tradition narrative can, at times, even refine the very concept of a virtue or a duty.

## The Framework: The Narrative Shape of the Self

We begin with an analysis of the work of Paul Ricoeur, a contemporary philosopher, who maintains that the identity of individuals and communities is essentially an identity constituted by narratives. It would be a mistake to imagine that philosophies of narrative identity are "the only game in town" and it is useful, if only to give some context, to indicate how they may be located within the broader field of philosophies of self. Kelly James Clark suggests that theories of self-identity fall into two basic categories: abstract theories and narrative theories.[4] Abstract theories seek what is essential in human nature and posit identity in terms of the dualist's non-physical souls, or the materialist's bodies with their spatio-temporal continuity. Both dualism and materialism can, in turn, be sub-divided and sub-sub-divided. However, they have in common a self which is not constituted in any significant way by its context but is an a-historical, a-cultural, a-social given. Vernon White[5] surveys recent academic work and concludes that this *purely* "abstract self" has had its day:[6]

> We are formed as individual persons, at least in part, by our conscious and unconscious relationship with the past and with other persons and social realities in the present. This is the massive consensus verdict of both sociological and psychological anthropology... This abstract self fails the tests of empirical evidence, common sense and conceptual analysis.[7]

Self-awareness varies greatly from one culture to another and does not seem to be a given but a construction.[8] After all, what would a self be like that had no cultural and social input?

---

4 Kelly J. Clark, "The Storied Self", unpublished paper. My thanks to Professor Clark for allowing me to see a copy of this paper.
5 White, 1996.
6 I hasten to add that I merely claim that abstract approaches on their own are inadequate and not that they need to be replaced by narrative approaches.
7 White, 1996, pp. 59, 61.
8 Ibid., pp. 60-61.

What are the prospects for a post-abstract self? It is here that narrative theories come into play. Several contemporary philosophers have championed the narrated-self including Charles Taylor, Alasdair MacIntyre and Seyla Benhabib. This book will focus on the work of Paul Ricoeur because he sets his philosophy of the storied self within a broader narrative hermeneutic, enabling us to set out more clearly how narrative ethically shapes audiences. I shall use Ricoeur's writings to establish theoretical support for the following claims: that individuals and communities do not come with ready-made identities but find their identities in and through narratives; that human life calls out to be transformed into narrative *and in turn (ethically) transformed by narrative*; that responsible ethical reading of stories requires both distancing of the horizons of text and reader as well as a merging of those horizons; that readers of stories cannot step outside a reading tradition, although they can innovate within traditions; that texts feed the ethical imagination of the reader by proposing "worlds" which the reader can explore and try out ways of evaluating actions. The second part of this chapter will then build upon the theoretical foundation laid by Ricoeur by clarifying different ways in which narratives can ethically refigure readers.

Ricoeur's thought is like a carefully spun spider's web in which all the parts interweave and interlock. The best way to proceed in the first half of this chapter is to enter the web through Ricoeur's philosophy of self. This will lead us quickly into criss-crossing the web of his narrative philosophy before exiting where we began. This method will allow us to see how the claims I wish to support can be situated within the context of a whole system of thought, the coherence of which lends some weight to the justification of its parts.[9]

## Paul Ricoeur on the Narrative Self

Throughout his philosophical career Paul Ricoeur has been preoccupied with what it means to be a thinking, reflective subject. His journey takes place in two complementary movements. In the first he employs a hermeneutic of suspicion in order to expose the illusions of the Cartesian self. In the second he attempts a post-critical reappropriation of the self through hermeneutics. Indeed he claims that the goal of *all* hermeneutics is *self*-understanding.

### The First Movement in the Search for the Self: Clearing Away the Rubbish

It has been traditional in philosophy since Descartes to see the self as having immediate and reliable access to itself by means of simple introspection. The Cartesian view sees the self as a "given" and perhaps as having what Ricoeur calls *idem* identity.[10] That is to say, the inflexible, static identity of a thing which stays the same. At the other end of the spectrum stands Nietzsche and his

---

9 I am not suggesting that coherence is sufficient for justification, but it is necessary.
10 Ricoeur, 1992, pp. 4-11.

deconstructive heirs who can doubt even more spectacularly than Descartes and dissolve the certainty of *cogito* in the deceitfulness of language.[11] Ricoeur wants to situate his hermeneutical philosophy of self at an equal distance from Descartes' *cogito* and Nietzsche's anticogito.[12] The Ricoeurian self is not a metaphysical substance and does not have direct access to itself via consciousness. In order to demolish the Cartesian privileging of consciousness Ricoeur brings Freud's psychoanalysis into play.[13] Freud demotes consciousness "from its focal position as the viewpoint from which all investigations of the internal mental life proceed."[14] Freud reduces everything *from* consciousness and in the process "wounds" the ego by displacing it from the centre. Consciousness is not the source of meaning but is, in fact, often *false* consciousness. As Freud says, "the subject is never the subject one thinks it is."[15] Ricoeur's search for the self begins by refusing the short cut offered by Descartes. This first step is negative and complicating, demoting the ego from being the master of its own house. Thus, for Ricoeur, Freud enters into his hermeneutics not in order to produce a so-called "psycho-analytic reading" but in order to destroy a certain notion of the reader. The readers do not come to a text complete and in full possession of themselves. On the contrary, they are open to being shaped by the text. After Freud, the task of self-understanding is going to be more of an effort - a long, indirect route that will never be completed, but still a legitimate undertaking.[16]

*The Second Movement in the Search for the Self - Ricoeur's "Long Road of Awareness"*
The second movement in Ricoeur's hermeneutics of self-understanding comes in a post-critical, "second naivete". He has deconstructed one "self" only to reconstruct another, but the whole notion of self-understanding needs to be rethought. Ricoeur writes, "The subject of self-reflection is not a given but a *task*."[17] That is to say, the self does not come into the world with a ready-made identity. Rather it is a dynamic, mutable self with self-sameness (character) and self-constancy (true to its promises) but not immutability. This notion requires some unpacking. In *The Symbolism of Evil*[18] Ricoeur argues that meaning does not originate in the subject but comes to the self from outside in symbols. The self is not immediately present-to-itself (contra Descartes) but is only indirectly present to itself in symbols mediated by a culture.[19] Later Ricoeur shifts his

---

11 Ibid., pp. 11-16.
12 Ibid., p. 23.
13 Ricoeur's main text on Freud is Ricoeur, 1970.
14 Blamey, 1995, p. 590.
15 Quoted in Madison, 1995, p. 80.
16 See especially, Dunne, 1996, on Ricoeur's mediation of Descartes and Nietzsche.
17 Quoted in Blamey, 1995, p. 596. Italics mine.
18 Ricoeur, 1967.
19 Madison, 1995, p. 78.

focus from symbols to metaphors[20] and then to texts.[21] The climax of Ricoeur's philosophy of the self is his closely argued work, *Oneself as Another*. The book is a "philosophy of detours"[22] which searches for answers to the polyvalent question, "Who?" This question can be posed as, "Who is speaking?" "Who is acting?" "Who is telling his or her story?" and finally, "Who is the subject of moral imputation?" Before examining the account of narrative identity developed in *Oneself as Another* we shall need to set out Ricoeur's philosophy of narrative hermeneutics, an account which reaches its pinnacle in *Time and Narrative*. This detour will enable us to see the supporting radial structures of the web upon which the philosophy of self can be woven.

### Ricoeur's Narrative Hermeneutic

How can story shape the actions of readers? Ricoeur's answer to this question is to consider the relation between the world of human living and the world of a narrative.[23] He begins with Aristotle's pairing of *muthos* (the activity of emplotment) and *mimesis* (the activity of representation). Aristotle pays great attention to the way in which action is transformed by *mimesis* in the act of emplotment. However, in *The Poetics* he pays little attention to the impact such narratives would have on their audiences. Ricoeur plans to rectify this oversight and develops Aristotle's notion of mimesis into a *three-fold* notion.[24]

- Mimesis$_1$ – the prefiguration.
- Mimesis$_2$ – the configuration.
- Mimesis$_3$ – the refiguration.

This three-fold notion is absolutely central to Ricoeur's project and is especially interesting for us. Hermeneutics must show how the text arises from "the opaque depths of living, acting, and suffering"[25] to its being received by readers who have their acting changed by it.[26] The prefiguration is the world of

---

20  See Ricoeur, 1978.

21  See Ricoeur, 1984, 1985, 1988.

22  Ricoeur, 1992, p. 17.

23  Although Ricoeur often discusses the elements of narrative he never sets out a simple definition. Hettema helpfully suggests Ricoeur's Aristotelian definition of narrative is as follows: "Narrative is a form of discursive communication which consists of heterogeneous elements that are arranged together by means of a plot; this plot causes the narrative to function as a certain mimesis of the world of action" (Hettema, 1996, p. 58). To this definition one would need to add that, for Ricoeur, the temporal unity created by a plot is a 'discordant concordance'.

24  "Mimesis and Representation" (1980 reprinted in Valdés, 1991) is a very helpful summary of the ideas this section and those which follow.

25  Ibid., p. 139.

26  Ibid., p. 140.

action prior to its narrative shaping in a text. Thus it is *pre*-figuration. The artist then shapes and transforms the prefigurative world of action through the mimetic activity (configuration). But that is not the end of the story. The readers then *re*-figure the action as they appropriate the narrative in the act of reading. Thus we can trace an arc of transformation: action is transformed by an author in narrative and then works its way back into the lived world as the reader finds his or her own action shaped by the narrative.

> I propose to show that mimesis$_2$ draws its intelligibility from the faculty of mediation, which is to conduct us from one side of the text to the other, transfiguring the one side into the other through the power of its configuration.[27]

We can already begin to see the potential of Ricoeur's hermeneutic for an understanding of how biblical narratives can refigure action by transforming the reader. We shall proceed to clarify the three-fold notion of *mimesis*.

*Mimesis$_1$ – The Prefiguration*

When speaking of mimesis$_1$ Ricoeur is drawing attention to the claim that human life cries out to be narrated. To perceive the proto-narrative structures of lived life helps us to begin to see *why* story is so powerful in reflecting and transforming it. Ricoeur sums up the heart of his claims about the prefiguration as follows:

> The composition of the plot is grounded in a pre-understanding of the world of action, its meaningful structures, its symbolic resources, and its temporal character.[28]

This quotation needs some unpacking.

- *Meaningful Structures of Prefiguration.* If plot is an imitation of action then we must already be capable of identifying the structural features of action - already capable of distinguishing action from physical movement. Action implies the existence of goals and motives and responsible agents. More than that action is always *inter*action - with others or towards others. So of actions we can ask, "What?" "Why?" "Who?" "How?" "With whom?" "Against whom?" There is a structural, conceptual network composed of the elements of action which we master in "practical understanding".[29] Now the configuration of action in narrative relates to this in two ways: First, every narrative *presupposes* familiarity by the reader with concepts like "agent", "goal", "circumstance", "help", "conflict". Second, narrative

---

27  Ricoeur, 1984, p. 53.
28  Ricoeur, 1984, p. 54.
29  Ibid., p. 55.

*transforms* the prefigurative structural network of action by means of the addition of plot. Ricoeur thinks of the network like a paradigmatic order in which terms relative to action are synchronic. The narrative is a syntagmatic order which is irreducibly diachronic. "To understand a narrative is to master the rules that govern its syntagmatic order."[30] This is more than simply to understand the semantic network of actions – it is to follow the plot. The prefigurative structure (mimesis$_1$) is thus the paradigmatic order whilst the configuration (mimesis$_2$) is the syntagmatic order and terms with a mere *capacity* for use in mimesis$_1$ receive an actual signification in mimesis$_2$.

- *Symbolic Resources of Prefiguration.* If human action can be articulated "it is because it is always already articulated by signs, rules and norms." Symbolism is not "in the mind" but "a meaning incorporated into action and decipherable from it by other actors in the social interplay."[31] Symbolic systems pre-exist texts and provide the context for actions. Certain actions "make sense" within symbolic contexts which invest those actions with particular significance. This makes action in the prefiguration a *quasi*-text.[32]
- *Temporal Character of Prefiguration.* Narrative time "grafts its configurations" onto prefigurative time. Prefigurative time calls out for narrative transformation but is not itself narrative in structure. We see in our lives "(as yet) untold" stories or potential stories. It is from this background that told stories emerge. Humans are "entangled in stories." "We tell stories because in the last analysis human lives need and merit being narrated."[33]

It should be clear that prefiguration does *not* refer to the unstructured world of action prior to any narrative figuration. It preludes narrative figuration but it is still figuration.[34] Some care needs to be taken in avoiding seeing too sharp a break between mimesis$_1$ and mimesis$_2$. It is only within a narrative context that "actions" are infused with meaning and become actions in the *full* sense of the word. Without such a context they are meaningless and thus not actions, for actions are performed for a *telos*. They have a beginning, middle and *end*. Plot gives actions their intelligibility.[35]

Alasdair MacIntyre shows how human actions cannot be understood apart from a narrative context that Ricoeur would term mimesis$_1$. Human action, he

30 Ricoeur, 1984, p. 56.
31 Ibid., p. 57.
32 Ibid., p. 58; "Life" in Valdés, 1991, pp. 433-434.
33 Ricoeur, 1984, p. 75.
34 Hettema, 1996, pp. 49-51.
35 Motive too requires a narrative context as motive requires the telos that plot provides. Ricoeur says, "it seems that for a motive to have explanatory force, it must be given in the form of a kind of small autobiography. By that I mean that I must put my motive under the rules of story telling." Ricoeur, 1984, p. 83.

argues, must be seen in terms of intentionality, and intentionality "cannot be characterised independently of the settings which make those intentions intelligible both to agents themselves and to others."[36] Thus an account of actions presupposes an account of intentions and an account of intentions presupposes an account of settings. By "setting" MacIntyre means to designate institutions or practices.[37] Critically all such "settings" have histories and the histories of individual agents have to be seen within these larger histories. Consider this example given by MacIntyre: Imagine looking at a man gardening and answering the question, "What is he doing?" One could give several answers – "digging", "gardening", "taking exercise", "preparing for winter" or "pleasing his wife". Some of these answers characterise the man's intentions, whilst others pinpoint unintended consequences of his action. His primary intention could be any one of the above and any of the above could serve as incidental consequences of his act. The same act could manifest very different kinds of behavior. If his primary intention is to prepare for winter then we must situate the episode in

> an annual cycle of domestic activity, and the behaviour embodies an intention
> which presupposes a particular type of household-cum-garden setting with the

---

36  MacIntyre, 1996, p. 206.

37  By a "practice" he means "any coherent and complex form of socially established co-operative human activity through which goods internal to that form of activity are realised in the course of trying to achieve those standards of excellence which are appropriate to, and partially definitive of, that form of activity, with the result that human powers to achieve excellence, and human conceptions of the ends and goods involved, are systematically extended. Tic-tac-toe is not an example of a practice in this sense, nor is throwing a football with skill; but the game of football is, and so is chess. Bricklaying is not a practice; architecture is. Planting turnips is not a practice, farming is. So are the enquiries of physics, chemistry and biology, and so is the work of the historian, and so are painting and music. In the ancient and medieval worlds the creation and sustaining of human communities – of households, cities, nations – is generally taken to be a practice in the sense in which I have defined it. Thus the range of practices is wide: arts, sciences, games, politics in the Aristotelian sense, the making and sustaining of family life, all fall under the concept" (1996, pp. 187-188). One needs to distinguish a practice (e.g. chess, medicine) from institutions (e.g. chess clubs, hospitals) which try to maintain the traditions of the practice (ibid., p. 194). To enter into a practice is to enter into a relationship with its past and present practitioners – to position oneself within a tradition (ibid., p. 194). Practice does for MacIntyre what the notion of human telos did for Aristotle (Nelson, 1987, p. 51). For MacIntyre the context within which the virtues may be specified is no longer a cosmic order but practices internal to human activity. A virtue is an acquired human quality which enables us to achieve goods internal to practices. The Christian may feel uncomfortable with this as the Christian metanarrative proposes a cosmic order of creation which forms the context for Christian virtues (see Chapter Two). MacIntyre is correct, however, to argue that such a there is no worldview-neutral place from which to discern this cosmic order.

peculiar narrative history of that setting in which this segment of behaviour now becomes an episode.[38]

On the other hand, if he is doing it to please his wife

the episode must be situated in the narrative history of a marriage... We cannot... characterise behaviour independently of intentions, and we cannot characterise intentions independently of the settings which make those intentions intelligible...[39]

MacIntyre thus argues that human action needs situating in two contexts: The actor's own history and the history of the setting(s), e.g. marriage or gardening as institutions.[40]

Peter Kemp has argued that the world of action is *already* storied.[41] Lived life prefigures the configuration more clearly than Ricoeur is willing to admit. Although not commenting on Ricoeur, MacIntyre makes the same point in *After Virtue* where he claims that "stories are lived before they are told."[42] Richard Kearney[43] has suggested that mimesis$_1$ is not so much *pre*-narrative as *ana*-narrative. That is to say that it does not come *before* narrative but *re-lives life in the light of narrative*. Once story feeds back into the lived world of hearers or readers, that world is transformed and is not pre-narrative any more. Indeed, I would maintain that there is no *actual* world that is pure pre-narrative. It is perhaps best to think of mimesis$_1$ as an abstract grammar for narrative which is actualised in human attempts to understand life whether written or not. However, this is not to say that lived life is *just* like a narrative. When we tell our stories we do *augment* experience, as will be demonstrated later, and to this extent Ricoeur is correct in distinguishing life from narrative. To summarise: the prefiguration, human life with its proto-narrative structure, calls out to be narrated and it is in response to this call that the story-teller responds in the configuration.

### Mimesis$_2$ – The Configuration

Mimesis$_2$[44] is the mediation between mimesis$_1$ and mimesis$_3$. Individual incidents become events when they find a place in a plot. A story thus places

---

38 MacIntyre, 1996, p. 206.
39 Ibid., p. 206.
40 Ibid., p. 208.
41 Kemp, 1989.
42 MacIntyre, 1996, p. 212.
43 In an email to me dated 16/6/99.
44 The reason that Ricoeur talks of mimesis2 as "configuration" is so as to side-step the notions of reference and truth at this stage in his enquiry.

events into an intelligible whole.[45] Ricoeur talks of how a plot unites *heterogeneous elements*. He has in mind things such as characters, events, incidents, motives, circumstances, actions and the like (the structural dimension of the prefiguration). Emplotting allows us to take a sequence of events in natural time and to see a story by "grasping together" the individual incidents, characters and actions as a unified, narrative-temporal whole or, what he calls, a concordance. In its chronology it reflects the episodic nature of life but such episodes are not simply seen one at a time but are also "grasped together".[46] Narrative thus holds in tension the episodic nature of cosmological time and the wholeness of human time. The reader is enabled to see the whole of the story from the end-point in a new light.[47] Now, this "grasping as a whole", the notion of beginning, middle and end in narrative, the exclusion of vacuous time and the ability to abandon chronology by use of flashbacks is very *unlike* lived life, arising instead from the activity of *muthos*. On the other hand, the episodic nature of narrative draws narrative time in the direction of the linear representation of time (then... and then... and then...).[48] So stories transform pre-narrative experience.[49]

So for Ricoeur, following Aristotle, narrative is a completeness, a wholeness or a concordance.[50] But Ricoeur wants to add a dimension of *discordance* within plot.[51] Narratives are full of surprise or fearful and tragic events that threaten the plot's coherence. "The art of composition consists in making this discordance appear concordant"[52] by placing it within the latter. Thus plot succeeds in precariously holding together elements which are constantly pulling the unity apart. So narrative is a discordant concordance and *mimesis* is not simply a copy of some pre-existing reality[53] but "creative imagination".[54]

---

45 Ricoeur, 1984, p. 65.

46 L.O. Mink's expression quoted in "Human Experience", in Valdés, 1991, p. 106.

47 "In reading the ending in the beginning and the beginning in the ending, we also learn to read time itself backwards" (Ricoeur, 1984, pp. 67-68).

48 Ibid., p. 67.

49 Subject to the qualifications mentioned at the end of the previous section.

50 Ricoeur, 1984, p. 38.

51 Ibid., p. 42.

52 Ibid., p. 43. The product of the literary artist is not a thing but a "quasi-thing", an "as-if", which Ricoeur describes as "the literariness of literature" (ibid., p. 45). But mimesis2 is not only a break with real life - it also connects to it. Praxis belongs to the lived world of ethics and the imaginary world of poetics so that we have "the 'metaphorical' transposition of the practical field by the muthos" (ibid., p. 46). Muthos indicates discontinuity with the pre-narrative world but praxis (by its double allegiance) assures continuity (ibid., p. 47).

53 Now Plato had a rather dim view of representation (mimesis) as it was, for him, two levels removed from reality. Thus a particular just action (say) is a dim reflection of the Form of Justice (reality) and the playwright's representation of the action is a dim reflection of the particular act: "a shadow of a shadow" ("Function", p. 130, "Mimesis",

The potential of narrative to shape readers is located in its potential to project "worlds" for them to "explore". To understand this we shall need to understand Ricoeur's thinking on sense and reference in texts. Writing, according to Ricoeur, totally changes the dynamics of the communicative situation as a result of the distanciation from the dialogical situation.[55] In a dialogical situation someone in particular is addressed and he or she has a chance to ask questions or respond to the speaker. Most of the texts which we read are not addressed to us in particular and the author is inaccessible to us for interrogation. There is in fact a "double eclipse" produced by the text as the writer is not aware of who in particular may read the text and the reader cannot gain access to the writer: "The reader is absent from the act of writing; the writer is absent from the act of reading."[56] The text generates its sense by its internal relations and *not* from its author's intentions (understood as private psychical experiences) thus it is liberated from being bound to one time or place. This sense, in turn, "projects" a "possible-way-of-being-in-the-world". It is this "world" projected by the text which is its referent and not items in the actual world as with spoken discourse. Indeed it is precisely *because* the referents in the dialogical situation are not available that this second level of reference is looked for. I find this attempt to obliterate authorial intention overstated. Recent works by Wolterstorff, Thisleton, Vanhoozer and Walhout have demonstrated that a Speech-Act Theory can reinstate authorial intention understood not as private psychical experiences, which Ricoeur rightly resists, but as public communicative action.[57] Walhout has shown that this need not turn us away from an examination of the "world" of a text but simply proposes that the world is projected *by an author's textually embodied intentions*.[58] So in following Ricoeur's thinking on world projection we need not follow him in rejecting all notion of authorial intention.

So what is this "world" which a text projects? Ricoeur seems to mean something like "the theme(s), values and possibilities for action presented to

---

p. 138 both in Valdés, 1991). It was not so for Aristotle and is not so for Ricoeur. Ricoeur sees art as more real not less real as it augments (condenses, spells out, develops) reality ("Function" in Valdés, 1991, p. 130). As Kearney explains, "Far from producing only weakened images of reality – shadows, as in the Platonic treatment of the eikon in painting or writing (Phaedrus 274e-277e) – literary works depict reality by augmenting it with meanings that themselves depend upon the virtues of abbreviation, saturation and culmination, so strikingly illustrated by emplotment" (Kearney, 1998, p. 161). For Aristotle mimesis is not an identical replica of reality (Ricoeur, 1984, p. 34) but produces muthos thus transforming pre-narrated action.

54 On Imagination in Ricoeur see especially Kearney, 1989 and 1998.

55 "What is a Text?" (1970) reprinted in Valdes, 1991, pp. 44-45.

56 Ibid., p. 45.

57 Vanhoozer, 1998; Wolterstorff, 1995; Thisleton, 1992; Walhout, 1999.

58 Walhout, 1999. Vanhoozer argues that Ricoeur himself hints in places at the importance of the author (1998, pp. 214-217).

the implied reader *by means of* the states of affairs linked by the plot and depicted in the text."[59] Vanhoozer writes that, "This notion of 'the world of the text' is perhaps Ricoeur's most important contribution to interpretation theory... It is 'the world of human values and existential possibilities'" – "the scope of our possibilities."[60] This world is

> that trait of every literary work by which it opens up a horizon of possible experience, a world in which it would be possible to live. A text... is the projection of a new universe, different from the one in which we live.[61]

Narrative fiction and poetic texts have a metaphorical reference, which is to say that they do not describe the world but they give new ways of seeing the world.

Ricoeur insists that both history and fiction are narrative in form, meaning that both use the plot to organise and unify their parts. He spends considerable time clarifying the similarities and differences between the two.[62] So as to avoid too sharp a distinction he proposes a "fictionalisation of historiography" and a "historicisation of fiction".[63] The key difference is on the level of reference. Fiction does not have any obligation to refer to *real* people or *real* events. By contrast history owes a "debt to the past" and is thus constrained in a way that fiction is not.[64]

---

59 Hettema describes the 'world' as "the presuppositions, norms and intentions which underlie actions in the text – the imaginative world in which the narrative agent lives" (Hettema, 1996, p. 32). It is, in Ricoeur's words, "a world that I might inhabit and into which I project my ownmost powers" (Ricoeur, 1984, p. 81, italics mine).
60 Vanhoozer, 1990, pp. 88-89, 91.
61 "Life" in Valdés, 1991, p. 431.
62 Ricoeur, 1984, 1985, 1988.
63 Fiction being presented "as-if" it had happened. "Narrative Function" in Valdés, 1991, provides a useful summary and see Ricoeur, 1988, ch. 8 for more detail.
64 Reference in history (See Petit, 1988, on Ricoeur and historiography): Ricoeur proposes an analogical theory of historiography. The past, being other, cannot be presented in the present but it can be represented. All history is a reconstruction of how the past could have gone – a sign that points beyond itself to a real past that the historian never adequately captures (Ricoeur, 1988, ch. 6). Thus history has an indirect reference to reality via traces, documents and archives. Ricoeur talks of history as quasi-narrative shaped by a quasi-plot including quasi-characters and quasi-events. The "debt to the past" inherent in historical narrative has ethical implications - a duty not to forget the stories of those who have suffered - which are highlighted clearly in the work of Richard Kearney (Kearney, 1996a, 1998).
     Reference in Fiction: Fiction has, at the level of the work rather than the sentence, a split level of reference. It does not refer to reality at a literal level but it generates a metaphorical referent (its world) which refers to reality through the reader. The "reality" that is shaped by the text is the "world" of the reader. But in Time and Narrative Vol. III Ricoeur shifts from the language of reference to the language of effects (Vanhoozer, 1990, pp. 98-99; Ricoeur, 1988, ch. 7, p. 159) and talks of how texts refigure the world

Ricoeur sometimes seems to speak of world-projection as a function of narrative texts in general but on other occasions seems to reserve the privilege of world-projection for fiction.[65] Of the two narrative modes he certainly seems to favour fiction.[66] It sets before the imagination situations that make up thought experiments by which we learn to join the ethical aspect of human behaviour to happiness and unhappiness.[67] "Ricoeur fears that descriptive language stifles the passion for the possible by confining us within the limits of the present, and closes our imagination to the future."[68] This preference for fiction is not something that a Christian should feel comfortable with. History too can transform its readers by offering possible ways of being-in-the-world which stand in contrast to their present experiences.[69] History *on its own* is not enough for the Christian imagination because human history is sin-infected and this limits our possibilities. Eschatology is a necessary "fictional" complement for history, but it is fictional in a special sense – in the sense that it outlines future, *as yet* unrealised, human possibilities but *not* in the sense that it is a human imaginative creation.[70] Fiction in the normal sense is also important, as Ricoeur says, but it is doubtful that stories about quasi-events provide *more* fruitful soil for the creative imagination than stories about actual events. Indeed the Christian claim is that it is the stories about actual events in salvation

---

of the reader rather than refer to it. Any "reference" to reality is indirect and via the reader. "The phenomenology of fiction has its starting point in the nothingness of the referent. This opens new ways of referring to reality." Not a "reproductive reference" (like history) but a "productive reference" ("Function", in Valdés, 1991, p. 121).

65 It seems to me that some fictional texts do not project genuine possibilities. For example, some fictions can present logically impossible worlds for the reader's consideration. As a possible example, think of science fiction stories in which temporal paradoxes are created (i.e., a man becomes his own father). There are some who do not see temporal paradoxes as logical contradictions but if this example is disallowed more could be produced. On top of that, some science fictions present futures which are not logically impossible but seem to me to be actually humanly impossible. Consider the Star Trek vision of a future paradise-like earth in which there is no crime, greed, hate or selfishness. This radical transformation is the result of technological development and human rationality. It is impossible given the nature of human sin. This Star Trek world, in this aspect at least, is consequently not a genuinely possible world.

66 "Could we not say, in conclusion, that by opening us to what is different, history opens us to the possible, whereas fiction, by opening us to the unreal, leads us to what is essential in reality" ("Narrative Function", in Valdes, 1991, p. 296). Thus "poetry is more philosophical... than history" (Aristotle quoted in ibid., p. 296. See Vanhoozer, 1990, pp.192-196) in that its stories reveal universal aspects of the human condition.

67 "Life" in Valdés, 1991, p. 428.

68 Vanhoozer, 1990, p. 282.

69 Thiselton, 1992, p. 357.

70 Christian theology roots its eschatological hope in the promise of God made in the resurrection of Jesus: a fact of history (or so the church has traditionally claimed).

history that form the most fruitful soil for imaginative reflection.[71]

Now, in fact, biblical narrative does not fit either of Ricoeur's narrative types. It is not historiography in the modern sense nor is it fiction in Ricoeur's sense. Ricoeur seems to polarise narrative such that it splits into "two radically distinct types."[72] I think that it is better to see Ricoeur's types as two ends of a spectrum with biblical narratives placed at different locations between the two.[73] Ricoeur himself seems to recognise that biblical narrative cannot be fitted into his duality of narrative types[74] although in practice he seems to treat it as fiction.[75] In this book it will be assumed that any narrative can project a world and that wherever we place Genesis 34 on the history-fiction spectrum its capacity to contribute to the ethical potency of the "world" projected by Genesis is not impeded.[76]

So story-telling both reflects and transforms the human experience of lived life. Stories project worlds that can transform lived experience through the act of reading. To this we now turn.

*Mimesis3 – The Refiguration*

"Narrative has its full meaning when it is restored to the time of action and of suffering in mimesis₃."[77] Mimesis₃ is what Gadamer[78] calls "application". It is "understanding" or the "intersection" of the world of the text with the world of the reader.[79] It is the climax of the hermeneutical arc when the text transforms its reader. It is also the place where we shall see how narrative shapes identity.

---

71 Vanhoozer argues that in Ricoeur's careful attempt to mediate between various binary oppositions he errs too much on the side of freedom, fiction, invention, the ideal and the possible over against the side of nature, history, discovery, the real and actual. The danger is that the historical deed, which can function as a foundation for the possible (as is the case with the work of Jesus), can lose its importance (Vanhoozer, 1990, p. 278).

72 "Function" in Valdés, 1991, p. 288.

73 Not only biblical narrative. Someone recounting events from their past is doing something which is neither pure history nor fiction.

74 Ricoeur, 1998c.

75 Vanhoozer, 1990, p. 239.

76 I would qualify this claim as follows: if the point is that readers should act mercifully (say) in imitation of the God who behaved towards Israel with mercy in the exodus then, if God did not in fact act with mercy in the exodus, the moral is undermined. Certain structurally key stories must be believed to be historical in order to sustain the worldview upon which the ethic grows. However, minor stories such as Genesis 34 are no less ethically useful if the reader regards them as fictional.

77 Ricoeur, 1984, p. 70.

78 On Gadamer see Thiselton, 1980, ch. 11.

79 It has to be said that I have not to date found any clear explanations in Ricoeur's writing of what he means by "the world of the reader". I take him to mean something like the prefigurative self-understanding, values and symbolic universe inhabited by the reader. It is that which is transformed in reading.

The act of interpretation of texts proceeds in two conceptually, if not practically, distinct movements which are like two sides of a single coin:

Explanation[80]
In this movement readers aim to distance the text from themselves. They examine the internal structures and plot so as to determine the sense of the text.[81] Semiotics and structuralism have a constructive role to play here in their uncovering of structures within the configuration of the text. Ricoeur's chief objection to structuralism (aside from its detemporalisation of stories[82]) is that it never progresses from explanation to appropriation. It examines the sense of the text at the expense of its reference. The focus in explanation is the configuration or mimesis$_2$. Interpretation *first of all* reads along the grain of a text sympathetically.[83] In Chapters Four and Five we shall focus on explanation of Genesis 34.

Understanding[84]
Having determined the sense of the text the readers aim to discern the referent of the text (its "world") and to allow it to intersect with their own "world".[85] The referent is projected *by* the sense. Hermeneutics aims to struggle against historical and cultural distance and alienation. It renders the dissimilar "contemporary" and "similar". Reading releases an "event of discourse".[86] This is the act of appropriation when the text is allowed to impact the reader and is achieved in the refiguration or mimesis$_3$. This is what Ricoeur means when he talks of interpretation taking place *"in front of"* the text." There seems to be some almost quasi-mystical dimension to "appropriation" in Ricoeur's thinking. Exactly how the "worlds" interact seems to be less than fully clear. This is quite possibly because it very much depends on the reader in question. Each reader is different and there are no simple rules on how to appropriate

---

80 The application of general rules and objectivism, science and methodology.

81 "Plot" relates to the sense of a text and not its reference.

82 "Narrative Function" (in Valdés, 1991, pp. 280 ff.) is one of numerous occasions when Ricoeur interacts with Structuralism. See Valdes for a dialogue between Ricoeur and Griemas.

83 Hettema, 1996, p. 35, Bartholomew, 1999, ch. 8.

84 Subjective comprehension.

85 It is obvious that Ricoeur has been deeply influenced by Gadamer's ideas on distancing and fusion of the horizons of the text and the reader. Ricoeur's "worlds" of the text and reader are equivalent to Gadamer's "horizons". Ricoeur does not think that the worlds of text and reader ever fully fuse into one but that some distance is always preserved (Hettema, 1996, p.26). The fusion of horizons is an interpretative ideal which, like the gold at the end of the rainbow, will never be attained.

86 "Appropriation" in Valdés, 1991, pp. 89-90.

texts.[87] The second main section of this chapter will bring some more clarity to the ways in which stories can ethically refigure readers.

Ricoeur likens the difference between explanation and understanding to that between (i) examining and explaining the structure of a Brahms symphony and (ii) the execution/enactment of the score.[88] "Explanation mediates a naïve preunderstanding and an "informed" understanding that has been educated by a structural analysis of the text."[89] We could employ the language of Gadamer here and speak of the act of distancing the horizons of the text and the reader and the act of fusing the horizons of the text and the reader. It does look at times like Ricoeur seems to envisage the fusion of horizons only occurring in the last act of interpretation – *first* explanation *then* understanding (fusion). This, though having some value, is somewhat misleading. The fusion of horizons is happening all the time even when we are seeking to distance the horizons. It is crucial to see that this fusion of horizons does not mean that any interpretation is a meaning-hybrid nor that the reader's horizon dominates the interpretation. Gadamer's point is that the original meaning is *only accessible through the fusion of horizons*. Readers deceive themselves if they think that they can bracket themselves out of interpretation and only ask about the contemporary application of a text at a later stage. Dan Stiver writes

> In fact, the image might better be conveyed as an expanding horizon, since one might infer from [Gadamer's] image that one can isolate the two horizons and then bring them together, which is precisely what Gadamer is concerned to reject. His work implies that our horizon is expanded in the encounter with another so that we understand the other horizon *through* ours. This dynamic process is open to a variety of results. We may reject the claims of a text; still, our horizon has been enlarged when we understand it enough to reject it. We may accept the claims of a text, which results in a reconfiguration of our horizon. Or we may appropriate the claims of the text in a creative new way... In each case a fusion of horizons is involved.[90]

Does it make sense then to speak of "distancing the horizons" or "explanation" or "objectivity"? Can we not make any real distinction between the ancient horizon of the biblical text and the modern horizon of readers? Is there no real difference between textual meaning and readers' appropriations? Stiver again

---

87 Hettema helpfully suggests that we see refiguration as the negotiation between text and reader of four dialectics. First, that of bondage to the text and freedom from the text; Second, that of Same and Other; Third, that of communicability and referentiality; Fourth, that of the stasis of and impetus to action (Hettema, 1996, pp. 88-100). There are numerous valid interpretations depending on how the dialectics are negotiated.

88  Vanhoozer, 1990, p. 88.

89  Ibid., p. 88.

90 Stiver, 2001, p. 47.

It seems that such a distinction is necessary, but in Gadamer's terms, it can only be a relative distinction. Even with Gadamer's model one can only make a relative distinction between what a text meant and what it might mean today... What Gadamer would insist on... is that the very understanding of [a text] already involves an idea of how this might be applied today. We gain access to [a text's] horizon by means of our own, but we do not thereby collapse [the text's] horizon into our own... Our understanding is always dialogical, involving a to-and-fro movement between two horizons that are never absolutely distinguishable, only relatively so.[91]

One can still speak of objectivity in interpretation for Gadamer and Ricoeur but it is not the modernist objectivity of verification but a postmodernist objectivity involving evidence and arguments but where certainty in judgements is underdetermined by such supports and one must speak in terms of probablitities. Ricoeur's account of "explanation" as an act in in which one distances the horizons of text and reader aims to makes space for such objectivity to interpretation.[92] Such an act allows us to approach the text with respect as "other-than-ourselves" and to avoid simply seeing our own reflection mirrored in it. However "explanation" cannot be distinguished so neatly in practice from "understanding" as it can in theory. A "fusion of horizons must occur at every point [even though] it is more thematic and pronounced at the last stage."[93]

In mimesis₃ we try out new ideas, new values, new ways of being-in-the-world in a free-play of possibilities.[94] In *Oneself as Another* Ricoeur speaks of the ethical dimension of refiguration as follows:

In the unreal sphere of fiction we never tire of exploring new ways of evaluating actions and characters. The thought experiments we conduct in the great

---

91 Ibid., p. 48.
92 Mark Alan Powell's work on reader response theory (Powell, 2001) in which narrative criticism brings controls that allow us to discern the interpretation a text "expects" of its implied readers can be positioned within Ricoeur's act of explanation. It allows us to discern when the interpretations of real flesh and blood readers are "expected" (i.e., in line with those of the implied readers) or unexpected (i.e., not in line within those of the implied readers). Unexpected readings, argues Powell, are not necessarily misinterpretations. For my views on reader response theories (see Parry, forthcoming c). However, it is crucial to understand that Powell's use of narrative criticism to "distance the horizons" of text and reader cannot eliminate the role of the horizons of the reader. Every attempt to discern the interpretation expected of the implied readers brings the horizon of the interpreter into play. Nevertheless, Powell's work illustrates well that a relative distinction between the horizons is both possible and important.
93 Stiver, 2001, p. 73.
94 "Function" in Valdés, 1991, p. 128.

laboratory of the imaginary are also explorations in the realm of good and evil.[95]

Consequently, narrative is a way of exploring characters and actions that our own life experience may not provide us with.

The reader is guided in his or her reading by traditional hermeneutical paradigms but it is the reader who completes the text. Texts are full of "holes, lacunae, zones of indetermination, which... challenge the reader's capacity to configure what the author seems to... delight in disfiguring... the reader... carries the burden of emplotment."[96] The work is completed in reading. Plotting is thus a *joint* work of text and reader: meaning is underdetermined by the text and needs readers to close the gaps and thus restrict the range of possible meanings.[97] "A text means all that it can mean"[98] but this is *not* to say that a text can mean anything the reader chooses for "the text is a limited field of possible constructions."[99] Interpretations can be possible or impossible, plausible or implausible, likely or unlikely, superior or inferior. The text has boundaries within which responsible interpretations play but the task of interpreting texts will never be completed. The interpreter's task is to navigate "between the Scylla of mechanical replication and the Charybdis of radical polyvalency and unconstrained textual indeterminacy."[100]

Tradition plays a crucial role in both the composition and the interpretation of texts and both writing and reading are situated within traditions. Ricoeur sees tradition as being composed of the elements of sedimentation and innovation.[101] By sedimentation he refers to established paradigms for writing or reading within a tradition. Every particular act of reading, to focus on the refiguration, takes place against the backdrop of inherited reading strategies for particular *kinds* of texts or sometimes of specific texts, as in the case of sacred texts and classic texts. But most acts of reading also break the mould and develop, or react against, part of the inherited paradigms. This is innovation and it is what stops the stagnation of traditions. But readers always innovate against the background of a reading tradition and thus there is no way to bypass tradition in interpretation except by means of a false objectivity.[102] New innovative readings are often laid down as sediment to be inherited by future readers and

95 Ricoeur, 1992, p. 164.
96 Ricoeur, 1984, p. 77.
97 For a useful summary of similarities and differences between Ricoeur and Derrida see Valdés (1991, pp. 21-30). Ricoeur is often seen as the best defence against deconstruction. Joy (1988), however, argues that Ricoeur's thinking needs more detailed development if it is to answer Derrida's challenge. At the moment, says Joy, Ricoeur and Derrida seem to be speaking different languages with different intentionalities.
98 Ricoeur, 1981, p. 176.
99 Ibid., p. 175.
100 Thiselton, 1999, p. 137.
101 Ricoeur, 1984, pp. 68-70.
102 See especially Lundin, 1999; Walhout, 1999, and Thiselton, 1999.

thus a tradition develops. Ricoeur here is influenced by Gadamer's rehabilitation of tradition in interpretation and the work of Hans Robert Jauss on "reception aesthetics" or, as it is more commonly known, "reception history".[103] To Jauss the history of the interpretation of a classic or sacred text within a community will close down some potential interpretations whilst providing fertile ground for innovative interpretations.[104] Chapter Three will sample the Jewish and Christian reception histories of Genesis 34 and Chapter Five will explore parameters for Christian interpretations of the passage.[105]

## Returning to Ricoeur's Narrative Self

Having overviewed Ricoeur's narrative hermeneutic we can return to the role of narrative in identity shaping.[106] In *Time and Narrative* Volume 3 Ricoeur

---

103 Jauss, 1982.

104 On Jauss see Parris (unpublished PhD, 1999) and Thiselton, 1999.

105 What is interpreted in a text is the proposed world that the reader could inhabit. Vanhoozer rightly worries that Ricoeur overplays the power of imagination to effect change in us. Ricoeur is correct in thinking that language and literature expand our consciousness of our possibilities yet humans do not have unlimited possibilities (as Ricoeur acknowledges). But "can the imagination free us from the bondage indicated by the symbols of evil and the doctrine of sin?" (Vanhoozer, 1990, p. 240). "Is regeneration really a matter of refiguring the imagination?" (Ibid., p. 247). For a Christian there are three conditions of Christian possibility: The historical deed of God in Christ which forms the foundation of the possible, the poetic word in Scripture which proclaims the deed, the Spirit which is the power that appropriates the word of kerygma.

Now the Spirit can use imagination but imagination alone is not enough to change sinful humans. This has implications for the ethical impact of biblical narratives. Some account of the role of the Christ and the Spirit in transforming readers must be given if the account is to be fully Christian (Ricoeur is not trying to produce a Christian account but this illustrates to me the error of his constant and principled attempt to keep his theology and his philosophy in separate, sealed conceptual compartments [Ricoeur, 1998a]. Such a division is neither possible nor desirable). This book will not explore the role of the Spirit but see Vanhoozer, 1998, ch. 7.

106 The reader may be helped by a brief sketch of the outline of Oneself as Another so as to be able to contextualise the role of narrative in Ricoeur's broader philosophy of identity. In phase one of the study the question is, "What is the nature of the self revealed by the philosophies of language and action?" Semantics reveals the person about whom one speaks to be a basic particular – irreducible to simpler components (The notion of basic particulars is taken from philosopher P.F. Strawson). Of such a person we attribute both physical and mental predicates (ch. 1). Pragmatics reveals a first-person speaker (an "I") who addresses another (a "you") (ch. 2). Both the "I" who addresses and the "you" who is addressed are also persons. Action theory reveals that the self is one who initiates action in the world (chs. 3-4). Nevertheless, a crucial temporal dimension is missing in the analytic descriptions given of the speaking, acting self thus far. The descriptive phase is limited to the prefiguration so Ricoeur moves

argues that the self is the *result* of a process of interpretation of symbols, metaphors and, most critically, narratives. Narrative places actions in the context of a life turning a mere paradigmatic order into a syntagmatic one and synchronic relations to diachronic ones. The notion of narrative is essential for understanding human action. Madison says,

> To understand an experience or an event is to make sense of it in the form of a story. As Hannah Arendt remarked, "The story reveals the meaning of what would otherwise remain an unbearable sequence of sheer happenings".[107]

> It is in telling our own stories that we give ourselves an identity. We recognise ourselves in the stories that we tell about ourselves. It makes little difference whether these stories are true or false, fiction as well as verifiable history provides us with an identity.[108]

---

beyond it to narrative configuration of the self in phase two (chs. 5-6). Two crucial features stand out: First narrative mediates the dialectic of the idem and the ipse and, second, narrative forms a crucial bridge between the description of the self in chapters 1-4 and the moral prescription of chapters 7-11. Only a storied self can be the subject of moral imputation. Phase three considers this moral dimension arguing that the teleological ethics of Aristotle take priority over Kantian morality in the good life (ch. 7). However, Kantian norms are needed as a sieve for the ethical aim to be tested (ch. 8). The complexity of real life situations often lead to an impasse of norms and morality needs to return to the ethical aim to make wise situational judgements (ch. 9). In this journey from teleology, through deontology and back the idea of self is taken to its highest pitch in the complex notions of ethical "self-esteem" and moral "self-respect" and their outworking in the three dimensions of (a) the aim of the good life, (b) with and for others, (c) in just institutions (Ricoeur, 1992, p. 172. The notions of self-esteem and self-respect tie the final three chapters into a unity as do the three dimensions of the ethical aim). One final point needs to be made in this sketch of the flow of Ricoeur's argument and that is the role of "the other" in the notion of self developed. At every stage in the enquiry but most particularly in the ethical-moral stage the notion of "the other" is implicated in the notion of the self. This is why the book is entitled, Oneself as Another. The "as" is not the "as" of comparison ("oneself similar to another") but the "as" of implication ("oneself inasmuch as being other") (Ibid., p. 3). A Ricoeurian self cannot exist complete in splendid isolation from "the other" as the Cartesian cogito can.
107 Madison, 1995, p. 83.
108 Quoted in Madison, 1995, pp. 80-81. Stroup (1981) develops an account very similar to Ricoeur's. He argues that personal identity is constantly being constructed by the individual from selected parts of their ever-enlarging history. Of course, the individual or the community can get into self-deception by repressing the past or mis-telling and mis-remembering it (ibid., pp. 124-131; Dunne, 1996, pp. 153-154). "In an individual's identity narrative... certain events are lifted out of that person's history and given primary importance for the interpretation and understanding of the whole. In every

Kathleen Blamey explains, "To the question 'Who?,' then, I reply by recounting a story, relating a life history. This history, in turn, is based on the recasting of other histories, those I have been told, those I have previously recounted."[109]

This ties in with Ricoeur's emphasis on the impact that narrative texts have on readers. They refigure or recast the experiences of the reader after the shape of the narrative's "world". Readers are changed and *formed* by stories. "To understand oneself is to understand oneself as one confronts the text and to *receive from it the conditions for a self other than that which first undertakes the reading.*"[110]

> To understand is not to project oneself into the text but to expose oneself to it; it is to receive a self enlarged by the appropriation of the proposed worlds which the interpretation unfolds. In sum, it is the matter of the text which gives the reader his dimension of subjectivity; understanding is thus no longer a constitution of which the subject possesses the key... if fiction is a fundamental dimension of the reference of the text, it is equally a fundamental dimension of the subjectivity of the reader: in reading, I "unrealise myself". Reading introduces me to imaginative variations of the *ego*. The metamorphosis of the world in play [in the text] is also the playful metamorphosis of the ego.[111]

The text, by presenting new visions of how to be-in-the-world, opens up possibilities for the reader consequently "enlarging" them. To some considerable extent "selves" are *products* of texts.

Ricoeur sees the nature of the narrative identity to be parallel to the nature of a narrative. Narrative is a dialectic of concordance and discordance held together by plot. Concordance in so far a range of heterogeneous elements (diverse events, intentions, causes, chance occurrences etc.) are bound into a temporal unity. Discordance in that reversals of fortune threaten to disrupt the unity from start to finish. Plot reconciles identity and diversity.[112] The identity of characters can be understood in a parallel way: "characters, we will say, are themselves plots... It is indeed in the story... that the character preserves

---

person's history there is a chronological order of sorts, yet no identity narrative includes all or even a majority of the events that have taken place in a single life..." (Stroup, 1981, p. 111). Stroup maintains that as personal identity is always an interpretation of personal history and that as history always has a narrative structure (so W.B. Gallie) then personal identity must always assume a narrative form (ibid., p. 112). For Stroup, as for Ricoeur, identity for individuals and communities is a hermeneutical concept – an ongoing task of interpreting one's history (ibid., p. 104).
109 Blamey, 1995, p. 599.
110 Quoted in Madison, 1995, p. 81. Italics mine.
111 Quoted in ibid., p. 82.
112 Ricoeur, 1992, pp. 141-143.

throughout the story an identity correlative to that of the story itself"[113] This is because, within character, identity is a dialectic which parallels that of concordance and discordance:

> This dialectic consists in the fact that, following the line of concordance, the character draws his or her singularity from the unity of a life considered as a temporal totality which is itself singular and distinguished from all others. Following the line of discordance, the temporal totality is threatened by the disruptive effect of the unforeseeable events that punctuate it...[114]

Caution is needed in seeing a human life as exactly like a story. Ricoeur criticises MacIntyre for speaking of the "narrative unity of a life" as the gathering together of one's whole life in the form of a narrative. Ricoeur thinks that there are several important dissimilarities between stories and an actual human life and this is really reflected in his distinction between mimesis$_1$, mimesis$_2$ and mimesis$_3$. First, in fiction, author, narrator and character are distinct voices, whilst in my life although I may be character and narrator, I am at best *co*-author of my life.[115] Second, in fiction, beginnings and endings need not be chronological, whilst in an actual life chronology is observed. Indeed, in life we cannot remember our beginning whilst our deaths can only be recounted by others. Life does not offer the opening and closure needed to grasp my life as a singular totality.[116] Third, I can trace in my life *several* plots (and not simply one) each of which lacks a sense of ending.[117] Fourth, different fictional worlds are hermetically sealed from each other being self-contained, whilst in life my life story interacts and is interwoven with those of others.[118] Life and narrative contrast but they also complement each other. It is precisely *because* of the unstable and open-ended nature of real life that we need fiction to organise life retrospectively. Any narrative formations we put on our lives are open to revision or extension, for life is an ongoing story.

We can also use fiction to provide models of how the lives of different characters can interact, to help us to see courses of action as having beginnings and endings, to provide models of good and bad deaths, to help us form projects, expectations and anticipations.[119] A life recounted autobiographically is always an unfinished narrative that is constantly being added to and revised. It is an ongoing interpretative project which moves in a hermeneutical spiral

---

113 Ibid., p. 143.
114 Ibid., pp. 147-148.
115 Ibid., pp. 159-160. In that the way my life story unfolds is in many ways out of my hands.
116 Ibid., p. 160.
117 Ibid., p. 161.
118 Ibid., p. 161.
119 Ibid., pp. 161-163.

between the vague and mobile horizon of our life plans (for our professional life, family life, leisure time and so on) and the more determinate models provided in a society for particular practices such as medicine, farming, mothering and so on. Narratives give form to the kinds of interaction proper to practices as well as models of individuals, considering how such roles fit in with their overarching life plans. This seems to be picking up on MacIntyre's reflections in *After Virtue* where we read

> We enter human society... with one or more imputed characters – roles into which we have been drafted – and we have to learn what they are in order to learn how others respond to us and how our responses to them are apt to be construed. It is through hearing stories about wicked step-mothers, lost children, good but misguided kings, wolves that suckle twin boys, youngest sons who receive no inheritance but must make their own way in the worlds and eldest sons who waste their inheritance on riotous living and go into exile to live with the swine [MacIntyre seems to have his sons muddled up here], that children learn or mislearn what a child and what a parent is, what the cast of characters may be in the drama into which they have been born and what the ways of the world are. Deprive children of stories and you leave them unscripted, anxious stutterers in their actions as in their words... [T]he telling of stories has a key part in educating us into the virtues.[120]

Education by story does not so much provide a collection of principles but a "capacity for judgement which the agent possesses in knowing how to select among the relevant stack of maxims and how to apply them in particular situations."[121]

---

120 MacIntyre, 1996, p. 216.
121 Nelson, p. 53. The sameness (idem) of identity provided by physical resemblance over time and spatio-temporal continuity (Ricoeur, 1992, pp. 116-117) is added to by the different kind of temporal endurance implied by selfhood (ipse). Idem tells us what endures over time but ipse tells us who endures and the latter cannot be reduced to the former. The permanence in time implied by ipse can be thought of in terms of two models: character and keeping one's word (Ibid., p.118). At the pole of character we have an enduring set of acquired dispositions (habits and identifications [Ibid., pp. 121-122. By identifications he means norms, ideals, models and heroes in which and by which the self or community recognises itself, ibid., p.122]) and here ipse can hardly be distinguished from idem (Ibid., pp. 118-121). Character is thus 'the what? of the who?' But it is a what? which cannot be separated from the who? in question as the what? of action can be. At the pole of keeping one's word or self-constancy we see ipse and idem split apart for one can be true to one's word even if one's desires, inclinations or opinions change. The polarity of these two kinds of self-permanence is traversed by narrative identity which oscillates between them. One contribution of narrative to the philosophy of self is its dialectic of the character and self-constancy. Literature contains a vast spectrum of characters (not to be identified with 'character' in the preceding

Narratives, for Ricoeur, also prepare the way for ethics in that the actions of characters are subjected to approval or disapproval and the agents are subject to praise or blame. In fiction, at least, we do not *actually* blame characters (for they do not usually exist) but we *experiment with ways of evaluating them*.[122] I will return in the next section to this theme of stories providing models for behaviour.

Individuals find their identity within a narrative framework but so too do social groups. Although this dimension is neglected in *Oneself as Another,* Ricoeur on other occasions uses the nation of Israel as an example *of a group whose identity was constituted within a narrative framework*. For example, "[R]eligious, and more specifically biblical, narratives do in their own way what all narratives do – they constitute the identity of the community that tells and retells the story, and they constitute it as a narrative identity."[123] He writes more generally of

> those events that a historical community holds to be significant because it sees in them an origin, a return to its beginnings. These events, which are said to be "epoch-making", draw their specific meanings from their capacity to found or reinforce the community's consciousness of its identity – its narrative identity, as well as the identity of its members. These events generate feelings of considerable ethical intensity, whether this be fervent commemoration or some manifestation of loathing, or indignation, or of regret or compassion, or even the call for forgiveness...[124]

In a similar vein MacIntyre observes that

> the story of my life is always embedded in the story of those communities from which I derive my identity. I am born with a past; and to try to cut myself off from that past, in the individualist mode, is to deform my present relationships. The possession of an historical identity and the possession of a social identity coincide... What I am, therefore, is in key part what I inherit, a specific past that is present to some degree in my present. I find myself part of a history and that is generally to say, whether I like it or not, whether I recognise it or not, one of the

---

discussion) ranging from those with a very fixed character that never changes to those who cease to have a definite character. Fiction submits identity to imaginative variations in "a vast laboratory for thought experiments in which the resources of variation encompassed by narrative identity are put to the test of narration" (Ibid., p. 122). By varying the relations between self-constancy and character they expose the differences between them (Ibid., p. 122).

122 Ricoeur, 1992, p. 164.
123 "Towards a Narrative Theology" in Ricoeur, 1995, p. 241.
124 Ricoeur, 1988, p. 187.

bearers of a tradition.[125]

We have traversed the Ricoeurian spider web in order to set forth theoretical foundations for our use of Old Testament narratives. We have seen that the Ricoeurian self, both individual and communal, is not a given but is constructed in dialogue with stories. Identity is thus not closed but constantly transformed and eschatologically orientated.[126] We have seen how (moral) action is transformed by being configured in story telling and refigured in reading. The responsible reader will aim to distance the text as well as to appropriate it in order to fill the gaps in such a way that its integrity is not violated. Such readers of texts will always be situated within a tradition of interpretative methods and also previous interpretations of specific texts. Finally, we have argued that the refiguration has ethical implications. It is this claim which shall be deepened in the next section.

## The Ethical Refiguration of the Reader

I wish to focus now on the ethics of mimesis₃. That is to say, the ways in which stories can ethically refigure readers, shaping their values and actions.

### *Story and the Exemplification of the General*

In this section I shall argue that stories of particular acts by particular actors in particular circumstances can be generalised and become models for the behaviour of other actors in analogous circumstances. I shall also maintain that the virtues and vices of characters also function as models to aspire to, or to avoid. I wish to suspend judgement on the meta-ethical debate concerning the priority of character or actions.[127] Clearly both are crucial to right living. Right acting can shape right character (through habit formation) and right character can shape right action. We thus find a virtuous circular relationship between action-imperative rules and virtues. As this book is concerned only with how narratives (and indirectly, laws) can shape the readers, it seems to me that we can leave the more foundational philosophical question open.

If we lose sight of this generalising potential and focus simply on the particularity of a story, any moral lessons that can be learned will be so specific

---

125 MacIntyre, 1986, p. 221.

126 Useful secondary texts relating to Ricoeur's analysis of the self are K. Blamey in Hahn, 1995; G. Madison in Hahn, 1995; E. Pucci in Kearney, 1996; J. Dunne, in Kearney, 1996 and D. Rasmussen in Kearney, 1996.

127 The question is, "Are right actions right because they are the actions a virtuous person would choose or is a certain individual virtuous because they tend to choose to perform the actions which are right?"

as to be useless.[128] Theo Hettema, in his Ricoeurian reading of the Joseph stories, claims that Ricoeur makes possible two ways in which narrative configures morality. These he calls model morality and metaphoric[129] morality. It is the former which concerns us here. Hettema writes,

> A configuration offers an arrangement of several elements of the world of action. This arrangement is a matter of imagination. It pretends to offer a better understanding of the character of reality than the prefigurative perception of morality may do. It has a claim to refer to the world of the reader; the imaginative arrangement implies that the reader might look and react to reality as the model shows. The configurative model also gives a prototypical example of behaviour. As a prototype it is a form of generalisation which the configuration makes to the reader. The configurative model invites the reader to analogical behaviour: in similar circumstances, the reader may act as the model has shown.[130]

Thus the characters (models) receive a sense of generalisation but must do so without undermining the specificity of the narrative, the complexity of the plot or of real life.[131]

In Genesis 37ff. Joseph is the model *par excellence.* He is the ideal son and brother, a model of obedience to his master, of sexual control, as well as the ideal believer.[132] Narrative makes proposals to the reader for their consideration. The reader, initially at least, seeks to play the role of the implied reader to explore new ways of evaluating characters and actions. Life does not provide us with as many experiences as we can imaginatively live in fiction and thus fiction helps train us for living. However, the reader is free to reject the models proposed by the narrator. Narrative does not *coerce* us even if it may try to. Rather readers *use* narrative to explore ethics. This is what Ricoeur means when he talks of how

---

128 Siebers, 1992, p. 40.

129 Metaphoric morality is a far less clear affair. It is the morality implied at the level of the world projected by a whole text (rather than individual episodes within it) as it interacts with the world of the reader. In Joseph the metaphoric morality is "laid down in the way the narrative imagines the creation of the possibilities of reconciliation" (Hettema, 1996, p. 249). It is "the literary creation of this form of [changed] personality, directed to the implied reader, through the experiences of time, evil, conscience and the mention of God" (ibid., p. 249). It aims to change the fundamental attitudes of the implied reader by inviting them to follow the course of action and accept the moral implications of the world of the text as elements of his or her own world (ibid., p. 250). The weakness of such morality is its lack of clarity and its inability to be generalised. It stands in tension with the clarity of model morality. Clearly Genesis may have a model morality but Genesis 34 will not have.

130 Hettema, 1996, p. 246.

131 Ibid.

132 Ibid., p. 247.

in the unreal sphere of fiction we never tire of exploring new ways of evaluating actions and characters. The thought experiments we conduct in the great laboratory of the imaginary is a way of exploring characters and actions which our own life experience may not provide us with.[133]

In his recent essay "Narrative Hermeneutics" Clarence Walhout has taken a very similar line.[134] Walhout says that what interests us about stories (fictional and historical) is that they provide us with "examples that will confirm or guide or explain or point out new directions for action."[135] In particular, what draws us is an interest in the ethical relationships between characters:

> The characters of fiction, like human beings in real life, form and discover their identities through their relationships with other characters. And more than this, they discover that their identities are dependent on the identities of others...[136]

We are especially concerned with the resolution of conflicts between characters for

> we are interested in how characters deal with their crises and aspirations, and thus we are interested in the authorial stance of the narrative, that is, the author's beliefs about how the situations of the characters can or cannot reach satisfactory resolution.[137]

Now narratives provide ethical models for our own actions but not in the traditional sense of prescriptive or exemplary patterns. Rather they provide "possible ways of understanding something"; heuristic sketches for "the possibilities of human action and possible ways of moving human actions towards resolution."[138] Thus whilst narrative does not *prescribe* models for our actions it does *provide* models for our *reflection*. Obviously then our interpretations of any stories will be influenced by our prior beliefs about ethics.[139]

Apart from the role given to the author here, this analysis is Ricoeurian through and through. It is also very useful and applicable to texts such as Genesis 34, or so I shall argue. However, it seems to me that the actions of

---

133 Ricoeur, 1992, p. 164.
134 He maintains that "the ethical response to texts embraces all other kinds of response, since responses are themselves actions and therefore carry with them ethical implications" (Walhout, 1999, p. 119).
135 Ibid., p. 122.
136 Ibid., p. 123.
137 Ibid., p. 125.
138 Ibid., pp. 125-126.
139 Ibid., pp. 127-128.

some scriptural characters *are* intended by the authors to be more than a mere models for reflection which readers are free to take or leave. They are models for imitation – exemplars of godly lifestyles whose actions are, in a loose sense, "rules" for the behaviour of readers. This is not to say that readers *have* to use such stories in this way but it is to say that authors can, and sometimes do, *intend* them to be taken in such a way. For instance, the story of Jesus' non-violent suffering is set out in the New Testament as an authoritative model for Christian living. Exactly how it applies in the myriad diverse cases of real life situations may vary considerably, but it is proposed as *more than a suggestion* to the Christian.

In the case of a *Christian* reading of the Bible, the issue of the authority of scripture raises its head at this point, for if an author intends the actions of a certain character to set forth an authoritative model for readers' own actions, is the Christian free to reject the model? At first glance we may answer with a "no", but in the next chapter I shall set up a hermeneutical grid which is based on the biblical metanarrative and may legitimise setting aside of some authoritative models on the grounds that they are not intended by God to be taken as authoritative in every era of history, or in every single situation.

It is clear from the above discussion that many biblical stories set up certain characters as models or "rules" to follow.[140] Waldemar Janzen has picked up on this insight and developed it in his fascinating book, *Old Testament Ethics: A Paradigmatic Approach*. He argues that certain central stories offer models of right behaviour that contribute towards building up five key paradigms: the familial, the priestly, the wisdom, the royal and the prophetic. The book opens with five brief case studies in which these models are set forth. Abram's behaviour towards Lot in Genesis 13 is a model of familial loyalty and support; Phineas' actions in Numbers 25 model zeal for Yahweh essential to the priestly model; Abigail in 1 Samuel 25 models wise behaviour; David models proper royal conduct in 1 Samuel 24, and Elijah acts as a true prophet in his conflict with Ahab over Naboth's vineyard in 1 Kings 21. A very helpful insight of Janzen's is that none of these characters are held up as perfect. It is not that Abram is a model of virtue. Rather he exemplifies right conduct in *a specific area of life* (in his case, the family) on a particular occasion.[141] A second crucial insight, and positive development of this idea, is that the Old Testament allows multiple stories, laws, aphoristic sayings, oracles, and the like to build up more complex models of appropriate familial, priestly, wise, royal and prophetic living. These models are somewhat abstract, being complex wholes constructed from the interaction of multiple-texts. No individual text sets out the grammar of any specific model in its entirety. One could possibly think of them as

---

140 Fowl (1988, p. 302) develops a very similar idea to what I am calling "model morality" in terms of Kuhnian exemplars. He examines Philippians 1:27-2:18 in terms of a part of the Jesus story being used as an exemplar.
141 Janzen, 1994, p. 20.

unconscious presuppositions of Israelite society and literature which may never have been consciously articulated in their entirety by any individual, but which manifest parts of themselves in laws, social structures, stories, psalms and so on. These models form guides to those for whom they are relevant. Clearly, not all the models will apply equally to all Israelites.

Janzen's paradigmatic approach to the Old Testament is a very constructive one. There are clear strengths to it, not least of which is the conceptual unity it brings to the diversity of genres in the Old Testament and the refusal to boil everything down to one model. The power of model morality in biblical narratives is illustrated very well throughout the book.

One should not think that Janzen is proposing a mining of biblical stories in order to abstract the gold of some theoretical models which then become the focus of ethics even as the stories themselves fade into the background. In Chapter Two I shall argue that the models are rooted in the stories and supervene[142] upon them. Perhaps we should think of the ethical models as *constituted*, in part, by stories just as statues are constituted by marble (or whatever). Just as one cannot keep the statue and discard the marble so one cannot keep the model without the story. And even if I am mistaken in this, an abstract model of ethical behaviour in different social realms is not going to have the *ethical-shaping impact* of stories and the rules embedded in them.

The next two sections will begin to show how stories in particular work in readers for good in a way that principles, rules and paradigms cannot. This is not to reject the use of abstract formulations. On the contrary, the moral life needs the conceptual clarity brought by the abstract as well as the character-shaping impact of the particular story. Robert C. Roberts likens the co-operation of the conceptual and the concrete to that of understanding one's location by looking at a map and by walking around. Maps can bring an understanding which lived experience cannot and vice versa.[143] We need the conceptual clarity of paradigms and grammars (on which see later). We also need the embodiment of them in stories and the like.

Stories not only provide models of good, wise and virtuous attitudes and behaviour. Sin, folly and vice along with their consequences are displayed in story for the hearer or reader to consider and avoid. One need only consider Nabal, Saul, David with Bathsheba or Abraham in Egypt to find such models.

It must be pointed out that biblical characterisation can function at various levels of complexity[144] but that at its most sophisticated we see that the same characters are capable of acts of virtue *and* of vice. Thus David, Saul, Samson, Moses, Abraham, Solomon and Joab could not be considered good or bad in any simplistic sense. They are more nuanced and complex characters – more

---

142 On the notion of supervenience see N. Murphy, 1998, pp. 127-148 (esp. pp. 132-138).
143 Roberts, 1999.
144 On characterisation in the Bible, see Berlin, 1983; Bar Efrat, 1997; Sternberg, 1987.

like real people than, say, Noah (the righteous man) or Goliath (the enemy). Some of their acts are paradigms of virtue, others are paradigms of vice, whilst others are ambiguous being neither fully black nor white. What are we to make of some of the behaviour of Jacob, for example? Extracting morals from his life is a precarious business. Genesis 34 will provide an example of such ambiguity.

To function well as a prescriptive model an act must be fairly clear-cut as far as its morality is concerned. The more ambiguous acts complicate the judgement of the reader and make simple imitation or avoidance impossible. This begins to intimate one of the limits of model morality but, as we shall see, in so complicating moral experience it opens up different, but equally fruitful and enriching, dimensions of the moral life which impact on the reader.

Thus, in stories we sometimes see displayed concrete examples of both abstract principles and abstract virtues. Stories serve to ground and illustrate as well as "fill out" and qualify the moral principle or the virtue. Robert C. Roberts writes,

> One of the most basic and natural media for presenting [the virtues] is narrative, in which connected sequences of actions, intentions, thoughts, and emotions are depicted in life-contexts that are the natural setting of such occurrences... The narrative display of a virtue is warmer, more immediately appealing, and more vivid than a philosophical display of it. For these reasons it enlivens the philosopher's imagination, and speaks to his heart, and keeps him close to the earth, thus correcting his occupational tendency to lose himself in the dusty clouds of abstract inference.[145]

Not simply virtues but also, as argued above, the problems and principles of action are displayed most clearly and naturally in narrative. Principles need narrative and narrative needs principles. Hauerwas writes,

> Though moral principles are not sufficient in themselves for our moral existence, neither are stories sufficient if they do not generate principles that are morally significant. Principles without stories are subject to perverse interpretation... but stories without principles will have no way of concretely specifying the actions and practices consistent with the general orientation expressed by the story.[146]

What are the limitations of model morality? First, as I have already indicated, it only functions well with clear-cut examples of good or bad characters and acts and thus cannot enable the more ambiguous stories in the Bible to ethically shape the reader.

Secondly, a related danger is that the clear-cut cases of model morality, if taken as the sum total of the narrative contribution to ethics, would

145 Roberts, 1999, pp. 473, 477.
146 Quoted in Brown, 1996, p. 19.

oversimplify the complexity and difficulty which sometimes marks the moral life. This, in turn, could lead to a reader/hearer with a very shallow ethical approach to life. Such shallowness can, as history shows, lead to great evils done in the name of righteousness. The clear-cut cases need balancing with the ambiguous cases.

A third danger is that of extracting an over-strong principle from a story. One can generalise from biblical stories but one cannot infer universally valid principles and it is a potential danger of model morality that one may attempt to do so. Thus, for example, to infer from the proposal that Elijah was right in killing the prophets of Baal that it is *always* right to have idolaters within God's people killed would be to overstep the mark considerably. In fact, killing apostate Christians on the basis of 1 Kings 18 seems dubious indeed for reasons which should become clear in Chapters Two and Five. Absolute rules cannot be inferred from particular narratives even if general principles can. This is not to say that there are no such rules, nor that narrative cannot illustrate an absolute rule, but merely that such a rule cannot be inferred from the narrative *alone*. This should not be considered a problem as there is far more to moral living than finding security in absolute moral rules, even if there is a place for some such rules. To reduce morality to the delineating and observance of universal principles is an impoverishment of morality.

Fourthly, a reader may find that they do not identify with the character or traits that the narrator intends (e.g. modern Christian readers find it difficult to fully relate to Phineas' violence in Numbers 25). Alternatively, they may identify with the intended character in *some* of their roles (e.g., Joseph in the family) but not others (e.g., Joseph in the court).[147] After all, Joseph's model behaviour in the court is relevant to a smaller group of people than his behaviour in the home. And even his behaviour in the home may not relate to readers in very different circumstances. This leads us on to consider the particularity of biblical narratives.

## Story and Particularity

Martha Nussbaum's work on narrative and ethics provides a way into a discussion of the particularity of narrative which is as important as its potential for generalisation considered above.[148] To Nussbaum, following Aristotle, the particular situation is prior to any rules, but without the general or universal it would be unguided.[149] Since, in our aspiration to grasp ethical truth, the

---

147 Hettema, 1996, p. 247.
148 The discussion of Nussbaum in this Chapter is a shortened version of parts of my article, "Greeks Bearing Gifts: Appropriating Nussbaum (Appropriating Aristotle) For A Christian Approach to Old Testament Narrative Ethics" in Parry, 2000a. On Nussbaum in Biblical Studies see also Barton, 1996, 1998.
149 Nussbaum, 1986, p. 306.

perception of concrete particulars is prior in authority to the general principles
and definitions that summarise those particulars, it will be natural for her to
suppose that the concrete and complex stories that are the material of narrative
fiction could play a valuable role in refining our perceptions of the complex
"material" of human life. Moral rules are important to Nussbaum but the good
novel reveals that the particular situation in all its nuances takes priority over
the rules. General rules are not fine-tuned enough to cover every type of
situation[150] being unable to account for:-

- new and unanticipated features in a situation.
- the context embeddedness of relevant features.
- the ethical relevance of particular persons and relationships.[151]

Absolute general rules would have to have so many exception clauses built into
them in order to absolutise them as to make them unusable.[152] Practical matters
are mutable and so specific situations require responses which are imaginative
and sensitive. A certain amount of improvisation by the wise agent is
essential[153] as "the concrete ethical case may simply contain some ultimately
particular and non-repeatable elements."[154]

Nussbaum has been accused by some of her critics of having no time for
rules.[155] This criticism is understandable given Nussbaum's emphasis on the
particular but is not really a fair representation of her work as a whole. In "An
Aristotelian Conception of Rationality" she accounts for rules as the distilled
wisdom of generations which deserve the utmost respect. However, rules are
"valid only to the extent to which they correctly describe good concrete
judgements, and [are] to be assessed, ultimately, against these."[156] So rules must
always be there as a moral guide but never as the final word.

Novels attend to the concrete and consequently embody a high evaluation of
the particular. They teach the reader to pay attention to the nuances of *specific*
situations. "The tonality of the action (or non-action) itself is particular and
enmeshed, and can hardly be well described (if we want to capture its
*rightness*) without the subtleties of the novelist."[157] The moral imagination

---

150 Nussbaum, 1990, p. 37.
151 Ibid., p. 38.
152 Ibid., p. 72.
153 Ibid., p. 71.
154 Ibid., p. 72.
155 Hilary Putnam talks of her "derogatory attitude towards rules" (Putnam, 1983, p. 193) and his concern that her approach may degenerate into "an absolutely empty 'situation ethics'" (ibid., p. 93).
156 Nussbaum, 1990, p. 68.
157 Ibid., p. 91.

is subtle and high rather than simple and coarse; precise rather than gross; richly coloured rather than monochromatic... the full specificity of the image is relevant. The very particular nuances of the image move us in a way which different wording would not. No paraphrase can capture it... Moral knowledge, James suggests, is not intellectual grasp of propositions... [nor] even simply... of particular facts; it is perception. It is seeing a complex, concrete reality in a highly lucid and richly responsive way; it is taking in what is there, with imagination and feeling.[158]

The Bible student must clearly deal with the place of the ethical rules that are to be found within the text of the Old Testament. In Chapter Two I shall argue that such rules need to be read within the narrative context that the Old Testament places them, but I should say at this point that it seems to me that some Old Testament laws are intended to be absolute prohibitions of the kind Nussbaum rejects.[159] But, even if one wishes to give a larger place to rules than Nussbaum does (and many ethicists do), one may still gain from a study of Nussbaum's focus on particularity, for it could be that careful attention to the particularity of cases may help the believer discern which divine imperative is the one to follow in a situation of conflict.

In this context it is worth introducing the work of Lawrence Blum and in particular his essay "Moral Perception and Particularity". Blum points out that even if, unlike Nussbaum, one accepts an ethical system that is rule-based, one must recognise the role of something to bridge the rule and the particular situation.[160] Kant referred to this "something" as "judgement". After all "it is not the rule but some other moral capacity of the agent which tells her that the particular situation she faces falls under a given rule."[161] Moral living

involves moral capacities, sensitivities, and judgement (1) to know which acts count as exemplifying particular moral principles, (2) to know how to carry out the act specified by the principle, and (3) to know when it is and isn't appropriate to instantiate given principles. These capacities go beyond possessing the principle (plus the strength of will to act on it); they are neither guaranteed nor encompassed by the commitment to the principle (plus strength of will) itself.[162]

However, even the supplementing of the principles with "judgement" is not enough.[163] Before one can get as far as bringing a principle to bear on a particular situation one must first be able to individuate the "situation". "It is

---

158 Ibid., p. 152.
159 For instance, the ban on worshipping false gods.
160 Blum, 1994, pp. 37-38.
161 Ibid., p. 38.
162 Ibid., p. 40.
163 Ibid., p. 38.

moral perception which does the individuating or construing of the situation, thus providing a setting in which moral judgement carries out its task."[164] Blum's essay shifts its focus to the importance of sensitive moral perception of particular situations – such perception is morally valuable *in its own right* as well as in its informing of right action.[165]

Now it is easy to get very mystical about the operation of moral perception and judgement but Blum aims to bring some clarity.[166] He resists the notion that situational perception is "a unified capacity", breaking perception down into a sensitivity to the presence of particular sorts of moral features. "The fact is, particular persons are better at perceiving certain *sorts* of particulars than other sorts."[167] For example, a person may be very sensitive to the exemplification of injustice in a particular situation but fail to perceive the affront to the victim's dignity. This decentralisation of moral perception opens the way for an exploration of "the ways that imagination, attention, empathy, critical reason, habit, exposure to new moral categories, and the like contribute to the formation of those sensitivities."[168]

The consequence of this is that even *if* one resists Nussbaum's insistence on the priority of the particular, one can still see that moral rules and principles are inadequate without the operations of the (partly) independent faculties of moral perception and judgement.[169] "It is not as if the principles themselves already fully contain the sensitivity needed to recognise their applicability, violation, and the like."[170] Consequently, one can appropriate Nussbaum's observations on how stories train us in moral perception, even if we wish to give a greater place to rules. Particularity is important in the ethics of narrative but, as I argued in the previous section, equally important, and underemphasized by Nussbaum, are the common features stories share: How an action on one occasion can provide a model for a similar act on a similar occasion. In fact, when approaching a new moral situation we *first* look for *similarities* in ethically significant features between the present situation and past situations so

---

164 Ibid., p. 42.

165 Ibid., p. 43.

166 Ibid., pp. 45 ff.

167 Ibid., p. 46.

168 Ibid., p. 46.

169 Ibid., p. 50. As a matter of fact Blum does want to move further from an ethics of rules than I indicate here (ibid., pp. 53 ff.).

170 Ibid., p. 51. In a postscript to the original essay Blum sets out seven steps that take a person from a given situation to an action based on moral principle. (1) The accurate recognition of the situations features, (2) The recognition of the moral significance of those features, (3) Asking oneself whether one should act, (4) Deciding whether one should act, (5) Selecting the rule or principle that seems applicable, (6) determining the act that best instantiates the principle one has selected, (7) figuring out how to perform the act specified. It is clear how crucial perception and judgement are in working with general principles.

that we have some idea how to proceed. Only then do we look for unique features which may modify our application of the previous paradigm. This emphasis on commonality is quite compatible with Nussbaum's focus on particularity. Consider Genesis 22. Abraham's act is a paradigm of sacrificial acts in later Israelite worship[171] yet it contains unique, non-repeatable features (human sacrifice being the most obvious). A narrative action can be partially paradigmatic like this because attention is paid to *both* the similarities *and* differences between the story and later partial parallels. Similar comments could be made about people and objects. We do, as Nussbaum says, appreciate them for their uniqueness and irreplacibility. However, we also value them, as Plato says, for what they have in common with other people and objects.

## Story and the Training of Emotional Perception

Nussbaum's essay, "An Aristotelian Conception of Rationality"[172] helpfully develops a notion of ethical rationality which has a key role for the emotions. She sums up Aristotle's view as being one in which "a person of practical insight will cultivate emotional openness and responsiveness in approaching a new situation" as emotion is a part of ethical "knowing".[173] Indeed "a reliance on the powers of the intellect can actually become an impediment to true ethical perception, by impeding or undermining these responses."[174] It can lead to inattentiveness to concrete responses of emotion and imagination to specific cases. It should be clear how this discussion on the role of emotion follows on directly from the discussion of particularity and perception.

In "Narrative Emotions: Beckett's Genealogy of Love" a stronger claim is made. There Nussbaum argues that we learn our emotional responses from our society: not only,[175] but primarily, through stories. Stories express the structure of emotions and teach their dynamics. They shape the way that life looks and feels.

> Indeed, it seems right to say... not only that a certain sort of story shows or represents emotion but also that emotion itself is the acceptance of, the assent to live according to, a certain sort of story. Stories, in short, contain and teach forms of feeling, forms of life.[176]

---

171 See especially Wenham, 1995.
172 Nussbaum, 1990, ch. 2.
173 Ibid., p. 79.
174 Ibid., p. 81.
175 Emotions are not learned in an ethics class but by interaction with parents and society. Such interactions provide paradigms of emotions and teach the cognitive categories that underlie emotion.
176 Nussbaum, 1990, p. 287.

[N]arratives are essential to the process of practical reflection: not just because they happen to represent and also evoke emotional activity, but also because *their very forms are themselves the sources of emotional structure, the paradigm of what, for us, emotion is.*[177]

Emotions find their place in human lives and must be learned from other human lives whether real or fictional.[178]

Narratives also evoke emotions in the reader and these emotions are, according to Nussbaum, epistemologically valuable. Here Nussbaum is in line with many recent philosophers and psychologists who maintain that emotions are strongly linked to cognition and are not mere animal instincts.[179] Emotions, according to Nussbaum, are linked to beliefs about what is valuable and the evaluative beliefs which ground our emotions are learned through early habitual exposure to complex social forms of life in which these beliefs are housed. I shall soon propose an important alternative to this claim but one which allows Nussbaum's insights on the importance of emotion to ethics to be maintained.

If emotion is crucial to living an ethical life which Henry James refers to as one that is "finely aware and richly responsible", and if stories are foundational

---

177 Ibid., p. 296, italics mine.

178 Nussbaum is certainly not claiming that emotion cannot lead us morally astray for it obviously can. If one's foundational beliefs are out of order then one's feelings will be also. Emotion is open to rational assessment but a rational assessment of an Aristotelian sort. That it to say that there is no Archimedian point from which to assess our beliefs and emotions. Such an assessment must be performed from within our human perspective. Our aim is to establish coherence among our beliefs, emotions and experiences. "The participants look not for a view that is true by correspondence to some extra-human reality, but for the best overall fit between a view of what is deepest in human lives... They seek for coherence and fit in the web of judgement, feeling, perception, and principle, taken as a whole" (1990, p. 26). Nussbaum trusts that our common humanity provides a sufficient basis for such a task to have hope of genuine progress. Thus "knowledge conveyed in emotional impressions must be systematised and pinned down by the activity of reflection" (ibid., p. 285).

179 Within the spectrum of psychological theories about emotion I would place Nussbaum, along with the majority of psychologists, between William James' emphasis on the primacy of physiology (1884) and Magda Arnold's emphasis on the primacy of cognition (1960). In 1964 Stanley Schachter proposed a two-factor theory of emotion. Schachter maintained that physiology did produce emotion but that it only provided the strength and heat of the emotion. Perception of arousal tells people that they are emotional and how strong this emotion is (to that extent James was right). However, cognitive interpretation of the situation provides the kind of emotion that is experienced (to that extent Arnold was right). Thus anger is experience of arousal in an annoying situation whilst euphoria is experience of arousal in an exciting situation. The role of cognition, however, is more than simply labeling bodily reactions. Cognition often precedes initial arousal and thus the emotion.

in learning appropriate emotions, then it follows that narrative is crucial for ethical living.

In explanation and defence of the claim that emotions play a key role in practical reasoning it will be necessary to say more about emotion, practical reasoning and the link between them.

In "Aristotle on Emotions and Ethical Health," Nussbaum makes out a case for the strong link between emotion and propositional belief. First she argues that certain beliefs are *necessary* for the experience of certain emotion. Take fear, as an example. One does not simply fear. One fears *something*. One fears some possible future unpleasantness, for example. Without being able to conceptualise the object of one's fear, to say what one fears, it seems odd to imagine that one can fear.[180] A possible counter-example to Nussbaum's claim are emotions such as angst which do not have an object. This calls for some nuancing of Nussbaum's view. One *may* have a sense of angst, for example, without having any *conscious* object for that fear. However, my amateur knowledge of psychology would lead me to suggest that such "fear" *would* have a *sub-conscious* object. It is the experience of psychotherapists that they can often help clients to recognise the unconscious objects of such feelings. Consequently, the counter-example fails.[181]

To see clearly the grounding of emotion in belief, imagine being angry at John for his insulting your mother. Your belief that he has insulted your mother is a ground of the emotional experience. If that belief were to change then the anger would modify or disappear as appropriate. Thus, if you came to believe that in fact John had intended a compliment but that you had misheard him then you would no longer be angry.

Nussbaum then goes on to argue that belief is not merely necessary for the experience of certain emotions but that it is actually a *constituent part of* those emotions.[182] She says that different emotions are individuated in terms of their beliefs not their "feely" quality. Take painful emotions. There is not a peculiar pain associated with fear, another with grief and another with pity. These emotions are differentiated primarily in terms of their propositional content. Thus we say that grief is pain *at the thought of* x whilst fear is pain *at the thought of* y. One cannot think of the emotion without the cognitive part of it.

It seems to me that this is insightful but overestimates the role of beliefs and propositions which I would claim are not necessary (though they may be

---

180 Nussbaum, 1994b, p. 86.

181 More convincing counter-examples would be moods or emotions which accompany musical experiences (on which Roberts' new book is very helpful, Roberts, 2003).

182 Nussbaum, 1994b, p. 88. So too Proudfoot, 1977, p. 348. The revivalist Jonathan Edwards talks of emotions as "the sense of heart where the mind is not speculative but experiences and feels" (quoted in Gilman, 1994, p. 221).

sufficient) for the experience of emotion.[183] Although it is usual for a belief or judgement *that x* to be connected with an emotion, it is possible to have an emotion without believing that x *actually is* the case. Consider the following example: my toddler picks up my mug of hot coffee and pours in onto my lap. I am very cross with her for a short while *even though* I know that she is not morally culpable. I do not have the belief that she has wronged me yet I feel angry with her *as if* I did have such a belief. To help account for this I propose that we use an alternative to Nussbaum's account of emotion.

The most insightful philosophical account of emotions that I have found is that of Robert C. Roberts outlined in his article, "What An Emotion Is: A Sketch."[184] Roberts defines an emotion as *"serious, concern-based*

---

183 There are several clear cases which cause problems for Nussbaum's belief-centred account of emotions. One of these is, surprisingly given Nussbaum's interest in literature, the emotion experienced during engagement with fiction. Nussbaum speaks as if to experience an emotion, fear say, one must believe that such and such is the case. However, it is a common experience for those reading fictional novels or watching a good film to feel emotionally moved. When we feel sad at the death of a fictional character we do not believe that the character is a real person who has actually died. When we feel fear as the slime creature approaches we do not think that such things even exist. So how are we to account for our emotional engagement with literature? Kendall Walton (le Poidevin, 1996, pp. 116-117) attempts to hold onto a belief-centred account of emotion by arguing that 'emotions' experienced during engagement with fiction are not real emotions. He argues that when we become involved in a fictional story, we engage in a game of make-believe. Just as a child may make-believe that the blanket spread over the chairs is the operating theatre of a hospital so we make-believe that a novel is reporting the truth. "Fiction... pretends to be making reference, and the reader accepts the pretence and co-operates with it... These conventions 'break the connection between words and world' that we expect of literal discourse" (Price, 1983, p. 2). This game of make-believe Price calls "the Fictional Contract". Now in a game the child may have the same or similar physiological responses as the real doctor trying to save someone's life. However, there is a crucial difference. The child does not really believe that the patient is dying. Thus, Walton says, the belief component of their "emotion" is different than in cases of real emotion. The child does not experience actual fear but quasi-fear. In just the same way, the person who engages with fiction experiences quasi-emotions. This account will not appeal to anyone unless they are already committed to a belief-centred theory. On Roberts' account we can construe the situation as X without actually believing that is really is X. Thus, the emotions experienced in fiction are real emotions. Granted, they are in important ways shallow emotions, for the construals "are bracketed, by the normal reader, with a proposition to the effect that this is fiction", but they are not second rate emotions. It seems to me, somewhat ironically, that we can give a better account of how stories impact us emotionally, if we abandon Nussbaum's hard-line on the propositional core of emotions.
184 Roberts' latest book (Roberts, 2003) on the analysis of emotions which develops his account in considerable detail. I am very grateful to him for sending me large sections of it for consideration whilst it was being written.

*construals.*"[185] This will need a little unpacking. The notion of construal Roberts takes from Wittgenstein's *Philosophical Investigations.* It is "a mental event or state in which one thing is grasped *in terms of*[186] something else."[187] Thus a person with whom I am tempted to be angry can be construed in various ways: "as a scoundrel who did such-and-such to me, as the son of my dear friend so-and-so, as a person who, after all, has had a pretty rough time of it in life, and so forth."[188] To each of these construals corresponds an emotion (anger, benevolence and pity respectively). This is the irreducibly propositional dimension of the paradigm cases of human emotion.[189] By "concern-based" Roberts means that the perceiver must *care* about the construal. For example, to feel guilt one must construe oneself as guilty *and* dislike being guilty. By "serious" Roberts means that the construal is compelling; having the appearance of truth.[190] Now I think that it is better to say that emotions necessarily involve a construal rather than a belief, because, although one will usually believe one's construal one may not. In the case of my toddler I feel angry briefly because I construe her as morally culpable *even though I do not really believe that she is.*[191] I remind myself that it is not her fault and thus cease to see her as culpable. To the extent that I succeed, the anger vanishes.

Roberts' account of emotion may indicate another way in which stories could shape emotion. Some stories may provide readers with new ways of construing people and situations. Such new construals will shape emotional responses to people. Consider Jesus' words, "Father, forgive them for they do not know what they are doing." Jesus construed those who crucified him as ignorant rather than as willfully rebellious against God. These construals are accompanied by different feelings and, by making such possibilities open to readers, new possibilities are opened up for seeing situations and people in contemporary life. This puts a different slant on Ricoeur's ideas about texts proposing new ways of being-in-the-world to the reader.

Biblical narratives do seem to consider emotion as a crucial aspect of ethical perception. Consider the reaction of David when Nathan brought home the point of his story with the words, "You are the man!" Had David had no emotional reaction but merely said, "Oh, yes I see your point," we would think that he had not perceived the significance of his deed at all. Consider the rape

---

185 Roberts, 1988, p. 209.
186 "In terms of" can have a perception, a thought, an image or a concept as its object (ibid., p. 190).
187 Ibid., p. 190.
188 Ibid., p. 193.
189 Roberts' new book explains in some detail that, although the paradigm cases of emotion have a propositional structure, this does not entail that all emotions are propositional. And some classes of emotion such as moods and emotions experienced through music are only analogically, at best, related to propositions.
190 Roberts, 1988, p. 201.
191 Ibid., p. 201.

of Dinah in Genesis 34. For the brothers to perceive the rape as "defiling" and as "folly in Israel" *is* to have an emotional reaction. If one did not feel these thoughts one has either not understood them or not accepted them. Adequate ethical perception *is* emotional perception

So the central question concerns the relation of emotion to practical reason. Emotion seems to play two conceptually distinct roles in moral living. First, and most obviously, it has motivational power. Emotion drives action. Emotion can drive both immoral[192] and moral action. It can send a person into a violent rage over a trivial matter or compel the prophet to speak out against an injustice. Gilman talks of how emotion involves a judgement about certain features of the world (emotional judgement) and about how it ought to be (emotional projects). Emotion is also the "energy" linking judgement and project. "Emotional energy, in other words, is the spark that ignites and drives humans to actualise the projects engendered by emotional judgements."[193] The power of emotion to drive action raises the critical issue of the education of the emotions to which we shall return shortly.

Second, emotional acknowledgement of certain features of a situation is the appropriate human acknowledgement of those features. A detached assent to the relevant propositions is an inadequate assent. To perceive a situation with one's moral perception is necessarily to engage one's emotions. One cannot be looking right if one does not feel as one looks.

We have argued above for the centrality of emotional perception to moral perception and of emotional education to moral education. The next crucial step is to enquire after the role of story in one's emotional education (and thus in moral education). Story can shape emotion in at least three ways.

First of all, the worldview which underpins the value beliefs upon which emotions are parasitic is (always?) narrative in framework. N.T. Wright, in *The New Testament and the People of God*, has written very insightfully here. As far as the Bible goes the metanarrative is absolutely crucial to spinning the worldview. Individual stories find their place in the bigger story. However, the individual narratives will play their role. A worldview and its values cannot be conveyed in a single narrative, but a single narrative can reinforce a worldview or challenge aspects of a worldview. It can strengthen a reader's ethical conceptions, stretch them, or shatter them. This is the importance of story at the level of the grammar of belief.

Second, and related to this point, is the way in which stories can play a role in the grammar of emotions. Narratives offer models of appropriate and inappropriate emotional responses which can shape an understanding of what emotion is, as well as generating the capacity for such responses in the reader. Of course, many factors influence the emotional life of a person and it would be

---

192 See Roberts, 1991b.
193 Gilman, 1994, p. 225. Of course, the role of judgement will be recast in terms of construal on Roberts' account. Many construals are judgements but they need not be.

folly to suggest that simply hearing a story will instantly mould the emotionality of the hearer. Nevertheless, we do learn our emotions *partly* from the emotions displayed by role models in narratives.

Third, stories engage the reader's emotions and give them the equivalent of an emotional work-out at the gym. Stories, both fictional and factual, can stretch and mould the emotional responses of the reader so as to shape them for better or for worse. This is not done by informing the reader or hearer (or viewer) how to feel on given occasions but by *eliciting* the feelings themselves.[194] Stories thus become like practice for facing situations we may face in life and the closer we see the parallel between our lives and the story the more impact they will have on us (consider the parable Nathan told David). Fiction encourages the reader to enter into the lives of the characters and to learn to perceive the best way forward in specific cases. Readers are encouraged to identify with the characters and thus to become more responsive in their own actual lives. We readers care for the particularity of the characters and in so doing become better perceivers in the situations in which we are embedded.[195] Literature thus trains the moral imagination.

## *Story and the Grammar of Ethics*

Stories can, as we have seen, display virtue in action but in some cases they do more than this. Within an ethical tradition such as Christianity certain central stories come to play a key role in the actual nuancing of the *meaning* of a virtue or vice. Robert C. Roberts borrows the notion of "grammar" from linguistics to explain this. The grammar of a moral concept is the set of rules, internal to a tradition, connecting and disconnecting it with the other moral concepts within that tradition. The grammar of a virtue is a conceptual map of how it links with motives, intentional objects, a concept of human nature, other virtues and vices and the like.[196] Roberts argues that "in some moral traditions some narratives play a role that goes beyond that of *displaying* virtues. They make up part of what is culturally distinctive about a set of virtues, by entering into the very grammar of those virtues."[197] In other words some stories do not merely *exemplify* a moral rule or a virtue but actually play a role in defining, for a particular community, what the rule or virtue *is*! Roberts mentions the exodus story and the Gospel narratives in the regard. With reference to the latter he writes,

---

194 One thinks of the catharsis associated with tragedy.
195 Nussbaum, 1990, p. 162.
196 See Roberts 1991b, p. 334 and especially Roberts, 1995.
197 Roberts, 1999, p. 478. In "Virtues and Rules" (1991b) he explains that "stories do not normally become part of the grammar of a virtue. Occasionally, they do, but only when the story is shared by a community and constitutive of a tradition" (p. 342).

The narrative of the incarnation, death and resurrection of the Son of God does not just dramatically display a set of virtues with a special grammar, but is itself taken up in the grammar of the virtues of those who accept the story and become members of the community. Compassion is seeing in the faces of the sufferers one ministers to the face of the incarnate Son who died for them; contrition is both sadness for sins committed against the God whose Son is the main character in the story and comfort that this man's death is one's own righteousness; gratitude is first of all for the act of God recounted in the story; hope is first of all for the resurrection for which the risen Jesus is the firstfruits... the main function of the narrative in the Christian community... is not to display the Christian virtues, but to take its place in the grammar of those virtues.[198]

It is for this reason that Roberts claims that "the idea of generic virtues, virtues which have only features that are non-specific to particular traditions, is a fiction."[199] Hauerwas and Pinches' book, *Christians Among the Virtues*, takes a similar line maintaining that we should refuse to talk of the virtues in an abstract sense as if there was a neutral, tradition-independent, account of them. Hauerwas and Pinches attempt to set out a *Christian* account of some of the virtues to indicate how it differs from accounts not informed by the Christian story (and the story of the cross in particular). In "Emotions Among the Virtues of the Christian Life" (1992) Roberts also fleshes out how the Christian narrative informs the understanding of the virtues.

Nussbaum[200] has challenged the claim that a tradition-neutral account of the virtues cannot be given, and a brief analysis of her contention will reveal an important qualification to the claims made above. Nussbaum indicates eight spheres of human life[201] that are almost impossible to avoid for human beings whatever their culture. To each of these spheres attach virtues which every human society must articulate. Granted that they may actually articulate the virtues differently, Nussbaum confidently hopes that an Aristotelian dialectic would, if employed, yield a virtue-system agreed by all rational people.

What Nussbaum does succeed in doing in her article, in my opinion, is showing that human nature (which could but need not be understood metaphysically[202]) should be expected to provide a *bare outline* of virtue which is culture-transcendent. Where she fails to convince is in her hope for a *full and rich* ethic to crystallise from an Aristotelian dialectic. Roberts points out, for example, how she "omits from the list of fundamental human experiences the need for a relationship to God. Presumably Nussbaum thinks that insofar as we

---

198 Roberts, 1999, p. 479.
199 Roberts, 1992, p. 37.
200 Nussbaum, 1993b.
201 Namely: morality, the body, pleasure and pain, cognitive capability, practical reason, early infant development, affiliation and humour.
202 See Nussbaum, 1995.

are rational persons we can be talked out of this sphere."[203] Few theists would agree here! This raises the suspicion that her attempt to find a universal morality by means of "neutral" reason is really a defence of one historical morality – notably a Western Liberal one.[204]

Nevertheless, we shall have to make space for a skeletal account of virtues which is culture-transcendent but which needs transformation within the narrative structures of traditions to turn it into a living morality. This explains the great commonalities between ethical systems as well as the divergences. Roberts puts the point as follows: "My view is that virtues have both generic and tradition specific features: that there is a 'general grammar' of the virtues, which specifies the features of trans-traditional virtue types, and a 'particular grammar' of the virtues themselves."[205] Indeed, the Christian narrative can easily accommodate a basic, generic ethic given its doctrine of creation. All people live within God's creation-order and are in God's image whether they realise it or not. Sin can only distort the structures of the world within certain limits.

The discussion so far has been in terms of virtues but I would like to add a small addition here. I shall argue in Chapter Two that key stories can also shape action-imperative-rules and principles in tradition-specific ways. A story can provide *a new motive* for obeying an old rule. Also a story can lead to *adaptations* of inherited laws and rules. On top of that, stories can lead to a rearrangement of the importance of a group of action-imperative-laws in relation to each other.

One may be tempted to think that this quasi-Wittgensteinian account of morals is to give way to relativism – that ethical truth is tradition-dependent. I would suggest that this need not be so. Christian virtues are rooted in the creation order and in its creator, both of which transcend human cultures. The ethic-shaping story that Christians tell is a story in which God has revealed himself and it is the doctrine of revelation that roots the Christian ethic in God himself.[206] Consequently, although a Christian will acknowledge that their ethic is shaped by their story, in just the same way that, say, Hindu ethics are shaped by Hindu stories, this does not, indeed *cannot*, amount to a claim that both sets

---

203 Roberts, 1992, p. 63, fn. 2.

204 So Hauerwas, 1989; Roberts (1992, p. 62, fn. 2) notes how attempts to find a universal morality by means of neutral reason tend to fall into one of two problems: (a) they are too general and thus they fail to present a morality anyone could live by, or (b) they become an unacknowledged apologetic for one specific, historical or philosophically constructed morality.

205 Roberts, 1992, p. 38; see also 1991b, p. 336 and Hauerwas and Pinches, 1997, p. 119.

206 On the imitation of God in the Old Testament, see Barton, 1994 and Birch, 1988 (though see Rodd, 2001, ch. 7 for a critique). For a philosophical attempt to root human virtues in the virtues of God see Zagzebski, 1998. I shall dispute this account in Chapter Two.

of stories (and the consequent ethics) are equally true.[207] Put differently, from the fact that there is no tradition-neutral way to *see* the truth about God, one cannot infer that there is no tradition-transcending truth about God, nor even that some people could be said to know what it is.[208]

Now, of all the ways in which narrative can function in ethics discussed above, this is the only one which does not apply to Genesis 34. Genesis 34 is, in Longacre's terminology, off-the-main-line of the narrative. It is, in terms of the plot of Genesis, an aside and consequently an unlikely candidate for contributing to the grammar of the virtues. As a matter of fact it has, quite rightly, not played such a role in the history of interpretation. We must look elsewhere for its ethical use.

### Conclusion: The Contribution of Narrative Form to the Ethical Life

From critical interaction with Ricoeur's work we have set up a framework in which it is possible to see how storytelling transforms (to some extent) the ethics of the proto-narrative world and how, in the act of reading, the reader is, in turn, transformed by the narrative text which presents new possibilities for the moral life. The reader can play with these proposals imaginatively allowing them to bring their shaping influence to bear.

I have argued that an appropriation of narratives in the moral life must stress *both* the generalisability *and* the particularity of stories. There are dangers in an overemphasis on either end of this spectrum and there is no scientific formula by which the "right" balance can be achieved. Sensitivity and spiritual wisdom in reading are skills much needed. We can generalise virtues and principles from stories, but we must not absolutise them. An overemphasis on generalisability will dull readers to the unique features of particular situations. An overemphasis on particularity makes it very difficult for a reader to make any appropriation of the moral dimension of the text other than the thought that decisions are made in very context-sensitive ways.

I have also argued that stories are capable of shaping the crucial emotional dimension of ethical rationality – a dimension sadly ignored or deliberately

---

207 Roberts (1991b) makes a related point when he writes, "nothing I have said rules out there being such a thing as the truth about human nature, and if this exists then the grammar of a set of virtues in fulfilment of that nature will be universally binding... moral rules." It may be possible to modify this claim slightly: Caleb Miller (1999) argues that we cannot infer from the claim that all humans have the same nature and telos that what is virtuous is the same for all people. Virtue ethics, he says, must remember the impact of the fall and to set impossibly high standards for sinful people is not redemptive. Instead, God will set realistic virtues which direct people in the direction of their telos even if not all the way there. Thus, virtues will be relative to individuals or groups. But even if correct, this relativism is limited. All true virtues must be pointing in the direction of the human telos as understood by Christian theology.
208 See Clouser, 1999.

suppressed in many Enlightenment systems of ethics. However, we must beware not to extol stories *at the expense of* rules or principles. Christian ethics requires both rules and narratives to be healthy and vibrant. The scripture provides not simply the exodus story but also the law of Moses; not only the story of Jesus but also the Sermon on the Mount. The urgent task of biblical theologians is to allow the narrative contexts to impact the principles/rules and the principles/rules to cast their shadow across the narrative. Only through such a creative dialogue can a Christian ethic claim to be biblical.

It remains to indicate how the insights gleaned in this Chapter will guide the study which follows. Our goal in an ethical reading of Genesis 34 is an appropriation of the text in which the worlds of reader and text intersect expanding the horizons of the interpreter. This thesis hopes to clear some ground to facilitate such readerly refiguration.

Ricoeur has maintained that individuals find their sense of self and their values within the stories told by the communities of which they are a part. Chapter Two will take this theme and explore the biblical metanarrative which delineates the contours of Christian identity. I shall argue that a Christian reading of individual stories within the Bible should always have the bigger plot as a context for interpretation. Chapter Five will apply the insights gained here to Genesis 34.

We have briefly mentioned the importance of reading traditions to Ricoeur. To ignore the contributions of past interpreters to our study of texts is misguided and thus Chapter Three explores the diverse ethical appropriations of Genesis 34 over a period of more than two millennia. This will enable the reader to situate my reading in a reading tradition - to see what is sediment and what innovation.

Mature understanding (in a Ricoeurian sense) of texts is mediated by explanation. Thus a structural and exegetical analysis of Genesis 34 is essential groundwork for informed appropriation of the story. Chapter Four will thus be devoted to such an "explanation". It will try to discern the boundaries set up by the text within which responsible interpreters can explore. Chapter Five tries to set up contours within which responsible *Christian* appropriations of Genesis 34 can occur. We shall consider the extent to which Genesis 34 provides models to imitate or avoid and the extent to which particularity and ambiguity come to the fore. The moral perceptiveness (or lack of it) of the characters involved will be considered. The ultimate goal of ethical reading is the refiguration of the reader and Chapters 2-5 have set out the parameters for such appropriations.[209]

---

209 However, we have seen that a reader may decline the invitation of the text if they cannot identify with the world being proposed. It is just such a problem which Chapter 6 takes up. There I examine the claim made by feminist scholars that Genesis 34 is patriarchal and androcentric and consequently a poor resource for the ethical life. I argue that the text can speak afresh to a post-androcentric Christian community.

# Chapter Two

# Biblical-Theological Reflections on Christian Ethical Appropriation of Old Testament Stories

*Narrative texts in the New Testament are fundamental resources for normative ethics... the narratives are more fundamental than any secondary process of abstraction that seeks to distil their ethical import.*[1]

*[T]he unity that we find [in the New Testament] is the... unity of a collection of documents that, in various ways, retell and comment upon a single fundamental story.*[2]

In this chapter we move from the realm of philosophical hermeneutics to that of theological hermeneutics. I hope to show, first of all, that story is the context within which Old Testament ethics lives and moves and has its being. I do this by proposing a way in which story is intimately connected with the three models for Old Testament ethics proposed by John Barton: divine commands, natural law and the imitation of God.[3]

---

1  Hays, 1996a, p. 295. I would qualify "more fundamental" by suggesting that it be understood to mean "more *epistemologically* fundamental" and not necessarily "more *ontologically* fundamental".

2  Ibid., p. 193. This chapter hopes to demonstrate the applicability of these two quotations to Old Testament ethics.

3 The reader may suspect that such a task is unnecessary given that Genesis 34 is obviously a narrative whether or not there is a link between these models and story. Surely all I need to do is to show that narratives can function ethically in order to show that Genesis 34 can. My justification is two-fold. First of all, I am seeking to outline and defend a *general* model for Christian ethical reappropriation of Old Testament texts. The model is then applied to a narrative case study (Genesis 34) but *the model itself needs to be able to handle a broader range of texts*. It will become clear that the model requires Christians to read individual narratives within the context of the whole canonical plot and this requires us to be able to clarify how the parts inter-relate (and, for our purposes, how narrative parts inter-relate with non-narrative parts). Second, it seems to me that studies of Old Testament ethics have seriously underestimated the importance both of

My second task is to outline the biblical metanarrative which plays a primary role in the shaping of Christian communal and individual identity. This narrative, so I shall argue, is that within which *Christian* ethical reflection must be done and through which *Christian* appropriations of individual Old Testament narratives should be filtered. I will defend the claim against the fear that reading the whole Bible as if it were one plot would force all the different narrative and non-narrative traditions into a soup in which distinctives are lost. I hope to show that the distinctive features of different parts of Scripture can be maintained within an overarching unity of plot. Chapter Five will apply the methodology of this chapter to Genesis 34.

## The Centrality of Story for Old Testament Ethics: Barton's Three Models for Old Testament Ethics

### *A Sketch of the Models*

The first task is to argue that story is central to different Old Testament models for ethics. In several works John Barton has suggested that three models for the basis of ethics can be discerned within the Hebrew Bible.[4] These models provide answers to the question, "*Why* should I act in such and such a way?" I shall argue that story is important to all three.

The first model is that of obedience to the declared will of God. Here the answer to the question is, "you ought to do such and such *because God commands it*." This lies at the root of the meta-ethical Divine Command Theory of ethics.[5] The Old Testament is full of direct commands from God and the clear impression given is that these commands ought to be obeyed simply because God gave them. The paradigm biblical texts which fit this model are clearly Old Testament laws.

The second model is that of "natural law". Barton understands natural law in a suitably loose way.[6] It refers to certain actions being right or wrong not because of a direct command from God but simply *because of the way the world is*. The focus in texts which pick up this strand of thinking is on the created order and the kinds of actions which do and do not accord with it. This

---

stories and of the narrative dimension of non-storied texts. In seeking to demonstrate the underpinning of legal, prophetic and Wisdom literature by story I am indirectly seeking to demonstrate that the pure narrative sections of the Old Testament ought to become more prominent in studies of Old Testament ethics.

4 Barton, 1978, 1994, 1998.

5 There has been something of a mini revival in Divine Command Theory in the past twenty years or so. See Robert Adams, 1979; Philip Quinn, 1978; Mark Murphey, 1998; William Alston, 1989, Ch. 12; Paul Helm, 1981.

6 Barton, 1994, p. 15.

ought not to be seen as secular ethics, for the created order is only as it is because of God's creative choice.[7] As examples of biblical texts in this tradition Barton singles out prophetic texts such as Amos 1:3-2:3; Isaiah 3:16-4:1; 31:1-2; 5:22; legal texts like the food laws in Leviticus 11[8] and Wisdom texts such as Proverbs. He concedes however that in the final form of the Old Testament canon the natural law texts have been assimilated by the divine command model.[9]

The third model is that of the imitation of God. Here the answer to our question is, "you ought to do such and such *because that is what God would do.*" Several Old Testament texts explicitly call for the imitation of God and ground ethical behaviour in such imitation. For example,

> Remember the Sabbath day and keep it holy... *for* in six days the LORD made heaven and earth... and rested the seventh day..."[10]

> If ever you take your neighbour's garment in pledge, you shall restore it to him before the sun goes down... And if he cries to me, I will hear, for I am compassionate.[11]

It looks here as though God's compassion for the vulnerable is the basis for Israel's.

> The LORD your God is the God of gods and Lord of lords, the great God, mighty and awesome, who is not partial and takes no bribe, who executes justice for the orphan and the widow, and loves the strangers, providing them food and clothing. You [also] shall love the stranger.[12]

These divine characteristics become normative for the lifestyle of the community of God: "Be holy *for* I the LORD your God am holy."[13]

In addition to these are texts that presuppose that God acts according to moral standards that humans also share.[14] The root of this idea could well be in the story in which God created humanity "in his own image."[15] To the extent to which humans image God they can assume that God lives by the same kinds of

---

7  Ibid., p. 17. For an overview of "creation" in 20th C Old Testament scholarship see Reventlow, 1985, pp. 134-154.
8  Assuming a Mary Douglas type of explanation for them. See Douglas, 1985.
9  Barton, 1998, pp. 74-76.
10 Ex 20:8-11.
11 Ex.22:26-27.
12 Deut 10:17-19.
13 Lev 19:2. See also Ps 25:8-9.
14 E.g., Gen 18:22-33.
15 Gen 1:27.

values.[16]

To this we can add Gordon Wenham's observation, that even though only a few texts make the moral imitation of God *explicit,* we can see that the qualities God seeks in his people are the very same qualities he has himself – mercy, justice, loyalty, generosity, love and so on.[17] We cannot infer from the fact that a particular law does not explicitly mention the imitation of God that the imitation of God is not a rationale for the law. We find that the *very same laws* are sometimes justified in terms of reflecting the divine character and sometimes not. For example, in Exodus 23:12 the Sabbath is simply commanded on grounds of compassion. No mention is made of the imitation of God. However, in Exodus 20:8-11 the *same law* is rooted in God's behaviour. This could *possibly* indicate that the imitation of God is far more implicit in Old Testament ethics than is sometimes thought.

How do these three models inter-relate? Barton sees the imitation of God as a "potentially unifying theme for much that the Hebrew Bible has to say about ethics... In a way it can hold together both obedience and natural law models."[18] This is because the laws could be seen as expressions of how natural law works out in practice and both could be rooted in the goodness of God himself.[19] With this I concur. The writers of the Old Testament documents never reflect on such abstract questions, but it does seem to be a legitimate readerly task to see if it is possible to unify the ethical strands found in the Hebrew Bible. This thesis does not stand or fall on my ability to do this but I shall put forward the following proposal to be tested against the text.

I propose that the ultimate foundations of all ethics are the virtues and goodness of the divine person. Out of his good nature God issues commands and laws. These commands lie behind the creation order itself which came into being with the fiats of God.[20] The creation thus reflects the order his words decreed and this may explain the assimilation of natural law to divine command which Barton observes. It also indicates an important qualification of natural law ethics as found in the Old Testament. The created order that provides the context for ethical deeds is the *theologically interpreted* creation order depicted in Genesis 1-2 and other texts such as Isaiah 40.[21] Thus an *adequate* interpretation of the natural law, from an Old Testament perspective, may well

---

16 Of course, this is not to suggest that these values exist independently of God for they are grounded in the divine nature itself.

17 Ex 34:6-7. G.J. Wenham, 1997, pp. 26-27.

18 Barton, 1994, p. 18.

19 Ibid., p. 19.

20 Gen 1. It should be noted that the notion of creation-order is not limited to Genesis 1 but pervades much of the Hebrew Bible (see Wolters, 1996). It should also be noted that the divine fiats are not arbitrary.

21 The most competent attempt I have found which defends a theological creation-order ethic is that of O'Donovan, 1994.

require *some* "special revelation".[22] Nevertheless, natural law is grounded in the order of the world, the order of the world is grounded in the commands of God and the commands of God are grounded in the nature of God.

I would maintain that natural law, as defined above, is what determines the "good" for humans. What is virtuous for a human *depends on what it is to be a human*[23] (which depends on the commands of God which depends on the nature of God). Divine commands to human beings such as the law of Moses I would see as expressions of the natural order of creation *as revealed in the biblical story.*[24] Where does the imitation of God fit into this scheme? Humans were made in the image of God and thus it is often the case that the *telos* of humans involves acting like God. By imitating God, the Israelites becomes closer to what God made them to be thus fulfilling the natural law. The reason why I do not want to maintain that the imitation of God is the ultimate grounding of ethics (as Barton seems to) is that there are numerous human virtues which simply cannot be grounded in divine virtues.[25] Courage, temperance, chastity and piety are all good for humans but it makes little sense to see God as brave, for example. Nothing can threaten God so he has nothing to fear. Whatever it is that makes courage a human virtue it is *not* that God himself exercises it and consequently, we are not courageous in imitation of God. Humans are to imitate God *only to the extent that we image God* but, as the God-human relationship is not symmetrical, some of God's virtues cannot be ours and some of ours cannot be his. The problem is solved if *"natural law"* or, as I prefer to

---

22 O'Donovan writes, "Knowledge of the natural order is moral knowledge, and as such it is co-ordinated with obedience. There can be no true knowledge of that order without loving acceptance of it and conformity to it, for it is known by participation and not by transcendence. In disobedience our perceptions of it assume false and strange shapes. Yet even in our confusion and error we remain, by the merciful providence of God, human beings... Even in confusion and error we do not simply cease to know... We will speak more truly of 'misknowledge', rather than of simple lack of knowledge... And the universe, though fractured and broken, displays the fact that its brokenness is the brokenness of order and not merely unordered chaos. Thus it remains accessible to knowledge in part. It requires no revelation to observe the various forms of generic and teleological order which belong to it. An unbeliever or a non-Christian culture does not have to be ignorant about the structure of the family, the virtue of mercy, the vice of cowardice, or the duty of justice... Nevertheless, such knowledge is incomplete unless the created order is grasped as a whole, and that includes its relation to the uncreated. If the creator is not known, then the creation is not known as creation" (O'Donovan, 1994, pp. 87-88).

23 This is similar to the Aristotelian line taken by Aquinas. On Aquinas see Lisska, 1997. My dispute with Aquinas is epistemological (see O'Donovan, 1994, pp. 85-89).

24 We shall see later that they may be qualified and limited expressions of such natural law. In its final form Psalm 19 suggestively juxtaposes creation order with the torah of Yahweh.

25 The argument which follows is, to my mind, a good reason to disagree with Zabzebski's (1998) attempt to root human virtues in the divine virtues.

call it, "creation order" grounds human *telos* and thus human virtues. Room is made for the imitation of God (for we are created in the divine image) and divine commands (which approximate to the creation order). But at the root of it all is the goodness of God himself which is reflected in the order of his creation. There is consequently no necessary conflict between the three models.

Be this as it may, my main contention in this section is that these three models only come fully into their own in an Old Testament context when situated within stories. Story provides the frame within which the models function. It will be easiest to demonstrate this by examining briefly the imitation of God, then natural law and finally divine commands.

### Story and the Imitation of God

When we consider the texts which call Israel to act in certain ways to imitate God, we see that this is always in response to certain ways in which God has acted, or acts, within the story of Israel itself. This is not always obvious, for some of the texts seem to refer to static qualities within God. However, God's virtuous character can *only* be demonstrated in historical actions which are necessarily storied. How are his mercy, justice, holiness and loyalty manifest? In acts of judgement and salvation. In exodus deliverance, exilic banishment and return from exile. In turn, God's virtues can only be imitated in human attitudes and acts *within the ongoing story of Israel and its individual "members"*. Apparently static virtues such as "justice" or "mercy" are, I suggest, shorthand references to their exemplification in divine acts of justice and mercy. Purely static divine virtues would not be virtues if they failed to manifest in action. This is a rather obvious observation but no less significant for that. When Israel imitates God it does so by remembering the story and allowing the behaviour of God to inform its own behaviour.

### Story and Natural Law

Natural law hardly seems to require story to situate it. However, in the Hebrew Bible the ordering of creation *is a part of the grand story that begins in Genesis 1.*[26] Creation is thus a story before it is a doctrine. When the natural order in

---

26 This is the case whether or not Israel's faith was a redemptive faith before it was a creation faith. There is a tradition of separating a creation ethic from a salvation-history ethic in Old Testament studies. For example, Eichrodt and von Rad emphasise "salvation history" at the expense of "nature" whilst some recent scholars have overplayed creation at the expense of Israel's story. Scholars tend to favour one or the other. The canon, in its final form, however sees creation as part of the same story as that in which we find the salvation of Israel. The division is a false and unhelpful one. The creation stories in Genesis 1-3 prefigure aspects of the later story of Israel anticipating redemption. However, Israel's redemptive faith was also seen in terms of creation. This is most clear in the prophecies of deutero-Isaiah. Thus there is a dialogical

gender relations and marriage is explained[27] it is done *via a story*[28] and the same could be said about the natural order in human-animal relations,[29] human-nature relations[30] and human-God relations. Think also of the example of Levitical food-laws that Barton mentions. It has been plausibly argued that the distinctions between clean and unclean animals were made on the basis of a theological interpretation of the natural order of the kind found in Genesis 1.[31] This is not to say that natural law thinking is exhausted by the early chapters of Genesis – that would be absurd. It is to say that natural law thinking was story-shaped and, *epistemologically*, story-grounded. It may be objected that there is no plot-development in the creation order and thus it seems to be too static to be labeled as storied. This is true in some senses. The creation is more like the stage on which the story occurs and its norms are a constant over *all* stages of the plot.[32] However, in the Bible the creation of this stage forms part of the story itself *and* we do have plot developments of a sort. We see that the norms of the creation are rebelled against in Genesis 3 ff.. In Christian systematic theological terms the creation is "fallen" and the harmony of Genesis 1-2 is shattered. The story of the Bible could be seen in terms of the restoration of the creation to a harmonious state even if not to its garden state.[33] And the twisting of the creation does have an impact on the ethics of the Bible which, as we shall see, have a measure of realism injected into them given the broken reality of the present "fallen" order. Thus it seems clear that a *biblical version* of natural law theory must be rooted in the biblical story of creation and fall.[34]

It could be objected here that the passages which Barton cites appeal to broader social convention or to an ethic which *transcends an Israelite*

---

relationship between creation and redemption theologies in the Old Testament. In the final canonical shape of the Old Testament creation comes first.

27  The creation order is ontologically structured through divine commands but it is known through story.

28  Gen 2:18-25.

29  Gen 1:26-28; 2:18-20.

30  Gen 1:26-30; 2:8-9, 15-17.

31  Mary Douglas herself makes this proposal and Douglas Davis makes a different but similar one (see B. Lang [ed.], 1985 for reprints of both articles).

32  This should be seen as a theological bulwark against historicism but should not be seen to rule out cultural and historical development. The Dutch philosopher Herman Dooyeweerd helpfully developed a notion of "opening processes" built into creation. This would see the creation as full of potential which must be brought out but in a way which does not run against its wisely constructed structures. On Dooyeweerd see especially Kalsbeek, 1975 and Clouser, 1991. For a short and simple explanation see Wolters, 1996, pp. 35-41.

33  Rev 21-22, 1 Pet 3:13; Rom 8:19-25.

34  Brown (1999) shows how creation and narrative are joined in an unbreakable bond in various Old Testament textual traditions. His approach is not quite the same as mine but complements it well.

*worldview* and which the nations *in general* can be expected to recognise. This is something epistemologically closer to what is normally called "natural law". For example, Amos' critique of the nations[35] presupposes their ability to see the injustice of their ways, yet they cannot be expected to do so within the story framework of Israel. Again, Amos imagines the rulers of Ashdod and Egypt called to watch and to be appalled at Israel outstripping even them in oppressing the poor.[36] He clearly expects them to discern some ethical truths without the knowledge of Israel's God. Now Barton does not actually claim that Amos' thinking here is fully-fledged natural law theology. In *Amos' Oracles against the Nations* he examines four rationales for the oracles against the nations[37] and rejects the following: the nations were condemned for opposing Israel; the nations were condemned because laws which apply to Israel were extended to apply to them; the nations were condemned for infringing a universal divine law. Instead, Barton proposes that the nations were condemned for infringing customs of war accepted, believed to be accepted, or which ought (in Amos' view) to be accepted by all nations.[38] So *cultural convention* is the grounding of the condemnation. What are we to make of this? Barton concedes that there is no evidence for any international agreements on conduct in warfare either legally ratified or not.[39] In fact, some nations such as Assyria seemed to glory in the cruel treatment of those they defeated.[40] And even if each nation did have its own standards for behaviour in war, they were certainly not universally shared, as Barton's contrast of the Assyrians and Hittites shows.[41] So, we cannot easily see Amos as appealing to *actual* quasi-universal social conventions. At best the oracles may appeal to what all the nations *ought* to know, even if in reality only some of them did know.[42] But this raises again the question of the basis of such an appeal. *Why* ought they to know these moral standards? Amos does not address that question directly. Perhaps he never reflected on it. But some reflection on the broader theology of Amos may suggest an answer *we* can give that is consistent with his thinking,

---

35 Amos 1:3-2:16. Hasel notes that scholars divide over the authenticity of these oracles but that the recent trend is clearly towards seeing them as coming from Amos' hand (1989, pp. 60-68). See Andersen and Freedman for an example of this trend (1989, pp. 206-211, 342-343).

36 Amos 3:9-11.

37 Barton, 1980, ch. 6.

38 So too J. Hayes, 1988, pp. 58-59. Hasel sees the options as follows: the oracles are grounded in natural law (J. Barr); the oracles are grounded in a universal covenant (R.E. Clements); the oracles are grounded in nationalism (M. Haran); the oracles are grounded in a universal morality (P. Humbert); the oracles are grounded in a universal law (K. Cramer); the oracles are grounded in international law (J. Barton) (Hasel, 1991, p. 69).

39 Ibid., pp. 51-57.

40 Ibid., p. 57.

41 Ibid., pp. 57-58.

42 Barton himself sees this (1980, p. 59).

even if he himself never articulated it.

## God of Creation

Amos has a clear theology of creation expressed in the hymnic fragments embedded in the book.[43] God is the creator of the mountains,[44] stars[45] and the heavenly chambers[46] and therefore has power in heaven and on earth to judge. He can bring drought,[47] or unleash floods[48] and earthquakes.[49] But he can turn his creation to bless his people with good harvests.[50]

## God of the Nations

God not only created the nations but also has been at work providentially in their stories even if they, unlike Israel, are unaware of this.[51] As creator and "guardian" of the nations he is their judge also.[52]

## God of Israel

Although the word "covenant" is not used to describe Israel's special relationship with God, Amos' message presupposes a covenant theology.[53] Yahweh speaks of "my people Israel"[54] whom he delivered from Egypt, guided in the wilderness, gave the Promised Land and sustained with the prophetic word.[55] Israel was thus more responsible than the nations and her failure more

---

43 Amos 1:2; 4:13; 5:8-9; 9:5-6. There is no scholarly consensus on the issue of whether these hymns were added in later or were placed there by Amos himself (Hasel, 1991, ch. 8). Andersen and Freedman argue that the non-hymnic sections clearly presuppose the creation theology of the hymns (1989, pp. 89-90) and thus have no problem in thinking that Amos himself placed the hymns in their present locations (ibid., pp. 42-43, 51-52, 72, 455-57, 486-90, 444-54). J. de Waard, 1977, sees the creation hymn in 5:8-9 as the centre of the whole book of Amos and structurally fully integrated into the main body of the text. If de Waard is correct this would support the view that Amos himself incorporated the hymns into their present context.

44 Amos 4:13.

45 Amos 5:8.

46 Amos 9:6.

47 Amos 1:2.

48 Amos 5:8.

49 Amos 9:5-6.

50 Amos 9:13.

51 Amos 9:7.

52 Amos 1:3-2:3. On Amos' God as the God of world history see Andersen and Freedman, 1989, pp. 90 ff..

53 This claim is, of course, controversial. Hayes sees no evidence of a covenant theology in Amos (1988, p. 38) whilst others see covenant as central to Amos (e.g. D. Stuart, D. Hubbard). Andersen and Freedman also see covenant theme as present in Amos (1989, p. 81, 91-93, 236 etc.).

54 Amos 7:8, 15; 8:2; 3:1; 4:12; 9:7.

55 Amos 2:9-11; 5:25; 9:7.

serious.[56] In spite of all Yahweh did for her, she became like the nations in pagan worship and rejected God's gracious provisions.[57] The covenant then is the basis for God's judgement of Israel and for them "salvation-history turns into judgement-history."[58] The covenant is also the basis of God's restoration of a remnant.[59]

Returning to our question, we see that Amos cannot appeal to the special covenant with Israel as a ground for God's judgement of the nations. However, part of the solution may be lurking in that neighbourhood. Andersen and Freedman argue that Amos 9:7 provides a vital clue. There Yahweh's gracious deliverance of Israel from Egypt is paralleled with his bringing the Philistines out of Caphtor and the Aramaeans from Qir. These gracious acts in the history of both Israel and the nations form the ground upon which their obligations to Yahweh rest. "Because he has acted on behalf of Philistines and Aramaeans he has a right to impose demands and to insist on compliance with rules and requirements, just as in the case of Israel."[60] In this case, Amos is not extending Israel's covenant obligations to the nations but seeing the nations as having their own duties to Yahweh (even if they do not recognise him as God). Whilst agreeing with Andersen and Freedman that God's providential grace probably forms *part* of the foundation of their obligations, I would not see this as incompatible with a grounding in creation-order (what Barton calls "a universal divine law").

William Brown has recently argued that Israel's laws were seen as a gracious response to God's salvation *and* as rooted in creation[61] and there is no reason why Amos' teaching need be seen as incompatible with this. Although he does not *explicitly* appeal to creation-order to ground his ethic such an appeal would fit with his overall theology. From a completed canon perspective I would observe that in the view of the bigger biblical story *all people are in God's image and live in the same created order*. Amos seems to concur with this. In less theological terms we have the same human nature and live in the same world. Even if many cannot appreciate the world from the perspective of Israel's story, they can still be expected to discern some of the norms of that same order from some other perspective.[62] Thus, *given a biblical story of creation*, Amos can expect a pagan nation to discern *some* of the creational norms. Human interpretations of the natural law can only go wrong (as one

---

56 Amos 3:2; 2:6-12.

57 Amos 2:6-8; 8:5.

58 Mays, 1969, p. 8.

59 Amos 9:8b-9. On the issue of the authenticity of this text see Hasel, 1991, ch. 11.

60 Andersen and Freedman, 1989, p. 352.

61 Brown, 1999.

62 This seems to fit with the implicit claims of texts such as Rom 1:18-20; 2:14-15; Acts 14:17; Ps 1:1-4; Isa 28:23-29.

thinking from within the biblical story would see it) to a certain extent and thus a common human morality, even if only very basic, could be expected. Nothing I have said about a theologically interpreted natural law should be seen as ruling out any insights into such order from other perspectives.

In summary, although Amos' ethic does not at first seem to have any narrative element, it can be argued that it does presuppose a story of God's creating and acting with gracious providential care in the histories of Israel and the nations. This story lies beneath the surface, but is needed to make adequate sense of his ethics.

Although Amos' "natural law" ethic may not be as narrative-free as it seems at first glance, it could seem that Israel's Wisdom Literature stands as a strong counter-example to the claim that natural law is linked to story in any significant way. I shall argue that appearances may be deceptive here also and that narrative and wisdom may be more strongly linked than is often thought.

Wisdom literature is grounded in a strong theology of creation[63] with little explicit place for Israel's story. The Wisdom "movement" was international[64] and Preuss even goes so far as to suggest that the God of Wisdom is not the God of Israel.[65] The Sages have been seen as proto-empiricists reading wisdom straight off the order of the world without any recourse to the special traditions of Israel. Arguably, this is a partial misunderstanding of Wisdom writings. The traditional sages, as Michael Fox has recently argued, were not empiricists at all.[66] They did use experience and observation but usually only to illustrate and urge obedience to truths *already known*: truths which were learnt from hearing the teachings passed on in the community and the family. "For the most part, the sages of didactic Wisdom sought not to discover truths but to inculcate them. This attitude is attested in Wisdom Literature throughout its history."[67]

---

63 Zimmerli, 1976.
64 See just about any introduction to Wisdom Literature for a discussion of non-Israelite Wisdom.
65 Preuss is discussed in Murphy, 1992, p. lxi. Blenkinsopp argues that the wisdom literature was originally religiously neutral and that it has been adapted under the influence of Yahwism (1995, pp. 24-29). This is questionable (F.M. Wilson, 1987) but it does seem to be the case that non-Israelite wisdom material (which should not be thought of as secular) was adapted within an Israelite context by placing it within a Yahwistic frame. On the "fear of Yahweh" and the religious dimension of Israelite wisdom see especially Murphy, 1987.
66 Fox, 1999, pp. 80-81.
67 Ibid., p. 84. Some qualification of this is required. Texts such as Job do indicate that experience could and did function as the actual source of knowledge rather than a mere illustration of it. Job's experiences form the ground of a rejection of a commonly drawn tight link between sin and suffering. It is generally thought that the book of Proverbs demonstrates this tight link although recently Raymond van Leeuwen has challenged that claim (Leeuwen, 1990).

Behind the wisdom literature lies the foundational assumption that there is a creation order established on wisdom[68] and discerned by wisdom.[69] God is the source of this wisdom and that explains why the start and end of Wisdom is the fear of Yahweh.[70] If one fears Yahweh, the God of Israel, *only then* can one begin *adequately* to discern the creation-order.[71]

> This note of fear is... to be identified with a... response to Yahweh... of total commitment within a framework of covenant relationships which Israel knew had been established. In the sense that such a response is a reaction to and a reflection of torah the identification of "wisdom" with "law", though not made overtly until the end of the biblical period, is something which is implicit from the beginning.[72]

Certainly, in their final form, texts such as Proverbs do presuppose the covenant of Yahweh with Israel and it is only the final form which has any authoritative function in the church.

Although it must be granted that not much is made of Israel's story in Wisdom texts, there are connections. Not only is the God of Wisdom Israel's

---

Fox argues that Qohelet stands in contrast to this epistemology and "is introducing a radical innovation into the notion of Wisdom: the notion that one may use his independent intellect to discover new knowledge and interpret the data of individual experience" (ibid., p. 76). Qohelet "looks to experience as a source of knowledge...; appeals to his own experience as evidence and testimony...; views knowledge as... dependent on perception" (ibid., pp. 76-77). Thus there is a tension between the epistemology of Qohelet and that of Biblical Wisdom in general. Qohelet's empiricism leads him to his famous *hebel* (Absurd!) conclusions on a range of issues. Exactly how to make sense of the contradictions in Ecclesiastes has been much discussed. Bartholomew (1999, ch. 7) develops Fox's insight in a different direction from Fox himself. To Bartholomew Qohelet juxtaposes two incompatible epistemologies with the "knowledge" that each yields. The empiricist "worldly wisdom" leads to absurdity whilst an epistemology founded on the fear of God lies behind the carpe diem texts. Qohelet displays the hermeneutical impact of two antithetical ways of knowing the creation. If this is correct then it coheres well with my contention that creation order cannot be read properly if one does not begin from theological assumptions. Qohelet then stands with rather than against texts such as Proverbs! It has even be argued that Ecclesiastes is an orthodox reflection on Genesis 1-3 and if this is correct it would tie in this particular wisdom work very closely with the biblical plot-line (Clemens,1994).

68 Proverbs 8 is a classic text linking creation order to the activity of divine wisdom.

69 Van Leeuwen, 1990. Human wisdom is to discern this order: "Wisdom is ethical conformity to God's creation", J. Flemming, quoted in Wolters, 1996, p. 26. Isaiah 28:23-29 is a fascinating text regarding creation-order. In it God is said to teach the farmer (through observation of the world) how best to farm the land.

70 Prov 1:7; 9:10; 16:6; 31:30; Job 28:28; Ecc 5:7; 12:13.

71 Bartholomew, "A God is for Life, and not Just for Christmas", unpublished paper, pp. 7-9.

72 Deut 4:6. Dumbrell, 1984, pp. 205-206.

God, Yahweh, but the figure of Solomon also links Wisdom Literature to the story of the nation.[73] Similarly Van Leeuwen has observed some links between teachings on land in Wisdom texts and in the Pentateuch, arguing that the former presupposes the latter.[74] Indeed

> [t]he values inculcated in Proverbs are much the same as those urged in the Pentateuch, e.g., commitment to God and God's divine order, love, justice, and honesty, caring for the poor and the needy, accepting life as a gift from God, despising and avoiding what is wicked and evil."[75]

The relation of wisdom and covenant material is two-way. Not only has the law shaped wisdom material but wisdom has shaped law. In the book of Deuteronomy "the legal and sapiential traditions flow together."[76] We have a legal text in a narrative frame which emphasises Israel's covenant relation with God whilst making use of a wisdom-influenced style. We also see the start of an identification of wisdom with obedience to torah and folly with disobedience.[78] The beginning of an identification of torah itself with wisdom is found in Deuteronomy[79] – an identification which matures in the work of Ben Sira.[80] It has also been argued that there has been some sapiential influence on Israelite prophets such as Amos[81] and Isaiah.[82] To this one may also add the observation that Wisdom traditions have also shaped some narrative material.[83] For example, scholars have drawn attention to Wisdom influences in Genesis 2-3,[84] in the Joseph stories,[85] in the Succession Narrative,[86] in the Solomon stories and in the book of Esther.[87] And some New Testament scholars have seen

---

73 Prov 1:1; Ecc 1:1; 1 Kg 1-4
74 Van Leeuwen, 1990, p. 122.
75 Witherington III, 1994, p. 24. Compare the Prov 11:1 and Deut 25:15-16 on justice in trade.
76 Blenkinsopp, 1995, p. 118.
77 Deut 4:6-7.
78 Deut 32:28-29.
79 Deut 30:11-14. Blenkinsopp, 1995, p. 152.
80 On which see ibid., pp. 162-167; and Witherington III, 1994, pp. 75-116.
81 S. Terrien, 1977.
82 J. Fichtner, 1977.
83 See D. Morgan, 1981.
84 L. Alonso-Schokel, 1976, pp. 468-480. Gen 2-3 not only employs wisdom motifs but weaves them in with anticipations of Israel's story, with covenant themes, with creation and with divine commands. It would be a fascinating study to consider how these are fitted together into a narrative unity.
85 Von Rad, 1977. See now especially Wilson, forthcoming.
86 2 Sam 9-20; 1 Kg 1-2. R.N. Whybray, 1968.
87 Talmon, 1963. Also Blenkinsopp, 1995, sees Esther (pp. 43-44) and Daniel (pp. 173-178) as having Wisdom influences. Against Wisdom influences see Crenshaw, 1977.

Jesus' self-understanding and early church christology as strongly shaped by Wisdom traditions.[88] The Wisdom of Israel, whatever its non-Israelite origins, has gradually been adapted and woven deeply into the story. Attempts to unweave it may be interesting from a tradition-historical perspective but must not be allowed to determine the relevance of these texts for the Peoples of the Book. Bartholomew writes,

> *From a canonical perspective*, wisdom begins with a holy reverence for the One who has rescued Israel and brought her to himself. Wisdom in this sense is not separate from Yahweh's redemptive acts but a response to them.[89]

In summary, the "natural law" ethic of Amos seems to presuppose a story of Yahweh's creation and providential care over Israel and the nations. The ethics of the Wisdom literature are also arguably deeply linked to narrative. We observe that Wisdom very often has a narrative exemplification in texts such as Job,[90] as well as in ordinary narrative texts like the Joseph or Solomon stories. We also observe how, in their final form, Israel's wisdom literature has been interwoven with the traditions of the covenant nation. We have argued that law, prophecy and narrative have absorbed a wisdom influence and that the God of the Wisdom texts is Yahweh, Israel's covenant God.

## Story and Divine Commands

The connection between Old Testament laws and stories will require fuller comment. It has been the case that work on Old Testament ethics in recent decades has been strongly biased towards Old Testament law. So much so, that for some scholars Old Testament ethics simply *is* law. A striking example of this is Walter Kaiser's work, *Towards Old Testament Ethics* which is structured around the decalogue. In this book non-legal texts hardly get a look in. Similarly, Otto's *Theologische Ethik des Alten Testaments*[91] is given almost entirely to discussion of legal and wisdom texts.[92] I shall argue that this focus leads to a distortion of Old Testament ethics.

It is helpful to begin our exploration of law and story with Paul Ricoeur's essay "Biblical Time."[93] Ricoeur is interested in the intertextual dynamics set in

---

88 E.S. Fiorenza's, 1995 (a theologically heterodox study); B. Witherington III., 1994.

89 Bartholomew, forthcoming.

90 Song of Songs arguably has a plot structure also.

91 Otto, 1994.

92 He writes, "In my view, the primary subject of an ethics of the Hebrew Bible... is the system of legal and ethical rules in the Covenant Code, Deuteronomy, Decalogue, and post-priestly Holiness Code." Quoted in Wenham, 2000, p. 109.

93 Ricoeur, 1998e. The original "Tempes Biblique" was published in *Archivio di filosofia* 53, 1985, pp. 29-35.

motion within the canon of the Hebrew Bible. He argues that whatever the original *Sitz-im-Leben* of the various texts they now have a new *Sitz-im-Wort* which deserves to be taken seriously.[94] He observes that the Yahwist school

> apprehended as one indivisible whole, as one unknotable knot, the whole constituted by the laws and the narratives. And from this union results both a narrativization of ethics and an ethicization of the narratives... Because of this, the law is not atemporal: it is marked by the circumstances of this giving and the very places of its injunctions, the desert, the mountain, the borders of Jordan. However, the opposite is no less important. The instruction issuing from the successive legislations, unified under the emblem of Sinai and Moses, colours the narratives themselves. These narratives, under the pressure of the prescriptive, become narratives of the march of a people with God under the sign of obedience and disobedience... the narrative does not constitute a separate genre. There is just the Torah....[95]

It seems appropriate to ask ourselves three questions: How does the narrative frame of Israel's laws impact them? How does the presence of the laws within the narratives shape the latter? What is the Relationship between law and moral ideals in the completed Old Testament?

*How Do the Narratives Shape the Laws?*

The first observation that needs to be made is that Israel's laws are located within the story of Israel's exodus and journey to the Promised Land. Israel is delivered from Egypt and led to Sinai where she is given the instructions from God via Moses. The very first command in the law is given a narrative frame: "I am the LORD your God, who *brought you out of the land of Egypt, out of the house of bondage*. You shall have no other gods before me..."[96] Janzen writes that "this brief characterisation of Yahweh as saviour is prefixed to the Ten Commandments as a reminder that they, and with them all the laws that follow, should be understood as interpreted by the story that it summarises."[97] Every set of laws found in the Old Testament is located within this plotline. Most are given at Sinai although Deuteronomic law is given on the plains of Moab prior to entry into Canaan.[98] Now this narrative context seems to stand in contrast to otherwise very similar laws from the ANE.[99] The laws of Hammurabi, for

---

94 Ricoeur, 1998e, p. 171.
95 Ibid., p.172. Similarly, Childs, 1985, p. 13.
96 Ex 20:2-3.
97 Janzen, 1994, p. 67.
98 For a discussion of how Deuteronomic law needs to be read within its narrative context see J.G. Millar, 1998, chs. 2-3.
99 On comparison of Ancient Near Eastern laws with Old Testament laws see J. Walton, 1989, ch. 3 and L. Epsztein, 1986.

instance, preserve very similar laws to those in the "Book of the Covenant" in Exodus 21-23. However, despite the presence of a prologue[100] there is no attempt to set Hammurabi's rules within a narrative. The same goes for all the other extant Mesopotamian laws.[101] Sonsino, in his study on motive clauses in biblical and Near Eastern law writes, "It is noteworthy that, unlike biblical laws, no cuneiform law is ever motivated by reference to a historical event."[102] Not only this, but Israelite law is unique in being presented as the commands of God rather than those of a human king. And not just any God, but the God of Abraham, Isaac and Jacob: the God revealed in the story of promise and deliverance. Thus the story-setting of Israel's laws gives them a uniquely distinctive flavour.

The impact of the narrative context on the shape of the laws themselves can be seen in occasional modifications of fairly standard Ancient Near Eastern ethical rules. Consider the following: "Honour your Father and mother that your days may be long *in the land which the LORD your God gives you.*"[103] Here we perceive that the motive given for following the rule is a motive specific to Israel's story.

We can also see that in several cases traditional rules are *changed so as to be consistent with the story of Israel.* Consider the institution of slavery. This was found in ancient Israel just as it was across the ancient world. However, Israel's laws on slavery were arguably more humanitarian than other slavery laws in the Ancient Near East.[104] What led to this modification of otherwise typical laws? I suggest that the answer is found in the story of the exodus. Israelites were not allowed to be enslaved because Yahweh says that "they are my servants, whom I brought forth out of the land of Egypt; they shall not be sold as slaves."[105] A Hebrew[106] slave is also to be treated well and released after six years for "You shall remember that you were a slave in the land of Egypt, and the LORD your

---

100 On the implications of which see Walton, 2002.
101 Those laws are as follows: I – Sumerian Laws 1. The Reforms of Uru'inimgina (c. 2350 BCE), 2. The Laws of Ur-Nammu (c. 2040 BCE), 3. The Laws of Lipit-Ishtar (c.1875-1846 BCE). II – Old Babylonian Laws 1. The Laws of Eshnunna (19th C BCE), 2. The Code of Hammurabi (1792-1750 BCE), 3. The Edict of Ammis aduca (1646-1626 BCE). III – Middle Assyrian Laws 1. Middle Assyrian Laws (compiled by Tiglath-pileser III, 1115-1077 BCE). IV Old Hittite Laws 1. Hittite Laws (1115-1077 BCE).
102 Sonsino, 1975, p. 174. Sonsino sees four kinds of motive clause in Old Testament laws: a) those which express God's authority, b) those which allude to the historical experiences of the people, c) those which instil a fear of punishment, and d) those which promise well being (ibid., pp. 109-117). It is b) which concerns us.
103 Ex 20:12.
104 C.J.H. Wright, 1983, pp. 178-182; 1990, pp. 239-259; Webb, 2001.
105 Lev 25:42.
106 Following Gottwald (1979, pp. 391-40) I take "Hebrew" here to refer not to ethnic Israelites but to "landless persons".

God redeemed you; therefore I command you this day."[107] In just the same way the kindness shown to foreigners in Old Testament laws[108] is explained as follows: "You shall not wrong a stranger or oppress him, *for you were strangers in the land of Egypt.*"[109] "You shall not oppress a stranger; you know the heart of a stranger, *for you were strangers in the land of Egypt.*"[110]

Some have proposed that the link between story and laws is even more intimate than I have suggested so far. Calum Carmichael has published several books defending his proposal that Old Testament laws are often generalizations from previously existing narrative traditions.[111] His proposals sometimes appear rather farfetched, but at other times they seem very plausible. At very least he has shown that Old Testament laws and narratives can mesh together more than is often realized. For example, an Old Testament story about the troubles that arise when a man marries two sisters[112] can become the foundation for a general ban on such a practice.[113] It matters little to me whether the story or the law came first. More important is the relation between them in their present context.

*How Do the Laws Shape Old Testament Narrative?*

But what of our second question? How do laws affect the stories in which they are embedded? I suggest that they drive the narratives towards what, in the previous chapter, we called model morality. That is to say that they set up the actions of the characters as models for imitation and rejection. The lives of the characters can become illustrations of faithful torah-observance or faithless disobedience. Gary Millar's book on the ethics of Deuteronomy[114] shows how the narrative frame of the book is taken up within its call to torah-observance. Certain events in the nation's history become warnings of the fate of those who disobey whilst other events become promissory anticipations of the future if Israel obeys the statutes and commands. Thus story comes to reinforce the importance of the laws. One can see the way in which laws have shaped the narratives when we consider Genesis. There we see several characters who model torah observance even before the torah is given (Abel, Noah, Abraham). The ancient traditions have been told in such a way that parallels can be drawn with the concerns of later periods.

---

107 Deut 15:15.
108 On which see Moucarry, 1988.
109 Ex 22:21.
110 Ex 23:9. On top of this are the commands to celebrate various religious festivals which are connected to the remembrance of the great story: Unleavened bread (Ex 23:14-15), Passover (Ex 12:3-20; Lev 23:6; Deut 16:1-8) and Tabernacles (Lev 23:34; Num 29:12-38; Ex 23:16; Ex 34:22; Deut 16:13).
111 Carmichael, 1979, 1985, 1992, 1996.
112 Gen 29-31.
113 Lev 18:18.
114 Millar, 1998.

*How Do Laws and Paradigmatic Ideas Relate?*

Recently, Gordon Wenham has made a proposal that could be put as follows: "There is a link between moral ideals and law, but law tends to be a pragmatic compromise between the legislators' ideals and what can be enforced in practice."[115] Wenham argues that *Old Testament laws set a minimum standard for behaviour rather than prescribing ideals for righteous living.*[116] This is not to deny that paradigmatic ideals[117] inform the laws. On the contrary, the laws are deeply shaped by the values of the writers. It is merely to claim that one cannot read off the moral goal of the biblical authors from simple outlines of the laws. In Wenham's words, there is a "gap between law and ethics" in the Bible.[118] The argument proceeds from the observation that typically laws set a minimum standard for moral living.[119] To demonstrate that this is so in the Old Testament Wenham considers three areas.

First of all, the worship of other gods. The law bans such worship[120] but the moral ideal is not the *mere* observance of the rule. The ideal is to love God with all one's heart – a love which includes *but goes beyond* mere obedience. The intimacy between God and humanity implied by the garden of Eden story and expressed in words such as, "My soul longs, yea faints for the courts of the LORD; my heart and flesh sing for joy to the living God"[121] is the ideal.[122]

The second area is found in the laws on homicide. The basic principle is found in the retributive "life for life" motif which reflects the value placed on human life by the biblical writers.[123] However, one could follow this law without living up to the ideal of positively valuing others. "[T]his is but the tip of an iceberg of an all-embracing ethic towards living creatures in general and human life in particular."[124] Some of the rest of the iceberg is spelt out in other commands and narratives.

The third area is that of sexual morality. Here the law grants more sexual freedom to men than to women in that it seems that men could not commit

---

115 Wenham, 1997, p. 18.

116 It is important to understand that Wenham does not include all divine commands found in the so-called "law codes" as "laws". By "laws" he refers to that sub-set of divine commands which, if broken, would lead to punishment inflicted by the community.

117 Janzen, 1994 and C.J.H. Wright, 1983.

118 Wenham, 1997, p. 20. It seems to me that Rodd's critique of Wenham (Rodd, 2001) is weakened by the fact that he criticizes an earlier version of Wenham's case (Wenham, 1997) rather than the fully developed one found in Wenham, 2000. Some of his criticisms apply only to the earlier version.

119 Ibid., p.18.

120 Ex 32; Lev 20:2.

121 Ps 84:2.

122 Wenham, 1997, p.19.

123 Gen 9:1-7.

124 Wenham, 1997, p. 22.

adultery against their wives[125] and could marry several women. On top of that, divorce seemed relatively simple.[126] However, the moral ideal expressed in narrative and wisdom texts is that of *lifelong, faithful, monogamy*. Prostitutes were to be avoided even though no *legal* sanctions would be enforced upon any man who went with a prostitute. Similarly, narrative texts such as Genesis seem to set up monogamy as the ideal[127] and polygamy as a problematic state of affairs (as illustrated by Lamech, Abraham and Jacob). Linking this to my earlier comments on the foundations of biblical ethics, we can say that Old Testament laws may point in the direction of natural laws, but often form compromises between the creational ideal and the broken reality of the human situation.[128]

Given that one cannot read the moral ideals off from the laws, the question then becomes, "Just how do we find the moral ideals of the implied authors of biblical texts?" Narrative texts have a key role here as does a central ideal of Old Testament ethics – the *imitatio dei*.[129] Wenham's new book *Story as Torah* develops the earlier article in very helpful ways. He argues that Old Testament narrative texts manifest the ideals of the implied authors but often not on their sleeve. We find characters who are complex, who combine vices and virtues in ways which mean we simply cannot assume that whatever a character does is approved of by the narrator. Even the greatest heroes of Scripture have feet of clay and the reader must be discerning. Nevertheless, Wenham thinks that given a sound rhetorical analysis of whole Old Testament books[130] one has a framework for discerning the wheat from the chaff in the behaviour of the characters. His goal is to see what the implied author thinks about their behaviour and he aims to avoid the pure intuition and subjectivism of an uncritical reader-response. The rhetorical analysis guides reading of the parts, but Wenham also proposes three guidelines to guard against misreadings. The behaviour pattern is probably approved of by the implied author if (i) it is repeated in a number of different contexts, (ii) these contexts set it in a positive light, (iii) remarks in other genres like legal codes, oracles and wisdom put the behaviour in a positive light (although such texts cannot be determinative for interpretation).[131]

The book then argues that when the method outlined above is employed on Genesis we can see that a paradigmatic ideal character is being recommended to the reader. He sums up,

---

125 Hugenberger has argued otherwise (1994, pp. 313-337) but for the sake of argument we shall follow the usual line.
126 Wenham, 1997, p. 23.
127 Gen 2.
128 Mt 19:3-8.
129 Wenham, 1997, pp. 26-28.
130 Wenham, 2000, chs. 2-4.
131 Ibid., ch. 5.

Thus out of the stories of Genesis we can build up a catalogue of the virtues as they are perceived by the [implied] author, an identikit picture of the righteous. He or she is pious, that is prayerful and dependent on God. Strong and courageous, but not aggressive or mean. He or she is generous, truthful and loyal, particularly to other family members. The righteous person is not afraid to express emotions of joy, grief or anger, but the last should not spill over into excessive revenge, rather he should be ready to forgive.[132]

I find Wenham's basic thesis to be convincing and very helpful in organising our thinking about how law and narrative interrelate. Both law and narrative manifest a Janzen-like value system and both must be read with great care when attempting to get at those values.

I would like to make some further comments by way of rounding off and summary. I have argued that Old Testament laws must be read within their narrative frame if we are to read them as the implied authors of the canonical texts intended. It seems that stories can shape laws in several ways.

First, the story sets a covenantal context for the laws, such that the laws become a way for Israel to sustain a relationship initiated by Yahweh.[133] This relation is narratively shaped and is the *raison d'etre* for the laws. Israel alone among the nations saw its laws as part of a covenantal relationship with its god. In fact, only Israel saw its laws as *revealed* by its god rather than given by a human king and merely *monitored* by the gods.[134]

Second, story can provide *a new motive* for obeying an old law. Here the narrative-informed motive clauses of Old Testament laws come into their own. Why should Israel care for the oppressed? Because Yahweh cared for Israel when she was oppressed. Why should Israel refuse to show favouritism? Because Yahweh refuses to show favouritism when he acts for *and against* Israel.

Third, story can lead to *adaptations* of old laws. It seems highly plausible that laws on slavery were made more humane in Israel in the light of the exodus narrative. The narrative takes a swipe at the notion of slavery itself, but the law sets a moral floor in allowing slavery subject to some humanising concerns. Thus, although the laws do not reflect the *fullness* of the ideal they do reflect its impact.[135] Or, somewhat differently, consider the story of the daughters of Zelophehad.[136] Their unforeseen circumstances led to an exception to the general rule and that exception was generalised into an adaptation.

Fourth, story can lead to a *rearrangement of the priority of various rules in relation to each other*. The shape of a general system of laws can be shaped in

---

132 Ibid., ch.5, p. 100.
133 See Walton, 2002.
134 Walton, 1989, ch. 3.
135 The best discussion of this is now Webb, 2001.
136 Num 27:1-11; 36:1-13.

tradition-specific ways by the stories told within community. Consider the centrality of property offences in the Laws of Hammurabi.[137] Despite the fact that the laws in the "Book of the Covenant"[138] are very similar to these laws, they clearly regard crimes against the person as far more serious than property offences. I suggest, and I leave it to others to explore and evaluate the matter, that the explanation lies in Israel's distinctive theology, shaped by its distinctive story. Has the story led to a reorganisation of the relative values enshrined in the laws?

Fifth, *stories can relativize the laws* in one of two ways: First, they can set out ideals which go way beyond the mere requirements of the law.[139] Second, they can illustrate situations in which the law should not be followed. One could get the impression that Old Testament laws are intended as rules that must never be broken. However, the narratives can serve to show that this is an overly wooden approach to such laws. Consider how the laws of primogeniture[140] are often overruled in stories (Abel over Cain, Isaac over Ishmael, Jacob over Esau, and so on). The law is undercut by its narrative enactment.[141] Dale Patrick argues that the legal codes of the Old Testament were not intended to be used as actual legal documents but rather as "instructions in the values, principles, concepts and procedures of the unwritten divine law."[142] Patrick thinks that actual legal decisions were guided by the principles enshrined in the laws but did not slavishly follow the rules to the letter.[143] In building up his case he draws attention to 2 Samuel 14. There the woman of Tekoa

> seeks what might be called an equity decision by pitting the principles of inheritance, lineal continuation, and the right to support from children against the principle of blood vengeance. David grants her son[144] immunity from blood vengeance... The story is important here because the king gives a ruling contrary to every law and principle in Scripture governing murder... Thus, not only does David's judgement not appeal to a rule of law, it is diametrically opposed to a known rule. It is given on the basis of the justice of the woman's cause. As she

---

137 In Babylonian laws crimes against the person and against property carry the same penalties whilst in Israel only crimes against the person carry physical penalties. For instance whilst in Hammurabi's law a thief who cannot repay is to be killed (no. 8) in Israel he is to be sold as a slave (Ex 22:1-4).

138 Ex 21-23.

139 So Wenham, 2000.

140 Deut 21:15-17.

141 So Stahl, 1995, p. 17. I must confess to finding the overall thrust of her discussion on law and narrative to be rather unattractive.

142 Patrick, 1985, p. 198.

143 Ibid., ch. 7.

144 It will be recalled that the case is an invention of Joab's designed to entrap David into taking Absalom back.

puts it, David "is like the angel of God to discern good and evil".[145]

R.R. Wilson has also drawn attention to the inconsistent way in which Deuteronomic laws are applied in the lives of characters in the Deuteronomistic History.[146] He concludes that, "factors other than allegiance to Deuteronomic law have played a role in the moral valuations that the historians have made of characters in the narrative... The Deuteronomic law appears to have been only one of the influences on the historians' evaluations of Saul and David."[147] Wilson's study is only brief and limited in scope but it opens up avenues of study which deserve further research. This non-rigid appropriation of Old Testament laws in narrative texts serves, as argued in Chapter One, to alert the reader to the fact that application of such rules requires moral sensitivity.

I hope that I have plausibly sketched a case for the claim that the ethics of ancient Israel are deeply rooted in the stories of the community: that one cannot adequately understand "natural law", the imitation of God or the commands of the torah apart from the stories recounted in the Hebrew Bible. In so doing I have already begun to talk not simply of individual stories but of the bigger story which they compose: the metanarrative. To this we now turn.

## The Priority of the Biblical Meta-Narrative in Shaping Christian Identity

### N.T. Wright's Hermeneutical Model

In his 1989 Laing Lecture, N.T. Wright launched an attack on hermeneutical strategies which "boil off certain timeless truths, models or challenges into a sort of ethereal realm which is not anything to do immediately with space-time reality in order then to carry them across from the first century to any other given century and re-liquefy them..., making them relevant to a new situation."[148] This stems, Wright feels, from Christians assuming that they know

---

145  Ibid., p. 195. It is of interest to note that David himself was not executed for murdering Uriah.

146  R.R. Wilson, 1988.

147  Ibid., pp. 72-73.

148  N.T. Wright, 1991b, p. 13. It may look at first sight that Janzen and Wenham are doing exactly this. However, it will become clear that within the biblical plot certain things remain constant such as the character of God and the creation order (which includes human nature). Thus the notion of story does not relativize everything as some maintain but makes space for both change and stability. This stability, however, is not a "timeless truth" if by that we mean truth which is somehow not integrally related to this temporal order. Rather it is a truth which does not alter in all the changes of the world. As a matter of fact Janzen and Wenham do not claim that their paradigms are unchanging. Given the image of God they could be so conceived but there is room for discussion.

what kind of text the Bible *ought* to be and thus proceeding to (mis)read it as if it were that kind of text. Scripture is largely narrative but Christians have often not known how to treat a story as an inspired scripture and thus perform interpretational acrobatics to knock the Bible into shape. After all "it is one thing to go to your commanding officer first thing in the morning and have a string of commands barked at you. But what would you do if, instead, he began 'Once upon a time…'?" [149]

Wright proposes a model for the authoritative function of Scripture and I shall use it as a foundation for the discussion which follows. He is worth quoting at some length here:

> Suppose there exists a Shakespeare play whose fifth act has been lost. The first four acts provide, let us suppose, such a wealth of characterisation, such a crescendo of excitement within the plot, that it is generally agreed that the play ought to be staged. Nevertheless, it is felt inappropriate to write a fifth act once and for all: it would freeze the play into one form, and commit Shakespeare as it were to being prospectively responsible for work not in fact his own. Better, it might be felt, to give the key parts to highly trained, sensitive and experienced Shakespearean actors, who would immerse themselves in the first four acts, and in the language and culture of Shakespeare and his time, *and who would then be told to work out a fifth act for themselves.* Consider the result. The first four acts, existing as they did, would be the undoubted "authority" for the task in hand. That is, anyone could object to the new improvisation on the grounds that this or that character was now behaving inconsistently, or that this or that sub-plot or theme, adumbrated earlier, had not reached its proper resolution. This "authority" of the first four acts would not consist in an implicit command that the actors should repeat the earlier parts of the play over and over again. It would consist in the fact of an as yet unfinished drama, which contained its own impetus, its own forward movement, which demanded to be concluded in its proper manner but which required of the actors a responsible entering in to the story as it stood, in order first to understand how the threads could appropriately be drawn together, and then to put that understanding into effect by speaking and acting with both *innovation* and *consistency*.[150]

The link with the biblical metanarrative should be fairly obvious. Wright sees the five acts as (1) creation; (2) fall; (3) Israel; (4) Jesus; (5) church. The New Testament would be Act 4, Scene One of Act 5 as well as hints about how Act 5 will end. I would slightly adapt and develop Wright's analysis of the biblical metanarrative as follows:

---

149 N.T. Wright, 1991b, p. 10.
150 Ibid., pp. 18-19.

ACT I: <u>Creation</u> (Gen 1-Rev 20)

ACT II: <u>Fall</u> (Gen 3-Rev 20)

ACT III: <u>New Humanity: Phase One</u>:
    *Scene One: The Abrahamic Covenant.*

 ACT IV: <u>New Humanity: Phase Two</u>:
    *Scene One:  Exodus and Sinai Covenant (Mosaic Covenant).*
    *Scene Two:  Conquest and Judges*
    *Scene Three:  Monarchy (and Davidic Covenant).*
    *Scene Four:  Exile and Return.*

ACT V: <u>New Humanity: Phase Three</u>:
    *Scene One:  Jesus (and New Covenant).*

ACT VI: <u>New Humanity: Phase Four</u>:
    *Scene One:  Church in NT period.*
    **Scene Two:  \*\*\* the missing section\*\*\***

ACT VII: <u>The New Creation</u> (hints found in Acts I-VI).

ACT VI, Scene Two is the one in which Christian Bible readers would locate themselves. They have the task of living out lives in continuity with the plot so far and the hints of what is to come.[151]

Now in considering the relevance of particular scenes within this plot it will be of crucial importance to see whereabouts in the overall story the Scene comes and how that part of the plot is linked to Act VI Scene Two.[152] Wright, in this regard, notes the crucial difference between how Christians relate to the New Testament and Old Testament. "The Old Testament has the authority that

---

151 Let me add here that the eschatological orientation of Christian ethics (ACT VII) cannot be overstated and few have exploited its implications as well as Stanley Hauerwas. Samuel Wells explains that for Hauerwas, "a teleological Christian ethic involves developing and sustaining the practices that conform to the [destiny] of the world" (Wells, 1998, p. 152). He argues that the church does not belong in a different space from the world (heaven) but to a different time (the new age) and that this has implications for our understanding of character, narrative memory and virtue (ibid., ch. 7). The church is to live in the present age but in the light of the victory of the Kingdom of God. Whilst I do not think that Hauerwas overstates eschatology in his ethics I do think that he understates creation and fails to properly appreciate the relationship between creation and eschatological redemption (on which see O'Donovan, 1994; Spykman, 1992; A. Wolters, 1996; Dumbrell, 1984).
152 See Hart on the importance of attending to the narrative of Scripture as a whole when interpreting any part of it (2000, pp. 196-201).

an earlier part of the play would have, no more, no less."[153] He criticises James Dunn for suggesting that Christians today should read the New Testament in the way in which New Testament authors read the Old Testament (*viz.*, with respect and cavalier freedom). The crucial difference is that New Testament authors believed that the coming of Jesus had marked a plot development of cataclysmic proportions. Their relation to the scriptures of Israel was changed in the light of this plot-twist. There is no similar plot direction change which separates us from the New Testament. Indeed the New Testament makes clear that the next act will be the new creation itself. Thus we are living in *the same Act as the New Testament but not the same Act as the Old Testament.*[154]

Consequently, the biblical metanarrative is set up by Wright as a hermeneutical grid for Christian appropriation*s* (the plural is important) of individual biblical narratives. For our purposes it would mean that any *Christian* considerations of the relevance of Genesis 34 must be done in the light of its place in the story of creation-fall and redemption.[155] None of this is to suggest that Wright's is the *only* valid model for biblical hermeneutics merely that it provides a powerful framework for *Christian theological* readings within which other methods and models could find a supportive role.[156] To slightly modify Brevard Childs, "There is no one hermeneutical key for unlocking the biblical message, but the canon provides the arena in which the [Christian] struggle for understanding takes place."[157]

---

153 N.T. Wright, 1991, p. 19.

154 Ibid., pp. 19-20.

155 One of the most powerful models for Christian appropriation of the Old Testament is the paradigmatic model developed by C.J.H. Wright in several texts (1983, 1990, 1995). Christopher Wright's model can be used profitably to fine-tune my considerations here. Despite its static appearance, the paradigmatic approach actually has a dynamic dimension which is sensitive to the plot changes in Biblical metanarrative. Indeed Christopher Wright has written of biblical story as a great unfinished symphony where the whole last movement is missing. Christian readers are to continue the symphony in the light of what has gone before and the composer's sketch of the grand finale (1995, pp. 24-25). I fully endorse the paradigmatic model but space prohibits a discussion of it.

156 I do not want to suggest that I consider other methods philosophically or even theologically neutral. The methods employed in biblical scholarship have often embodied subterranean philosophical assumptions which are questionable from a Christian perspective (see esp. Bartholomew, 1999; Evans, 1996). It has often been assumed that such methods are neutral and help with non-biased description from which theology can build if it so wishes (see Watson, 1994, ch. 2 for a critique). However, I would question this claimed neutrality and hope that one could develop sociological and historical-critical methods which are more compatible with a theistic perspective. It is these which could complement or supplement the theological methods proposed here.

157 Childs, 1985, p. 15. In Childs, 1979 (p. 76) there is a distinction drawn between the use of the Bible for reconstructing ancient history and reading it as sacred Scripture. Different methods are used for different goals.

I am in agreement with the hermeneutical strategy of N.T. Wright and will proceed to set out its strengths and some qualifications needed to avoid dangers inherent in the model.


## Evaluating the Model

There are various strength to Wright's model. First, it takes the narrative genre of much of Scripture seriously, allowing it to "be itself" rather than allegorising it or ignoring it for the more systematic pastures of Paul's epistle to the Romans. Whatever one's doctrine of Scripture, one must not allow it to force scripture into a mould it does not fit. A doctrine of scriptural inspiration and authority needs to be crystallised in dialogue with the actual phenomena of the text itself, rather than decided *a priori* and then used to manhandle the text. Of course, non-narrative texts are misread if they are read *as* stories, but biblical psalms, epistles, laws, prophecies and the like are very often reflections on elements of the metanarrative. They are non-narrative reflections on narrative and thus find a place within a meta-narrative contextualisation.

Second, Wright's model also takes into account clear development in the biblical story of God and his people and refuses to read all texts as if Christian readers can relate to them in the same way. In fact, one could develop Wright somewhat and note that some individual stories are crucial on-the-line[158] parts of the plot (e.g. the disobedience of Adam and Eve, the exodus deliverance, the crucifixion stories) whilst others are very much off-the-line and not so important (e.g. the story of Judah and Tamar). I shall show, if it were not intuitively obvious, that Genesis 34 clearly falls into the latter category. I thus hope to demonstrate in this book how even peripheral stories can be fruitfully read by modern Christians.

Third, Wright's model grants a very clear sense of authority to biblical stories but one which is appropriate to the nature of the beast in question.[159]

Fourth, Wright's model allows for a range of authentic, Christian appropriations of the stories without opening the door to just any reading. Readings of stories can be shown to be either implausible or illegitimate *Christian* readings and thus rejected.[160] Obviously careful thought is needed

---

158 The notions of on-the-line and off-the-line are from the field of linguistics. By an on-the-line story I mean a story which advances the main plot line. By an off-the-line story I mean one which is more of an aside.

159 Attempts to develop a notion of narrative authority can be found in Stroup, 1981; Bauckham, 1999b.

160 For a defence of the legitimacy of Christian interpretations of the Bible guided by orthodox theology see Wall, 2000a. Wall argues that the church's Rule of Faith which guides such interpretations is "narrative in shape, trinitarian in substance, and relates the essential beliefs of Christianity together by the grammar of christological monotheism" (ibid., p. 101). God's acts in creation and salvation which I refer to as the metanarrative form part of this Rule of Faith.

here to set out more clearly how this would be done in practice with the biblical metanarrative. One example should suffice for now. Contemporary Zionist readings of the Joshua narrative are to be seen as illegitimate as *Christian* interpretations for after Christ the *land* of Israel is not something which is of significance as far as the plotline goes.[161] Joshua should be appropriated in very different ways by *Christians* from the way it was by its first audience. On the other hand there may well be a wide range of authentic Christian appropriations of Joshua.

Objections to reading the Bible through the grid of the metanarrative may come in different forms. I wish to consider two objections under the titles (i) a postmodern objection to Wright's model and (ii) a modern objection to Wright's model.

### A Postmodern Objection to Wright's Model

Some postmodern thinkers have objected to the notion of master narratives that organise our thinking on a whole range of issues. Walsh and Middleton explain that for many thinkers metanarratives are merely social constructions:

> particular moral visions dressed up in the guise of universality. And in falsely claiming universality whilst being bound to their own constructed character, metanarratives inevitably privilege unity, homogeneity and closure over difference, heterogeneity, otherness and openness. The result is that all kinds of events and people end up being excluded from the way in which the story gets told. No metanarrative, it appears, is large enough and open enough genuinely to include the experiences and realities of all people.[162]

Behind the claims to truth and "totality" lie plays for power which silence "the other". Given that metanarratives are the root of such evil there is a moral imperative to deconstruct, subvert and relativise such big stories allowing all voices to be heard in "the carnival of postmodern culture."[163]

Walsh and Middleton respond to this objection with three arguments.[164] They begin by noting that local narratives which make no claims to universality can legitimate large scale violence to match any metanarrative. Consider the ethnic cleansing of the Balkans and Rwanda.[165]

Second, they observe that postmodernity itself has its own implicit but unacknowledged metanarrative. Such thinkers are "caught in a performative contradiction, arguing against the necessity of metanarratives precisely by

---

161 This claim is controversial given that many Christians do in fact read the Bible in Zionist ways but is well defended by Chapman, 1983; Burge, 2003 and P. Walker, 1996.
162 Walsh and Middleton, 1995, pp. 70-71.
163 Ibid., p. 73.
164 N.T. Wright himself makes very similar points in a popular book, 1999, ch. 3.
165 Walsh and Middleton, 1995, p. 75.

(surreptitious) appeal to a metanarrative."[166] Humans have a need to make sense of their lives in terms of a bigger picture.

Third, they feel the force of the postmodern objection and attempt to set out the Biblical Metanarrative in a way that is not only non-totalizing and non-violent but has the resources to "shatter totalizing readings."[167] I would agree with this with the caveat that this "shattering" must not come at the price of relativising the claim of the biblical super-story to be *the true story* of the world. This is an exclusivist claim which confronts alternative worldviews and cannot be tamed.[168] I shall assume that their attempt is successful allowing us to proceed to a second objection to Wright's model.

*A Modern Objection to Wright's Model*

Christians always have, and continue to,[169] read the Bible as a unity: a single book with a single plot line.[170] Indeed, classical Christian positions and those of the vast majority of living Christians see the Bible as, *in some sense*, the product of a single divine author.

It is fairly easy to trace the contours of the biblical metanarrative and to see why the church felt that the biblical books, taken together, bore witness to a single story. However, there is a tendency for Christians to synthesise biblical books too easily and to ignore, or interpret away, the distinctive perspectives and theologies of the diverse biblical texts. It is exactly this worry which came to fruition with the impact of modernity on biblical studies. There was a swing away from the perception of unity in the canon to an emphasis on distinctiveness and diversity.[171] Until relatively recently the dominant view in

---

166 Ibid., p. 77.

167 Ibid., chapter 5.

168 On which see Carson, 1996. The book is, to my mind, somewhat overstated and unnecessarily conservative but essentially on the right tracks.

169 There is always a temptation for academics to take changing fashions in the academy as representing significant changes for the church at large. Such temptations must be resisted as delusions of grandeur.

170 See Motyer (2000) for a helpful discussion of the pitfalls of attempts to integrate the teachings of all the biblical texts and the need to hear such an integrated biblical voice addressing us. Motyer sets out five helpful theses for the ongoing project of a biblical theology (pp. 158-163).

171 Childs sees the publication of Semler's book *Abhandlung von Freier Untersuchung des Canons* (1771-76) as pivotal in the change: "He succeeded in seriously damaging the central pillar on which Protestant orthodoxy – to a lesser degree Catholicism – had sought to construct its house. Semler argued that a theological interpretation of the Hebrew canon as a unified, accepted body of authoritative Jewish writings rested upon historical misconceptions, and that it should be replaced by a strictly historical definition whose content would be established according to its true historical development" (Childs, 1979, p. 35). On the development of Old Testament theology see J. Hayes and F. Prussner, 1985.

the academy was that each text (or hypothetical source) was to be read on its own terms and not to be seen as part of a larger, unifying whole. There is a theology of P and a theology of J and of E and D and each must be considered separately. Redaction criticism opened up the way for literary approaches which consider the theology of a final text such as the book of Genesis. Clearly the final redactor of the text selected and organised his materials to shape a finished product which can be seen as a unity. Indeed it may even be possible to see a group of texts as a unity of this sort. Genesis to Numbers is one such example and Deuteronomy to 2 Kings another. To take the latter example, although each book may have to be studied in its own right as a discrete unit[172] there is a clear set of "family resemblances" which runs through Deuteronomy to Joshua to Judges to 1 and 2 Samuel to 1 and 2 Kings.[173] The theology and vocabulary is very similar and the books seem to slot together into a single story. Given the canonical placing of Deuteronomy as the conclusion of the Pentateuch[174] with it picking up where Numbers leaves off we could even read Genesis-2 Kings as a single history. However, to suggest that all the other narrative texts in the Bible can be linked into this story is to enter difficult waters. In one sense the Chronicler tells part of the same story as the authors of Samuel and Kings. However, the story is told from a different perspective. In a real sense they tell *different stories* just as the four Gospels could be said to. To read them as a single story invites blurring of distinctives.

The philosophical and hermeneutical shift which came with modernity brings both benefits and problems for traditional Christian ways of reading scripture. The importance of allowing discrete units of the Bible to establish their own identity cannot be underestimated. Attempts to set out the theology and ideology of Genesis, of Deuteronomy, of Isaiah 40-55 (66?) and of John's Gospel have been immensely helpful. This is not, in and of itself, a problem for reading the Bible as a unity. It only becomes a problem if the diversity is thought to be full-blown, irreconcilable conflict between ideologies, historical plotline or the like. The unity of scripture can bear considerable diversity that falls short of this extreme. The legitimate fear of many biblical scholars is that a return to reading the whole Bible as a unity is either to attempt the impossible, given the results of biblical criticism, or comes at the price of denying those results. Wright himself could not be accused of blurring the distinctives of different biblical authors and books, but his model does lend itself to such a possibility. The Shakespeare play has a unity *because it has a unity of author* up until the missing section. Each part was written in the light of the whole. Such cannot be said of the Bible. It has diverse authors who did not all have some clear sense of the whole to which they, unknowingly, contributed. Any

---

172 After a spate of reading Deuteronomy-2 Kings as a single work (following Noth) there is a shift back to analyses of the individual books in their own right.
173 See McConville, 1993.
174 Childs, 1979, pp.127-132.

attempt to read the Bible as united by a metanarrative must not side-step this
objection but move beyond it to a post-critical sense of the whole: a unity
which allows diversity within. I shall briefly sketch a justification for seeking
such a unity.

I would maintain that the authors of the narrative (and prophetic) books of
the Old Testament and New Testament knew themselves to be telling segments
of the *ongoing* story of their people. There are no Old Testament narrative texts
that have a sense of closure. The promises to the patriarchs are famously only
*partially* fulfilled within the Pentateuch,[175] awaiting a future realisation. Judges
ends in chaos, looking to a future King.[176] The historical books of Samuel-
Kings end in the exile without a return, yet with the *hope* of one.[177] Ezra and
Nehemiah continue but do not finish the story for the glorious return from exile
was not so glorious as had been hoped.[178] Even a book such as Ruth, which
looks self-contained, plugs itself into the bigger story by being set within the
period of the judges[179] and anticipating the reign of David.[180] Each Old
Testament story is part of a bigger whole and *the writers were quite conscious
of this.*

It was this sense of an on-going, bigger plot which inspired the Old
Testament writers to write about the earlier parts of their story in the light of
later events. This is perhaps nowhere clearer than in the patriarchal stories of
Genesis, where the Israelite authors told the story in such a way as to anticipate
and link with events of their own day.[181] For example, the sacrifice of Isaac in
Genesis 22 is told as a paradigm of obedient sacrificial worship at the
Jerusalem Temple.[182] This way of retelling stories in the light of later events
was seen as quite legitimate on the shared assumption that the later parts of the
same story open up some of the "surplus of meaning" in the earlier parts. This
is similar to the way in which we read a detective story. As new events are
revealed the reader has to return to rethink the significance of earlier parts of
the book.

N.T. Wright has shown[183] how such an assumption was also prevalent in the
Judaism of the first century and is the key to first century Jewish biblical
hermeneutics of the time. He, along with other recent scholars,[184] also shows in

175 D Clines, 1997.
176 Judges 21:25.
177 1 Kg 8:33-34, 46-53.
178 Isaiah 55-66 make this clear (see P. Hanson, 1979).
179 Ruth 1:1.
180 Ruth 4:17-22.
181 Walter Moberly brings this out very well in Moberly, 1992a.
182 See Moberly, 1992a, ch.3,; Wenham, 1995.
183 See N.T. Wright, 1991, 1992, 1996.
184 Richard Hays, 1989 and Witherington's, 1994, study Paul's use of the Old
Testament make very similar proposals. Although epistles are not narrative in form they
are theologically founded on the Old Testament story and the Jesus story. On the New

detail that the New Testament authors worked with the same hermeneutic. What marked the Christians out was that they believed that the story of Jesus was the climactic scene in the whole story of Israel. Wright shows how his story sent the early Christians back to re-examine the Old Testament in the light of this new development.

So far so good. All I have done is describe (far too briefly) how the biblical writers of Old Testament and New Testament saw their own writings as part of an ongoing plotline. This, they felt, legitimated re-reading earlier parts in the light of later parts. Many would have no problem with such claims. The traditional Christian contention is only one step beyond this. Christian readers of the Bible should agree with the New Testament writers that Christ is indeed the dramatic fulfilment of the story up until that point. Consequently, they would agree that it is right to read the previous sections of the story in the light of his life. This procedure should not be objected to as a violation of the integrity of Old Testament texts.[185] On the contrary, *it is in line with the assumptions of those very texts. If* one sees the Christ-Event as part of the plot *then* one is obligated to allow it to cast its significance back onto our understanding of earlier texts.[186] Those texts find themselves in a bigger inter-textual context and consequently find new meanings liberated from their pages. One could justify such a procedure on the literary grounds of intertextuality[187] and the theological grounds that the Christian community would privilege the intertextual relationships between the canonical books over those between canonical books and other "texts" (taken in as broad a sense as the reader

---

Testament in general see Beale (1989) and on the Synoptic use of exodus, conquest, Temple and kingship motifs see especially Swartley, 1994. On the impact of Old Testament narratives on Paul's ethics, see Hays, 1996b.

185 Consider the concern of Wernberg-Moller: "The use of the Old Testament in the New is the concern of the New Testament scholar and not the Old Testament scholar; the latter should not go to the New Testament except in isolated instances for the purpose of textual criticism and should never for a moment forget that, so far as he is concerned, it is the original meaning of the text that matters, and not the use that was later made of it in the New Testament" (quoted in Bruce, 1976, p. 11). More recently David Jasper has criticised Brevard Childs for reading Old Testament texts within a Christian tradition which is "ultimately alien to the Jewish writings themselves" (Jasper, 1995, p. 17). This claim is astonishing as it seems clear that Christian theology is organically related to the Jewish tradition of the Old Testament texts.

186 Childs maintains that his canonical method "does not assume a particular stance or faith commitment on the part of the reader" (1979, p. 72). This seems to me to be both true and false. It is true in that anyone could employ the method if so disposed but false in that there is no compelling reason why someone who is not a Christian would feel obligated to read the Bible with Christian theological assumptions (and Childs is well aware that it is Christian theological assumptions his method presupposes [Childs, 1985, Ch. 1]).

187 For an overview see O'Day, 1999.

wishes).[188]

Francis Watson helpfully explains how traditional historical criticism focuses on the prehistory of parts of the text, seeking their meaning in some postulated prior (linguistic, literary, social and historical) context. "The 'sources' are the sites of primary, primal reality... The outcome is the relative unreality of the final form of the text, whose veil of illusion one must penetrate in order to attain to reality itself."[189] However, this value-system is reversed if one focuses on the way that the parts have been integrated into a canonical whole:

> The textual artefact is the product of the welding together of disparate raw materials, and the possibility that the marks of their various origins can sometimes still be faintly discerned in no way detracts from the final form as the primary site of their reality. *It is the prehistoric forms of the text which possess only a shadow reality, and not the final form.*[190]

But will this not lead us to neglect the riches offered by biblical criticism – riches acquired only by reading the texts, as best we can, as the implied readers of those texts? Possibly, and that is why it is necessary to set up safeguards. Attempts to understand Genesis, for example, as it was originally intended are valuable for their own sake, but from a Christian perspective they are merely a *crucial preliminary* to reading it in the light of the bigger plot. I would maintain that a *Christian* reading of an Old Testament text must, except in unusual cases, work by extending meanings intended by the original redactors or authors.[191] Thus establishing such meanings first helps guard against Christian distortions of Old Testament texts.

This claim is best illustrated with an example. Take the words of God to Abraham that the promise was to him and his "seed."[192] To what does the word "seed" refer? It possibly refers to the Davidic King[193] although it seems to me more plausible to take it as referring to the people of Israel. That was what the

---

188 The method proposed here is not identical with the much discussed canonical approach of Childs (see esp. Childs, 1979, 1985). Childs focuses on the final form of books and on the canonical context (as I do). However, he emphasises the historical joints within texts thus synthesising a final form reading with redaction criticism (so Bartholomew, 1999, p. 106). I am not here concerned with the results of source or redaction criticism. On Childs see Scalese (1994); Seitz (1998, ch. 9); Bartholomew (1999, pp. 99-107); Watson (1994, ch. 2); Barton (1984) and Barr (1983b).
189 Watson, 1994, p. 34.
190 Ibid., p. 35. Italics mine. For this reason I am surprised to see that Brown's excellent volume on *The Ethos of the Cosmos* is organised around the theology of the no-longer, if ever, existent sources (P, J, deutero-Isaiah etc.) rather than that of the final form.
191 See Moberly, 1994.
192 Gen 12:7.
193 Alexander, 1995.

author intended. However, Christ fulfils the mission of Israel. He *is*, to New Testament writers, Israel-as-God-intended-it-to-be. Consequently, Paul feels free to argue that when Genesis talks about "seed" it talks about Christ.[194] Now my claim is that a Christian reader can happily agree with Paul. Genesis does talk about Christ. Such a reader is *not* claiming that the author *knew* that they wrote about Christ. The claim is rather that the promise made by God *was* about Israel and was fulfilled in Christ *as* the representative of Israel. Thus Paul could understand the promise *better* than the original author! Notice that the Christian interpretation does not work by ignoring the originally intended meaning. On the contrary, it only works by *acknowledging* the original meaning and seeing the fulfilment of that in later events. If the reader is a Christian then not to push past standard exegesis would be to *under*read the Genesis text even if not to *mis*read it.

It is important to emphasise that what I am proposing is not an examination of what ancient Israelites *actually* believed, or how they actually *behaved* at any particular point in time or space. Such a study is perfectly legitimate but not my concern here. I am proposing a study of the ethics of biblical documents (which may or may not coincide with the ethics of ancient Israelites[195]) but more than that, I am proposing a *synthesis* of the ethics of all the biblical documents.[196] Such a synthetic task is not easy and my proposals may well need some modifications if they are to do justice to the texts. It may be objected that the final result is a mere abstraction: a theological construction *of the interpreter* rather than something identical with the ethics of any single biblical author. This may be so, but it is merely the reply to an invitation issued by the biblical documents themselves. We must not forget that the idea of a metanarrative is not an alien imposition upon texts, but arises from a dynamic present *within the texts*. This, to my mind, legitimates a Christian attempt to perceive a unity in the overall story. It runs the *risk* of flattening the distinctives

---

194 Gal 3:16. I am following N.T. Wright, "The Seed and the Mediator: Galatians 3.15-20" in N.T. Wright, 1991a, pp. 157-174. Wright argues that the title "Christ" is being used collectively of the saints in Christ their representative.

195 Millar, 1998, p. 26.

196 Barton is right to raise the question of the extent of the canon: Christians do disagree over the canonical status of the apocryphal books (see Bruce, 1988). There are "no methods 'internal' to biblical study which will enable us to decide what ought to be in the canon" (Barton, 1984, p. 93). Thus a canonical approach like Childs' or Wright's is only useful once we have delineated the contents of the canon. Scalese (1994, pp. 64-67) proposes a flexible view concerning the exact content of the canon depending on which books different Christian communities use as authoritative scripture. A Protestant could work without the apocryphal books and a Catholic or Orthodox Christian with them. Interpretative results may differ but not massively for the addition of the controverted texts would not make any serious changes to the plotline (principally filling out Act IV, Scene 4). And even a Protestant would need the apocryphal books as background for interpretation of the New Testament.

of individual texts but it need not do so. To see why, we need to return to the
original problem. Does the metanarrative approach to the Bible run roughshod
over diversity? It would be useful to have some typology of the diversity and
"contradictions" one may find within the Old Testament. John Goldingay
suggests the following kinds of diversity:[197]

- Diversity in the meaning of concepts, themes and institutions.
- Diversity in the messages brought by different Old Testament books
  and traditions.
- Diversity in the significance found in particular events or motifs.

The reasons for such diversity are diversity of authorship and of audiences,
diversity in the situations books were written to address, diversity of the
external context of Israel's world, diversity in how God chooses to act on
different occasions given his sovereign freedom and the complexity of the
realities addressed by Old Testament texts.[198] His typology of "contradictions"
is as follows:[199]

*Formal Contradiction*
This is a contradiction at the level of words but not substance. For example, the
Old Testament states and denies that God changes his mind even in the *same*
chapter![200] However, "both the affirmation and the denial are part of a coherent
analogical description of God's involvement in the world, and each would be
misleading without the other."[201]

*Contextual Contradiction*
This "denotes a difference reflecting the variety of circumstances which
different statements address; if the two speakers were confronting similar
circumstances, one might find them speaking in similar terms."[202] Goldingay
suggests that the contrasting attitudes of Isaiah and Jeremiah towards the
Temple exemplify this kind of contradiction.

*Substantial Contradiction*
This is a true divergence of viewpoint which cannot be explained in terms of
formal or contextual contradiction. However, these differences arise within the
same worldview and the parties are, in a real sense, on the same side.
Chronicles and Isaiah 55-66 are proposed as an example of such substantial

197 Goldingay, 1995b, pp. 2-12.
198 Ibid., pp. 12-15.
199 Ibid., pp. 15-25.
200 1 Sam 15:11, 29, 35
201 Ibid., p. 17.
202 Ibid., p. 19.

contradiction.

*Fundamental Contradiction*

This is what we could call a contradiction at the level of worldview. The contradiction between Yahwism and Baalism would illustrate such a clash of worlds. Goldingay does not suggest that the Old Testament exemplifies this kind of contradiction.

Now the metanarrative approach can quite happily acknowledge the kinds of diversity mentioned above. There is no need to see a concept such as the "Kingdom of God" or "creation" or "covenant" as being *identical* in every book of the Bible. Clearly concepts change and develop allowing us to examine the concept of "messiah", say, in different texts.[203] So long as some kind of harmony could be established between the different uses there is no problem. As suggested earlier, a Christian could legitimately see Jesus as fulfilling the divine promise to David in 2 Samuel 7 without suggesting that the implied author had a single, future messianic deliverer in mind. There is no need to imagine that the message of every book need be the same, nor that every author will see the same significance in the exodus or the exile. The metanarrative model allows for changes and plot developments and consequently we would expect diversity.

Formal contradictions are not undermined by the model and nor are contextual contradictions. Indeed, the model is very sensitive to *certain types* of contextual change; namely the turning points marked by the changes between the Acts. However, the model does need some refinement here. Clearly, within a single Act there can be very diverse situations which require different "words from the LORD". N.T. Wright's model could be misread to suggest that within an Act there is a unity of context. But the plot moves on even within the same "dispensation" (to switch metaphors). This is most clear in my ACT IV. This Act includes Israel in the wilderness, in the land, in the united and divided monarchies, in exile and after. It is obvious that the previous parts of the narrative can be appropriated in diverse ways *within the same Act*.[204] The "heretical" interpretation of the exodus given in Amos 9:7 is just one such example. There is an important point for Christian readers of the Bible in this. *All* Christians have lived in the same part of the plot (my Act VI, Scene Two) and relate to the previous parts (Act I-Act VI, Scene One) in the same way. However, the very diverse contexts within which Christians read cannot be ignored as though all Christians should appropriate the Bible in the same way.

---

203 See the essays in (eds.) Satterthwaite, Hess and Wenham, 1995, for the kinds of idea proposed here in relation to the concepts of "messiah".

204 Perhaps it is here that historical criticism, social scientific methods and the like can play a helpful role in helping us to discern contextual differences other than dispensational plot changes.

The metanarrative model provides essential contours for a Christian appropriation, but interpretation is underdetermined by the metanarrative. There is not one, timeless Christian reading of the Bible and it is a defect in the model *if* it suggests that there is. I would advocate Wright's proposal (as I am sure he intended it) as a framework *within which* Christian interpretations can take place. So far, the recognition of the diversity of scripture has led only to an enriching of our model and not a negation of it.

Things become less clear with substantial contradictions as they pose more of a threat to the unity of the whole, but as they are differences within a broader unity, they can perhaps be accommodated.[205] Certainly Goldingay sees no serious problem with them, although I must confess to preferring to see such contradictions as reducible to formal or contextual ones. Wright's model would, I think, incline a reader to try to harmonise conflicts first.[206] If, however, such attempts at harmonisation led to a disrespect for the integrity of the texts; if the texts simply will not naturally yield to harmonisation then the substantial contradictions must be allowed to stand as *valid alternative reactions to certain situations.*

The only kind of contradiction which the model really cannot handle at all are fundamental contradictions. I shall provisionally maintain that there are no examples of such diversity in scripture. Any suggested examples of such contradictions will have to be considered on an individual basis.

In summary, I hope that I have set up some fundamental parameters within which *Christian* readings of Genesis 34 should take place. The Christian reader will want to know just how that individual story fits into the bigger story which commenced in Genesis 1 and is still ongoing. They will also reflect on their own context and ask how, if at all, this story could bring a word from the Lord into their situations.

## Conclusions

In this chapter I have argued that divine commands, natural law, and the imitation of God are best understood within the context of the story Israel told about herself and the world. Abstracted from such a context they wither and die or mutate into something quite different. I then went on to argue, following Wright, that Christian readers need to read individual stories in the Bible within the context of a single metanarrative, within which they locate both the biblical stories and themselves. I finally made some provisional comments in defence of this hermeneutic to allay fears that it would lead to a flattening of the

---

205 Many would maintain that substantial contradictions are very constructive theologically in that they do not allow us to absolutise any particular theological formulation or story. See especially Bruegemann, 1997, Part II, entitled "Israel's Counter-Testimony" and Walsh and Middleton, 1995, ch. 8.
206 See Marshall, 1988; Carson, 1983.

distinctive features of individual biblical books.

From this discussion it seems that a *Christian* reader of Genesis 34 needs to ask the following questions:

How does Genesis 34 fit within the context of the Jacob Cycle? Of Genesis 12-50? Of Genesis 1-50? It is at this point that we could raise Wenham's questions about whether the behaviour of a character is being set out by the implied author of Genesis as a paradigm of virtue or vice. We also need to ask, "How does Genesis 34 fit into the context of the Pentateuch? Of the Old Testament? Of the New Testament? How does the story fit in with legal texts, prophetic texts and Wisdom texts? We shall ask such questions in Chapters Four and Five. In so doing we try first to establish a sound exegesis of the text (Chapter Four) as a preliminary for a whole-canon interpretation (Chapter Five).

What is the context in which my community finds itself? How, if at all, can Genesis 34 be a word of the LORD to *us*? Obviously, there is no one "right" answer to this and I shall leave readers to find their own.

**Part Two**

# The Rape of Dinah as a Case Study

# Chapter Three

# A History of the Interpretation of Genesis 34 with Special Reference to its Use in Ethics

*[Genesis 34] is one of the least illustrated chapters in Genesis and I have never heard it given in an Anglican lesson nor mentioned in any sermon and the commentators themselves who cannot evade their duty show by the startling variety of their comments the uncertainty that weighs upon this incident's interpretation.* Julian Pitt-Rivers. [1]

It was briefly argued in Chapter One that all readers of texts are located within reading traditions both in terms of reading methodology and sometimes in terms of interpretations of specific texts. Chapter Two examined a method for appropriating the Old Testament with roots in the Christian tradition. This chapter explores how Genesis 34 itself has been interpreted by Jews and Christians over the centuries. When reading a biblical text it is always wise to remember that one is not the first person to have "made sense" of the text. Genesis 34, when not neglected, has been used, as Pitt-Rivers notes in the epigraph, in many varied ways over the centuries in guiding ethical conduct. I propose to take some brief, historical samples of Jewish and Christian readings of the passage, from about 150 BCE to the present day, with the intention of identifying some of the central questions. No attempt has been made to be exhaustive but I have given more space to the origins of the traditions of interpretation.

### c.150 BCE – c.100 CE: Second Temple Jewish Readings

There are no explicit[2] references to Genesis 34 in the Hebrew Bible outside Genesis nor in the New Testament. Our first recorded references to the Dinah episode are found around 100 BCE in the books of *Jubilees, The Testament of Levi, Theodotus* and *Judith*. Slightly later readings are to be found in *Josephus, Philo* and *Pseudo-Philo*.

---

1 Julian Pitt-Rivers, 1977, p. 146.
2 Possible allusions to the chapter elsewhere in the Old Testament will be discussed in Chapter Five. In this survey I limit myself to explicit discussion on the Dinah story.

## The Book of Jubilees on Genesis 34

The Book of Jubilees was probably written by a priest in Hebrew some time between 170 and 140 BCE.[3] The aim of the book was to defend Judaism against the disintegrating effects of Hellenism. Primarily the Dinah story is used as the basis for a diatribe against Israelites who give their daughters to marry Gentiles. Before and after the issue of the massacre is mentioned we are told that the justification for it is Shechem's dishonouring of Dinah. This has the clear effect of justifying the slaughter. It is of interest that no mention is made of the circumcision of Hamor and Shechem. This may be because it would be harder to justify the massacre if Hamor and Shechem had agreed to be circumcised - it would certainly not fit with the point that the author of Jubilees wishes to draw out from the story. Having outlined the story, our author now begins to apply it – "And thus let it not be done from henceforth that a daughter of Israel be defiled."[4] Why? Because "judgement is ordained in heaven against them that they should destroy with the sword all the men of the Shechemites because they wrought shame in Israel."[5] God's approval of the sons' actions and his disapproval of the Canaanites could not be more clearly put. Later in the chapter Simeon and Levi's act is extolled in a way that parallels them with Phineas in Numbers 25.[6] We are then told that Levi's deeds will be recalled for a thousand generations.[7]

Jacob's rebuke is recalled out of faithfulness to Genesis 49:5-7, but it is relativized by noting firstly, that Jacob's motive was fear of Canaanite revenge[8] and secondly, that the fear of the Lord fell on the surrounding cities so that they did not attack the Israelites. Thus Jacob's rebuke was unwarranted and the sons' actions vindicated - God looks after his own.

Getting back to the flow of the argument which we left in v. 6, we see that the application of the story is clear - any man in Israel who gives his daughter or sister to marry a Gentile acts shamefully and ought to be stoned to death.[9] The Mosaic ban on intermarriage with Canaanites is recalled[10] and is given as the logic behind the sons' words in Genesis 34:14: "we will not give our daughter to a man who is uncircumcised; for that were a reproach to us."[11] This, for the author of Jubilees, is the verse that unlocks the relevance of the story. The crime for Jubilees is not rape, but sex and marriage with a Gentile. Simeon and Levi are the paradigm for faithful Israelite behaviour.

---

3 Vanderkam, 1992, p. 1030 (contra Charles, 1913, p. 1).
4 30:5.
5 30:6.
6 30:17b-19. So Pummer, 1982, pp. 180-181.
7 30:20, 23.
8 30:25.
9 30:7.
10 30:10-11.
11 30:12.

## The Testament of Levi on Genesis 34

In Chapters 6 and 7 of the *Testament of Levi*[12] we find Levi talking in the first person about the Shechem incident. The first thing of interest is that, contrary to Genesis 34, Levi opposes the circumcision of Shechem and Hamor: "I counselled my father, and Reuben my brother, to bid the sons of Hamor not to be circumcised; for I was zealous because of the abomination they had wrought on my sister."[13]

6:6-7 records Jacob's disapproval of the massacre. He "was wroth, and he was grieved in that they had received the circumcision, and after that had been put to death, and in his blessings he looked amiss upon us. For we had sinned because we had done this thing against his will, and he was sick unto that day." It looks as if Levi is confessing the error of the act but not so. It may have been against *Jacob's* will but not against God's. 6:8-11 explains: "But I saw that the sentence of God was for evil upon Shechem; for they had sought to do to Sarah [and Rebecca] as they had done to Dinah our sister, but the Lord prevented them." Levi thinks that his father's assessment of the situation suffers from a lack of historical perspective. Shechem has a catalogue of abuse against strangers (not least patriarchal and matriarchal ones) going back years. Levi's massacre was justified on the basis of these past crimes. None of these crimes are recorded in Genesis, although they may be based upon some Genesis narratives such as the wife-sister stories. The reason that this discussion is interesting is that our author obviously thinks that Jacob has a point in his critique. That the Hivites were circumcised is a big problem for any attempt to justify the massacre, because it de-sacralises what was seen as a rite of supreme significance in Judaism at this period. He must come up with some *other* justification for the deed because the forceful abduction of Dinah alone is not enough.

Chapter 7 has Levi addressing his father taking the massacre as a prefigurement of the Lord disinheriting the Canaanites. John J. Collins writes,

> The rape of Dinah becomes a kind of original sin for the people of Shechem, which still has its effect in the author's own day. The folly of the Shechemites was a common Jewish taunt, as we know from Ben Sira's reference to "the foolish people that lives in Shechem" (Sir. 1:26).[14]

---

12 "The Testaments of the Twelve Patriarchs were written in Hebrew in the latter years of John Hyrcanus - in all probability after his final victory over the Syrian power and before his breach with the Pharisees - in other words, between 109 and 106 BCE. Their author was a Pharisee who combined loyalty to the best traditions of his party with the most unbounded admiration of Hyrcanus" (Charles, 1908, p.282).

13 6:3-4.

14 J.J. Collins, 1980, p. 96.

These "foolish Shechemites" of the author's day were, of course, Samaritans.[15]

## The Book of Judith on Genesis 34

The book of Judith was written some time between 150 and 100 BCE. In chapter 9 the heroine prays to God and refers to the massacre in Shechem in her prayer to legitimate her ruse against the "Assyrians". Pummer writes that

> in the text of Judith one can discern allusions to several Old Testament stories about the use of stratagems, such as Rebekah... Tamar.... Ehud... and Simeon and Levi. It is as if the author wanted to show that in comparison with all those other figures, Judith did not commit an evil act but used a ruse against an unjust aggressor.[16]

In 9:2-4 she prays:

> O Lord God of my father Simeon, into whose hand you gave a sword to take vengeance on the strangers, who loosened the girdle of a virgin to defile her, and uncovered the thigh to her shame, and profaned the womb to her reproach. For though you said, "It shall not be so"; yet they did so: so you gave their rulers to be slain, and their bed, which was ashamed for her that was deceived [or "their deceit"], to be dyed in blood...

Judith prays that she might be able to smite Israel's contemporary enemies by the deceit of her lips,[17] presumably as Simeon and Levi had done to the Hivites. Clearly the story is seen as having moral import - in defence of Israel, deceit and violence are justified in the name of Yahweh. God unreservedly approved of the massacre of the Canaanites as the latter are, in Judith's view, without redeeming features. There is no mention of the circumcision of the Hivites, nor of their desire to legitimise the relationship of Shechem and Dinah, nor of Jacob's condemnation of the deed.

## Josephus on Genesis 34

Josephus (37 CE to 97 CE) was a soldier, writer and statesman born in

---

15 On the *Epic of Theodotus* see John J. Collins, 1980 (the quotation is from p. 96). The main thesis of Collins' article is to argue that Theodotus' reading of Genesis 34 is used to support the violence of Hyrcanus against Samaria and its capital Shechem in the second century BCE. I shall return to this in my summary of Jewish interpretations of this period. On *Liber Antiquitatum Biblicarum* or *Pseudo-Philo* see Pummer, 1982, p.179.
16 Pummer, 1982, p. 181.
17 9:10

Jerusalem to an aristocratic Jewish family. The *Jewish Antiquities* (20 volumes) was his second major work in which his aim is to tell the honourable history of his people from the creation to 66 CE – "a history comparable, nay, in antiquity far superior to that of Rome."[18] Working *mainly* from the Hebrew text of the Bible (at least as far as Book 10) Josephus paraphrases the inspired text under the influence of traditional interpretations despite his repeated claims to have added nothing to the biblical narratives.[19] Josephus paraphrases Genesis 34 in *Antiquities* 1.21.1-2: He tells how Dinah went out to the city during a festival (the influence of Theodotus[20] may be felt here) to see the finery of the women of the country. She was seen by Sychem son of king Emmor. According to Josephus the "ravishing" of Dinah put Jacob in a dilemma. On the one hand, in view of Emmor's rank, he could not refuse the marriage request. On the other hand, he thought it wrong for Dinah to marry a Gentile. He asked permission to consult his sons. The King left and Jacob broke the news to the sons about Dinah and the request for marriage asking them for their advice. Josephus tells us that Jacob opposed marriage to a Gentile and he makes no mention of the Hivites getting circumcised.

We are told that the attack was without Jacob's sanction and that he was "aghast at the enormity of these acts and indignant at his sons." However, God steps in and indirectly supports the sons' actions: "God appeared beside him (Jacob) and bade him take courage, purify his tents and perform those sacrifices which he had vowed to offer when at first he set out for Mesopotamia and had seen the dream."[21]

## Philo on Genesis 34

Philo Judaeus (c. 20 BCE - 50 CE) was an aristocratic Jew from Alexandria with a dazzling knowledge of classical Greek literature and philosophy. He "chose to cast the greater part of his treatise in the form of a detailed philosophical exegesis of the Pentateuch."[22] His hermeneutic was indebted to his Greco-Roman philosophical heritage, being inspired by the allegorical tradition initiated by Theagenes of Rhegium (2nd half of sixth century BCE) and expanded by the Stoics.[23] Philo will read a story at the literal level but he argues that the truer meaning is the deeper, mystical one that is found through allegorising. Thus persons are often seen as representing abstract ideas.

---

18 Introduction by Thackery in Josephus, 1943, p. ix.
19 Ibid., p. xii.
20 We know that Josephus was aware of the work of Theodotus - see *Contra Apionem* i.216.
21 For an interpretation of Josephus which sees him as supporting Jacob against the sons see Wenham, 2000.
22 Winston, 1981, p. 2.
23 Ibid., pp. 4-5.

Following the Stoics, Philo tries to discover what a person or place represents by extensive use of etymologising.

Philo discussed Genesis 34 on two occasions. We shall first examine the *Migration of Abraham* which is a treatise on Genesis 12:1-4, 6. Genesis 34 arises in Philo's discussion of 12:6 where Abram goes to Shechem. Philo reads God's call to Abram in 12:1-4 as the call to a person to leave their body (land), sense (kinsfolk) and speech (father's house) and head towards higher realities. The promise is that God will cause a "multitude of qualities" (great nation) to reach full maturity in that person. God will also give mastery of language (I will bless[24] you) and magnify the individuals outward (make your name great) as well as their inner person.

Abram was seventy-five at this time and according to Philo this means that the soul must progress through reason (symbolised by 70) and the senses (symbolised by 5) as it "travels through" the whole of ethical philosophy (the land) in its search for wisdom. In Shechem (meaning "shoulder" and thus symbolising work) we find a symbol (the oak) of the solid labour such a search for wisdom entails. At this point Philo's mind wanders across to Genesis 34. The man Shechem symbolises the opposite kind of work from that noble work which the oak represents.[25] His father is Hamor meaning "ass": "practising folly and nursed in shamelessness and effrontery."[26] Thus Shechem, son of Hamor, is the toil of folly and irrationality. Dinah means "judgement"[27] and Shechem "ravished" her thus he symbolises the defilement of "the judgement faculties of the understanding."[28]

Simeon and Levi are described as the "hearers and pupils of sound sense"[29] who were too quick for Shechem. First they "made secure their own quarters"[30] and then they overthrew the city "when still occupied in the pleasure-loving, passion-loving toil of uncircumcision."[31] Philo is taking liberties with the text here for in Genesis 34 Shechem and Hamor were actually circumcised at this point. Colson and Whittaker suggest that for Philo the "circumcision of the truly wicked is only illusory."[32] These passion-loving fools tried to "carry off

---

24 The Greek word for 'bless' in the LXX is ευλογησω which includes the word λογος. Thus Philo links blessing with speech.

25 Philo, Vol. IV, 1968, p. 223.

26 Ibid., p. 224.

27 Ibid., p. 223.

28 Ibid., p. 224.

29 Ibid., p. 224.

30 Ibid., p. 224. Colson and Whittaker (ibid., p. 264, fn. b) note that Philo is probably referring to the disablement of the Shechemites by circumcision (except that he does not refer to circumcision) to make the point that "virtue must fortify itself against vice before it can take the offensive."

31 Ibid., p. 224.

32 Ibid., p. 265, fn. D.

unobserved the virgin soul (Dinah)"[33] but failed thanks to the "hearers and pupils of sound sense." For Philo Dinah was not actually defiled. The soul (Dinah) *"seemed* to have been shamed" but "became again a virgin. Seemed, I said, because it never was defiled."[34] Because the soul did not intend the wrongdoings then the unwilled sufferings are not real defilements.[35] The moral of this story is that one should work to honour and not to ravish judgement and sound sense.

In *On the Change of Names*[36] Philo uses the story a second time in a slightly different way. He is discussing those who speak noble words but whose actions are "most vile and their methods equally so."[37] The archetype of such a one is Shechem, son of Hamor. He symbolises, as we know, the "toil which is fathered by unintelligence" and which is "miserable and full of affliction." Now in Genesis 34:2-3 Shechem humbles Dinah and then speaks kindly to her. The juxtaposition of the terrible deed and the affectionate words was "to show that his actions were the opposite of his words."[38] Dinah represents "incorruptible judgement, the justice which is the assessor of God, the ever virgin."[39] The "fools who attempt to seduce her seek by means of specious talk to escape from conviction."[40] All this fine talk is useless as "the vindicators will come strong and doughty, inspired with zeal for virtue."[41] These vindicators (Simeon and Levi) will tear off the bandages of false talk from the Shechems of this world and behold "the soul naked in her very self"[42] thus exposing "all her disgraces."

Philo is not primarily interested in an ethical evaluation of the events recorded in the story. Nevertheless, he is concerned to use the story in ethical reflection. He tries to see how the characters' actions signify timeless truths that can guide the soul in its journey towards God. The story, for Philo, guides one towards a unity of word and deed in the pursuit and honour of virtue, reason, judgement and wisdom. Shechem does not practice what he preaches and despises wisdom, thus he seals his fate. There are clear implications for the soul on its journey to God. In line with other Jewish readings of the time, Shechem is made more villainous than he is in Genesis 34, and the sons of Jacob become more idealised. Elements in the story which place Shechem in a better light are either ignored (e.g., the narrator's comments that he *truly* loves Dinah) or used to damn him (e.g., his affectionate words to Dinah in 34:3). Also no mention is made of his circumcision. In fact, Philo actually says that he was

---

33 Ibid., p. 224.
34 Ibid., p. 225.
35 Ibid., p. 223.
36 Philo Vol. V, tr. Colson and Whitaker, 1968. pp. 193-200.
37 Ibid., p. 193.
38 Ibid., p. 194.
39 Ibid., p. 194.
40 Ibid., p. 195.
41 Ibid., p. 199.
42 Ibid., p. 199.

uncircumcised.[43] Simeon and Levi are the heroes of the story and nothing is allowed to detract from the glory of their deeds. Even Jacob's curse in Chapter 49 is used in such a way as to enhance their unity! Dinah is held in honour as a symbol of virtue, judgement and wisdom and thus Philo honours her (or at least the ideal she represents). Shechem's attempts to defile her are futile and wrong. In no way is she to blame for the attack although Philo does not think that a genuine ravishing took place (at least in the spiritual reality).

### *Summary of Second Temple Jewish Interpretations of Genesis 34*

We may now stand back to notice some "persistent features" in the various Jewish retellings of the Genesis 34 story from this period.[44]

We may recall the fact that the circumcision of the Shechemites is usually ignored or even denied (Philo). The only occasion on which it is acknowledged (T. Levi) we see the lengths that the author goes to in order to circumnavigate the problem that this causes. Circumcision would have been seen in this period as a sign of conversion to Judaism and clearly, if the Hivites had converted, it becomes hard to justify the deeds of Simeon and Levi.

We may also notice that without exception the massacre is justified. This justification arises from three sources:

First, there is the general desire to present the patriarchs in a good light. Second, the praise of Simeon and Levi's *zeal* is in line with Jewish piety of the time, one of the characteristics of which was zeal for God.[45] Finally, Collins' key contention is that the interpretations use the Genesis story to provide a precedent for justifying violence against Shechem at the time the texts under discussion were written. They formed part of an anti-Samaritan polemic. Shechemites are "foolish" (T. Levi). "The story of Genesis 34 became, in the phrase of Kippenberg, the Magna Carta of Jewish violence against Samaritans."[46]

We may notice that the mechanism used to justify the killings is that of putting the sons of Levi in a very good light and the Hivites in a very bad light. Different strategies are taken for dealing with the issue of Jacob's disapproval.

---

43 Philo, Vol. IV, 1968, p. 224.

44 Collins, 1980, pp. 97-98.

45 T. Levi 6:3; Jub 30:18; Judith 9:4. Pummer, 1982, p. 180.

46 Collins, 1980, p. 98. Reinhard Pummer concedes that Theodotus is "a strict and exclusivist Jew" but disagrees with Collins' claim that his work should be seen as an anti-Samaritan polemic (Pummer, 1982, p. 178). Instead it is, according to Pummer, an inculcation of the prohibition against mixed marriages (ibid., p. 182). Several of our texts do highlight the issue of Jew-Gentile intermarriage in their interpretations of the story. A prohibition on such unions was certainly part of the perceived ethical message of Genesis 34 in this period. Whatever is the case in this debate it is clear that the story was used to guide ethical behaviour.

It is either not mentioned or it is relativised in some way.

Philo represents a very different hermeneutic from the others and he is very much less concerned with the issues that preoccupy them. This leads to a much more individualised and interior ethic extracted from the tale. Nevertheless he follows the same pattern of reading the Israelites as saints and the Canaanites as sinners. This tradition of evaluating the characters has continued until the present day in both Jewish and Christian interpretations.

## 100 CE – 1000 CE: The Early Christian and Orthodox Jewish Readings

### The Early Church on Genesis 34

#### Tertullian

The New Testament makes no mention of the Dinah incident and the Fathers of the church rarely allude to it. Tertullian (c. 160 CE - c. 220 CE) in Chapter X of his *An Answer to the Jews* makes use of Genesis 49:5-7 and 34:25-31 as a typological foreshadowing of the execution of Christ by the Pharisees. Strictly speaking Tertullian is not interested in ethical guidance in his use of the text. Nevertheless, he indicates a strong disapproval of the action of Simeon and Levi in the massacre of the Shechemites, at least in that it prefigures the massacre of Jesus by the Jewish leaders. Simeon and Levi represent zealous Jews both to the Jewish interpreters and to Tertullian but, of course, one's attitude towards zealous Jews will have some impact on one's evaluation of their action.

#### Ambrose

Ambrose (339 CE - 397 CE) the Bishop of Milan makes three references to the story. His thinking is developed most clearly in *Duties of the Clergy* Book I, Chapter XXV.[47] He is discussing the four virtues of wisdom, justice, courage and temperance. All four are instantiated in Abraham and in Jacob. The virtue of temperance is evidenced by Jacob's response to the rape of his daughter.

> What moderation (is as) true as his, who acted with such moderation as regards time and place, as to prefer to hide his daughter's shame rather than avenge himself? For being set in the midst of foes, he thought it better to gain their affections than to concentrate their hate on himself.

This passage is fascinating because it is the first attested interpretation of Genesis 34 (as far as I am aware) where the marriage alliance is approved of

---

47 The other references are in *Duties of the Clergy* Book II chapter V and *On Belief in the Resurrection* Book II (v. 23).

and the massacre condemned. Ambrose clearly feels that Jacob's reasoning in 34:30 is sound.

*Jerome*

Jerome (c. 340 CE - 420 CE) makes three references to Genesis 34. Of most interest is Letter CVII.6 to the mother of Paula the Younger. Jerome is explaining the duties that parents have towards their children. He writes,

> If you take precautions to save your daughter from the bite of a viper, why are you not equally careful to shield her from "the hammer of the whole earth" (Jer 1:23)? to prevent her from drinking the golden cup of Babylon? to keep her from going out with Dinah to see the daughters of a strange land? to save her from the tripping dance and from the trailing robe.

Parents must keep their daughters from "frivolous girlfriends and bad company."[48] In his letter to the virgin Eustochium he says,

> Go not from home nor visit the daughters of a strange land, though you have patriarchs for brothers and rejoice in Israel as your father. Dinah went out and was ruined. I would not have you seek the bridegroom in the public squares. I would not have you go about the corners of the city (Letter XXII:25).

So women should remain at home and "avoid the dangers of the public sphere."[49]

*St Gregory's Pastoral Rule*

Chapter XXIX of Gregory's Pastoral Rule concerns the instruction of those who deplore the sins of deed and those who deplore the sins of thought. For the former category, Gregory advises self-judgement and repentance to avoid the judgement of God. The great danger is to lose the sense of sorrow that drives one to repent. To illustrate that danger, Gregory makes allegorical use of Genesis 34:1-3. Dinah represents the foolish soul that puts itself in sin's way and ends up violated and Shechem is the devil who, after uniting himself with the sinning soul, deceives it so that it loses its sorrow and penitence. Beware of this type of scenario, warns Gregory.

## Genesis Rabbah *on Genesis 34*

Jacob Neusner describes *Genesis Rabbah* as

the first complete and systematic Judaic commentary to the book of Genesis. In normative and systematic Judaism, that is, the Judaism that reached its original expression in the Mishnah, ca. A.D. 200, and came to final and full statement in the Talmud of Babylonia, ca. A.D. 600, *Genesis Rabbah* therefore takes an important position. Specifically, this great rabbinic commentary to Genesis, generally thought to have been closed ("redacted") at ca. A.D. 400, provides a complete and authoritative account of how Judaism proposes to read and make sense of the first book of the Hebrew scriptures."[50]

*Genesis Rabbah* thus set the direction for subsequent Jewish exegesis of Genesis. The text, though completed at about 400 CE, contains material from considerably earlier.[51]

The discussion on Genesis 34 begins with some reflections by the Rabbis on 34:1, "And Dinah went out to see the daughters of the land." Yose of Onayyah writes,

> it is written, "And Leah *went out* to meet him" (Gen 30:16). She went out all made up to meet him, just like a whore. That is why it is written, "And Dinah, daughter of Leah, whom she had borne to Jacob, *went out*".[52]

Just as Leah "went out" like a whore to seduce Jacob so Dinah "went out" like a whore.

Dinah is clearly held to have been responsible for all the terrible results that followed from her whorish behaviour in going out. However, the commentary now shifts the blame back a stage to Jacob. 34:1 points to three figures: Dinah, Leah and Jacob. The Rabbi's take each as responsible, in some way, for the events. In LXXX: IV.1 Rabbi Judah sees Dinah's rape as a result of Jacob's overconfidence in Genesis 30:33. Rabbi Huna blames Jacob for not marrying Dinah off earlier to a circumcised man. The punishment for that was her sexual relation with an uncircumcised man.[53] Rabbi Simeon ben Laquish believed that Jacob's pride was punished by his daughter's rape.[54]

Bringing the blame back to Dinah, Rabbi Joshua of Sikhnin (in the name of Rabbi Levi) asks why God made woman from a rib. God thought to himself,

---

50 Neusner, 1985, pp. ix-x.

51 We can learn much from the text about Judaism at the time of the final redaction - a critical period in its history. It was at this time that Palestine shifted from pagan rule to Christian rule and the new rulers "adopted that politics of repression of paganism that rapidly engulfed Judaism as well" (ibid., p. ix). The basic hermeneutic of *Genesis Rabbah* reflects this situation.

52 LXXX: I.Y. The reference system hereafter is Neusner's.

53 LXXX: IV.2

54 LXXX: IV.3

We should not create her beginning with the head, so that she is not frivolous, nor from the eye, that she not be a starer [looking at men], nor from the ear, that she not be an eavesdropper, nor from the mouth, that she not talk too much [as a gossip], nor from the heart, that she not be jealous, nor from the hand, that she not be light-fingered, nor from the foot, that she not be a gadabout, but from a covered up piece of man.[55]

The Rabbi then spells out at length that despite God's counsel women have become all the things that God did not desire. The climax is the thought that woman may not have been made from the foot "yet she *is* a gadabout."[56] To illustrate this Dinah is mentioned as "going out." A typical woman!

Rabbi Berekhiah in the name of Rabbi Levi then compares Dinah's "going out" with someone who goes outside with some meat and exposes it. Once it is exposed a bird (Shechem[57]) swoops down and grabs the meat. Dinah exposed herself to danger by "going out."[58] LXXX: VI uses Proverbs 11:12 to indicate that Jacob's silence in 34:5 is a mark of wisdom. The sons' anger is also justified.

With regard to the sons' deception, Rabbi Samuel bar Nahman denies that this was a case of lying because the text says "...*because* he defiled their sister." Shechem's evil deed somehow made the deception not a deception.[59] I take this to mean that it was a *justified* deception. The massacre is defended even more strongly by suggesting that the Hivites were planning to double-cross the Israelites. On the basis of Hamor's words, "Will not their cattle, their property and all their beasts be ours" we read that "The [people of Shechem] had in mind to cheat but were themselves cheated."[60]

LXXX: XI looks at how the sons "took Dinah out of Shechem's house and went away."[61] Rabbi Yudan explains that "They dragged her out." Clearly the Rabbis wanted to know why Dinah had not left on her own accord and had to be "taken". Rabbi Huniah said that "a woman who has had sexual relations

---

55 LXXX: IV.4.C

56 LXXX:IV.4.E-K.

57 LXXX: VII.1 parallels Shechem's response to Dinah (cleaving, loving, delighting in and speaking to the heart of - vv.4, 8, 19, 3) with God's reaction to Israel (cleaving, loving, delighting in and speaking to the heart of - Deut 4:4; 7:7; Mal 3:12, Isa 40:12). Neusner describes this as "a stunning and daring contrast - yet common place" (Neusner, 1985, p. 152). The parallel could have been seen to Shechem's credit (loving Dinah as God loves Israel) were it not for the fact that he is explicitly he describes as "a wicked person" (F, M). Thus the parallel is a contrast of the carnal love of a wicked man and the pure love of God although it is a curious comparison in that the focus is on the common features exhibited by such different characters.

58 LXXX: IV.5

59 LXXX: VIII.1

60 LXXX: VIII.3. See Chapter Four for a discussion of this.

61 Gen 34:26

with an uncircumcised man finds it hard to leave." Simeon steps in and marries her to take away her shame. This gets Simeon "off the hook" for in Gen 46:10 we read that Simeon had a son named Saul by a *Canaanite* woman. If Simeon had had sexual relations with a Canaanite then he had disobeyed later Mosaic law and looked rather hypocritical in his reaction to Dinah. However, the Rabbis took it that *Dinah* was in fact the Canaanite mentioned. This was because she had sexual relations with a Canaanite and acted as the Canaanites do and thus became as they. In order to protect Simeon's reputation Dinah is stripped of her full Israelite status. Ironically his marrying his *full sister* would hardly put him in Moses' good books anyway.

Louis Ginzberg has compiled Jewish Haggadot from the second to the fourteenth centuries from which it is clear that Jewish re-tellings of, and elaborations upon, the story of Dinah continued in the tradition of *Genesis Rabbah*.[62] The Hivites are painted as vile and deceptive and the sons of Jacob are held up as paradigms of virtue. The Genesis story undergoes some interesting transformations in order to maintain the purity of the sons' motives and the justification of their deed. It was really only in modernity that some Jewish readings began to express a disapproval of the massacre.[63]

## 1000CE – 1300CE: The Mediaeval Period

### *Bernard of Clairvaux on Genesis 34*

Saint Bernard (1090 - 1153 CE), the Cistercian monk and founding Abbot of the monastery at Clairvaux (in 1115 CE) makes use of Genesis 34 in his first published work *On the Steps of Humility and Pride* (1125 CE). The work charts the downward path of a proud soul. The first of the twelve steps of pride is "curiosity about what is not one's proper concern."[64] In section X.29 Bernard explains that "There are two reasons why you might raise you eyes which have no blame attached to them: to ask for help or to give it."[65] This claim is backed by biblical references. Then he writes, "If you raise your eyes for some other reason I should have to say that you are no imitator of the prophet, or the Lord, but of Dinah or Eve, or even Satan himself."[66] Bernard elaborates on Dinah, as we shall see in a moment, then begins section IX.30 with the words "You, too, Eve..."[67] and compares Eve with Dinah in her wrongful raising of the eyes.

---

62 Ginzberg, 1937. See too Graves and Patai, 1963.
63 See Salkin, 1986, p. 287.
64 Bernard of Clairvaux, 1987, p. 100.
65 Ibid., p. 124.
66 Ibid., p. 124.
67 Ibid., p. 124.

Section X.31 begins, "You, too, Satan..."[68] and compares Satan's wrongful looking with Dinah's and Eve's. So we have three biblical case studies of the terrible results that follow from curiosity. Jean Leclercq says that Bernard "speaks to (Dinah), but far from reproaching her, he questions her gently, neither hurting nor humiliating her... Then he goes on to speak in the same way to Eve... These two women symbolise any human being who succumbs to sin's temptation."[69] Nevertheless, "Bernard reveals his underlying assumptions about rape. The attack was provoked by the victim and her curiosity, making her the cause of the sin."[70] About Dinah, Bernard says,

> For when Dinah went out to pasture her goats she was snatched away from her father, and her virginity was taken from her (Sg 1:7). O Dinah, you wanted to see the foreign women (Gen 34:1)! Was it necessary? Was it profitable? Or did you do it solely out of curiosity? Even if you went idly to see, you were not idly seen. You looked curiously, but you were looked upon more than curiously. Who would believe that idle curiosity[71] of curious idleness of yours would not be idle in the future, but so terrible in its consequences for you and your family and for your enemies too (Gen 34:25)?[72]

### Ancrene Wisse *on Genesis 34*

*Ancrene Wisse* (meaning roughly "a guide for anchoresses") is a text written in the West Midlands of England some time between 1200 and 1230 CE by an anonymous Augustinian canon. It functioned as a guidebook for the anchoresses - "religious women who lived as enclosed hermits in cells which were next to, or formed part of, churches."[73]

Anchoritic literature emphasises the need to take continual care to avoid sin. "Fear also governs her attitude to the outside world. So far as is possible she must avoid looking at it, or listening to it or letting her heart dwell upon it."[74]

---

68 Ibid., p. 125.
69 Leclercq, 1989, p.10.
70 Schroeder, 1997, p. 777.
71 Richard of Saint Victor (d. 1173) interpreted Dinah's going out to 'see' "as prideful comparison with the beauty of other women" (Schroeder, 1997, p. 776). He also thinks that initially Dinah struggled not to enjoy the rape but that Shechem drew her into "perverse and scandalous delight" (ibid., p. 780). It was apparently a common view of rape that the victim was innocent unless they came to enjoy it; in which case they shared in the sin of lust (see ibid. on Augustine, pp. 784-785).
72 St. Bernard, 1987, p. 124.
73 Savage and Watson, 1991, p. 8. The Council of Reims in 1157 used the Dinah story to support the strict enclosure of nuns to protect them from rape and seduction (Schroeder, 1997, p. 776).
74 Savage and Watson, 1991, p. 18.

Lechery is a key enemy to be opposed according to these texts: sexual temptation and fantasy lurks around every corner and must be dealt with strictly. These concerns rear their head in the section with which we are concerned.[75] The issue of particular concern is that of the anchoresses peeping out of their narrow windows at the outside world. This brings two dangers: the impact on them of what they see and, this is where Genesis 34 comes in, the consequences of their *being seen*. What makes peeping out evil is the evil which results from the initial act. Consider "what harm has come of peeping: not one harm or two, but all the woe that now is and ever was and ever will be - all comes from sight."[76] Lucifer saw his own beauty, became proud and was reduced to a devil. Eve saw the fruit, desired it and now all humanity suffers.[77] The story of Eve shows how *one* look can ruin the world and gives the lie to the claim that one *only* intends to look and not to act. To look at a man is to put oneself in the same position of Eve looking at the fruit.[78] At this point we read:

> "A maiden, Jacob's daughter, called Dinah," as it tells us in Genesis, "went out to look at strange women" - yet it does not say that she looked at men. And what do you think came of that looking? She lost her maidenhood and was made a whore. Thereafter, because of the same act, the pledges of the high patriarchs were broken and a great city was burned, and the king, his son and the citizens were slain, the women led away. Her father and her brothers were made outlaws, noble princes though they were. This is what came of her looking. The Holy Spirit caused all such things to be written in the book to warn women of their foolish eyes. And take note of this: that this evil caused by Dinah did not come from the fact that she saw Hamor's son, whom she sinned with, but came from her letting him lay eyes on her - for what he did to her was very much against her will at first.[79]

All the above evils came "not because women looked foolishly on men, but // because they uncovered themselves in the sight of men, and did things through which they had to fall into sin."[80] A woman's face, neck, hands and words are compared to a pit into which an animal (a man) may fall and which must be covered.[81]

> The judgement is very severe on whomever uncovers the pit, for she must pay for the animal that has fallen in. She is guilty of that animal's death before our Lord,

---

75 Ibid., pp. 66-92.
76 Ibid., p. 17.
77 Ibid., p. 67.
78 Ibid., p. 67.
79 Ibid., p. 68.
80 Ibid., p. 69.
81 Ex 21:33-34

and must answer for his soul on Doomsday... you who do anything by which a man is carnally tempted through you, even if you do not know it, fear this judgement greatly.[82]

The explicit assumption in the above texts is that any sexual incident is the woman's fault. Men are like wild animals with an uncontrollable desire for sex, so if a man rapes a woman then she has only herself to blame.[83] This is the ethical message which the Dinah incident is used to support and illustrate.[84]

## 1500 CE – 1600 CE: The Reformation

### *Martin Luther on Genesis 34*

Luther's lectures on Genesis 34 were quite likely delivered at Wittenberg in the autumn or winter of 1542-43.[85] He writes at great length and comments on the story as it develops but I propose organising his ideas around his thoughts about the different characters in the story.

#### *Luther's Comments on Dinah*

Luther was very concerned with the age of Dinah when she was raped. He considered her to have been 11 or 12.[86] In Luther's day girls were allowed to marry at 12 "but at that age they do not even know that they are alive or that they are girls."[87] In his view a girl was ready "for bearing the pains of childhood in her seventeenth or eighteenth year... the defilement inflicted on a girl almost still an infant is a very great disgrace."[88] Her only sin is curiosity[89]

---

82 Savage and Watson, 1991, p. 69.

83 The standard biblical reference book in the middle Ages, the *Glossa Ordinaria*, glosses the biblical text to fill out Dinah's character so as to portray her as "careless, negligent and easily seduced." After the seduction (violence was not used) she chooses to remain with Shechem so as to continue enjoying the sensual pleasures he offers (Schroeder, 1997, pp. 779-780). Nicholas of Lyra (1270-1340) also blames the "wandering curiosity of Dinah." However, unlike the *Glossa Ordinaria*, he sees a rape and not a seduction (ibid., p. 780).

84 Savage and Watson (1991) try to put these attitudes in some perspective. They explain that "the anchoresses are only meant to be concerned with their own guilt, not that of those they unwittingly tempt into sin, so that the question of male responsibility is mostly irrelevant here" (p. 349, fn. 13). This, however, only goes a small way to removing the offence of the passage to modern ears.

85 Schroeder, 1997, p. 780.

86 Luther, 1970, p. 187.

87 Ibid., p. 188.

88 Ibid., p. 188.

which led her to leave the house alone without her parents permission![90] "The disobedience and curiosity of the girl is punished quite severely."[91]

> By nature girls find pleasure in the society of other maidens of equal age in the neighbourhood... Accordingly, it is an example which should be carefully noted and inculcated in girls. They should not form the habit of strolling about and looking out of the window (cf. 2 Sam 6:16) and lounging around the door, but should learn to stay at home and never to go anywhere without the permission of their parents or without companions. For the devil is laying snares against the modesty of this sex, which by nature is weak, irresponsible, and foolish and hence exposed to the snares of Satan."[92]

After the rape Shechem tries in vain to win her love but she remained "in her grief and sorrow."[93]

*Luther's Portrait of Shechem*

Luther's Shechem was still a boy;[94] an arrogant and spoiled little brat, who "must have been brought up in a wanton manner."[95] In his royal arrogance "he thought that anything was permitted to him as a prince."[96] He is a friend and neighbour of Jacob[97] and as a noble member of his father's house one would expect him to behave honourably.[98] These factors make his crime more shocking and unexpected. Now "the rape of a virgin is a capital crime of itself by all law, divine and civil"[99] and the rape of a king's daughter (as Luther considered Dinah) is worse than the rape of a peasant's daughter.[100]

Shechem then loves Dinah with his "juvenile love",[101] but fails to win the grieving girl's heart so he carries her "off in a most unjust manner"[102] and holds

---

89 According to Luther she wanted to see games, dances and weddings in the city (ibid., p. 192).

90 Ibid., p. 192.

91 Ibid., p. 194.

92 Ibid., p. 193.

93 Ibid., p. 195.

94 Ibid., p. 190.

95 Ibid., p.194.

96 Ibid., p.195.

97 Ibid., p.190.

98 Ibid., p.191.

99 Ibid., p. 201. Luther thinks that rape was considered a capital offence in that whole area of Canaan and that consequently the locals were deeply offended that so saintly a guest (Jacob) was dishonoured in this way (ibid., p. 197).

100 Ibid., p. 202. To seize property and reduce men to slavery is a lesser crime than rape (ibid., p. 208) in Luther's eyes.

101 Ibid., p. 194.

102 Ibid., p. 201.

her "captive at his house."[103] The salt in the wounds comes with Shechem's total lack of remorse and repentance: "He does not repent yet but still increases his sin... No confession is heard, no repentance. No, he thinks that he has acted rightly or that it is a small sin to rape a maiden and defile her."[104] His death is a just punishment.

### Luther's View of Jacob

Luther has a very idealised view of Jacob's godliness[105] holding him up in the commentary as a paradigm of virtue and devotion to God. Luther, as Ambrose before him, reads this story primarily from Jacob's imagined perspective.[106] "Let anyone guess for himself how great is the grief of the father who has an only daughter and what a cross to see her defiled and dishonoured in a most shameful manner... a most atrocious and intolerable trial."[107] Joy Schroeder helpfully suggests that Luther's interpretation of the story may have been influenced by the recent death of his own thirteen year old daughter, Magdalena.[108] He shared with Jacob a fatherly love for his daughter and knew about deep loss.

When the news reached him Jacob was silent. This, according to Luther, is because he was "smitten with great sorrow"[109] so he patiently waits for counsel and a remedy from the Lord.[110]

Jacob is angry at his sons Simeon and Levi for two reasons. First, they have acted unjustly towards the Shechemites. Indeed he is deeply moved on account of so many murders.[111] Second, they have put the whole family in great danger. This threat nearly broke Jacob's faith in God's ability to protect. His faith struggles but he does not fall into unbelief. This is a necessary trial of a kind which the faith of all the saints must endure at times.[112]

### Luther's Perspective on Hamor and the Hivites

Hamor brought up his son with too much license and the lack of discipline ruined the lad.[113] God has ordained it that parents are responsible to look after their children and to control their desires and morals.[114] "Therefore parents are

---

103 Ibid., p. 197.
104 Ibid., pp. 195-196, see also pp. 199-200.
105 Ibid., pp. 191, 192, 197.
106 However, Luther is aware that not only Jacob but the whole family "suffered great grief... Leah especially was deeply grieved" (ibid., p. 196).
107 Ibid., p. 196, cf. 187, 190.
108 Schroeder, 1997, pp. 780-781.
109 Luther, 1970, p. 196.
110 Ibid., p. 196.
111 Ibid., p. 219.
112 Ibid., p. 219.
113 Ibid., p. 194
114 Ibid., p. 194.

to learn that they should not be too indulgent towards their children but that they should restrain them."[115] Hamor is a failed parent for when he finds out about his son's sin he does not reprove him and thus "becomes a partaker of another man's sins and agrees with him. This is the worst aspect of the matter."[116]

Hamor then approaches the Israelites despising Jacob in comparison with himself.[117] He "acknowledges no guilt; he does not confess the sin, and much less does he plead an excuse. He is too proud and for this reason the sin is aggravated."[118] When he is talking to his own people he says that that the Israelite property will belong to them. This is either a lie to his people or else he planned to double-cross Jacob.[119] Either way his sin is increased.

The people of Shechem come out little better in Luther's account. None of them urges Hamor to return Dinah to Jacob and "so also this people agrees with its rulers, and for that reason they suffer and perish together, and justly too."[120] It seems that Luther thought that the people of Shechem were sinners whom God had decided to punish. He thus allowed Shechem to sin and become a catalyst for punishment on the whole town who were caught up in the sin of the leader.[121]

### Jacob's Sons In Luther's Commentary

"The brothers had a just cause for their indignation and wrath. But they will be too cruel in exacting vengeance..."[122] They repay Shechem sin for sin and so "neither side follows what is just and right."[123] The sons perform justice but in an unjust, indeed "atrocious and cruel,"[124] manner[125] and thus incur their father's indignation. The "high and mighty rascals"[126] do not acknowledge their sin and justify it by making Shechem's deed sound worse than it was, for he only wanted Dinah as a wife, but they accuse him of wanting her as a whore![127] Simeon and Levi are, in Luther's opinion, full of what he considers typical Jewish arrogance about their status as God's people.[128]

---

115 Ibid., p. 198.
116 Ibid., p. 196.
117 Ibid., p. 196.
118 Ibid., p. 198 and see pp. 199-200.
119 Ibid., p. 208.
120 Ibid., p. 208 and see  p. 209.
121 Ibid., p. 207.
122 Ibid., p. 196.
123 Ibid., p. 201.
124 Ibid., p. 204.
125 Ibid., p. 201.
126 Ibid., p. 219.
127 Gen 34:31
128 Luther, 1970, pp. 202-203. In two relatively recent (1990; 1991) publications Ilona Rashkow has argued that the translations  of the 'classical' period (1525-1611) of

*God in Luther's Account of Genesis 34*

God is not mentioned in the text of Genesis 34, but that very absence becomes the start of Luther's reflections on the character who ought to have been present, yet was not.

> God and his angels close their eyes and pretend not to see. God ignores the matter and acts just as if he did not know or see the daughter being dragged away and defiled. For he permits this to be done whilst his angels rest and do nothing."[129]

Appearances are not as they seem. Luther's God never lets go of the steering wheel of his creation. It seems that several purposes are served here. God had decided to punish the Hivites for their sins and allowed the "sins of the Amorites to become complete" by the rape of Dinah. He used the sinful reaction of the sons of Jacob to punish the city. The unjust massacre is "also the secret judgement and wrath of God by which he permits all the citizens to be slaughtered."[130] Although the sons of Jacob act unjustly, nevertheless, God is not unjust when he punishes the Shechemites[131] because he warned them not to sin.

Finally God uses Jacob's trials so that we observe his wise reactions and learn similar patience.[132] Trials though, are still, by their very nature, painful and we still feel the absence of God even though he is never truly absent.

## *John Calvin on Genesis 34*

Calvin's Genesis commentary (1554) sees Dinah's rape as another trial for God's servant Jacob. His daughter's loss of chastity would "inflict the deepest wound of grief upon his mind."[133] As was common in the treatment of this story Calvin begins by drawing moral lessons from Dinah's "going out".

> Dinah is ravished, because, having left her father's house, she wandered about more freely than is proper. She ought to have remained quietly at home as both the Apostle teaches and nature itself dictates; for to girls the virtue is suitable,

---

English Bible translation - the Tyndale Pentateuch, the Coverdale Bible, the Geneva Bible, the Rheims-Douay Bible and the King James Version - are all influenced by the sexism and anti-Judaism of the translators. Genesis 34 is her test case but her arguments fail to support the weight of her thesis. She does, however, demonstrate that they took a similar line to Luther and Calvin in condemning the sons and disapproving of Dinah's 'going out'.

129 Luther, p. 191.
130 Ibid., p. 210.
131 Ibid., p. 214.
132 Ibid., p. 192.
133 Calvin, 1965, p. 218.

which the proverb applies to women, that they should be... keepers of the house. Therefore fathers of families are taught to keep their daughters under strict discipline, if they desire to preserve them free from all dishonour; for if a vain curiosity was so heavily punished in the daughter of holy Jacob, not less danger hangs over weak virgins at this day, if they go too boldly and eagerly into public assemblies, and excite the passions of youth towards themselves. For it is not to be doubted that Moses in part casts the blame of the offence upon Dinah herself, when he says, "she went out to see the daughters of the land;" whereas she ought to have remained under her mother's eyes in the tent.[134]

Concerning Shechem Calvin thinks that "although he embraced Dinah with real and sincere attachment, yet, in his want of self-government, he grievously sinned... when she was unwilling and resisted, he used violence towards her."[135] However, he came to his senses and tried to redeem the situation.[136] His deference to his father's will[137] is laudable and from it we infer "that the right which parents have over their children is inviolable."[138] In the negotiations with the Israelites, the Hivite delegation is presented by the narrator in such a way as to gain our sympathy, and thus to harden us against Dinah's brothers' continued anger.[139]

Jacob, when he hears the news, is silent with grief.[140] It is for the sons, however, and their response to the rape, that Calvin reserves most of his comment.

Shechem, indeed, had acted wickedly and impiously; but it was far more atrocious and wicked that the sons of Jacob should murder a whole people, to avenge themselves of the private fault of one man. It was by no means fitting to seek a cruel compensation for the levity and rashness of one youth, by the slaughter of so many men... Perfidy was also superadded, because they proceeded, under the pretext of a covenant, to perpetrate this enormous crime."[141]

Calvin draws a moral point from this for his audience: "Therefore we must beware, lest, after we have become severe judges in condemning the faults of others, we hasten inconsiderately into evil. But chiefly we must abstain from violent remedies which surpass the evil we desire to correct."[142] Calvin thinks

---

134 Ibid., p. 218.
135 Ibid., p. 219.
136 Ibid., p. 219.
137 Gen 34:4
138 Calvin, 1965, p. 219.
139 Ibid., p. 222.
140 Ibid., pp. 219-220.
141 Ibid., p. 220.
142 Ibid., p. 221.

that, as a matter of fact, it would have been wrong for Dinah to marry Shechem[143] but that the motivation of the sons is wrong.

Hamor does not come off well in Calvin's treatment. "He ought, in the beginning, severely to have corrected the fault of his son; but he not only covers it as much as possible, but yields to all his wishes."[144]

The Shechemites are castigated for being so willing to transfer allegiance to an unknown God ("they knew that, by a new sacrament, they would be committed to a different worship of God"[145]) by the hope of gain. They did so because they were blinded by an evil conscience.[146]

Despite this the Israelite massacre was unjustified. "Under the pretext of a covenant, they form a design against friends and hospitable persons, in a time of peace, which would have been deemed intolerable against enemies in open war."[147] Indeed the massacre is even worse because that cannot be ascribed to anger.[148] To their cruelty we may add the sin of avarice.[149]

Jacob's *apparent* selfish rebuke to Simeon and Levi was probably an attempt to draw them to repentance by the fear of punishment. He saw them terror-stricken at their recent crime and suited his words to their state of mind.[150] Their reply is very much to their discredit: it "not only breathes a barbarous ferocity, but shows that they had no feeling."[151] They excuse themselves on the basis of a crime committed by one man and they treat their father with contempt. Not only that but they are unconcerned about the danger in which they have put the family. "Thus we are taught, how intemperate anger deprives men of their senses. We are admonished, that it is not enough for us to be able to lay blame on our opponents; but we must always see how far it is lawful for us to proceed."[152]

So in Calvin's reading all except for Jacob are put in a bad light but his chief objects of horror are the sons of Jacob.

### 1600 CE –1800 CE:  Post-Reformation Readings

To show how diversity of interpretations was preserved in the Christian tradition in the post-Reformation period we shall juxtapose the work of two Anglican writers: Gervase Babington and Matthew Henry.

---

143 Ibid., p. 223.
144 Ibid., p. 223.
145 Ibid., p. 225.
146 Ibid., p. 225.
147 Ibid., p. 226.
148 Ibid., p. 227.
149 Ibid., p. 228.
150 Ibid., pp. 228-229.
151 Ibid., p. .229.
152 Ibid., p. 229.

## Gervase Babington

The themes which surface in the work of Bishop Babington of Worcester (1615) are ones with which we are now well familiar. Dinah's typically female curiosity was her downfall as it is for so many women. Her "going out" followed by her rape was "a profitable example to warne all youth... to beware, and to keep within for it is fafe..."[153] "Libertie and loofeneffe hath fpoiled many as one, as it heere did her."[154] Parents should be strict with their daughters and marry them off as soon as possible.

Jacob acts as a wise man should: he "rufheth not by and by into actions according to his greefe..."[155] His sons are righteously angry, hating sin as we ought.[156] Although their action was "a great murther in mans eies worthy of great blame" we must see in it the justice of God who will not allow those who attack his people to escape unpunished.[157] That having been said, the sons should "have been orderly, and with their Fathers aduice, vvho cheefely vvas wronged, and vvhofe vvifedom and difcretion vvould better have guided his Sonnes..."[158] Their anger darkened their minds leading them to act irrationally.

Hamor is a "fond Father" but he ought to "fharply have punifhed fuch behauiour in his Childe."[159] The moral being "a mally Father, maketh a wicked Childe."[160]

## Matthew Henry

Matthew Henry's influential biblical commentary on Genesis (1725) makes familiar moral applications.

Dinah was the "Darling of the family" "yet she proves neither a joy nor a credit to them" when she went out with her mother's connivance.[161] "She went to fee, yet that was not all, fhe went *to be feen* too... with fome thoughts *of the Sons of the land too*... NOTE, the Pride and Vanity of young People betrays them to many Snares."[162] She was taken by surprise by Shechem but *not by force*. The moral is that "young women muft learn to be chaft, keepers at home."[163]

---

153 Babington, 1615.
154 Ibid., p. 140.
155 Ibid., p. 140.
156 Ibid., p. 140.
157 Ibid., p. 141.
158 Ibid., p. 143.
159 Ibid., p. 140.
160 Ibid., p. 140.
161 Henry, 1725, original edition available from Worcester Cathedral Library, p. 112.
162 Ibid., p. 112, italics mine.
163 Ibid., p. 112.

Jacob is the wise man who holds his peace[164] whilst his sons are the fools. They sinfully misuse the covenant symbol of circumcision to murder the relatively innocent Hivites. "NOTE: Bloody Defigns, have oft been covered and carried on with a Pretence of Religion... But this diffembled Piety is doubtlefs double iniquity. Religion is never more Injur'd, nor God's Sacraments more Prophan'd, than when they are thus ufed for a Cloke of Maliciofnefs."[165] Their "infolent Reply" to Jacob in v. 31 requires the answer "no" but it hardly justifies the deed.

> It was true that Shechem had wrought Folly againft Ifrael, in defiling Dinah, but it ought to have been confider'd how far Dinah herfelf had been acceflary to it. Had Shechem abufed her in her own Mother's Tent, it had been another Matter, but fhe went upon his Ground, and perhaps, by her indecent Carriage, had ftruck the Spark which began the Fire: when we fevere upon the Sinner, we ought to consider who was the Tempter.[166]

Shechem tries to atone honourably for his deed and the Hivites were honest in their dealings with the treacherous Israelites.[167]

## 19th – 20th Century Trends in Interpretation[168]

### *Source Criticism and Genesis 34*[169]

The great revolution in Biblical Studies that came to be known as Higher Criticism soon made its presence felt in the study of Genesis 34. Although there has been a shift in recent years away from such approaches, they still play an important role in Old Testament studies. Such studies have had a clear impact on the study of the ethics of the text.[170] As far as Genesis 34 goes basically two

---

164 Ibid., p. 112.
165 Ibid., p. 113.
166 Ibid., p. 114.
167 Ibid., p. 113.
168 Susanne Scholz, in a recent article (1998), has argued that 19th Century German commentaries on Genesis 34 reflect the perspective of the powerful and not the subjugated on rape. The forensic medical texts of the time reflect a similar male attitude towards rape. Scholz proposes reading the chapter from the perspective of the victim (Dinah) to show the rape in all its horror. This chapter does not allow space to examine these commentaries.
169 Some of this material is taken from the introductory section of my article "Source Criticism and Genesis 34" (Parry, 2000b). My thanks to the Tyndale Bulletin for permission to use it here.
170 For a detailed, point by point refutation of source-critical studies of Genesis 34 see Parry, 2000b.

main positions were held:-[171]

- A documentary solution which held that the chapter was composed of two *separate* stories which were blended together by a redactor, and
- A supplementary hypothesis which held that the original story has been substantially modified by major additions from a later hand.

*Documentary Accounts*

Essentially two sources were thought to compose the chapter and although critics disagreed over the details of which verses should be in which source there was a broad agreement.

Source One

The oldest of the two sources (in the majority opinion) is often referred to as the Shechem variant of the story as its main character is Shechem. Precisely how this variant goes will depend on which verses one thinks ought to be included in the source but basically the story would have gone as follows:

Shechem rapes Dinah (v. 2b[172]) and then falls in love with her (v. 3) and he abducts her (v. 26). Jacob hears of his daughters' defilement whilst his sons were in the field (v. 5). When they hear the news they return home in great fury because Shechem had wrought folly in Israel (v. 7). Shechem speaks to her family and offers generous gifts if only they will agree to let him marry the girl (vv. 11-12) but they refuse his offer as marriage to an uncircumcised man is a disgrace (v. 14[173]). Nevertheless, the enthusiastic Shechem decides to get circumcised anyway such is his love for Dinah (v. 19). Simeon and Levi (presumably the other brothers have been appeased by Shechem) decide to attack Shechem and kill him and take Dinah out from his house (vv. 25-26). Jacob however, is not pleased and he rebukes the two brothers (vv. 30-31). Some think that the original conclusion is now lost. [174]

Source Two

This more recent source (in the majority opinion) tells the story as follows:

Dinah went out to see the women of the land when she was seen by

---

171 Von Rad, 1972, p. 325. Both such approaches begin by trying to account for the same features of the text which are considered to count against the unity of the narrative. According to the Higher Critics Genesis 34 exhibits two types of such features:-

Doublets. That is double accounts of the same event.

What Gunkel calls 'difficulties' (Gunkel, 1997, pp. 3, 57) and Westermann 'a whole series of inconsistencies' (1986, p. 535).

172 Westermann would have vv. 1-2a as part of the Shechem source also (1986, p. 535) as would Delitzsch (1978, p. 218) although in this they are in the minority.

173 Delitzsch includes v. 14 in the Hamor source.

174 E.g., Skinner, 1930, p. 417

Shechem (vv. 1-2a). Some think that there was no sexual relation between Shechem and Dinah (i.e. vv. 2b-3 do not belong to this source) - Shechem merely saw Dinah (v. 2a) then asked his father to request her hand in marriage for him (v. 4). [175] Others think that the words וַיִּשְׁכַּב אֹתָהּ from v. 2 also belong to this source and thus, Shechem saw *and* raped Dinah then fell in love with her. [176] He did not, however, abduct her. The abduction is found in v. 26 from the Shechem source and thus Dillmann and Gunkel[177] argue that וַיִּקַּח אֹתָהּ from v. 2 belongs in the Shechem source and not the Hamor source. Most critics would include v. 4 but not v. 3 in the source[178] and thus Shechem seeks Dinah's hand in marriage through his father. Hamor sets out alone for Jacob's household (v. 6) where he proposes an alliance between the two groups (vv. 8-10). The sons reply deceitfully (v. 13) by agreeing to the alliance on the condition that the Shechemites are circumcised (vv. 15-17[179]). Hamor is pleased with the deal (v. 18) and goes to his city to persuade them to agree to the terms (vv. 20-24). However, three days after they are circumcised (a fragment of v. 25) all the sons of Jacob descend on the town (v. 27), kill all the males (a fragment of v. 25 relocated in v. 27), and plunder the town (vv. 27-29). The conclusion of the story is 35:5 where God protects the family from the retribution of angry locals.

### The Redactor's Hand

Clearly, to sustain such a division of the text, one needs to appeal frequently to the work of a redactor who smoothed over the cracks. Westermann pays more attention to the redactor than most identifying him as C in contrast to source A (Shechem variant) and B (Hamor variant). Westermann's redactor has his own ideological agenda which is not identical with either of his sources though closer to the Hamor source. [180]

### *Supplementary Accounts*

Noth argues that a J account had been expanded by later supplements (vv. 4, 6, 8-10, 15-17, 20-23, 27 as well as the mention of Hamor in v. 13a, 18, 24, 26). Others who have followed in his trail include de Pury,[181] Kevers,[182] Blum,

---

175 E.g., Driver, 1904, p. 303; Westermann, 1986, p. 356.
176 E.g., Gunkel, 1997, p. 358.
177 Gunkel, p. 358 (as Driver, 1904, p. 303 and Westermann, 1986)
178 Though Westermann is an exception and does the opposite (1986, p. 535).
179 Delitzsch includes v. 14 (1978, p. 218).
180 The redactor "wants to narrate an example of the execution of the law of Deuteronomy. He wants to take a stand in express opposition to the possibility of any peaceful or contractual agreement with the inhabitants of the land such as was at him in the tribal account" (Westermann, 1986, p. 544).
181 Pury, 1969.
182 Kevers, 1980.

Vawter[183] and Zakovitch.[184] Vawter thinks that an original text (vv. 3, 5, 7, 11-13 [minus the reference to Hamor], 18 [minus the reference to Hamor], parts of vv. 24-26 and vv. 30-31) has been supplemented by vv. 1-2, 4, 6, 8-11, 14-17, 20-23, fragments of 24-26 and 27-29. This does not follow the documentary analysis exactly but in essence Vawter sees the Shechem source as the basic story that has been changed by the "Hamor sections". The latter, however, never existed as an independent source and were added to fit J.

Yair Zakovitch has recently argued for a more moderate supplementary analysis in which an original story (which he thinks is most of the chapter) has been expanded by a few additions (vv. 2b, 5, 7b, 13b, 17, fragments of 25-26, 27 and 30-31). His analysis differs quite considerably from the traditional one.

*Source Criticism and the Ethics of Genesis 34*

It is obvious that if one divides up a story into two different sources one now has three different stories - source A, source B and the final redaction. In the case of Genesis 34 the ethical dynamics of the resulting texts differ. One can no longer simply investigate the ethics of Genesis 34 but must look to the ethics of the source documents. This was a radically novel way of reading the ethics of the story and that point was not missed on source critics.[185] For example, S.R. Driver after explaining what he considers a *Christian* interpretation of the text *as a whole* in which all the characters come out less than blameless, he goes on to say that

> *these judgements will naturally be somewhat modified, if the modern critical standpoint is adopted.* In J, Simeon and Levi slay only Shechem and his father; and though this punishment was greater than what Shechem's act deserved (Ex xxii.16f), it might perhaps be excused on the part of two high spirited, martial youths, eager to avenge an outrage on their sister, and whose moral standards could not be expected to be in advance of those of the age in which they lived... In the representation of P, the treachery and cruelty are much greater; and probably, - like the terrible narrative of Nu. xxxi - it is merely an *ideal* picture of the manner in which the priestly writer conceived that a people hostile to Israel... ought to be treated.[186]

Gunkel actually uses the differing moral stances of the different sources to date them relative to each other.[187] He believes that the Hamor variant approves of

---

183 Vawter, 1977.
184 Zakovitch, 1985.
185 In what follows the differences between the critics quoted are a result of differences over which verses to assign to which sources.
186 Driver, 1904, p. 307.
187 Gunkel, 1997, p. 361.

the attack as a just punishment for rape. God himself sides with the sons.[188]
"Thus the legend thinks; every pagan city in which a daughter of Jacob is
violated should be destroyed."[189] The Shechem variant is less positive about the
attack. The crime is bad yet Shechem is prepared to atone for his sins and most
of Jacob's sons (it is assumed) warm to him. Jacob himself is enraged by the
attack. At the other end of the spectrum the 49:5-7 variant is wholly against the
massacre and views the future demise of the two tribes a fitting punishment. On
the assumption that later texts idealised the patriarchs and had a less positive
view of foreigners, Gunkel thinks that 49:5-7 is the most ancient version,
followed by the Shechem version with the Hamor version as the most recent.
The final redactor of the story had more sympathy with the tough line of the
Hamor variant and so he used the Hamor variant as the basis interspersing it
with the Shechem variant. Minor changes were made to create a "passable
unity."[190] So Genesis contains three different narratorial ethical evaluations of
the attack on the city.

An article by Yair Zakovitch illustrates the impact of a rather different
supplementary approach from the usual. His two stories are somewhat different
from the above. The original

> story tells of Shechem's innocent attraction to Dinah and Jacob's sons'
> treacherous exploitation of the situation in order to plunder the city. That
> Shechem raped Dinah is neither mentioned nor even hinted at by either party in
> the course of the negotiations between the families. It seems that the rape element
> was added because the editor assumed that the brothers must have had a
> justifiable motive for their deceit and cruelty; what the motive was he inferred
> from the analogous story in 2 Sam 13.[191]

So the story originally saw the sons in a very dark light and Shechem as an
innocent, exploited victim. The expanded version slurs Shechem and justifies
the sons. Two very different stories with two very different ethical dynamics!

Another recent approach of this type is that of Wyatt. He aims to strip the
story down to his reconstruction of its purported original, pre-Israelite
version.[192] The original version is simply presented for us with very little by
way of argumentation. It has, we are told, been expanded at least three times[193]
with the final story bearing little similarity to the original. The proto-story was
a selection of parts from vv. 1-3, 11-12, 14, 18-19, 26. The story tells of a King

---

188 Gen 35:5.
189 Gunkel, 1997, p. 361.
190 Ibid., p. 362.
191 Zakovitch, 1985, p. 188.
192 Wyatt suggests that the original version may have been Hurrian from the Amarna
period, 1990, p. 456.
193 Ibid., pp. 449-58.

called Shechem who makes love (Wyatt does not think that Genesis 34 is about a rape[194]) to Dinah, a woman of noble stock from among his people. Such is Shechem's love that he offers to pay the bride-price and the bride's own dowry. The price he must pay is a hard one - he must be circumcised. In the original story this has nothing to do with a covenant with Israel. Rather it is a marriage rite performed on the bridegroom by his future father-in-law.[195] Instead the father-in-law-to-be kills Shechem. However, this is no revenge killing but a human sacrifice![196]

> We have here, I believe, an account of the archetypal marriage rite, the sacred marriage, in which the bride-groom is sacrificed. The rite of circumcision as a marital rite would have its importance in its being a substitute with all ordinary husbands for their lives. But in undergoing circumcision they would, ideally, remember the sacrifice their archetype had to endure on their behalf.[197]

Under pressure of Jewish nationalism the story was adapted so that a message of restoration for the Hivites (the "third day" in 34:25 originally alluded to the restoration motif of Hosea 6:2[198]) "is now ironically to be turned into their annihilation."[199] Wyatt writes that the

> original meaning, concerning the redemptive significance for the community of the sacrifice of its king, continues to operate subliminally through the successive appropriation of the motif by the community collectively, and its subsequent reassessment as the legitimisation of land-seizure and community isolation from neighbours. The tragedy of the story is that in its surface language it has become a warrant for genocide.[200]

One impact of such source division is that the whole notion of biblical narrative ethics changes, for the actual story that we have before us in the text is passed over very quickly for greener pastures. The source-critic does not present us with differing biblical evaluations of the same story but *different stories* with different evaluations. Elsewhere I have attempted to make a detailed refutation of Source-Critical conclusions regarding Genesis 34,[201] but here I shall simply state that, whatever the prehistory of the text, it is the ethical dynamic of the *finished* text that interests me. Where the source critic leaves us with an

---

194 Ibid., pp. 435-36.
195 Ibid., p. 438.
196 Ibid., p. 439.
197 Ibid., p. 439.
198 Ibid., p. 457.
199 Ibid., p. 457.
200 Ibid., p. 458.
201 Parry, 2000b.

unstable text that does not present a coherent stance, I shall attempt to show moral complexity and ambiguity in a unified text.

## New Literary Readings of Genesis 34

Recent years have seen a dramatic shift away from diachronic analysis of biblical narratives towards synchronic ones. The final form of the text has been seen, once again, as a legitimate subject of study.

### Sternberg

Of all the "literary" readings of Genesis 34 one of the most important is, without doubt, that of Meir Sternberg. Sternberg sees the story as a classic example of how a biblical narrator seeks to persuade his readers to change their views by the use of skilful rhetorical techniques.

> The narrator needs no telling that if he lets the facts "speak for themselves", it is the victims of the massacre that are likely to gain most of the sympathy: the reader could hardly help condemning Jacob's sons for the shocking disproportionateness of their retaliation.[202]

> Precisely because the narrator is aware that we bring our habitual norms and scales of value to the reading, his main concern has been to subject them to such pressure as will modify and transform, if not invert, automatic response. He has deployed his masterly rhetoric to shape the reader in his own image, to bring their viewpoint into alignment [with his own].[203]

So the narrator aims to "take his readers on" and subvert their automatic condemnation of the massacre by storing up so much sympathy for the brothers and such antagonism towards the Hivites that when the massacre occurs the readers support it because it is seen as restoring moral equilibrium.[204]

Sternberg argues that the narrator presents the rape in very negative terms (v. 2) so as to store up sympathy for the brothers.[205] The positive comments about Shechem's attitude to Dinah in v. 3 do "not quite counterpoise, still less cancel out, the impact of its predecessor."[206] That we are told of Shechem's love for Dinah *after* the rape makes us less sympathetic than if we were told before.[207]

---

202 Sternberg, 1987, p. 455.
203 Ibid., p. 470.
204 Ibid., p. 466.
205 Ibid., p. 446.
206 Ibid., p. 447.
207 Ibid., p. 477.

In vv. 5-7 "Jacob's response is conspicuous by its absence."[208] As paterfamilias he ought to have acted,[209] or at least felt angry,[210] but he is emotionally indifferent. Hamor, in contrast, is an exemplary father[211] which only intensifies the readers shock at Jacob. The sons' anger also exposes their father's lack of feeling. The reader, claims Sternberg, will feel sympathy with the aggrieved brothers.[212] V. 7 serves to "elicit maximum sympathy for [the narrator's] heroes"[213] by making it impossible to decide if we are presented with the brothers' perspective on the crime or his own. The text makes many redundant comments about the relation of Jacob to Dinah and the sons all with the aim of focusing attention on him.[214]

The Hivites are sincere but come across in a bad light because they make no apology for their deed,[215] because the recurrent verbs (take, give and go out) recall the crime in vv. 1-4 setting up unfavourable echoes,[216] and because, the reader later finds out, they have taken Dinah captive and, Sternberg assumes, are using her as leverage. To Hamor the whole situation is a business opportunity. In contrast to him, Sternberg sees the sons as religious idealists who stick to their religious principles (v. 14). The speech made by Hamor and Shechem to the Hivites (vv. 20-24[217]) serves to lessen our sympathy for them. They make the deal sound as great as possible to the town people, making several changes to the original deal, so that the readers suspect their dubious intentions. The claim that the Hivites would have the Israelite possessions (v. 23) indicates that they planned to turn on the family at the nearest opportunity.[218]

The reader is now in a position such that the narrator can tell of the massacre in all its horror without turning the reader against the brothers.[219] The massacre was not revenge but rather was forced upon Simeon and Levi. They had to deal with resistance and any possible future retaliation.[220] It is important to see though that Simeon and Levi do not join in the illegitimate looting of the town - they cling to their principles (unlike the other brothers[221]). All the other characters in the plot (Jacob, the Hivites, the other brothers) only serve to

---

208 Ibid., p. 448.
209 Ibid., p. 448.
210 Ibid., p. 449.
211 Ibid., p. 451.
212 Ibid., p. 453.
213 Ibid., p. 455.
214 Ibid., p. 450.
215 Ibid., p. 456.
216 Ibid., p. 456.
217 Ibid., pp. 464-466.
218 Ibid., p. 466.
219 Ibid., p. 467.
220 Ibid., p. 468.
221 Ibid., p. 469.

highlight the narrator's two heroes, Simeon and Levi, by contrasting poorly with them.[222] In vv. 30-31 Jacob speaks at last "only to reveal himself as the tale's least sympathetic character."[223] His concerns are pragmatic and selfish not moral and idealistic like the brothers. The narrator gives his last word (v. 31) to Simeon and Levi leaving "no doubt where his sympathy lies."[224]

*Fewell and Gunn*

In direct contrast to this, Fewell and Gunn in 1991 argued that Genesis 34 is a text open to divergent, competent readings of which Sternberg's is only one. They propose a reading in which Shechem, after committing a terrible crime, acts so as to redeem the situation. The "narrator tips the balance in Shechem's favour."[225] Jacob too is portrayed favourable as the wise man who eschews "action-orientated heroics" out of a sense of responsibility to his family and their safety.[226] Dinah herself was wronged by Shechem but he manages to woo her (34:3) and she comes to see a marriage as the best way forward.[227]

The Hivites (Hamor, Shechem and the townsfolk) are portrayed as sincere people deceived by the true villains of the piece – the sons of Jacob. These angry, young men care nothing for Dinah as a person but merely for their own honour.[228] They reject the only realistic (given the culture in question) solution to the problem (marriage) and act wickedly by killing innocent people, plundering and raping the survivors[229] and then taking Dinah *against her will* from Shechem's house.[230]

*Caspi*

Another important literary interpretation of the chapter is Caspi's, "The Story of the Rape of Dinah: The Narrator and the Reader" (1985). "In this story we witness the earliest development of a society's moral stand concerning the defilement of a woman's honour and body."[231] "The narrator uses the story as a medium for transmitting values sanctioned by society... thus the story is offered to the reader from a traditional viewpoint."[232] This contrasts with Sternberg's view in which the narrator tries to subvert the traditional values of the reader. Having said that, Caspi, like Sternberg and for very similar reasons, thinks that the story is told in such as way as to "win the reader's approval of the

---

222 Ibid., p. 473.
223 Ibid., p. 473.
224 Ibid., p. 475.
225 Fewell and Gunn, 1991, p. 197.
226 Ibid., p. 208.
227 Ibid., p. 196.
228 Ibid., p. 206.
229 Ibid., p. 205.
230 Ibid., p. 211.
231 Caspi, 1985, p. 25.
232 Ibid., p. 31.

punishment."[233] He departs from Sternberg in arguing that the plunder is also approved of by the narrator.[234]

## Feminist Readings of Genesis 34

One of the features of contemporary Old Testament studies is its diversity. One current trend is the production of ideological interpretations of texts. That is to say, reading a text and evaluating it in terms of a particular ideology held by the reader. Feminist interpretations of the Bible are part of this movement. As I shall be devoting Chapter Six to feminist hermeneutics I shall simply note here that Dinah's lack of a voice, the attitude of the men towards the women in the story and the issue of rape loom large in such readings.

## Social Anthropology and Genesis 34

Three works have appeared which attempt to apply the work of social anthropologists to Genesis 34.

### Julian Pitt-Rivers[235]

Pitt-Rivers argues that Genesis 34 needs to be seen within the discussion of endogamy and exogamy which spans Genesis. He sees a shift from earlier patterns in which Israelite women could be given to non-Israelite men to a later "restricting the access of foreigners to Israelite women."[236]

> [T]he sister-wife stories depict a situation that is typical of nomadic people living in political and economic dependence upon townsmen who extort a sometimes grudgingly given sexual hospitality from their visitors in exchange for tolerating their presence.[237]

The honour of men is linked to the sexual behaviour of their mothers, sisters, wives and so on.[238] Thus the issue of who the women could be "given" to was a pressing one for sex symbolised group power-relations and was thus a political issue.[239] Genesis 34

> records how, when the Israelites first attempted to become sedentary, they ceased to allow their women to be preyed upon by their more powerful neighbours and

---

233 Ibid., p. 32.
234 Ibid., p. 41.
235 Pitt-Rivers, 1977, pp. 126-171.
236 Ibid., p. 157.
237 Ibid., p. 160.
238 Ibid., p.165.
239 Ibid., p. 170.

abandoned the custom of offering sexual hospitality in the way that went with
their nomadic condition. As a result the conception of marriage they subsequently
adhered to was opposed to the notion of exchange... The fate of Shechem then
marks the transition from an elementary to a complex structure of kinship, from a
closed system to a system of marriage strategy dominated by political values, and
the adoption by the Israelites of the concepts of honour and shame which go with
that system.[240]

Abraham used marriage in a conciliatory way whilst Simeon and Levi use it in
a very politically aggressive way: they no longer "give" their women but they
still "take" foreign women. Yahweh, on the other hand proposes a defensive
strategy for marriage to avoid idolatry in which Israelite women are not "given"
to foreigners nor foreign women "taken" as wives.[241] The Old Testament
reveals that the *practice* of Israelite men was often not Yahweh's strategy but a
loose form of endogamy[242] which tolerated marriage to foreign women.

*Naomi Steinberg*[243]

Steinberg's basic thesis is that, in the light of anthropological studies of kinship
structure, it seems that marriage in Genesis functions to establish patrilineal
descent within the line of Terah rather than to form alliances. In her view,
Genesis 34 addresses the question of appropriate spouses for Israelite women.
The conclusion is that they "should not marry outside the circle of kinship
reckoned through the patrilateral genealogy of Terah."[244] To marry outside the
family (as Esau had) breaks down the family solidarity. For Dinah to marry
Shechem "destroys lineage solidarity and deprives a member of the Terahite
line of a potential wife."[245] Jacob is to blame for agreeing to the marriage but
the sons object out of a sense of family honour (which is linked to the control
of the sexuality of women).

When Shechem violated the honour of Dinah, the honour and safety of her entire
family were threatened. Anthropological studies suggest that men who are thought
to be unable to control the sexual honour of their women from outsiders are also
thought to be unable to defend themselves against attacks from outsiders. In an
attempt to prove their ability to protect themselves, Simeon and Levi... show the
sons of Shechem their power in a mass attack on the men of the city.[246]

240 Ibid., p. 170.
241 Ibid., pp. 166-167.
242 Ibid., pp.162 ff.
243 Steinberg, 1993.
244 Ibid., p. 109.
245 Ibid., p. 110.
246 Ibid., pp. 110-111.

Prewitt, on the other hand, believes that the Levirite law is the basis for the massacre.[247] If there was no massacre then Dinah would have had to marry another man from Hamor's line.

### Lyn Bechtel[248]

Building on her earlier work on shaming[249] and her anthropological objection to interpreters reading Genesis 34 from an "individual-orientated" perspective Bechtel proposes a radical new look at the chapter. She makes a reasonable case for the minority report that Dinah was not actually raped but consented to Shechem's sexual advances.[250] The story must be read from a group-orientated perspective. Dinah "is both a figure who 'goes forth' and crosses her group boundaries and a marginal figure who engages in sexual activity outside the group."[251] The brothers consider Dinah to be polluted with "outside stuff." Tribal custom has been transgressed and shame brought on the tribe.[252] Not only that, but to lose her sexual power, which continues the existence of the group, to an outside, uncircumcised group is also shaming. The brothers seek to redeem the family honour by killing the Shechemites (the crime was perceived as a group crime and thus the punishment was a group punishment[253]). Simeon and Levi foolishly endanger the group by the attack. Jacob "displays the proper group-orientated behaviour. He is quiescent, passive, dependent on his community and co-operative. He does not carry out independent action, but waits for mutual support. He co-operates with Hamor; he is willing to listen."[254] He is also willing to allow outsiders to become insiders if they accept the group values. Dinah and Jacob, Hamor and Shechem are mediating figures between the two groups - those who are willing to cross the boundaries. Jacob and Hamor reach an honourable compromise enabling bonding and peace.[255] In Bechtel's story then the sons are the villains of the piece. The story challenges their militant attitude which is threatened by outsiders - an approach which threatens the survival of the group. The heroes are Jacob and Hamor, the flexible and tolerant leaders. One could draw clear moral lessons from this story with contemporary application.

---

247 Perwitt, 1990, p. 109.
248 Bechtel, 1994, pp. 19-36.
249 Bechtel, 1991. This article is the best work that I have found on the subject of shaming in the Old Testament.
250 Bechtel, 1994, pp. 19-31.
251 Ibid., p. 32.
252 Ibid.
253 Ibid., p. 34.
254 Ibid., p. 35.
255 Ibid., p. 35.

## Summary

It is clear from the above discussion that the moral lessons drawn from Genesis 34 vary and depend on the assessments of the characters and their behaviour. Disagreement at the level of character analysis leads to disagreement on the level of moral application. We could summarise the issues as follows:

- *Dinah:* is she the innocent victim of male sexual violence or the immoral temptress who was "asking for it"? Alternatively, is she the lover who crossed social boundaries in the pursuit of her man?
- *Jacob:* is he the godly, wise character in the story or the morally compromised father who cares not for his daughter and the family honour? Is some mediating position possible or desirable?
- *Shechem:* is he a young man who tries to honourably atone for his errors or an unruly, unprincipled Casanova who thinks that he can take what he wants with impunity? Is some mediating position possible or desirable?
- *Hamor:* is he an honest, if somewhat business-minded, leader or an unscrupulous manipulator who uses his hostage, Dinah, as leverage in order to negotiate a deal which he plans to renege on when the opportunity arises? Is some mediating position possible or desirable?
- *Hivite menfolk:* are they those who incur guilt by refusing to speak out against injustice or the innocent victims of Israelite aggression?
- *Jacob's sons:* are they the true heroes motivated by a zeal for the LORD and a concern for Dinah or the villains who act in a treacherous, irreligious and cruel way to defend their male pride? Is some mediating position possible or desirable?

Given the divergence in character assessments one has to raise the question whether the biblical text is so indeterminate that *all* of the above assessments are legitimate readings. Clearly the concerns of the day, from anti-Samaritan polemics in the inter-testamental period to feminist interpretations in the current period, do influence the assessment of the passage. There is indeed a level of indeterminacy in texts but the text does place limits on the range of meanings one can find. In Chapter Four I shall argue for what I take to be the narrator's implicit assessment of the characters. I shall argue that some of the above mentioned interpretations simply do not do justice to the actual text and are consequently to be regarded as inadequate readings.

# Chapter Four

# An Interpretation of Genesis 34

Before we can attempt to use Old Testament narrative in modern ethical discourse we need, as far as is possible, to allow the text to set its own agenda. In Chapter One we saw that to avoid seeing only our own faces reflected in the text it is important to seek to distance the horizons of the text from our own horizons. This chapter seeks to interpret Genesis 34 in its literary and historical context. The exegesis defended here is further supported by the detailed discourse analysis of Genesis 34 found in Appendix 1.

To prepare the ground for this close reading of Genesis 34 we first need to see the structural outline of the text and how it functions in its literary context.

## The Structure of Genesis 34

It is amazing that so little work has been done on the literary structure of the Dinah story. In what follows I shall assume that the way that other commentaries divide up the text for comment gives some clue as to their views on literary structure.

### Scene Divisions in Genesis 34

The first task that requires our attention is to sort out the scene divisions in the story. This is not as simple a task as it seems and there are several points of disagreement.

- *Problem One:* Does Scene One start at 33:18 or 34:1?
- *Problem Two:* Is v. 4 the end of a Scene or the start of a Scene or neither?
- *Problem Three:* Following from problem two is the problem of vv. 5-7. Are they, with v. 4, the end of a Scene or, without v. 4, the start of a new Scene?
- *Problem Four:* Are vv. 18-19 the end of a Scene or the start of a Scene?
- *Problem Five:* Are vv. 30-31 a separate Scene or not?
- *Problem Six:* Does the story end at 34:31 (the majority view) or 35:5 (the minority view)?

Let us take these issues in turn and attempt to resolve them. We need some criteria to decide the issues. I propose that the following features, or combinations of them, can mark a change of scene: a change of location, a change of characters, a change in time, linguistic markers such as those identified by Longacre as below band 1 in the narrative rank scheme (see Appendix 1).

On top of these we need to recognise that a common story-telling technique in Hebrew narrative is to end a scene with a trailer for the next scene.

*Problem One*

34:1 clearly marks a change in direction in the narrative. We are introduced to a new actor (Dinah) embarking on a new action (going to see the "daughters of the land"). The verb of motion is not uncommon in settings for scenes[1] and a change in geographic location is indicated. Given the common practice of ending scenes with a lead-in to the next scene, we can safely take it that 33:18-20 is the end of the previous story and 34:1 is the beginning of the Dinah story. This is reinforced by the observation that the focus is on Jacob in 33:18-20, whilst he is very much in the background in the off-line narrative of Genesis 34.

*Problem Two*

We may assume a change in location between v. 3 and v. 4 (presumably Hamor was not present during the defilement incident). However, no mention is made of a change in location and the shift from v. 3 to v. 4 is not linguistically marked in any way to indicate that a new scene is beginning. Given that the actor in vv. 2-3 is the same as in v. 4 (Shechem) we are unwarranted in taking v. 4 as the beginning of a new scene. It is better to think of it as a separate section within Scene One.

*Problem Three*

It seems that vv. 5-7 are linguistically marked and informationally crucial as a setting for what follows. There is a geographic shift from the town to Jacob's dwelling outside the town. There is also a shift in the characters from Shechem and Hamor to Jacob and sons. Thus I take vv. 5-7 to be the Setting for Scene Two.

*Problem Four*

Given that in vv. 18-19 we have neither change in location nor a change in characters we ought to see it as the end of a scene rather than the start of another. V. 20 has a clear shift in location to the town with a verb of motion. Scene Two thus ends with Hamor and Shechem agreeing to the Israelite terms for an alliance (vv. 18-19). This view is reinforced when we notice that Scene

---

1 Longacre, 1989, p. 87.

Three ends with the Hivites agreeing to the Israelite terms set out by Hamor and Shechem (v. 24).[2] Thus Scenes Two and Three balance: both are negotiations ending with the sons' conditions being accepted. I suspect that the reason many commentators have taken vv. 18-19 as the start of a scene is that they have not been sufficiently aware of the practice of ending a scene in such a way that it leads into the next. Vv. 18-19 clearly lead into vv. 20 ff. but that alone does not indicate that they are part of the same scene.

*Problem Five*

There is a strong similarity between the shift from v. 29 to v. 30 and the shift from v. 3 to v. 4. Here, as there, we can assume a change in location but no explicit mention of one is made. V. 29 is set in the city whilst v. 30 (we assume) is set at Jacob's house. V. 30 is not linguistically marked in any way to indicate that a new scene is starting so, given the parallel with Scene One, I think it best to take vv. 30-31 as part of Scene Four, even if they are a separate section within the Scene. Thus both Scene One and Scene Four end with the offensive sons (Shechem in v. 4 and Simeon and Levi in vv. 30-31) talking to their fathers. This balance in content reinforces our decision not to separate vv. 30-31 too strongly from vv. 25-29.

*Problem Six*

Although 35:1 is not linguistically marked as the start of a new story it is clear that the conversation between Jacob and sons is over and a new one between God and Jacob has begun. The topic of discussion changes from the prudence and ethics of the massacre to the call to go to Bethel. The fact that 35:5 alludes back to 34:30 is not a good enough reason to make 35:1-5 part of the same scene as 34:30. Better, I think, with the majority to take 34:31 as the dramatic climax to the Dinah story with 35:1-5 as a link between the story near Shechem and the altar near Bethel.

*The Structure of Genesis 34*

The above considerations supports the analysis of G.J. Wenham who analyses the chapter as follows:[3]

---

2 All commentators agree that v. 25 is clearly marked as the beginning of a new scene. There is a change in characters, in pace and a circumstantial clause marking a temporal shift (three days later....).
3 Wenham, 1994, pp. 307-308.

Narrative
*Scene 1:* Shechem rapes Dinah and seeks to marry her (1-4)
      Speech to father: "Get this child for me to marry" (4)
Dialogue
*Scene 2:* Hamor and Shechem propose a marriage alliance with Jacob's family
(5-19)
      Hamor's speech (8-10)
      Shechem's speech (11-12)
      Jacob's sons' speech (14-17)
      Hamor and Shechem consent (18-19)
Dialogue
*Scene 3:* Hamor and Shechem put the terms for a marriage alliance to the
townsfolk (20-24)
      Hamor and Shechem speak (21-23)
      Townsfolk consent (24)
Narrative
*Scene 4:* Jacob's sons rape the town (25-31)
      Speech to father: "Should he treat our sister as a prostitute?" (31)

I consider Wenham's analysis to be a very helpful way to look at Genesis 34
but I think that we can fine tune it further. Brueggemann[4] divides the story up
as follows:

   33:18-20. Introduction: settlement in Shechem
   34:1-12. Seduction and negotiations by Shechem
   34:13-29. Retaliation by the sons of Jacob
   34:30-31. Conclusion: dispute between Jacob and sons

What is intriguing in this rather idiosyncratic analysis is that Brueggemann
clearly divides a scene in half. That is to say Wenham's Scene Two (vv. 5-19)
is split after v. 12. Brueggemann designates 34:13-29 as "the sons' revenge"
because their deceitful speech is the beginning of their strategy that leads to the
massacre. I think that Brueggemann has seen something here and I propose an
analysis of the structure of the chapter that is essentially in line with Wenham's
but which incorporates this shift in v. 13. Genesis 34 is, in my view, organised
in a palistrophic pattern as follows:

---

4 Brueggemann, 1982, p. 274.

**Scene One**

A        (v. 1 Setting: Dinah "went out...")

         vv. 2-3 Shechem "takes" Dinah

         v. 4 Shechem and his father discuss the situation

**Scene Two**

   B     (vv. 5-7 Setting: Hamor "went out..." and Israelite anger)

         vv. 8-12 Hamor and Shechem speak to Jacob and sons:
         give Israelite and "take" Hivite daughters.

      C  vv. 13-17 The deceptive response:
         If you are circumcised we'll "take" Hivite daughters.
         If not we'll "take" our daughter and "go out"
         *vv. 18-19 Result: Step One towards retribution*
         *Hamor & Shechem agree to the terms.*

**Scene Three**

   B1    (v. 20 Setting: Hamor and Shechem "came"
         to those who lived in their city)

         vv. 21-23 Hamor and Shechem speak to the Hivites:
         "take" Israelite and give Hivite daughters.
         *v. 24 Result: Step Two towards retribution:*
         *those who "went out" of the city gate agree to the terms.*

**Scene Four**

A1       (v. 25 Setting: Simeon and Levi "take" sword and "come" upon the city)

         vv. 26-29 They "take" Dinah and "went out". They "take" booty.

         vv. 30-31 Simeon and Levi and their father discuss the situation.

The above analysis highlights the use of key words that are used in the narrative to dramatic effect.

*A and A1*

A describes the crime in which Shechem "takes" Dinah and demands that his father "take" her as a wife for his son. A1 reverses that "taking" when the brothers of Dinah "take" her back and also "take" booty (having "taken" their swords to slay the men). In A Dinah "went out" and was "taken" whilst in A1 she is "taken" and "goes out" of Shechem's house. This reversal of word order draws attention to how the massacre is a reversal of the original crime. Both A and A1 end with a conversation between the "takers" and their fathers.

*B and B1*

In B Hamor and Shechem go to the Israelites to negotiate and in B1 they go to the Hivites to negotiate. In B and B1 the conversation is about an alliance in which daughters are given and "taken".

*C*

In v. 13 the narrator gives a very elaborate multiple-verb-frame quotation formula. If the Hivites do not agree to Israelite modifications to the deal they will "take" their "daughter" and "go out". They do exactly that in A1.

*Scenes Two and Three*

B and C are both part of Scene Two, whilst B1 is Scene Three. Both Scene Two and Scene Three end with a step towards plot resolution: Shechem and Hamor in C and those who "go out" of the gate of the city in B1 agree to be circumcised. Shechem and Hamor's agreement may have looked neater in B instead of C, but the plot would not allow that. However, the order is preserved by having each scene of negotiations end this way.

*Settings*

In the Settings of A and B the characters "went out", whilst in the Settings of B1 and A1 they "came to/upon". B1 and A1 thus reverse A and B by having the verb אצי later (v. 24 in B1 and v. 26 in A1). This accentuates the way in which C turns the plot around.

Each scene opens with some individual or party crossing the group boundaries between Canaanite and Israelite dwellings. In Scenes One and Four we see Israelites cross the boundaries, whilst sandwiched between in Scenes Two and Three it is Hamor and Shechem. When Dinah "went out" to see the Canaanites she was defiled, so when her brothers "came upon" the Canaanites they killed and looted. When Hamor "went" to see Jacob he was deceived and signed his death warrant. When he "came to" his city he unintentionally deceived his people and they too put their names to the death warrant. One fateful crossing of the boundaries led to three more of escalating seriousness.

## The Peak of the Story

An important aspect of Longacre's work on discourse linguistics is his notion of the peak of a story. This feature is claimed by Longacre to be a "language universal":

> Essentially, *peak* is a kind of zone of turbulence... in which predictable discourse features are skewed so that certain typical features are removed or partially suppressed, while other features are introduced. It represents a kind of gear shift in

the dynamic flow of a discourse."[5]

Obviously such features exists at a discourse level and as little work has been done at this level we need to be tentative in our thinking. Essentially Longacre is claiming that the key part of the story can be marked in various ways. There is no simple formula here. One must look for combinations of the kinds of features mentioned below as syntactic clues:[6]

(a) Episode introduced by *wayehi*
(b) Repetition of participant name
(c) Greater descriptive detail to build suspense
(d) Chiastic structures often follow peaks
(e) Multiple tellings of the same story
(f) A crowded action line is typical. "Peak is marked essentially by a change in pace or character of a narrative."[7]

I suggest that the peak of the Dinah story is 34:25-27 whilst 34:28-29 and 30-31 are post-peak episodes 1 and 2.[8] The reason for this is that after introducing the episode with *the only wayehi* in the chapter (feature (a)) the action suddenly speeds up from the very slow pace of the speeches in the preceding two scenes - speech being a feature designed to maintain and build suspense (feature (c)). We have a burst of action (feature (f)) which is followed by a very detailed chiasmus that slows the pace right down and marks the end of the peak (feature (d)). These syntactic features combine perfectly with the actual content of the peak, for it is in this section that the decisive action is taken to resolve the inciting incident in vv. 2-4. So syntax and content combine to mark vv. 25-27 as the climax of the story. That is A1 on the palistrophe.

Some may protest that the very chiastic structure would imply that the focus of the story is the sons' speech in C. This would, in my view, be to misunderstand the function of the patterning in the narrative. The centre of a palistrophe may indeed be the focus of the story but it need not be the climax. Often the centre of a narrative chiasmus serves to indicate the moment when the tide turns. This is literally true of the flood narrative, which reaches its centre with the flood beginning to recede.[9] It is true also of the Jacob cycle as a whole (on which see below) and it is the case here. The sons' speech is not the climax of the story but the turning point. The climax is clearly what the story has been building up to throughout, as my discourse analysis in Appendix 1

---

5 Longacre, 1989, p. 18.
6 Ibid., pp. 30-35.
7 Ibid., p. 39.
8 Winther-Nielsen has suggested to me in conversation that his analysis of Joshua 6:20b-21 is very similar.
9 Gen 8:1. See Wenham, 1991, p. 156.

demonstrates.

Having made a provisional analysis of the structure of Genesis 34 it is appropriate to look at the function of the Dinah story in the structure of the Jacob cycle as a whole.

## Genesis 34 in its Context

### *Clues on the Context of Genesis 34*

What is the story of Dinah doing where it is? How does it contribute to the flow of the Jacob cycle?[10] Brueggemann writes that "it seems to have no relationship with anything before or after"[11] but despite the fact that its *raison d'être* is not initially obvious, Genesis 34 is clearly no stray boulder. There are numerous links between it and its context that clearly indicate that it has always occupied this position in the final redaction of Genesis. Wenham[12] provides a comprehensive list of features which indicate that Genesis 34 presupposes what precedes it and is itself presupposed in what follows.

- the geographic setting in Canaan presupposes that Jacob has returned there.
- the family relationship of Jacob's marriage to Leah and the resulting children is assumed.
- Jacob's lack of love for Leah is the background for his lack of concern for Dinah (contrast his later attitude to the loss of his favourite wife's son, Joseph). This tension also explains the overreaction of Dinah's full brothers.
- in 30:21 Dinah's birth is mentioned (this is only done for a woman if she is to figure prominently in the subsequent narrative, cf. 22:23) and thus 30:21 anticipates Genesis 34.
- the necessity of circumcision for inclusion in the Israelite community presupposes Gen 17. "Indeed the phraseology of 34:15, 'let all your males be circumcised' seems to be a direct quote from 17:10, and the other passages about circumcising males in 34:17, 22, 24 also seem to echo 17:10,12."[13]
- it is customary in Genesis to close an episode by having a trailer for the next. 33:18-20 fulfils this function for chapter 34.
- 35:1-5 (especially v. 5, cf. 34:30) presupposes the events in chapter 34 with the enraged Canaanites out to destroy the Israelites in revenge for the Shechem massacre.

---

10 Gen 25:19-36:43.

11 Brueggemann, 1982, p. 274.

12 Wenham, 1994, pp. 308-309.

13 Ibid., p. 308.

- 49:5-7 is Jacob's second condemnation of Simeon and Levi for the massacre in 34:25-26.

Thus Genesis 34 is an integral part of the Jacob cycle.


## *Steps in the Right Direction*

In 1975 two works were published which advanced the discussion somewhat. J.P. Fokkelman presented a very insightful structural analysis of the Jacob cycle in his book *Narrative Art in Genesis*. He had little to say about Genesis 34 but he did notice that two stories that seemed to intrude into the Jacob cycle - Chapter 26 and Chapter 34 - are symmetrically placed in the flow of the cycle. "Both are exactly two scenes away from the boundaries."[14] This observation led Fokkelman to observe certain similarities between Genesis 26 and 34. Both are about generations other than Jacob's - his parents (Ch. 26) and his children (Ch. 34). The effect of this is to tie the Jacob cycle into the book of Genesis. Not only this but both stories make the theme of the blessing of Abraham (the promise of land) thematic and in both the problem for the promise arises within the land - its inhabitants: Philistines (Ch. 26) and Hivites (Ch. 34). Indeed in both stories the prospect of intermixing with Canaanites is raised as an issue.

The second work was Michael Fishbane's[15] "Composition and Structure in the Jacob Cycle (Gen 25:19-35:22)."[16] Fishbane saw the Jacob Cycle according to the following pattern:

---

14 Fokkelman,1975, p. 240.

15 Others have seen such structures. For example Brueggemann (1982), writing after Fishbane but apparently unaware of his article, draws the following pattern (p. 213).

    A - Conflict with Esau

     B - Meeting at Bethel

      C - Conflict with Laban

       D - Births

      C1 - Conflict and covenant with Laban

     B1 - Meeting at Penuel

    A1 - Reconciliation with Esau.

This, however, does not show how Gen 26 and 34 fit into the scheme.

16 Which was reworked for Fishbane, 1998.

---

**A:** Oracle Sought; Rebecca struggles in childbirth; *bekorah* –
Birthright; birth; themes of strife, deception, fertility (25:19-34)
  **B:** Interlude; strife, deception; *berakhah*, blessing; covenant with a foreigner (26)
    **C:** Deception; *berakhah* stolen; fear of Esau; flight from the land (27:1-28:9)
      **D:** Encounter; (verb: *paga'*) with the divine at a sacred site near border; *berakhah* (28:10-22)
        **E:** Internal Cycle Opens; arrival; Laban at border; deception; wages (29:1-30)
          **F:** Jacob's wives fertile (29:31-30:24)[17]
          **F1:** Jacob's flocks fertile (30:25-43)
        **E1:** Internal Cycle Closes; departure, Laban at border; deception; wages (31)
      **D1:** Encounter (verb: *paga'*) with divine being at sacred site near border; *berakhah* (32)
    **C1:** Deception Planned; fear of Esau, *berakhah* - gift returned; return to land (33)
  **B1:** Interlude; strife, deception; covenant with foreigner (34)
**A1:** Oracle Fulfilled; Rachel struggles in childbirth; *berakhah*, death, resolutions. (35)

---

So the Jacob cycle forms a massive chiasm in which chapter 34 finds its place. Like Fokkelman, Fishbane is also led to compare Genesis 26 and 34 noticing a range of parallels. This list has been more recently expanded by Gary Rendsburg.[18] Evidently Genesis 26 and 34 are off the main-line of the Jacob plot and Fokkelman, Fishbane and Rendsburg demonstrate that they serve the two-fold narrative function of (a) integrating the Isaac *toledot* with the Terah *toledot* (Gen 26) and the Jacob *toledot* (Gen 34) and (b) giving a dramatic pause at key points at either end of the story. We shall need to go further than this though. Why were these particular stories chosen to perform this function?

The theme of the blessing of Abraham is really the key theme that runs through the Jacob cycle: the macro-structural idea that organises the whole. Longacre writes that "every text, if it truly is a text, has a germinal idea (or closely related complex of germinal ideas) that acts as an overall plan in the development of that discourse."[19] Each episode in the story plays its part in

---

17 I have made a minor adaptation to Fishbane's pattern here as suggested by Rendsburg (1986, p. 53, fn. 3).
18 Rendsburg (1986) notices nine more verbal and thematic parallels between chs. 26 and 34, some of which seem rather tenuous whilst others appear reasonably plausible (pp. 55-56).
19 Longacre, 1989, p. 17.

contributing to this macro-structural idea. It is by pursuing this thought that we shall come to see more clearly the function of Genesis 34 in its context. I would argue that each story in the Jacob cycle contributes either directly or indirectly to the theme of "the transmission of the divine promise to Jacob and its outworking."

## Taking the Discussion Further

Genesis 26 is not just any interruption into the tensions between Jacob and Esau. In Genesis 25:19 ff. Jacob takes Esau's *bekhorah* (birthright) whilst in 27 he deceives his father into giving him Esau's *berakhah* (blessing). According to Fokkelman, Genesis 26 is "demonstration material."[20] It demonstrates what the blessing of Isaac is and how it works in practice. Genesis 26 models the blessing of Abraham just prior to Jacob's deception of his father to get that blessing.

That Jacob inherits this promise becomes very clear in 28:3-4 when Isaac blesses Jacob before he flees Esau: "May you take possession of the land where you now live as an alien, the land that God gave to Abraham." At the borders of Canaan in Bethel the fleeing Jacob encounters Yahweh in a dream.[21] Yahweh promises "I will give you and your descendants the land on which you are lying... I will bring you back to this land."[22] Thus Jacob walks from the land with the words of God clearly in his mind. It is obvious that Jacob's residence outside the land is a temporary, abnormal state of affairs.[23]

It is clear that in Paddan Aram God really is with Jacob and he is blessed with offspring. After the central episode of the palistrophe[24] with the focus on fertility, the very next move is to bring Jacob home.[25] As Jacob fills out the details of this message to his wives, it is significant to notice how God calls him home. God is reported to have said: "I am the God of Bethel... Arise and leave this country and return to the land of your clan."[26] Bethel has clear associations with the divine promise. In 13:14-17 Yahweh reiterates the promise of descendants and particularly land to Abraham whilst he is near Bethel. The next occurrence of Bethel is where God transfers that promise to Jacob in 28:10-22. Now in 31:13 we read that the God of Bethel calls Jacob back to the land. In Genesis 35 Jacob returns to Bethel and it comes as no

---

20 Fokkelman, 1975, p. 114.

21 Gen 28:10-22.

22 Gen 28:13-15.

23 In some ways Jacob's experience of exile, servitude, fertility and return prefigures that of the exodus generation.

24 Gen 29:31-30:43.

25 Gen 31:3.

26 Gen 31:13.

surprise that we find the promise reiterated yet again.[27]

One can think of the cycle as a journey in which Jacob begins and ends in Mamre with Isaac.

1. With Isaac in Mamre

2. Flee Canaan via Bethel (divine promise)

3. Paddan Aram (God of Bethel call Jacob home)

(4. Enter Canaan at Shechem)

5. At Bethel (divine promise)

6. Bury Isaac at Mamre

Obviously the conflict with Esau is a potential threat to the divine promise and that issue dominates chapters 32-33. God protects Jacob and reconciles the divided brothers.

So by 33:18-20 it looks like all the plot threads are being tied up. The conflict with Esau which drove Jacob away is resolved, he has begun to experience the fulfilment of the promise of descendants and now he returns to the land. And just to drive home the point that the promise of land is the focus here, Jacob buys a plot of land[28] as his grandfather had.[29] Indeed the parallel with Abraham does not stop there. It is, in my opinion, no coincidence that Jacob returns to Shechem before moving on to Bethel and Mamre. When Abraham first entered the land of Canaan in 12:5-9 the first place at which he stops is Shechem.[30] It is here that the very first explicit promise of land is given: "To your offspring I will give this land." Thus Abram builds an altar to Yahweh. Next he moves to Bethel[31] where he builds another altar. Similarly as Jacob enters the Promised Land he travels first to Shechem[32] - the very place

---

27 Gen 35:11-12.

28 To underline the symbolic significance of this land purchase as a foretaste of the Israelite inheritance of Canaan we must notice that when Joseph's bones are returned to the promised land for reburial they are buried on this very plot of land (Joshua 24:32).

29 Gen 23.

30 Gen 12:6. This is the only mention of Shechem before 33:18.

31 Gen 12:8.

32 Some commentators do not think that the Dinah story is set in Shechem at all. The controversy centres around 33:18 which could be read in one of the following two ways:-

(a) "Then Jacob came to Salem, the city of Shechem"

(b) "Then Jacob came in peace to the city of Shechem."

where God first promised the land. There he purchases some land and builds an altar to *El Elohe Israel.*[33] After Chapter 34 God calls Jacob to move onto Bethel[34] where he is to build an altar to the LORD. Ultimately he, like Abram, ends up in Mamre. If this parallel is intended it is possibly interesting that prior to God's promise of the land to Abram at Shechem in 12:7 the editor has alerted the reader to the fact that "the Canaanites were in the land at that time."[35] It is these same Canaanites at Shechem who throw a spanner in the works in Chapter 34. Jacob, as Abraham, may have set his feet on the land but he, like his ancestor, was not alone: the Canaanites were in the land.

This parallel with Abraham explains the significance of Shechem and Bethel in the plot. The very places draw our attention to the promises of land and descendants.

So by the time that the reader reaches 34:1 they feel at ease. All that is needed now is that Jacob return to Mamre via Bethel and the death of Isaac to close the cycle in the usual way.[36] Chapter 34 is a rude and dramatic interruption in this predictable ending. The divine promise is suddenly thrown into jeopardy yet again.[37]

Chapter 35 can, after the interruption, bring the Jacob cycle to its expected

---

Is שלם (a) the name of a town or (b) an adverb meaning "in peace" or "safely"? The issues are complex but I tentatively favour translation (b) on the grounds that the Samaritan Pentateuch reads *salom* clearly taking the word as an adverb. There are some stronger reasons for not taking *salem* to be the name of the city. Firstly, 35:4 assumes that Jacob's family are in Shechem which indicates that this is the city where they have been all along. Also Joshua 24:32 tells us that the plot of land that Jacob purchased from the sons of Hamor was in Shechem. The question as to whether "Shechem" in 33:18 refers to the man or the city is more ambiguous. Even if Shechem does refer to the man rather than the town this does not, of course, mean that the town was not Shechem. If we take *slm* as an adverb, as I do, and "Shechem" as a personal name then all we can conclude from 33:18 is that the town is not named. The context (35:4) and texts like Joshua 24:32 will name the city for us. It seems to me that the ambiguity may be deliberate. There is a certain satisfying symbolism if we take "Shechem" as the name both of the city and of the one who represents the city. The acts of the man are not the acts of an individual but the acts of the group he represents. On Shechem see E.F. Campbell and J.R. Ross, 1963; G.E. Wright, 1964.
33 Gen 33:19-20.
34 Gen 35:1.
35 Gen 12:6.
36 Notice some of the parallels between the close of the Abraham cycle and the close of the Jacob cycle. There is the death of a patriarch's wife (Sarah and Rachel), the purchase of some land, a list of the patriarch's sons, the death of a patriarch, burial by his geographically separated sons in Mamre and a genealogy of the non-elect son of a patriarch (Ishmael and Esau).
37 S.P. Jeansonne (1990) is one of the few who notices the link with the promise of land. See too Brueggemann (1982, p. 274) and Vawter who notes that it is God and not Hamor who is to give the land to Jacob (1977, p. 357).

conclusion with the return to Mamre via Bethel. The cycle closes with the death and burial of Isaac at Mamre.

The above conjectures seem to bear out the comments of Bar Efrat:

> An isolated incident receives its significance from its position and role in the system as a whole. The incidents are like building blocks, each one contributing its part to the entire edifice, and hence their importance. In the building which is the plot there are no excess or meaningless blocks. The removal of any one may cause the entire structure to collapse or at least damage its functional and aesthetic perfection.[38]

Having considered the place of the story in its context and indicated my conviction that the issue of exogamy and its implications for the divine promise of descendants and land inheritance is relevant to the story's interpretation we can proceed to lay out a reading of the text.

## Genesis 34: An Interpretation

### *Genesis 34 Scene One (34:1-4)*

*Genesis 34:1 - Dinah Goes Out*

The story opens with Dinah "going out" to see the daughters of the land. Abraham did not want Isaac to marry "from the daughters of the Canaanites" (27:46) whilst Rebecca does not want Jacob to marry from "the women of the land" (27:46-28:9). It is thus possible that the term "daughters of the land" denotes those not acceptable as marriage partner's for the Israelites and draws our attention to the issue of exogamy.

That Dinah is identified as "daughter of Leah" is not insignificant. Nowhere else in the story is she identified this way and Leah herself plays no role in the narrative. It is very rare for a character to be identified primarily in terms of their mother, as Dinah is in v. 1.[39] When we recall that Leah was Jacob's unloved wife we have one key to help us unlock the familial dynamics of the narrative.[40] Jacob's apparent lack of appropriate concern may be because Dinah is the daughter of his unloved wife.[41] This key also unlocks the reason why Dinah's full brothers, Simeon and Levi, are so concerned about the matter. Thus the narrator subtly alerts us to consider how the tense relationships between Jacob and his wives affect the behaviour of the different parties in the

---

38 Bar Efrat, 1997, p. 93.
39 Laffey, 1988a, p. 41.
40 Caspi, 1985b, pp. 28-29.
41 Jeansonne, 1990, p .91.

rape of Dinah.

## *Genesis 34:2 - Shechem Rapes Dinah*

The action commences when Shechem "sees" and desires Dinah. He is introduced to us with a very full participant reference. We realise that he is probably one of the sons who sold Jacob the section of land near the town[42] and was thus known to the family. He is identified by his father (Hamor), his father's group identification (Hivite[43]) and social position (Chief[44] of the Land). Shechem is a man of noble birth and of importance in the area in which the Israelites dwell. He is also a Hivite. I have argued above that the context indicates that his Canaanite status is significant for the interpretation of the story. He "takes her". This phrase can be used in the sense of "taken in marriage"[45] although the context clearly indicates that it was not marriage in which Dinah was taken. In retrospect this "taking" may refer to his taking her to his house[46] but on a first reading of the story it simply refers to his taking her for sexual intercourse. We need to be aware of the resonances set up within the text by the use of this key word. Possibly the sequence "he saw her... and he took her" alludes to the sinful paradigm of Eve who "saw" the fruit of the tree and "took" it,[47] the sons of God who "saw" the daughter of men and "took" them as wives[48] and Achan who "saw" the devoted items and "took" them and thus, like Shechem, did "folly in Israel."[49] If so, then the reader is alerted to the sinfulness of this "seeing" and "taking". We then read that he "lay (with) her" and "he shamed her."[50] Aalders thinks that Shechem's behaviour is in accord with the customs of the times.[51] It is, however, not the case that rape (anticipating a later conclusion) was approved of at the time. 34:7 tells us that what constituted Shechem's folly was his "lying (with) Jacob's daughter". The Hebrew description in v. 7 is the verb שׁכב (to lie) plus the object marker. The verb שׁכב is often used as a euphemism for sex in the Hebrew Bible. It can either be שׁכב + עמ (lie with) or, as here and in the narratorial description of v.

---

42 Gen 33:19.
43 Campbell and Ross (1963, p. 9); Speiser (1969, p. 264-267) and Hoeffner (1973, p. 225) prefer LXX "Horite" = Hurrian. Margalith tries to identify Hivites as the Ahhiyawa of Western Anatolia (1988, p. 60-77) and Hostetter suggests that they may have been a Bedouin group (1995, p. 76). The fact is that we are unsure who the Hivites were.
44 On this translation see Speiser, 1969, p. 264 and Westermann, 1985, p. 538.
45 Cf. Gen 34:16.
46 Wyatt, 1990, p. 439.
47 Gen 3:6.
48 Gen 6:2.
49 Josh 7:21, 15.
50 Scholz (1998, p. 165) sees an ascending scale of violence in the verbs in v. 2. In fact, none of the verbs is reserved for violent acts but given that in this context we have a rape her claim is plausible.
51 Aalders, 1981, p. 154 and p. 159.

2, שׁכב + את (lay + object marker). Is there any significance to this distinction? We ought to consider the pool of Hebrew terms for intercourse from which the writer selected this one. One could use the verb קרב (to approach), בוא (to go into), ידע (to know) or שׁכב (to lie). Now the first three terms usually have quite positive associations.[52] Most of the uses of שׁכב עם in a sexual context, however, have negative connotations. Noble writes,

> As far as I can discover שׁכב עם, like its standard translation "lie with" is an evaluatively neutral expression which can be used both of the normal relationship between an man and his wife (e.g. Gen 30:15, 16; 2 Sam 11:11; 12:24) and of various sexual acts which are explicitly condemned (e.g. Ex. 22:18 [English 22:19], Deut 27:20-23) In contrast [to שׁכב אמ] שׁכב את is used only of acts that are in some way irregular.[53]

A survey of all the uses of שׁכב plus the definite object marker reveals the following:

    (a)  Incest. [54]
    (b)  homosexual relations.[55]
    (c)  adultery.[56]
    (d)  sexual relations with a woman that one knows is having a period.[57]
    (e)  in 1 Samuel 2:22 Eli's sons "lay (with)" the women who served at the entrance of the Tent of Meeting. This is an evil (v. 23) and a sin against Yahweh (v. 25), leading Israel to transgress (v. 24).
    (f)  when Amnon rapes Tamar we read - "he shamed her and lay (with) her."[58]

The death penalty was prescribed for incest, homosex and adultery. God himself killed Eli's sons and Absalom killed Amnon. In the case of the menstruant both the partners were "cut off". I would say that, with the

---

52 Context can twist them of course, e.g. the cynical use of ידע by the base men in Gen 19:5 and Jud 19:22.

53 Noble, 1996, p. 178. William Williams (1997, p. 102. See also Naude, 1997, pp. 1199-1200) thinks that שׁכב אמ and שׁכב את are both negative. He thinks that Noble's positive uses are exceptions to the rule. I shall follow Noble in taking שׁכב אמ as neutral in itself with the context determining the overtones. I shall argue that שׁכב את is always negative in its overtones.

54 Gen 19:33-34. Other incestuous relations described with שׁכב את can be found in Lev 20:11 (a father's wife) and v.12 (a daughter-in-law). Both warrant the death penalty.

55 Lev 20:13.

56 Num 5:11-31; Ez 23.

57 Lev 20:18. The penalty is for both to be "cut off". If a man has sexual relations with a menstruant by accident in that the period starts during intercourse (Lev 15:24) he is made unclean for seven days but not "cut off" (the woman is not defiled by this as she is unclean already).

58 2 Sam 13:14.

exception of Leviticus 15:18[59] (and 20:18) it refers to irregular sexual acts that generate major defilement.[60] Divine boundaries outside of which sex should not occur are crossed.

שכב עת is used by both the narrator (v. 2) and the sons (v. 7) clearly implying agreement on a very negative evaluation concerning Shechem's deed.

Finally we read that "he shamed her" (ענה). Bechtel is correct in saying that this verb "indicates the ['abuse'], 'humiliation' or 'shaming' of a woman through certain kinds of sexual intercourse including rape though not necessarily."[61] Women can be shamed through consensual sexual activity[62] but the verb can be used in rape cases also.[63] We shall see that the Tamar case alludes to Genesis 34 and I will argue that Dinah is similarly shamed by a rape. Longacre argues that the use of a verb with a pronominal suffix (as we have

---

59 Lev 15:18 is an anomalous text. Here we read that normal sexual intercourse between husband and wife, an act not sinful in any way, is described with שכב & the object marker. How are we to account for this? I think that the answer lies in the connection of the phrase שכב את with the phrase טמא (defile). When we consider all the occasions where שכב את appears it is almost without exception describing an act which defiles. Consider Leviticus 15:18; Numbers 5:11-31; Ezekiel 23:8,17; Genesis 34:3-5. Indeed all the outlawed sexual acts in Leviticus 18 are said to defile (v. 24) and thus Leviticus 20:11-13, 18; 2 Samuel 13:14 and probably Genesis 19:33-34 (see Hartley, 1992, pp. 293-294) can also been seen as שכב את acts which defile. Thus (almost?) all sexual acts described by שכב את are defiling acts in some way. In Genesis 34 we are told twice that Shechem lay (with) Dinah (v. 2, v. 7) and three times that he "defiled her" (v. 5, v. 13, v. 27). I suggest that in Leviticus 18:15 we find שכב את used because we are being told that normal sexual intercourse produces minor defilement (why it should do so see G.J. Wenham [1983] and R. Whitekettle [1996]). Leviticus 15:18 is still an anomaly because no sin has been committed. Clearly the level of defilement produced by other שכב את texts is in another league from Leviticus 15:18 (the unintentional contact with menstrual blood in Lev 20:18 falls between the extremes). Dinah's defilement would not have been such an issue if it was the minor defilement of a regular sexual act. So שכב את is a term usually used for a sexual act that is outlawed by Israel's later laws and to engage in such an act defiles those involved.

60 We cannot agree with Caspi (1985b, p. 32 followed by Ross, 1996, p. 572 and Fokkelman [quoted in Scholz, 1998, p. 166]) who claims that "the use of the direct object draws attention to the force used in the crime." Clearly, most of the uses of שכב את involve no force. Also in the rape case in Deuteronomy 22:25-27 where force is used the act is described by שכב אמ. This is not to say that force was not used in Genesis 34:2 - only that the use or non-use of the object marker is unrelated to that question. We also cannot agree with Sternberg (1987, p. 446) and Scholz (1998, p. 166) who think that the use of the direct object marker "reduces the victim to a mere object." Clearly this is not the case in most of the occasions in which the phrase is used. Longacre argues that this use of the object marker is, in itself, neutral as far as power relations go (1989, pp. 155-157).

61 Bechtel, 1994, p. 24.

62 Deut 22:23-24; 22:28-29.

63 2 Sam 13:11-14.

here) indicates the dominance of the actor over the one acted upon.[64] Thus the climax of Shechem's act is fittingly described by ויענה - Shechem stands in dominance over the girl he has just shamed. This would fit with the rape interpretation.[65]

## Excursus - What Was Shechem's Crime?

It has always been taken for granted that Dinah was raped, but in recent years that view has been called into question. Thus it is necessary to digress and to ask, just what was Shechem's crime in Genesis 34? Such a digression will require us to step outside of Scene One but a proper interpretation of the story requires a clear view of the nature of the crime.

It is agreed by all interpreters of Genesis 34 that Shechem has sexual intercourse with Dinah (v. 2) and in doing so committed an act that her brothers saw as being a heinous crime (v. 7). What exactly was it about that sexual encounter that so angered Jacob's sons? On this point interpreters cannot agree. The problem is that it has three different aspects that may singly or together be the cause of offence:

(a)   Dinah and Shechem are not married.
(b)   Shechem, the majority of interpreters claim, rapes Dinah.
(c)   Shechem is a Hivite and Dinah is an Israelite.

At the two extremes of the interpretative spectrum we could place Paul Noble, who believes that exogamy was not an issue at all and that the crime was essentially rape,[66] and Bechtel, Wyatt and Frontain[67] who believe that Dinah was not raped and that the offence was entirely that of a sexual relationship between an Israelite and a Hivite. Between these two poles we find the majority of interpreters. The problems arise from the difficulty of disentangling the different dimensions of the crime. The first task we must undertake is to outline Old Testament attitudes towards pre-marital sex.

---

64 Longacre, 1989, pp. 155-157.

65 Bechtel argues that ענה is never used of rape itself (1994, pp. 26-27 and against her comment above). The only rape cases where the verb is used we find that the defilement is produced by some other aspect of the act. Her argument precedes as follows: Deuteronomy 22:23-24 and 22:28-29 are two cases of consensual sex that shame (ענה) the woman (in fact, it is not clear whether the latter case concerns consensual sex or rape). In Deuteronomy 22:25-27 we have rape but no shaming. Tamar is the exception, but it is the incest that shames her. Now we will see later the problems with seeing ענה as the result of incest in 2 Samuel 13. To this we may mention that the Levites' concubine was "shamed" (ענה) during a rape and in Lamentations 5:11 we read how the Babylonian invaders shamed (ענה) the women of Zion clearly by raping them. I am not arguing that ענה means "rape" but that rape can 'humiliate' (contra Bechtel).

66 Noble, 1996, p. 183.

67 Frontain, 1991, pp. 178-179.

*Pre-Marital Sex: Old Testament Attitudes*

Gordon Hugenberger[68] has argued that we must distinguish two distinct relationships involved in the formation of marriage.

(a) a contract between the husband to be and the girl's father. The מוהר is a key element here. It is not a bride price as if the young man were buying the woman from her father but is better thought of as a betrothal present. In this stage the wife-to-be is an object which the man acquires from her father (he "takes" her, she is "given" to him).[69]

(b) a sexual relationship between the man and woman. This is the marriage proper and here the woman is not an object but an active partner in the union. Marriage is not primarily a relationship between a husband and the girl's father but a covenant between a man and a woman.

Now pre-marital sex is partaking in relationship (b) without relationship (a).

This is not a good thing because the father of the girl has not been consulted at all and he has authority over his children. In a situation where the girl has engaged in sexual activity prior to her father and the fiancé entering into a covenant, then the relationship must be formalised. The young man must pay the מוהר "which, if accepted, constitutes the *ex post facto* approval of the union by the girl's parents and extinction of their parental authority over her."[70]

Exodus 22:15-16 [ET 16-17] discusses the seduction of an unbetrothed girl. The crisis is resolved by the payment of the מוהר. The man cannot refuse to pay but the girl's father can refuse to accept the marriage (in which case the man still pays).

Clearly pre-marital sex was not approved of. If it occurred the man had to marry the woman (if the father allowed - Exodus). There is no doubt that Dinah and Shechem engaged in pre-marital sexual activity. This is why Shechem aims to pay a very generous מוהר to formalise the relationship. He assumes that her family have the right to refuse the marriage (as in Ex 22:15-16) so he will pay whatever it costs to have her. In doing so, it seems that he is doing exactly the right thing, and if pre-marital sex were all there was to this incident, the matter would rest there.

*Old Testament Attitudes Towards Rape*

Apart from Genesis 34, the Old Testament provides us with two clear rape accounts and one (possibly two) laws relating to rape.

---

68 Hugenberger, 1994, ch. 6.

69 In the Old Testament marriages were often arranged by parents both for daughters and sons. However, practice was flexible. Sons often could choose their own wives even if the formalities of parental arrangement were still followed. This seems to be what happened in Shechem's case (34:4). On the issue of parentally arranged and self-initiated marriages see V.P. Hamilton, 1992.

70 Hugenberger, 1994, p. 251.

The first story is that of the Levite's concubine in Judges 19. She and her husband were staying at the house of an old man in Gibeah. The men of the town wanted to gang-rape the Levite. Instead, he throws his concubine out to them. They abuse her all night and humbled her (ענה 19:24, 25) and as a result of this act she died. This act was described as "folly in Israel."[71]

The second story is the rape of Tamar in 2 Samuel 13. Amnon desires his half-sister Tamar and prepares a trap so that he can get her alone. He seizes her and, despite her protestations, her humbles her (ענה), lays (with) her and thus becomes as one of the fools in Israel. Then he hates her and will not agree to marry her. This, cries Tamar, is an even greater evil than his raping her! She remained desolate in the house of her brother Absalom.

Deuteronomy 22:25-27 considers the case of a man who rapes a betrothed virgin. This is treated in the same way as the case of adultery in vv. 23-24 except that only the man is stoned. The woman is not responsible for what has happened to her and thus is not culpable.

Deuteronomy 22:28-29 is a controversial text. Some consider it to be about the rape of an unengaged woman.[72] There are problems, however, with this reading of the text and some support an interpretation which does not involve rape.[73] I think that the situation is such that one cannot say for sure whether these verses concern rape or not.

What are the implications of this discussion of Deuteronomy 22:28-29? If it concerns the rape of an unbetrothed girl then we have clear Old Testament guidance on this kind of situation. Indeed, put together with 22:25-27 we could say that rape was treated as a case of extra-marital sex, with the exception that the woman was not held responsible. Thus, if she was betrothed then the man was stoned for adultery, but the woman was morally blameless. If she was not betrothed, then it was treated as a case of pre-marital sex except that the woman was not blamed. To protect her from the problem of not being able to find a husband now that she was no longer a virgin and, from the greater likelihood of divorce, the man was forced to marry the girl and was not allowed to divorce her. If 22:28-29 does not concern the rape of an unmarried woman then we simply do not know how such cases were regarded.[74]

---

71 Jud 20:6.

72 E.g. Laffey, 1988a, p. 41; Cragie, 1976, p. 295; Westbrook, 1992; Ridderbos, 1984, p. 227 (but c.f. editors comment in fn. 39).

73 Against rape see Mayes, 1979, pp. 312-313; Carmichael, 1979, pp. 38, 42; Hugenberger, 1994, pp. 255-257.

74 Hugenberger (1994, p. 257) thinks, on the basis of 2 Samuel 13, that the preference was for marriage but if the man did not agree to this then he was liable to the death sentence. Unfortunately texts like 2 Samuel 13 are not so straight forward as this. That was a case of incest and this complicates the situation. Indeed there is not a judicial death sentence in 2 Samuel 13 but rather a personal vendetta. We cannot be sure that Absalom was carrying out a sentence that David ought to have. Similarly in Judges 19: this is rape but the severe judgement carried out on Benjamin afterwards is complicated

I suspect that Hugenberger is wrong to imply that the death sentence was standard for those who would not marry but in our case it does not matter. In Genesis 34, Shechem will bend over backwards to marry Dinah. Thus, even if Deuteronomy 22:28-29 would not compel him to, convention would wish him to and he is doing the "right" thing.

### Was Dinah Actually Raped?

There are three clues that, if present, would put the matter beyond dispute:-
  (a)  If the scene of the crime was "in the countryside"
  (b)  If Dinah is said to "cry out", or
  (c)  If we are told that Shechem seizes her.

None of these are present but their absence does not mean that Dinah was not raped. In Hebrew there is no technical term for rape so clearly all the terms used to describe this act (נבלה עשה בישראל, טמא, ענה, שכב, את לקח) can be used in non-rape situations. Nevertheless, there are good reasons to retain the traditional interpretation of the passage even if such arguments only yield a probability and not a certainty.

Firstly, the phrase "folly in Israel" in Dinah's case[75] may well indicate rape. Chou-Wee Pan explains that

> often *nbl* and its cognates in the Old Testament refer to one who acts foolishly in a moral or religious sense, breaking social orders or behaving treacherously towards God... the action is commonly expressed in the idiomatic phrase *nebala beyisra'el*, sacrilege in Israel, which describes a person who "commits an act of crass disorder or unruliness".[76]

Anthony Phillips explains נבלה as "a general expression for serious disorderly and unruly action resulting in the break up of an existing relationship."[77] He suggests that in Shechem's case the folly was the breaking of customary law which separated one clan from another.[78] The term נבל and the phrase "folly in Israel" (נבלה עשה בישראל) are often applied to sexual acts. It is clear that Shechem's folly consists in his sexual behaviour, but what exactly was it about the act that qualifies it as "folly"? The phrase "folly in Israel" is used of several sexual crimes.

---

by various factors. This was a gang rape in contravention to the expected hospitality. The woman was married and thus this counted as adultery and did warrant the death sentence (Deut 22:25-27). She also dies which also brings a death sentence. Thus Judges 19 will not tell us what attitudes were towards the rape of an unengaged woman.

75 Gen 34:7.
76 *New International Dictionary of Old Testament Theology and Exegesis*, Vol. 3, p. 11.
77 Phillips, 1975, p. 241. See too M.W. Roth, 1960.
78 Ibid., p. 238.

(a)  adultery.[79]
(b)  the desire for homosexual relations is "folly".[80]
(c)  rape.[81]

In each of the above cases a sentence of death was passed (in Amnon's case there was no official sentence but Absalom carried out his own unofficial one). Clearly this term is reserved for very serious sexual crimes.

Can the other uses of the term help us? Well clearly homosex is not relevant and Dinah is not engaged so adultery is not an issue. Rape is a clear possibility. We have two clear cases (see above) where a rape was described as "folly in Israel". In Tamar's case one could argue that it is not the rape so much as the fact that Amnon was her half-brother that makes the act "folly". This would be a mistake however. It is Tamar herself who describes the act as "folly in Israel" and yet she sees no problems in a sexual relationship with Absalom within marriage (contrary to Lev 18). Thus it cannot be the incestuous dimension that qualifies the act for the description "folly in Israel". It seems to be that the act is an act of rape. One could argue that it is the pre-marital dimension of the act that makes it "folly" rather than the non-consensual dimension. Ancient Israel clearly disapproved of pre-marital sex between an engaged woman and another man[82] and an unengaged woman and a man.[83] In the former case the sentence was death. The latter case was not so serious. It warranted the man paying the bride price to the girl's father and, if the father wished it, having to marry her. However, pre-marital sex between two unmarried people (as in Dinah's case) hardly warrants the very serious description "folly in Israel": a crime for which a life is often taken.[84] It seems that it was the nature of the sex act *as rape* that draws such condemnation. A young woman is compelled into an unfitting sexual liaison (pre-marital or extra-marital) - that is folly.[85]

---

79 Deut 22:21; Jer 29:23.
80 Jud 19:23.
81 Jud 20:6,10; 2 Sam 13:12.
82 Deut 22:23.
83 Ex 22:16-17.
84 Deut 22:21; Jud 20:6,10; 2 Sam 13:12.
85 Dinah is also said to be 'defiled' by Shechem. Defilement in some cases is ritual (Ex 19:15; 1 Sam 21:4-5; 1 Sam 11:11-13) and in others seems to be a metaphorical extension to refer to sinful behaviour Leviticus 18:24 notes how all the sexual crimes reviewed typify the way in which the Canaanites defile themselves. In Chapter Five I explore the theological implications of the plausible suggestion that the category of defilement is anachronistic in Genesis 34. Neither the term טמא nor את שכב tell us whether this act was wrong because of the pre-marital aspect, the rape dimension or the inter-group aspect. Every sexual act (putting Genesis 34 to one side for the moment) in which טמא is used is one in which both parties consent. This could be used as an argument against the claim that Shechem raped Dinah. The one שכב את case where force

Secondly, and most powerfully, we may note the intertextual allusion to Genesis 34 in 2 Samuel 13. Absalom's rape of Tamar clearly alludes to the Dinah story in the following ways:-

(a) there is a man who wants a woman and had sex with her.

(b) in both cases the woman's brother is angered, hides his anger and then, using deception, executes the criminal.

(c) in both cases we find fathers who do nothing about the crime (although David, unlike Jacob, is angered).

(d) we find a contrast in the attitude of the male partner after the act - Shechem loves Dinah whilst Amnon hates Tamar. Of the two rapists Amnon is portrayed as more evil than Shechem.

(e) In particular, we find the same terminology, used to describe the sexual act. The act "shames" (ענה) the woman.[86] The words in 2 Samuel are "and he shamed her and he lay her" - the exact reverse of Genesis 34:2. Indeed these two occasions are the only times in the Hebrew bible that we find שכב plus the object marker with 3 feminine singular suffix.

---

is used (2 Sam 13) and thus where we would expect to find טמא is the one in which we do not see it. It could be argued that Tamar was raped and thus she was not defiled as she did not consent to the act. If it is the case that a wrongful sexual act to which a woman did not consent does not defile then we can conclude that because Dinah was defiled she cannot have been raped. However, for several reasons I think that this conclusion cannot be drawn. For a start, arguments from silence are less than secure. We know that incest "defiles" (Lev 18) yet the word "defiled" is not used in connection with Lot and his daughters (Gen 19). We know that homosex "defiles" (Lev 18) yet the term is not used in Leviticus 20:13. That we are not told that Tamar is defiled does not mean that she is not. Secondly, we know that incest defiles and thus we know that Absalom, being Tamar's half-brother, did defile her. The narrator's not mentioning this does not imply that no defilement took place. That Tamar herself did not see the incestuous marriage as a problem does not imply that the narrator took such a view. Also Ezekiel 22:10-11 talk of a man who violates (ענה) his sister and another who defiles (טמא) his daughter in law. It seems here that ענה and טמא overlap considerably. That Tamar was violated (ענה) is clear and this implies that she was also 'defiled' (טמא) Thirdly, although all the texts where someone is explicitly said to be "defiled" through a sexual act concern consensual acts this does not mean that a person cannot be defiled through no fault of their own. Clearly one can be ritually defiled without intentionally doing anything wrong. Consider the man who is defiled by a woman's period which starts during intercourse (Lev 20:18). One can be accidentally defiled by coming into contact with an unholy thing. So from the phrase "he defiled Dinah" we cannot deduce that Dinah was raped nor can we deduce that she was not. All that we can say is that the sexual act was wrong. It transgressed boundaries set up by God (or, at very least, the social customs of the Jacobites).

86 Gen 34:2; 2 Sam 13:12.

(f)   the men's actions are described as "folly in Israel."[87]

Bechtel thinks that it was the incestuous aspect of Amnon and Tamar's sex that shames her. Tamar, as already noted, seems to think otherwise. She sees the rape as humiliating (ענה) but has no objection in principle to a marriage with Amnon. It is clear that for her it was not the incest that was the aspect of the act that would humble her. It could be replied that her pleas for marriage were a bluff in an attempt to get out of the situation. Against this possibility we may note that after the rape she begs Amnon not to throw her out. This indicates that she still thought a marriage was possible and would redeem her honour. If she was bluffing there would be no point in continuing the bluff. Thus I think that we can take it that Tamar really did believe an incestuous marriage to be acceptable. These links between Genesis and 2 Samuel make it more than likely that the author of 2 Samuel saw the Dinah story as a rape.

Third, we may recall that the narrator tells us not that Dinah went out to see the local men or Shechem but that she went to see the "*daughters* of the land".

Fourth, we remember that nowhere in the text is Dinah blamed for her behaviour, whilst Shechem is blamed for his. If Dinah had consented to the liaison she too would have borne the blame.[88]

Finally, the expression "he spoke to her heart" (v. 3) implies that Dinah was distressed which would support the rape interpretation.[89]

So I shall take it that Dinah was raped by Shechem.[90] However, we have seen reasons to think that even in a rape case some sort of redemption could be found, perhaps through marriage. That option is rejected by the sons and I suggest that his Hivite identity was the complicating factor. Genesis 34 is about the rape of an unbetrothed Israelite girl by a *Hivite* man. *It was a triple-layered crime.*

*Was Exogamy An Issue?*

In defence of the importance of exogamy as an issue, consider the following:

First of all, Shechem is immediately introduced to the reader as "Shechem, son of Hamor the Hivite - prince of the land."[91] Right from the first he is Shechem the Hivite and through the rest of the story he is continually linked with his father Hamor. We are thus constantly reminded that he belongs to the Canaanite group. The identity of the rapist matters in this plot. He is not just a man. In fact, he is not just a Hivite: he is the son of the Hivite ruler. The plot

---

87 2 Sam 13:12, Gen 34:7 see also "folly" and ענה in Jud 19.
88 The intertextual allusion I shall later develop between Genesis 34 and Numbers 25 strengthens this claim.
89 See Fischer, 1984.
90 There is no reason to follow some of the rabbis in claiming that Shechem sodomized Dinah (see Salkin, 1986, p. 286).
91 Gen 34:2.

would not develop as it does were this not so. It is also no coincidence that the name of the man is the also the name of his city.[92] Within the story Dinah is not just a woman - she is the daughter of Jacob, the father of the Israelite nation. Her identity as belonging to the Jacobite group is constantly underlined by her participant references.

Secondly, in Genesis the issue of the relationship of Abraham's family to the local Canaanite population is already an issue. In particular, the issue of intermarriage with Canaanites has been raised several times and the option is rejected each time. Abraham will not allow Isaac to marry a local - his wife must be a descendant of Terah.[93] Similarly, Isaac and Rebecca are heart broken when Esau marries Canaanite women[94] and insist that Jacob must marry a descendant of Terah.[95] It is interesting to note that this disapproving reference to Esau's exogamy occurs in Genesis 26 which, according to the structure of the Jacob cycle we considered earlier, is to be read alongside Genesis 34. Later Pentateuchal texts explicitly forbid the marriage of Israelite daughters to Hivites.[96] Marriage to most foreigners who live outside of Canaan is not objected to in Deuteronomy.[97] These contextual indicators provide a context for reading this story.[98]

Thirdly, the narrator spends a large amount of time on the issue of a potential alliance between the Hivites and the Israelites. This would be an alliance in which the two groups would exchange daughters in marriage and become as "one people". Now if the issue is simply one of rape and revenge this element would only serve as the mechanism by which revenge comes. It certainly is that, but the narrator dwells at such length on this issue that one begins to suspect that it is more than just a mechanism for revenge. Three times we are treated to the wife-exchange speech[99] and twice to the idea of the groups becoming as "one people".[100] The content of these speeches is obviously something that the narrator wishes to draw the listener's/reader's ear/eye to. What would the narrator make of such an alliance? I think that the answer must be that it would be perceived as a serious threat to the covenant family. Steinberg has argued recently that "The marriage pattern in Gen 11:27-50:26 is consistent with anthropological theory on kinship relations: social contexts that emphasise inheritance maintain endogamy."[101] Alliance-marriages are found in

---

92 Kass, 1992, p. 32.
93 Gen 24:3-4.
94 Gen 26:34-35.
95 Gen 27:46-28:2 and 28:6-9.
96 Deut 7:1-4.
97 Deut 21:10-14 and 23:7-8 and 23:2-6 if we interpret that to mean that intermarriage between Israelites and Moabites was postponed for ten generation.
98 Rightly Ross, 1996, p. 275.
99 Gen 34:9, 16, 21.
100 Gen 34:16, 22.
101 Steinberg, 1991, p. 51.

groups practising exogamy[102] and are not the pattern in Genesis 12:27-50:26. Abraham, Isaac and Jacob all marry within the patrilineal line of Terah: thus, she argues that legitimate heirs were those who (a) were born of those unions and not others (consider Abraham's children other than the one born to Sarah) and, (b) were themselves married within the line of Terah (contrast Esau).

> The emphasis on inheritance, both of lineage and of property, allows us to infer that marriages are formed to keep inheritance of land within certain kinship boundaries... fragmentation of family holdings diminishes the family's ability to survive economically and socially... In peasant culture, economic survival and social status are attached to property and property rights."[103]

If the twelve sons marry Canaanites then the whole line of promise is thrown into chaos. Israel would lose its distinctiveness and be assimilated into the Canaanite population. Any *post-Mosaic* audience would see the obvious danger here. Steinberg maintains that the marriage of an Israelite daughter to a Canaanite would be problematic also. Now it seems clear to me that the brothers never even contemplate this alliance. Their action is not performed to avoid an alliance but to avenge the rape of their sister. Nevertheless, it does highlight the narrator's interest in the issue of intermarriage.

Finally, our earlier discussion of the literary context of Genesis 34 indicated that the issue of a threat to the divine promise to Abraham is part of the *raison d'être* of the story.[104]

---

102 Ibid., p. 48.

103 Steinberg, 1993, p. 11 and 23.

104 Showing that exogamy is an issue for the narrator is not to show that it was an issue for the brothers. However, I think that we have reasons to think that they considered it to be a problem also, even if not for exactly the same reasons as a post-Mosaic audience. First of all, to anticipate a later conclusion, the claim in v. 14 that it would shame the Israelites if their sister was married to an uncircumcised man must be taken as a true statement and not a part of their deception. There is no possibility of Dinah marrying Shechem the Hivite as far as the sons are concerned and this makes Shechem's act especially serious. Second, the sons perceive Shechem and Hamor as an indivisible unity and, as rulers of the city, they represent their whole group. This explains their belief that the whole city was involved in the defiling of Dinah. They see the rape as the attack by one group (Hivites) upon a representative of their group. Shechem has attacked the honour of their sister (v. 31), their father - the group head (v. 7) and the community of Israel (v. 7) by his action. It seems clear that the sons are aware of the group dimension of what they perceive as a crime and their response is clearly directed at the group of Shechemites (vv. 25-29). Finally, we notice in several of our word studies, that the idea of having sex outside acceptable social boundaries was an issue. This could be seen in terms of the Israelite-Canaanite divide. It was crossing over this boundary that was part of Shechem's crime. It has been objected to these claims by Fewell and Gunn (1991, p. 206), followed by Noble (1996, p. 183), that exogamy cannot have been an issue because the sons themselves had no qualms about marrying

One could object to this suggestion by arguing that if Shechem's Hivite identity ruled out marriage why did her family simply not refuse the marriage and demand a *mohar* anyway, in line with Exodus 22:15-16? This objection overlooks the particular dynamics of the situation. The Hivites, we shall learn in v. 26, already have Dinah at Shechem's house. All the parties involved in the negotiations know this (though the reader does not realise until later) and it casts its shadow across the talks. I do not think that the Hivites are overtly using Dinah as a hostage (contra Sternberg). Hamor would prefer genuinely friendly relations with the Israelites and a unity between the peoples - to use Dinah as a hostage would not really help him achieve this goal. Hamor and Shechem had the leverage in terms of numbers and in terms of Dinah, but they chose not to use it. Instead they made some very generous offers. Nevertheless, the potential for things to turn nasty if marriage was refused must have been obvious to the Israelites such that a straight refusal of marriage would have been a big risk.

We have seen that the very language used to describe the crime ("saw... took, lay, shamed") carries with it a negative evaluation of what happened. This leaves us in no doubt as to the narrator's stance on the crime.

### Genesis 34:3 - Shechem's Desire for Dinah

V. 3 thus takes the reader by surprise. The man whom we have just taken a strongly negative attitude towards is described in terms that seem to put him in a sympathetic light. The relationship between v. 2 and v. 3 has caused a number of reactions amongst interpreters.

    (a)   Bechtel thinks it indicates that v. 2 does not describe a rape at all. Rapists do not love their victims. Rape is not about love and sex, but about power.

    (b)   Sternberg, on the other hand, thinks that to tell readers of the love of

---

Canaanites. The story adduced to support this is Genesis 38 in which Judah's son marries Tamar, a Canaanite. Sternberg (1992) has shown that the narrative actually undermines the wisdom of such intermarriage and is in-line with the main-stream of Genesis. Noble complains that a marriage still took place (1996) but this need indicate no more than that the sons were hypocritical. Indeed Judah was quite happy to treat women as prostitutes - a crime Shechem is chastised for. Judah is portrayed in Genesis 38 as the hypocrite *par excellence*. It could also be objected that Joseph marries an Egyptian (Gen 41:45). However, that problem can be mitigated somewhat when we recall that (a) Joseph had been living in a foreign land for an unusually long period, (b) the Pharaoh arranged the marriage so Joseph could not easily refuse, and (c) later Mosaic law did permit marriage to Egyptians (Deut 23:7-8) but not to Canaanites (including Hivites, Deut 7:1-3). So I think that it is certainly possible that the desire to avoid exogamy was part of the sons' motivation for the deception and massacre (so too Adar, 1990, p. 124). However, the text presents the primary reason as their anger at the dishonour done to Dinah, their family and their group.

Shechem before the rape would have made the reader less condemnatory about the crime. To tell of it after allows the reader to feel the full horror of the crime before making the judgement more complex.[105]

(c) Fewell and Gunn suggest that it relativises our anger at the rape and draws our sympathy towards Shechem. He may have done wrong but at least he now loves the girl and is willing to atone for his mistake.[106] They write that "one must acknowledge that the narrator tips the balance in Shechem's favour..."[107]

(d) Scholz suggests that v. 2, read with a feminist analysis of rape as an act of violence, will not allow us to read v. 3 in such a way as to give any sympathy to Shechem. V. 2 provides the context for a negative reading of v. 3 in terms of Shechem's sexual lust.[108]

I have already indicated my disagreement with (a) and although I find (d) interesting I think that it is a most unlikely interpretation of the intended meaning of the narrator. For a start, the rest of the story makes it clear the lengths Shechem will go to legitimise (as he sees) the relationship. He is prepared to pay whatever is required and undergo a painful surgical operation without a second thought because he "loves" Dinah. The phrases used by the narrator and the subsequent behaviour of Shechem indicates that his feelings are not being presented in a negative way. Indeed, if the storyteller had wanted to give a negative evaluation, as Scholz suggests, there are many clearer ways in which he could have done so. The phrases in v. 3 indicate that the narrator is going to lengths to get the reader to see just how much Shechem desired (in a more positive way) Dinah.

So where does this get us? The contrast between v. 2 and v. 3 is odd to say the least. In v. 3 we read that Shechem's soul clung to Dinah and that he loved the girl. Are we to think that Shechem "loved" Dinah before the rape but that the narrator chose to withhold that information until now? Caspi thinks as much - "Shechem acted out of wild, consuming love."[109] Or is it that Shechem sexually desired Dinah, raped her and then found a deeper attraction than the mere sexual?[110] There is no way to answer that question with certainty but either way we are forced to ask, with Sternberg, what impact the order of the disclosure of information has on the reader's evaluation of the situation? Sternberg is sure that Shechem would come off better if we had been told that

---

105 Sternberg, 1987, p. 447.
106 Some Jewish traditions (Midrash Sekhel Tov on Gen 34:4) state that Shechem repented and desired to marry Dinah to make amends.
107 Fewell and Gunn, 1991, pp. 196-197.
108 Scholz, 1998, pp. 168-171 & see Kass, 1992, p. 32.
109 Caspi, 1985b, p. 33.
110 So Jeansonne, 1990, p. 92; Vawter, 1977, p. 357; Aalders, 1981, p. 154.

he loved Dinah before he raped her. Whether or not he loved her prior to the rape we are not told. Fewell and Gunn, on the other hand, think that a rapist who loves cannot be regarded sympathetically, whilst a rapist who learns to love does win some qualified respect. It is here that the reader's own perspectives play an important role. Sternberg does seem to be guilty of assuming that the readers of biblical texts are all the same. Some may indeed feel that to love then rape is not so bad as to rape then love. My sympathies lie with Fewell and Gunn: to rape out of "love" does not make me sympathetic to the rapist whilst a rapist who learns to love is taking steps in the right direction. What Sternberg and Fewell and Gunn agree on is that the rape is viewed negatively (although Fewell and Gunn underestimate the extent of the negative evaluation) and that v. 3 presents Shechem in a sympathetic light.[111] V.3 does not reduce the negative evaluation of the crime, as v. 7 makes clear, but it does serve to complicate the reader's judgement.[112] I would say that v. 2 does create some legitimate cynicism about the quality of Shechem's love[113] yet the narrator will not allow the villain of the piece to be caricatured. Rather "he is made more human for the reader."[114] The "bad guy" turns out to be a more complex character than we may like to think.

It is also worth noting that although Dinah's feelings are never explicitly referred to they can be inferred from v. 3 to some extent.[115] We are told that Shechem "spoke on her heart" (דבר על־לב). Fischer is absolutely right to see here a reference to Shechem's attempt to calm down a distraught young woman.[116] The phrase is always used in cases where the party spoken to is very distressed. Thus, by implication, the reader sees Shechem's attempt to calm a very upset Dinah. Dinah, as an Israelite, would probably see her status in the same terms as the other Israelites in the story - as defiled. Fewell and Gunn think that Shechem's speech is a perlocutionary act indicating that Dinah was won over by his affection.[117] Sternberg has demonstrated that they are wrong in this claim: To "touch the heart" is a perlocutionary act whilst to "speak to the

---

111 Caspi, 1985b, p. 33.

112 Kidner, 1967, p. 173.

113 Cf. 2 Sam 13; Scholz, 1998, pp. 169-170. אהב can mean 'desire' and not 'love' depending on the context.

114 Von Rad, 1972, p. 326.

115 And as far as Dinah's fate is concerned, all we know is that she went into Egypt with her family to live. Jewish tradition provides us with several imaginative endings to her story (see Salkin, 1986, pp. 288-289).

116 G. Fischer, 1984. Scholz says, "The phrase appears in the context of fear, anxiety, sin or offence, when 'the situation is wrong, difficult, or danger is in the air.' Someone speaks to the 'heart' of the fearful character to resolve the frightening situation. 'Talk[ing] against a prevailing (negative) opinion.'" (1998, p. 170). The phrase occurs in the following texts - Gen 34:3; 50:21; Jud 19:3; 1 Sam 1:13; Isa 40:2; Hos 2:16; Ruth 2:13; 2 Chr 30:22; 32:6

117 Fewell and Gunn, 1991, p. 196.

heart" is an idiomatic phrase simply meaning "to speak good words of some kind... designed to move the addressee's 'heart'."[118] None of the biblical uses of "speak to the heart" meet J.L. Austin's criteria for perlocutionary acts. This means that we cannot know from v. 3 how successful Shechem was at wooing Dinah. The term only describes what Shechem *tried* to achieve (to soothe her) but it tells us nothing about what he *actually* achieved.[119]

The narrator's focus, however, is not on Dinah's distress but Shechem's attempt to disperse it. Exactly what he said to Dinah we do not know. *Genesis Rabbah* suggests that he may have offered to marry her. Ordinarily, although such a proposal may seem, to our ears, to add insult to injury, such a move may have been seen as the best way forward. Many interpreters read Deuteronomy 22:28-29 as teaching something along these lines, and even if we reject such a reading of that text, the rape story in 2 Samuel 13 makes the point clear. Tamar does not want to have sex with Amnon, but once he has raped her she begs him to let her stay so that she can marry him. His refusal is seen by her as an act even more heartless than the rape itself, because now her hopes of marriage are dashed forever. To marry Amnon would at least give a quasi-normal life and make the best out of a tragic situation. Many women today would find such an attitude impossible to understand, but we must be careful not to interpret the experience of ancient women as if they are modern women waiting for the chance to express themselves.[120] Given that in the next verse Shechem asks his father to take Dinah for him as a wife, it seems that *Genesis Rabbah* may be correct. We do not know what Dinah thought of Shechem's proposal of marriage. I have suggested above that his Hivite status would have been a problem. Quite how much of a problem it was for her we shall never be sure. From our narrator's perspective her feelings about Shechem are not important *to the story he tells.*[121]

*Genesis 34:4 - Shechem and his Father*

Shechem is the focus in Scene One. He is the actor. He sees, takes, sleeps with and humiliates. He clings, loves and speaks. Finally, he speaks to his father. He requests, in a rather rude and abrupt way, that Hamor "get the child for [him] as a wife". The request itself and the manner in which it is made clearly indicates Shechem's burning desire and just possibly indicates Shechem as dominating his father.[122] It is not clear if the word "child" is used in a slightly patronising way in Shechem's request, as we have so few attested examples of the word. It may be slightly patronising given that the narrator uses the term for a young woman (נערה) and that Shechem himself uses that term when negotiating with

---

118 Sternberg, 1992, p. 477.
119 Ibid., pp. 477-478 followed by Noble, 1996, p. 179.
120 See Stone, 1996, pp. 115-116.
121 See Chapter Six.
122 Jeansonne, 1990, p. 92.

the Israelites.[123] Caspi thinks that the word indicates that Shechem knows that Dinah has not yet reached puberty.[124] This is not at all certain though it remains possible. The use of the word לקח ("take") has negative echoes given the first illegitimate taking of Dinah.[125] This casts a shadow over Shechem's attempt to legitimise the relationship. The reader awaits Hamor's reply. Will he rebuke his son for the crime against Dinah and her family? As a father he is responsible for his son's behaviour and, given the seriousness of the crime, the least we can expect is a stern rebuke even if Hamor then agrees to ask Jacob for Dinah's hand in marriage.[126] The narrator keeps us in suspense with the use of what Longacre calls a simple unresolved dialogue.

### Excursus: Genesis 34 as a Twisted 'Betrothal Type-Scene'

Robert Alter has proposed that "there is a series of recurrent narrative episodes attached to the careers of biblical heroes that are dependent on the manipulation of a fixed constellation of predetermined motifs."[127] One such type scene is the Betrothal Type Scene.

> What I would suggest is that when a Biblical Narrator... came to the moment of his heroes betrothal, both he and his audience were aware that the scene had to unfold in particular circumstances, according to a fixed order. If some of those circumstances were altered or suppressed, or if they were actually omitted, that communicated something to the audience as clearly as the withered arm of the twelfth sheriff would say something to a film audience." [128]

Alter proposes that the Betrothal Type Scene included the following elements:-
- (a) The future bridegroom (or surrogate) journeys to a foreign land.
- (b) There he encounters a girl (the term נערה "invariably" occurs unless the maiden is identified as so and so's daughter) at a well.
- (c) The man or girl draws water from the well.
- (d) The "girl" or "girls" rush home ("hurry" "run") to bring the stranger's arrival to her family's attention.
- (e) A *mohar* is negotiated and a betrothal concluded after he has had a meal.

---

123 See J. MacDonald, *JNES* 35, 1976, pp. 147-170, "The Status and Role of the *na'ar* in Israelite Society."
124 Caspi, 1985b, p. 35.
125 So Sternberg and contra Sarna who thinks that "this 'taking' is to make amends for the other" (1989, p. 234).
126 Luther, 1970, pp. 194,198.
127 Alter, 1981, p. 51.
128 Ibid., pp. 51-52.

Alter's data base is rather small[129] and this makes some of his conclusions more ambitious than they ought to be. For example, in Genesis the travelling to a foreign land (a) is tied to the specific plot element in which the heirs of promise had to marry from Terah's line. It may not be an essential element of a betrothal scene. However, let us tentatively accept the existence of such a Type-Scene. I propose that Genesis 34 may possibly be seen as a major distortion of a Betrothal Type-Scene. It is a story about the negotiations over a marriage: the very kind of story where one would expect to find such a Type-Scene. The details may bear this thought out.

First of all, the potential bridegroom "sees"[130] a girl (נערה) but instead of a normal meeting we have a shameful sexual act before the professions of love to the girl. There is no well[131] but there is a girl, Jacob's daughter, in a foreign land (a reversal).

Second, Shechem and Hamor hurry to negotiate with Jacob. Although the words "hurry" and "run" are not used the narrative makes it likely that they set out before the sons arrive home and perhaps even before they find out. It is significant that we do not have Dinah running back to introduce her family to the men. If Alter is right about the Type-Scene, then the very lack of a mention of Dinah's return home would raise suspicions on the part of the readers. Why do Shechem and Hamor come alone? Where is Dinah? It is not until v. 26 that we are explicitly told that she is in Shechem's home but right at the start of Scene Two the narrator may, in his very silence, create an unease on the reader's part.

Third, there is no welcoming meal but negotiations over a betrothal and *mohar* begin immediately and one is sorted out (or so it seems).

However, as the initial meeting was distorted so the actual marriage is distorted. Instead on a uniting of two peoples we have a massacre. If I am right in my suggestion then the story gets some of its power by its *not* following the Type-Scene pattern at key places.

### Genesis 34 Scene Two (34:5-19)

*Genesis 34: 5-7*

The question which the reader is now asking is likely to be, "What will Dinah's family do when they find out?" Thus the Setting for Scene Two opens with the words, "Now Jacob heard that he had defiled Dinah his daughter."

We should note that Shechem's "love" for Dinah does not make what he did any the less defiling. Now Jacob is not so insensitive as not to care at all - he

---

129 Gen 24:10-61; 29:1-20; Ex.2:15b-21; Ruth; 1 Sam 9:11-12; Jud 14.
130 Cf. Gen 29:10.
131 In the parallel text in Genesis 26 there are wells in abundance.

realises to some extent the offence of the rape. But he also knows who it is that has defiled his daughter and herein lies his problem. Jacob is a man who is responsible to protect his whole family and he fears the possible repercussions of opposing a man of such local stature as Hamor's son. This assessment is clear from his comment in v. 30.

His sons are out in the field when he hears the news and so he keeps still until they return. How is the reader to deal with Jacob's keeping still on hearing the news? Sternberg has argued that it is a moral criticism of Jacob - he hears and he does nothing.[132] Given that it is his "daughter" about whom we are reading such inactivity is surprising. Fewell and Gunn argue that it could just as well reflect his wisdom. Perhaps, out of caution rather than apathy, he waits to consult his sons.[133]

Sternberg gives other reasons for his negative assessment of Jacob.

- In contrast to his sons (v. 7) none of Jacob's feelings are mentioned.[134] This also contrasts sharply with his strong emotional outburst at the loss of Rachel's son, Joseph (37:34-35) and with David's anger at the rape of Tamar (2 Sam 13:21).[135] Given that the narrator has already drawn our attention to the fact that Dinah is Leah's daughter (v. 1) the lack of an emotional response is not such a surprise.
- v. 5c tells us that Jacob was silent "until" his sons returned. The irony is that as it turns out he was silent after they returned as well.[136] Even if we can understand the initial silence the subsequent inactivity is inexcusable.
- The story places Jacob at the centre of attention and activity when everybody else converges on his home to talk with him. All the familial terms draw attention to him as the key figure. Thus, his inactivity is accentuated.[137]
- Hamor, by acting on his son's behalf, contrasts and thus shames Jacob who is silent in his daughter's defence.[138]
- Sternberg thinks that v. 7 is ambiguous about the timing of the sons' return. Should we translate it as, "and the sons of Jacob came in from his field when they heard" or "and the sons of Jacob came in from his field. When they heard, the men were grieved"?[139] This is a permanent gap, says

132 Sternberg, 1987, p. 448.
133 Fewell and Gunn, 1991, p. 198. So too Carmichael, 1979, p. 33. Kass (1992, p. 32) thinks that Jacob is too distressed to do anything. The text leaves a gap here for the reader to fill at this point. Clearly how one fills it (and both a] and b] are fillings with long histories. If anything b] is the majority position in the history of interpretation) has major repercussions for one's moral assessment of Jacob.
134 Sternberg, 1987, p. 449.
135 Ibid., p.449
136 Ibid., p. 449
137 Ibid., pp. 450-451.
138 Ibid., p. 451.
139 Ibid., p. 452.

Sternberg. On the first reading we have to ask, "but who told them? Was it
Jacob or not?" This raises questions about Jacob's concern. On the second
reading we see that Jacob had not even bothered to send for his sons. Both
closures of the gap reflect badly on Jacob. I have to say that at this point
Sternberg fails to convince. For a start, his second translation, in which
Jacob does not bother to send for his sons, is an unnatural way to take the
Hebrew text. Far more natural is the reading in which the sons return when
they hear. Second, even though the text does not explicitly say that Jacob
sent for his sons, it seems likely that the reader is intended to infer that he
did. We have been told that Jacob has found out and he waits for his sons
to return. We then learn that they too hear and return home. It seems likely
that Jacob sent for his sons and awaited their return and this does not
reflect badly on him. The possibility that they heard in some other way
must remain open, but it is neither explored nor accentuated by the
narrator.

- Finally Sternberg perceives another permanent ambiguity in the relation
  between v. 6 and v. 7. Are they sequential? If so, then Hamor came to see
  Jacob, but as the latter "kept silent" he had to wait until the sons
  returned.[140] Are they simultaneous? If so, then Hamor leaves as the sons
  return all converging on Jacob, thus drawing attention to his "keeping
  silent". Thus we have a permanent ambiguity with unitary judgement.[141]
  Sternberg is correct that the relationship between v. 6 and v. 7 can be
  construed in the ways he mentions, but I feel that the implications which he
  draws from this may be over subtle.

Nevertheless, other than the final two, these considerations, plus the fact that at
no point in the story does Jacob make mention of Dinah, make Sternberg's
interpretation of the silence plausible. However, it seems to me that he is wrong
to argue that Fewell and Gunn's reading is not a possible gap-filling. When the
reader first comes across the silence of Jacob he or she has not read far enough
to bring most of his other considerations to bear. I propose that Fewell and
Gunn's gap-filling can be used in such a way to fit Sternberg's general poetics
(though he himself did not notice it). Sternberg writes about the reasons for
David's invitation to Uriah as follows:

> Does the king wish to confess to Uriah? To ask his forgiveness? To bully or
> perhaps bribe him? The informational gap leaves room, at this stage, for various
> conjectures - some of them "positive" - about the king's motives. His true
> intentions once clarified, the positive hypotheses will boomerang; and this shift
> from the meritorious to the villainous will then help to sustain the chapter's

---

140 So too Sarna, 1989, p. 234.
141 Sternberg, 1987, pp. 448 ff..

overall ironic thrust.[142]

Why could one not see Jacob's silence in the same way? When we read about Jacob's inactivity in v. 5 we are not sure whether it is a culpable silence or a wise silence - either gap-filling is legitimate at this stage. However, as we progress it becomes clear, for reasons given by Sternberg, that the silence is wrong and the positive gap-filling boomerangs against Jacob. This could be another

> example of potential gap-filling, artfully exploited even though it does not become actual. For the effect produced on the reader by a literary text does not rest only on the final conclusions he reaches on turning the last page; it embraces all the impressions, true or false, generated in the course of reading.[143]

In v. 5 we learn that Jacob knows. Just as we are kept in suspense about what Hamor's reaction will be, so too we are kept in suspense about what Jacob's reaction will be, as the narrator takes us back to Hamor in v. 6. Here we learn that Hamor is on his way to see Jacob. Why? Has he come to fulfil his sons' request? Has he come to apologise? Yet again these questions are left unanswered as we move across to the brothers in v. 7.

As soon as they hear the news they return home, presumably to see their father. In this very significant verse we learn firstly, that they are deeply grieved by the news and secondly, that they are very angry. The narrator then gives us the reason for these deep emotions - "for he had done folly in Israel by lying (with) the daughter of Jacob, a thing that should not be done." Sternberg writes,

> The opening "*ki* he had committed an outrage in Israel" would appear to originate with the narrator, particularly since at this time "Israel" had not yet become a nation. The characters can hardly think and judge in terms of a category shrouded in the future, but no such limitation hampers the omniscient teller. [Alternatively, we could read "Israel" as referring to Jacob]... For rhetorical reasons the narrator chooses to ambiguate where he could elucidate, since the undecidable perspective enables him to elicit maximum sympathy for [the sons].[144]

Clearly this is the reason that the sons felt as they did. However, it is equally clearly the narrator's own assessment of Shechem. Thus the narrator is in total agreement with the sons' diagnosis of the crime. V. 7 "goes a long way towards aligning *at this stage* the viewpoints of the brothers, the narrator, and the

---

142 Ibid., p. 199.
143 Ibid., p. 199.
144 Ibid., p. 455. The hermeneutical significance of this anachronism will become clear in Chapter Five.

reader..."[145] The "love" of Shechem for Dinah does not in any way make the crime "OK" from the narrator's perspective nor, when they find out about it, from the sons'. Thus it seems that we can say that the narrator thinks the grief and anger of the brothers is a natural and correct reaction to the incident.

Now all of the above has simply been setting the Scene for the negotiations. All the characters have been manoeuvred into place and the tension has been ratcheted up as a potentially explosive encounter is about to commence. The reader is intended to share the brothers' horror and anger at the crime, whilst being open to a possible resolution of the dilemma by an apology and restitution. There is some sympathy for Shechem and this will be both added to and reduced in the negotiations which follow.

*Genesis 34:8-10*

Hamor, having gone to speak with Jacob, finds Jacob's sons at home too and so speaks to them (v. 8). Our questions concerning his response to Shechem's request in v. 4 are immediately answered as he opens with the words, "Shechem, my son - his soul clings to your daughter. Please give her to him as a wife." What is lacking in Hamor's whole speech is any reference to the crime of v. 2. Shechem is strongly drawn to Dinah, he says, but there is nothing said about how he has already taken her. Fewell and Gunn say that this is understandable given the delicate negotiations in which he must engage. To bring up the rape may have induced a confrontation and made progress very awkward.[146] However, given the serious dimensions of the crime, this can hardly be acceptable. At the very least one would expect an apology yet nothing of the sort is forthcoming. This, in my estimation, counts against the Hivites.[147]

The rest of Hamor's speech is very telling in helping us sketch his character. Having made the primary request Hamor changes the subject. He broadens out the discussion from one particular marriage to an alliance between the two peoples, in which the Israelites give their daughters to Hivite men and the Hivites give their daughters to Israelite men. The verb לקח (take) recalls the original crime thus not allowing the readers to forget it.[148] The two groups will live together and the land will accommodate them both. Hamor urges the Israelites to dwell, to travel and to trade[149] in the land. Von Rad comments, "the opportunity to settle in... territory [is] a great privilege, for which the poor nomads with small cattle strove at all times."[150] Hamor sees his son's love for

---

145 Ibid., p. 453, italics mine. See also Caspi, 1985b, p. 33.
146 Fewell and Gunn, 1991, p. 199.
147 So too Jeansonne, 1990, p. 93; Sternberg, 1987, p. 456; Noble, 1996, pp. 181-182; Sarna, 1989, p. 235; Luther, 1970, pp. 195-196, 199-200.
148 Sternberg, 1987, p. 456.
149 "Acquire holdings" - Sarna, 1989, p. 235.
150 Von Rad, 1972, p. 327.

Dinah as an opportunity to create an alliance between the two groups which will be mutually beneficial. The emphasis in this speech is on the benefits for the Israelites. They will have the freedom of the land and a trade alliance as well as a pool of eligible wives. Their only obligations are to agree to Shechem's marriage and to give their daughters to the Hivites as wives. Hamor is a "business man" - an opportunist. He recognises the significance of this large and wealthy family and he is aware of how a strong alliance with them would benefit his people. Dinah has provided him with the opportunity and he proceeds to seize the day. There is no reason to think that Hamor is being dishonest in his proposal[151] and I shall defend his honour against the excessive attacks of a range of scholars later. I think that the narrator portrays Hamor as a man who has every intention of honouring his word. The blame attaches not to his honesty but to his insensitivity to the moral offence his son has caused. A good business opportunity blinds Hamor to the feelings of the offended family. He hopes that they will be too eager to sign up to the deal to make too much of a fuss over a "little indiscretion". This was his fatal mistake.

*Genesis 34:11-12*

Before the Jacobites can reply, Shechem interjects with an impassioned plea for Dinah's hand in marriage. Shechem is consistently portrayed in the story as an eager and passionate young man. He lacks the maturity to control his drives. This was so in the rape, in his rude request to his father, in his interruption here and in the content of the speech. Finally, the eagerness with which he submits himself to circumcision comes as no surprise for a man so driven by his passions. Shechem addresses not Jacob and his sons but "*her* father" and "*her* brothers" for this is how he sees them. For him their only significance lies in their relationship to the woman he wishes to marry. He begins politely - "May I find favour in your eyes" - and then proceeds to offer to pay a *mohar* and gift of any price the family wish to name.[152] This is not a man who has the time or patience for negotiations to get a good deal. He has his eyes set on one thing and he immediately plays his trump card.[153] As far as Dinah's financial value to the family goes they could not have got a better deal anywhere else. Of course, the sons are not interested in Dinah's financial value but Shechem offers them what he thinks may quash any concerns they have over the unfortunate incident of the rape. He ends with a desperate appeal - "I will give whatever you ask of me just give me the girl as a wife!" Fewell and Gunn, following Westermann,[154] suggest that Shechem is offering this money as compensation and as a kind of penance.[155] This seems not to be the case.[156] The terms refer to the normal

---

151 So Von Rad (ibid., p. 328) and contra Sternberg (1987) and Berlin (1983) *et al*

152 The מוהר price was normally fixed by custom, Sarna (1989, p. 235).

153 Caspi, 1985b, p. 36.

154 Westermann, 1985, p. 540.

155 Fewell and Gunn, 1991, pp. 200-201. So too Sarna, 1989, p. 235.

*mohar* and present to the bride.[157] The text gives a reason for the offer
(Shechem's love for Dinah) and thus there is no need to supply another (a
desire to make amends). As with Hamor there seems no recognition of the
offence that he has caused the family of Dinah. I do not imagine that this was
deliberate but was simply that he could not see beyond his own desires to
recognise the seriousness of what he had done.[158] Shechem has no interest in
Hamor's alliance (except as a means to an end): his love for Dinah had given
him tunnel vision so that he lacks the perspective to recognise his own sin.[159]
Ironically it is his love for Dinah that blinds him to the danger in her brothers.
Ultimately, and with some poetic justice, his desire for her is his undoing as it
was hers in v. 2.

So the Israelites are being offered a very tempting package if they agree to
the marriage: not only a potentially beneficial alliance but also a very
handsome *mohar*. They stand to benefit greatly from the rape of Dinah.
Shechem is, of course, doing the "right" thing by offering to marry Dinah. I
argued earlier that such a solution after a rape may have been seen as the way
to make the best of a bad situation. However, as we shall see, his Hivite identity
proved to be a complicating factor and his lack of penitence does not endear
him to the reader. Nevertheless, I think that the narrator is trying to elicit some
sympathy for Shechem. He has no interest in harming the Israelites. He will
treat them with honour and respect even if for an ulterior motive. He will give
whatever it takes to have Dinah's hand in marriage. Such a passion stimulated
Jacob to work seven years for Rachel and one does feel some sympathy for the
infatuated young man.

## Genesis 34:13-17

V. 13 marks the turning point in the narrative. It is here that the tide turns
against the Hivites without their realising it. It is here too that it becomes very
difficult to discern where the narrator's sympathies lie. Does he approve of the
sons' actions? Does he disapprove? The history of interpretation, as Chapter
Three has shown, is littered with those, ancient and modern, who have seen one
or the other view endorsed.

Jacob remains silent. Given that he is the head of the family and that it is his
responsibility to speak at this point, his silence is noticeable. The sons speak in
his place. V. 13 introduces their speech in a significant way. Firstly we learn
that they answer Shechem and Hamor deceitfully and then we are reminded
why they do so - because he defiled Dinah their sister. Now there is an

---

156 Noble, 1996, p. 181.
157 Westermann, 1985, p. 540; Sarna, 1989, p. 235. Speiser sees a hendiadys -
"not...two separable items but as one payment of the amount due the family for the
release of the girl" (1969, p. 265). Even if this is correct my argument stands.
158 Noble, 1996, p.192; Sarna, 1989, p. 235.
159 Vawter, 1977, p. 357; Noble, 1996, p. 192.

epistemological divide between the Hivites and the reader as the following speech is considered. We know what they do not - that the sons are still seething with anger at their sister's mistreatment and that what the brothers say is not true.

Sternberg is correct to see the claim that "he defiled Dinah their sister" as both the sons' reason for deceit[160] and the narrator's judgement on the rape. He is also correct that this reminder does serve to mitigate, somewhat, the reader's disquiet at the comment that the sons spoke deceitfully. Does the defiling of Dinah justify the deceit? That, I suggest, depends on the nature and purpose of the deceit. At present the reader knows neither. The narrator helps us to sympathise with the sons - to see it from their side. This does not necessarily mean that he wants the reader to end up by endorsing the sons' actions. It "may not excuse their deceitfulness but it at least makes it understandable."[161] Whether that it the case will be investigated later.

The sons begin by flatly refusing the possibility of a marriage between Dinah and Shechem. The reason they give is that Shechem is not circumcised and for an Israelite woman to marry an uncircumcised man would be deeply shaming to the Israelites (including Dinah[162]). Is this claim a lie? Does the narrator's claim that the sons spoke deceitfully include this claim? Some argue that it does[163] whilst others that it does not.[164] In canonical context, indeed in the context of Genesis itself, it is indeed true that for an Israelite woman to marry an uncircumcised man is shaming. Genesis 17:9-14 makes circumcision essential for being a part of Israel. The sons go on to quote the covenant chapter Genesis 17:10 as their speech progresses (which makes the suggestion of Westermann that circumcision was not a religious rite in Genesis 34 most unlikely[165]) so it seems to me virtually undeniable that they spoke truthfully here. At very least they draw attention to something which they believe to be the case in theory, even if they use it as a ruse. This conclusion is reinforced by our earlier discussion of exogamy. So wherein lies the deceit? The sons proceed by immediately making an exception to their refusal: "if you will be as we are by circumcising to you every male." That is to say, every potential marriage

---

160 "It has been pointed out that sisters play a particularly potent symbolic role in male-male relations in a number of societies. In particular, the ability to guard against threats to a sister's sexual purity or to avenge sexual misconduct against one's sister is often an index of masculine honour." (Stone, 1996, pp. 106-107).

161 Noble, 1996, p. 184; Jeansonne, 1990, p. 94.

162 So Noble, 1996, p. 183, fn. 25 contra Fewell and Gunn, 1991.

163 Fewell and Gunn, 1991, p. 202; Noble, 1996, pp. 182-183.

164 Sternberg, 1987.

165 Westermann, 1985, p. 540. The odd thing is that Westermann himself draws attention to the Genesis 17:10 quote in the sons' speech. Let me qualify my critique. Whilst claiming that circumcision was a religious rite in Genesis 17 I would not maintain that it had the developed exclusivist overtones as are found in Mosaic Yahwism (see Chapter Five).

partner of an Israelite woman (the males) could qualify for marriage if they remove the foreskin. To remove the foreskin is to remove the offence and thus the barrier to marriage. If this is done then, and only then, will the Israelites give their daughters to the Hivites (and, by implication, Dinah to Shechem) and take Hivite daughters for themselves. Then they will dwell and the two groups will be as one people. To this conditional agreement the sons append a warning - if the Hivites do not agree to the circumcision condition then they will take Dinah and go. Now it is worth pointing out that this thinly veiled threat takes on a fuller significance when we look back to it from the perspective of v. 26. The reader could read the threat to take Dinah and go as implying that Dinah is with the Israelites. Alternatively it could imply that the Hivites still have her. The reader is uneasy but, as yet, unsure about Dinah's whereabouts. When v. 26 is reached the gap will be filled and the true nature of this threat will become clear - the Hivites still have Dinah at Shechem's house. Once that is realised we re-read the negotiations with different eyes. We now realise what we did not on the first reading but what both parties to the negotiations did - that Dinah is in Shechem. The question is, in what capacity is she there? As a prisoner[166] or out of her own choice?[167] Fewell and Gunn think that given that he "spoke to her heart" in v. 3 "it is simpler to assume that she is now in Shechem's house of her own accord. Nor, if she is a hostage, does it make sense for the Hivites to be offering the Israelites such open-ended terms for the bride-price or even to be offering terms at all - the Hivites are the ones who have the strength of numbers."[168] I argued at the end of *Excursus 1* that Dinah was not being used as a hostage but was a *potential* hostage.

We still have to identify the deceit in the sons' speech. On a first reading of the story it is not clear where the deceit lies until we read of the massacre. It is only then that we realise that the lie is that the sons were going to "take Dinah and go" whether the Hivites agreed to be circumcised or not. They never had any intention of entering into the alliance proposed by Hamor. The pretence of going along with the proposal was a ruse to get the Hivites circumcised, and thus to make them easier to defeat when Dinah was taken back. Sternberg wonders whether their intention may have originally been to make the conditions of marriage so difficult that the Hivites would refuse and Dinah would be returned.[169] That is not likely. There is no indication that it was merely the return of Dinah that the sons were after, but retribution for the rape.

What about the claim that an Israelite woman could marry a non-Israelite if he was circumcised? Although the sons lied when they said that they would agree to such a solution, would it have been acceptable in normal

---

166 So Sternberg, 1987; West, 1980, pp. 148-149 (which he takes to show that Shechem did not love Dinah); Caspi, 1985b, p. 41; Luther, 1970, p. 197.
167 So Fewell and Gunn, 1991; Vawter, 1977, p. 359.
168 Fewell and Gunn, 1991, p. 200.
169 Sternberg, 1987, p. 464.

circumstances? In other words, if we were not dealing with a situation in which a group of angry brothers plan to get revenge, could a non-Israelite, by getting circumcised, make himself an eligible marriage partner for an Israelite? This question cannot be answered with certainty on the basis of Genesis 34. Given that the speech is deceitful we cannot be sure whether the suggested "solution" was actually a lie (i.e. a Gentile getting circumcised would not actually make an acceptable marriage partner) or whether it was true, but that the sons were lying about their willingness to accept the "solution". That Jacob did not object to their suggestion may suggest that he found it quite acceptable. The answer depends partly on the extent to which circumcision was seen as an act of conversion to Yahwism. Second Temple Jewish interpretations, by their very silence about the circumcision, indicate that circumcision would have been considered a sign of conversion. The silence was because the massacre would then have been put in a very bad light if a town of converts had been massacred. However, such interpretations may have been reading back later attitudes to circumcision into the text. By submitting to circumcision were the Hivites simply following an Israelite custom for ulterior motives, or were they agreeing to worship the God of Israel? From Genesis 34 the former seems to be the case. There is no indication that the Hivites were converting their religion to become the equivalent of early God-fearers. Most likely circumcision was seen as a marriage rite by the Hivites rather than a religious covenant symbol.[170] Mere circumcision would surely not make a Gentile acceptable as a marriage partner. To be fair, the brothers do not require religious conversion from the Hivites - the Canaanites do all that was required of them. So it may have been dishonest of the brothers to suggest that circumcision alone, without religious conversion, would qualify the Hivites for an alliance with Israel.

What is the reader intended to make of this deception? On the one hand the narrator wants to elicit a certain degree of sympathy for it. The sons certainly had good reason to be angry and given the political power of their guests it may have been imprudent to have taken a more direct approach. On the other hand, there are a number of factors that could not but lead the reader to feel uneasy about the sons' action.

Firstly, the very fact that they are engaged in a deception is slightly disconcerting - "it indicates a limited complication of judgement"[171] - but the reader may be willing to tolerate that given the circumstances.[172] The Old Testament certainly does not have an ethic such that it is wrong to lie regardless of the circumstances, though it does place a premium on speaking the truth.[173]

---

170 Geller, 1990, p. 10.
171 Sternberg, 1987, p. 459.
172 Contra Sarna, 1989, p. 236.
173 Wenham, 2000, takes a stronger line, arguing that within the rhetoric of Genesis the deception would certainly have been seen as unacceptable. If he is right then it strengthens my point, but I prefer to be more cautious.

Secondly, once it becomes clear where the deception is leading, one cannot help but feel that it is a calculated overreaction to the situation. The rape of Dinah was a terrible crime but what the Israelites do in retribution hardly reflects the law of the tooth - a principle which the readers may have been expected to believe in. The sons behave more like Lamech in Genesis 4 who slew a man for striking him and repaid seventy-seven times.

Third, the use of the covenant symbol of circumcision in the deception is at once clever in its effectiveness and irony, and at the same time a cruel and perhaps cynical abuse of the symbol. Did the narrator consider the use of circumcision merely to disable the male community of Shechem to be an irreligious distortion of its purpose? Certainly in the history of interpretation there is a long tradition of reading the story in that way.

Fourth, did the narrator think that making an agreement with the Shechemites (into which they entered in good faith) and then breaking it was wrong? Certainly in the book of Joshua, once an agreement had been made with the Gibeonites there was no way in which it could be broken, even if the Israelites may have regretted the deal.[174] Breaking alliances and covenants was treated as a very serious crime in ancient Israel. There is some reason to think that the story in Joshua 9 may consciously allude to Genesis 34. Immediately prior to the story we read about a covenant ceremony near Shechem.[175] Straight after that the tale of the *Hivites* from Gibeon is recounted, but this time the situation in Genesis 34 is reversed. In Genesis 34 the Israelites deceive the Hivites in order to slaughter them, whilst in Joshua 9 the Hivites deceive the Israelites in order to avoid slaughter. In Genesis 34:25 the Hivites discover the ruse *after three days,* just as the Israelites do in Joshua 9:16. The Genesis covenant is not kept by Israel and dooms the Hivites, whilst the Joshua covenant *is* kept by Israel and *saves* the Hivites. If these parallels are sound then Israel's loyalty in Joshua 9 puts their disloyalty in Genesis 34 in a negative light.[176] It seems unlikely that the narrator would have approved of Simeon and

---

174 Josh 9:3-27.

175 Josh 8:30-34.

176 Did God want to save the Hivites in Joshua 9 perhaps to balance out the Genesis 34 massacre? At first sight one may think not (Josh 9:14) but the following considerations may indicate otherwise: First, the "curse" for their deception is for them to work in the sanctuary of Yahweh. They were involved in some sense in the worship of Israel's God – hardly a cruel "curse". The Gibeonites returned with the exiles to rebuild Jerusalem (Neh 7:25) indicating long-lasting loyalty to this God in whom they confessed some kind of faith (Josh 9:24). Second, it is Israel's covenant with the Gibeonites that precipitates Israel's important defeat of the Southern coalition in Joshua 10 indicating Yahweh's providential use of the Hivites' salvation. Finally, we know that Israel's victories had led the Amorites to fear them (Josh 2:11; 5:1). This may have led them to seek peace with Israel exactly as the Gibeonites did in Joshua 9. Joshua 11:19-20 explains that in order to avoid this Yahweh strengthened the resolve of the Canaanites giving them the courage to fight and thus driving Israel to destroy them (e.g. Josh 11:1-

Levi's covenant breaking. [177]

These four aspects of the sons' response must have been expected to raise moral questions given the beliefs of both the narrator and his implied reader. Both believed in truth speaking as the ideal. Both believed in the law of the tooth. Both believed in the religious centrality of circumcision and both believed in the importance of keeping oaths and agreements. And yet, the crime was serious and the situation difficult. Did that justify the retribution? I shall leave that question unanswered for now. [178]

### *Genesis 34 Scene Three (34:20-24)*

*Genesis 34:20-24*

Hamor and Shechem returned [179] to their city gate to speak to the men of their city. The central question for us is, "How are the Hivites portrayed in this Scene?" Several writers agree that this scene is here to harden the reader's attitude towards the Hivites. [180] This is supposedly done by:

(a)  making subtle changes from the speech Hamor made to the Israelites so that Hamor now presents a deal which is primarily to the advantage of his people rather than vice versa. The demands of Jacob's sons are softened. Caspi goes as far as to claim that Hamor offers a very different deal to each of the two groups [181] but his reasoning is very fragile.

(b)  the lack of reference to Dinah and Shechem which is taken to be deceitful. [182]

(c)  by the ominous mention that all the Israelite property would belong to the Hivites if they agree to the deal. This, we are told, indicates that the Hivites had no intentions of keeping the deal and would turn on the

---

5). In other words God strengthened the fearful hearts of the Canaanites to stop them doing precisely what he allowed the Gibeonites to do. This could indicate divine sanction for their salvation perhaps to compensate for Genesis 34.

177 Of interest here is Andersen's interpretation of Jacob's curse in Genesis 49:5 which he reads as: "Simeon and Levi: Brothers they destroyed; They were violent to their covenant partners" (Andersen, 1966). This would make the violation of the agreement an inexcusable violation of covenant.

178 For comments on vv. 18-19 see Appendix 1.

179 NB the singular verb (lit., "he came, Shechem and Hamor his son" ) indicating their unity in the eyes of the narrator.

180 E.g. Caspi, 1985b, pp. 36-38. Caspi even suggests that the sons realise that Hamor has such deceitful intentions!

181 Caspi, 1985b, p. 37.

182 Von Rad, 1972, p. 329. Supporting the "deceitful Hivite view" see also Sarna, 1989, p. 237 and Kass, 1992, p. 35.

Israelites at the first opportunity. Sternberg thinks that this "may well
reflect the hidden intention of the speakers all along."[183]

I shall argue that, on the contrary, this scene clearly depicts the Hivites as very
genuine about the agreement and totally deceived by the sons of Jacob.

In response to (a) we can simply note that Hamor's twisting of his original
speech makes no changes of substance to the agreement. It simply puts the
most favourable "spin" on the deal so as to sell it to those who have the most to
lose by it (i.e., their foreskins). The softening of the demand is also
understandable for the same reason and does not amount to a change in the
agreement. This speech is "a ... diplomatic masterpiece."[184] Hamor is portrayed
as a skilled rhetorician but surely not as a liar!

Similarly, in response to (b) we may say that it was again for reasons of
credibility with his people that no mention is made of Dinah. She may have
been the catalyst of the deal, but from Hamor's perspective she was merely a
means to an end; simply the first example of a broader alliance in which
daughters are exchanged. It is that alliance which truly interests him and it is
that which he sells. On top of that, if it was suspected that Hamor had ulterior
motives for this covenant, namely the marriage of his son, that would not help
him in his cause to persuade the men to get circumcised. So the omission is for
understandable reasons and does not amount to a major deception on his part.

More serious is the claim that the Hivites are shown as not intending to keep
the deal. This claim is most unconvincing because the comment that the
Israelite property will now belong to the Hivites is open to an alternative
interpretation, which makes more sense of the evidence. Namely that once an
alliance is made with the Israelites, it will not only be daughters which are
exchanged but property also. On this reading, Hamor's comment relates to
trade with the Israelites and not theft. Fewell and Gunn, rightly in my view,
suggest that "we may as readily understand the clause to mean that once the
Israelites are part of the community the total market will have been swollen by
the amount of goods that the Israelites bring to it."[185] This interpretation is
made all the more likely when one considers the following:

- Here we have Hivites talking alone with no Israelites present. This is the
  opportunity *par excellence* for the narrator to have them hatch their
  devious plot to double cross Jacob's family.[186] On Sternberg's reading the
  narrator is aiming to harden attitudes to the Canaanites as much as possible
  prior to the massacre. If that is what he is trying to do then he does a rather
  poor job. There is no mention at all of pretending to enter into an

---

183 Sternberg, 1987, p. 466. See too Berlin, 1983, pp. 76-78; Ross, 1996, p. 274.
184 Von Rad, 1972, p. 328.
185 Fewell and Gunn, 1991, p. 204.
186 Cf. Gen 37:18-36 when Joseph's brothers plot and then deceive their father.

agreement. That Sternberg has to reach for a subtle interpretation of one slightly ambiguous sentence in itself ought to be a warning.

- On the other side of the coin is the fact that Hamor strongly urges his people to accept the Israelites and to agree to their terms. We need to remember that the Hivites are being asked to agree to a painful surgical operation. If the deal was done to lull the Israelites into a false sense of security it is an extreme way in which to do it. If it was simply plunder the Hivites wanted they could have out-numbered the Jacobites any time.[187] The comments of Hamor to the effect that the land can accommodate both groups is a clear indicator that he was trying to persuade his group to let the Israelites have the freedom of the land. If double-crossing was on his mind the conversation would have proceeded very differently.
- Hamor's call to the Israelites to "trade in the land" indicates that this comment here, to his people, is really spelling out the consequences of healthy trade relations with a wealthy family living locally.

All of these factors make the suspicious reading of Scene Three most implausible. So what can we say about the Hivites? They are willing to go along with the agreement for what they stand to gain out of it (hardly surprising and not a serious offence): a pool of potential wives and more open trade opportunities. Hamor comes over as a pragmatic leader who can put a skilful twist on the facts to make them as attractive as possible, but without making substantial changes or lying. He really believes that this deal is in the best interests of both groups and he has every intention of keeping his side of the bargain. This Scene does not harden attitudes towards the Hivites and possibly makes the reader more sympathetic towards them. At least they seem sincere, even if selfish.

It is possible that there is a subtle criticism of the local men here. Just possibly we are expected to think that they are well aware of what has happened to Dinah and thus their not mentioning it implies implicit approval. There is no criticism of Shechem's behaviour from his father nor from his people. Thus they too share in his guilt to some extent.[188] Their agreeing to get circumcised may implicate them to some degree in that they too are prepared to get some mileage out of the rape of Dinah. That the rapist was the son of their leader may also associate them with his guilt as Shechem is their representative.[189] He represents the city of Shechem and thus his attack on Dinah is, by implication, the attack of the city of Shechem on the Israelites as a family and as a nation. These thoughts may explain the otherwise odd remark in v. 27 that in Shechem *"they"* had defiled Dinah. In the eyes of the brothers of Dinah she had been defiled, not simply by the rapist, but by the city which

---

187 Fewell and Gunn, 1991, p. 204.
188 So Luther, 1970, pp. 208-209.
189 Ibid., p. 206.

he represented, which held him in honour and which sat by in silence prepared to gain out of the experience. However, some of this speculation is based on the idea that the men of the city knew about the rape of the girl. We do not know whether they did or not and the narrator certainly makes nothing of the issue of their knowledge. It is not something to which our attention is drawn. Indeed, the lack of mention of Dinah in Hamor's speech may indicate his desire to keep her out of their thoughts. Her absence in this scene is noticeable as she dominates the rest of the story. The attentive reader cannot help but notice her absence and this may indicate that although she is in Shechem's house, the locals are not really cognisant of this fact. Be that as it may, there is very little in this scene to harden attitudes towards the Hivites.[190] The reader does realise though that the end of the Scene has the Hivites falling right into the trap of the brothers. The Scene ends in suspense as we wait to find out exactly what it is that they have let themselves in for. We are not kept waiting long as Scene Four hastens to release all the suspense which has been built up.

*Genesis 34 Scene Four (34:25-31)*

*Genesis 34:25-29 - The Attack*

The final Scene opens three days after the Hivites have been circumcised and are in great pain. The action begins as Simeon and Levi take their swords and descend upon the city which is unaware of, and unprepared for, their violent arrival. Simeon and Levi are introduced as "two of the sons of Jacob, Simeon and Levi, brothers of Dinah." The reminder that they are Dinah's brothers is no idle repetition - Simeon and Levi are two of the girl's full brothers and thus they feel especially responsible for her and angry at her rape. The reader is reminded yet again of the reason for the attack: the rape of Dinah. Clearly the sons' motive is not simply an opportunity for enrichment by plunder. They attack out of the belief that their sister, and their group, have been wronged.

The massacre is not dwelt on but is passed over very briefly. We simply read that they killed every male including Hamor and Shechem, his son. Shechem certainly, and Hamor probably, were killed in revenge for the rape, but why kill the entire male population? There are two possibilities which spring to mind:-

(a) They too were considered guilty by the sons in some way.[191] Was this simply because in their eyes Shechem, as the representative of the city, brought the whole city into guilt by association? Perhaps the Israelites perceived the crime as an attack by one group on their own group and thus the whole group is responsible. Was it because they did not speak up about Shechem's behaviour and thus implicitly agreed to the rape and aimed to profit from it? The sad part of this is that Scene Three

190 König, 1919, p. 641.
191 Ross, 1996, p. 274; Kass, 1992, p. 35.

makes it clear that the Hivites did not want to harm the Israelite group but had a vested interest in keeping on good terms with them. *They* did not perceive the situation as an attack on the Jacobites.

(b) The massacre was not done in revenge at all but was a pragmatic move. If the brothers only killed Shechem and Hamor then the Shechemites would have responded violently against the Israelites in retaliation for the murder of their leaders. Thus this potential threat had to be removed. If Dinah was to be rescued, the massacre was a necessary evil.[192]

The fact is that our text does not tell us why all the males were killed, and we cannot be sure whether (a) or (b) was the primary reason.[193] 34:27 explains that the other sons considered the city to be "where *they* defiled their sister".[194] This forms the only reason for the plunder which the narrator explicitly mentions and it seems to indicate that the townsfolk where considered guilty in some sense for the attack on Dinah. On the other hand, I do not think that we can rule out utilitarian motives as well. I propose that the sons probably killed all the men *both* because they thought them guilty in some sense *and* because they wanted to remove the threat of possible future revenge attacks.

After the killings the sons "took Dinah from the house of Shechem and they went out". Fewell and Gunn see this "taking" as against Dinah's wishes. However, we do not know that they took her by force.[195] Their claim depends upon an over-reading of v. 3 as we have already seen. Similarly, Laffey's comment that they "take all their possessions, including Dinah"[196] is very odd. Dinah was not one of the Hivite possessions! Indeed, I would contend that wives were not the property of their husbands in Old Testament Israel.[197] Jeansonne also writes of their taking as "unfair to Dinah" on the basis of Deuteronomy 22:28-29.[198] We have, however, already seen that Deuteronomy 22:28-29 is not applicable in this case. All of these critical evaluations of the return of Dinah are unfounded.

The crucial question is, "Does the narrator approve of the massacre?" There are no explicit comments on the rights or wrongs of the killings but then this

---

192 Kass, 1992, p. 35. West thinks that the original plan was not to kill all the men but merely to make them powerless to resist the rescue of Dinah (West, 1980, p. 151). How he knows this is not clear. The claim has no textual foundation and if it is true it is hard to see why the sons did end up killing all the men.

193 Kass opts for both, 1992, p. 35.

190 Alter (1996, p. 194) sees the plural form of the verb in v. 27 (they defiled) as free indirect discourse – the language of the narrative used to explain how the brothers felt about the crime.

195 Sternberg, 1992, p. 478, fn. 13.

196 Laffey, 1988a, p.42.

197 So C.J.H. Wright, 1990, ch. 6.

198 Jeansonne, 1990, p. 95.

silence is standard practice for biblical narrators and does not indicate the lack of a moral stance, nor the lack of an intention to communicate one. Unfortunately the matter is highly ambiguous.

*Hints That the Narrator Did Approve of the Massacre*

First of all the structure of the story makes it clear that this scene parallels the rape scene and is an act of retribution for that. This in itself indicates some justification for the killing. The initial crime is the problem which is partially resolved in this scene. The balancing of crime and punishment is also indicated by the use of key words - just as Shechem "took" Dinah so the sons now "take" their swords, kill the offender and "take Dinah" back. Thus the imbalance of the first taking is corrected by the second. There is also the poetic justice in the fact the Shechem's crime began with his penis and his punishment begins in the same place: "As Shechem sinned through sex so he is brought low by a rite involving a wound to his sex."[199]

Secondly, the narrator has made it very clear just how serious Shechem's crime was. We have seen how he is presented negatively to begin with and, despite some softening of that original picture, he never shakes off the narrator's disapproval. Hamor too entangles himself in the guilt to some extent, as we have seen. The narrator constantly reminds us that the sons attack for motives which we are not only expected to sympathise with, but also to agree with.

After the massacre we read that the brothers "took Dinah from Shechem's house." This is the first time in the story where Dinah's location is clear. I argued that the reader has previously been given two very subtle hints that something may not be right, but now the truth is revealed. Armed with this new information the reader casts his thoughts back to the negotiations and sees them in a new light which does not reflect well on the Hivites but does gain some sympathy for the sons.[200]

There is also the sense in which the massacre at Shechem serves as a type of the later conquest of Canaan.[201] We have the sons of Israel having just entered the promised land; the sexually immoral Canaanites; the complete destruction and the burial of gods under the tree at Shechem. On the other hand, the Canaanite cities were to be totally put under the ban and that is not the case here as all the women and children are spared. Chapter Five will explore the Conquest typology and its relevance to the ethics of Genesis 34 more carefully.

The implied reader could hardly have been expected to agree with the Hivite deal. The thought of Israel becoming "one people" with the Canaanites would have been seen as a serious threat.[202]

---

199 Geller, 1990, p. 2; Sarna, 1989, p. 236.
200 Sternberg, 1987, p. 467.
201 West, 1980, pp. 151-156; Ross, 1996, p. 275; Geller, 1990, p. 5.
202 Aalders, 1981, p. 159; Sailhammer, 1992, p. 200.

The logic is expounded fully in Ex 34: "Make no treaty with the inhabitants of the land lest, when they go whoring after their gods and sacrifice to them, they invite you to share the sacrifice. Then you may take some of their daughters for your sons and, when those women go whoring after their gods they may make your sons go whoring after them likewise." Peaceful contact leads first to intermarriage and then to "whoring", the pungent term covenant tradition employs to describe the sexual rites of the Canaanite fertility religion.[203]

The sons were not primarily concerned about this but their deed did put an end to a threat which a post-Mosaic audience would perceive.

The above arguments conspire to draw a considerable amount of sympathy for the actions of Dinah's brothers. To my mind there is no doubt that the narrator wants the reader to take their action seriously and sympathetically. However, none of the above makes the matter a straightforward approval on the narrator's part and Chapter Five will attempt to show how the support gained from the above considerations is significantly undermined when Genesis 34 is put into intertextual communion with the rest of the Old Testament.

*Indicators That the Narrator Does Not Want the Reader to Approve of the Massacre*

First of all we may note that the plot resolution (the massacre) is not, in fact, a complete plot resolution. There is no "and they all lived happily ever after." On the contrary, the sons' solution generates two more problems, the first of which Jacob draws attention to in v. 30. By killing the Hivites the sons have made the whole family vulnerable to attack from the other local Canaanites. However, they do not really care about such consequences: paying back the defiler of Dinah is their only thought (v. 31). The second problem is that they increase the tensions within their own family and set themselves at loggerheads with their father. The story ends suspended in the middle of a fierce family argument about the massacre leaving the reader with the sense that their deed has stirred up trouble at home which hangs over the rest of the narrative.[204] The Joseph story develops the family tensions between Rachel's sons the sons of the other three women. 49:5-7 makes it clear that the family dispute sparked by the Shechem massacre was never resolved and continued to boil away over the years until Jacob could contain his anger no more.

The narrator would have expected his readers to have been aware of the *lex talionis* and to have considered it an essential principle of justice instituted by God himself.[205] It seems highly probable that the obvious imbalance between the crime and the punishment would have been important in assessing the appropriateness of the Israelite response. Andre Neher calls their act "an

---

203 Geller, 1990, p. 3.
204 Brueggemann, 1982, p. 279.
205 Even Sternberg agrees with this (1987, p. 445). See also Noble, 1996, pp. 192-193.

outrageous escalation in that it goes beyond all bounds of morality."[206] A girl is raped and in response the men of an entire city are killed and the town is then plundered![207] It may be drawn to our attention by the very key word we mentioned above. Shechem "took" Dinah and in response the sons "took" swords, "took" Dinah and "took" plunder. May this excess of "taking" indicate an over-reaction?

The plunder account in vv. 27-29 goes into lavish detail about what the Israelites took from the Hivites. The pace is slowed and the reader is forced to ponder all the booty. Sternberg is of the opinion that the repetition gives the impression of an "orgy of looting ... The greed portrayed by the plunderers reduces them to the moral level of the Hivites."[208] There is a touch of irony in that the Hivites had hoped to get hold of the Israelite possessions through trade and yet the Israelites now possess all the Hivites possessions through conquest.[209] However, this may actually turn to reflect badly on the Israelites. The Hivites would have taken Israelite goods in a peaceful and legitimate way whilst the Israelites take the Hivite goods in a violent and illegitimate way. One may ask how the plunder of the town could be considered a balancing of the crime committed by Shechem. Granted that the motive is not simply greed but a desire to right a genuine wrong (v. 27) that does not mean that the action was appropriate. The "taking" of one Israelite woman led to the "taking" of all the Hivite women and a modern reader, at least, may be led to be suspicious just how pure their motives were.[210] This is especially so given that although later laws allowed Israelites to marry foreign women prisoners of war, Canaanite women were not to be married. Genesis 34 does not tell us what happened to these women but, at least from a Mosaic perspective, inter-marriage was out of order.

The very fact that the killing and plunder is achieved by the use of a deception, which also involved the possible cheapening of Israel's covenant symbol, puts a question mark over the aggressive act.[211] Delitzsch writes that "the whole story ... shows us the disgrace of the promised generation not hiding how Simeon and Levi abused the sacred sign of the covenant as deception for their private execrable revenge."[212] This is an overstatement but it does draw attention to a significant feature in the text.

The final word in Genesis on the massacre is found in Genesis 49:5-7 and that is damning in its condemnation. Jacob's comments given there are set at a

---

206 Quoted in Salkin, 1986, p. 287.
207 Fewell and Gunn, 1991, p. 205.
208 Sternberg, 1987, p. 471. See too Brueggemann, 1982, p. 278; Noble, 1996, p. 195.
209 Caspi, 1985, p. 41; Davidson, 1979, p.197; Sarna, 1989, p. 238.
210 Brueggemann, 1982, p. 278 and Noble, 1996, p. 195 talk of selfish gain.
211 Brueggemann, 1982, pp. 277-78; Plaut, 1974, p. 337; Ross, 1996, p. 569; Wenham, 2000; König, 1919, p. 641.
212 Die Genesis, 2nd Ed., 1889, p. 341 (trans. Scholz, 1998, p. 157).

much greater distance from the danger than his comments in 34:30. As the motives of expediency are removed his comments are more considered and normative than those in 34:30. We shall examine them in more detail in Chapter Five.

The readers seems to be put in a rather awkward situation by the narrator. They cannot simply condemn the action of the sons without reflection. Indeed they are being led to sympathise with it to some extent. On the other hand, there cannot be a triumphalist agreement with the deed, for it jars against the scales of justice and proportion which the implied readers would have. The narrator very skilfully refuses to caricature the Hivites as demons deserving whatever they get. His presentation of them complicates the reader's evaluation of the massacre. The sons do seem to be over-reactionary.

*Genesis 34:30-31 - A Family Dispute*

The Scene then moves from the city to Jacob's house as we overhear the argument between Jacob and Simeon and Levi. Jacob is furious with his sons because they have put the family in serious danger from Canaanites out for vengeance. Simeon and Levi are infuriated by their father's rebuke. They respond with the biting rhetorical question, "Should he have treated our sister as a prostitute?" Jacob seems to have forgotten Dinah in his response to the crisis and the brothers will not allow that. They did what they did to defend her honour and the consequences be damned!

What did the narrator intend the reader to make of Jacob's rebuke? On the one hand it seems clear that he did not want the readers to align themselves with Jacob. Given the less than complimentary way in which he is portrayed earlier in the story, we cannot assume that his view here will be condoned by the narrator - perhaps the opposite. Also, the fact that no mention is made of Dinah and the seriousness of the crime underlines the idea that he has constantly underplayed the offence of the rape during this incident. His words here also do not hint at any moral complaint to his sons.[213] Jacob is not primarily concerned at the injustice of the deed but rather at the inconvenient consequences for his family. He makes no mention of the plunder which was equally as objectionable as the massacre. On top of this, the constant use of the first person personal pronoun indicates a possible selfish concern for his own life. All of these things serve to stop the reader aligning their view with Jacob's.[214] Nevertheless, it is possible to overplay the distance the narrator puts between his view and Jacob's. It would be misleading to indicate that Jacob's response is pure selfishness.[215] Even more misleading is Kidner's suggestion that Jacob swallows his scruples so as to profit from the alliance.[216] True

---

213 Plaut, 1974, p. 337; König, 1925, p. 642.
214 Contra Brueggemann, 1982, pp. 278-279 and Sailhammer, 1992, p. 202.
215 As Noble does (1996, p. 184); König, 1919, p. 642.
216 Kidner, 1967, p. 173.

enough he says "I" and "me" frequently to indicate the object of his concern but we must beware here of making the move that many scholars have made by suggesting that the "I" is Jacob himself. Jacob is the head of his household, the "I" who represents the family. His concern is for the family and not simply himself. This is clear in the comment "yet I am only a small number" where the "I" must refer to Jacob's group and not Jacob as an individual. This indicates that all the "me"s which follow, except for the last where it is distinguished from the family ("me and my house"), refer to the whole group. In fact the final "me and my house," I suggest, explicates what Jacob has meant by "me" in the preceding comments - "they will destroy me, *that is to say*, me and my house." Jacob's final outburst makes much sense of his behaviour earlier in the story. We now see that he is a pragmatic man who feels the responsibility that is his to ensure the safety of his family. This Dinah episode was not simply a sin against the family but, given Shechem's status, a potential threat to their very existence if he was refused. His silence over his sons' deceitful agreement indicates that he probably thought that it was the best way forward and now the situation is a thousand times worse. The reader can surely empathise with this stance even if they cannot endorse it fully. Jacob does have a point.[217] God steps in to protect the family from the attack which he feared and thus the threat is defused[218] but this is not to say that Jacob's stance is devoid of value or that he lacked faith in God. He simply does not wish to tempt providence.

The final word for now goes to the sons and this clearly indicates that the narrator wants the reader to ponder long and hard over what they have to say.[219] They justify their murderous action as an appropriate response to the man who treated their sister as a prostitute. "Was he right to do this?" they ask and both Jacob and the reader are expected to answer, "Of course not". There is a problem in discerning exactly what the sons had in mind when they accuse Shechem of treating Dinah as a prostitute. Prostitutes were women who were paid for sex. They were not considered adulterous although adultery can be metaphorically described as prostitution. Prostitutes were not under the authority of a husband or father, thus although their activities were not approved of, they were not criminals.[220]

The problem is that it is not at all clear in what way Shechem treated Dinah as a prostitute. He did not pay her for sex. By volunteering to pay the *mohar* and marry her he recognised her position within the 'Father's House'.

One could argue that one rapes prostitutes and thus Shechem treated Dinah as a prostitute by raping her. This is wrong. One does not rape prostitutes. "Harlots engage in sexual relations for business purposes; there is mutual

217 Fewell and Gunn, 1991, p. 207; Vawter, 1977; Noble, 1996, pp.184-185; Brueggemann, 1982, p. 279.
218 Gen 35:5.
219 Kass, 1992, p.36; Sternberg, 1987, p. 475.
220 Bird, 1997, pp. 221-225.

consent. Harlots are not raped."[221]

Kass translates v. 31 as, "as a Harlot should *one* treat our sister?" He writes, "the sons are asserting that their failure to defend their sisters' honour would be tantamount to regarding her as if she were a prostitute ... in rape - and in indifference to rape - a man, or a community, treats a woman the way that a harlot treats herself."[222] Kass' thought is vague but the idea seems to be that prostitutes treat themselves with a lack of respect. In raping Dinah Shechem treats her without respect just like one treats a prostitute. The brothers are claiming that if they ignore the crime they too would be treating her with a lack of respect. The idea boils down to this: to treat someone as a prostitute is to treat them (their sexuality?) without respect. Kass seems uncertain who treats Dinah as a prostitute. Certainly, the brothers, if they do not avenge the crime (should we treat her as a prostitute?). He also implies that Shechem does by raping her ("...in rape...") and perhaps the town in ignoring the rape ("...in indifference to rape ... a community..."). This seems too all embracing. The text actually says, "should he" not "should one". The brothers are not thinking about their treating their sister in this way but about Shechem doing so. One could make this option more plausible if the text were translated, "should he (Shechem)..." Thus "to treat as a prostitute" means to treat with a lack of respect. There is value in this analysis but it is too general and requires some fine-tuning to be useful.

Sternberg, developing an idea similar to that of Kass, writes,

> 'Damn the consequences', they say, and their response vibrates with the sense of injury that drove them to seek redress in the sword. Shechem treated Dinah like a whore not only in his cavalier way with her virtue but also by his subsequent offer of 'gifts' to her protectors. The idiom for harlots' pay (*etnen zona*) eloquently rhymes with that key verb (*ntn*) of the Hivite blandishments.[223]

The problem with this suggestion is that Shechem's offer to pay a (generous) *mohar* after a rape would not constitute, by itself, treating someone as a prostitute. In itself the practice was probably acceptable. Noble thus modifies Sternberg's view as follows:

> The brothers' objection, then, is not to the offer of money per se, but to it being offered as a routine bridal payment (rather than as compensation or restitution) which simply ignores the fact that Shechem has already forced her to have sex with him. This forcing has defined a particular relationship between Shechem and Dinah - namely, rapist and victim ... the antecedent relationship that needs to be

---

221 Bechtel, 1994, p. 31.
222 Kass, 1992, p. 36.
223 Sternberg, 1987, p. 474; Wenham, 1994, pp. 316-317; Caspi, 1985, p. 30; Ross, 1996, p. 274.

transformed is not the normal one of unbetrothed man and woman, but a highly irregular one of rapist and victim. This cannot be put right when some of the relevant parties refuse even to acknowledge its existence; in attempting to do so they succeed only in transforming it into an irregular relationship - namely, that of client and prostitute - thus adding insult to injury.[224]

The problem here is that a rape situation probably *can* be transformed by a *mohar* and marriage and, as mentioned earlier, prostitutes were not raped.

Bechtel proposes an alternative which we could set out as follows:

(i)      harlots engage in consensual sexual activity outside the bonding and obligation of the marital/family unit: the central social structure of society.

(ii)     Consequently they potentially threaten the cohesion of the social structure.

(iii)    Dinah engaged in consensual sexual activity (recall that Bechtel rejects the rape interpretation) outside her society and (from her brothers' perspective) without the possibility of bonding.

(iv)     Consequently she threatens the social structure.

(v)      Conclusion: *in this way* Dinah has become like a harlot.

This looks convincing at first until one begins to reflect upon it and then the cracks begin to show. Bechtel's argument focuses attention on Dinah's behaviour. By consenting to sex with a Hivite she has intercourse outside acceptable social boundaries with no possibility of marriage. Thus she has threatened the social boundaries. But the text focuses attention on *Shechem's* behaviour not Dinah's. She has not acted like a prostitute, he treated her like one.[225] She has not endangered social boundaries but *he has*. It was quite possible for a woman to "play the harlot in her father's house" but Dinah is not accused of this. Also harlots were not women who had sex without the possibility of bonding. It was quite possible to marry a prostitute (unless you were a priest[226]). That Dinah could not marry a Hivite would not make her parallel to a prostitute.

Most likely, in my view, is the simple suggestion that Shechem treated Dinah as if she were not subject to some man - in her case, Jacob.[227] Prostitutes' "activity violates no man's rights or honour" whilst pre-marital sex by a daughter was understood as an "offence against her father and family, whose honour required her chastity."[228] Shechem treated Dinah without regard to her

---

224 Noble, 1996, p. 194.
225 A point apparently also missed by Carmichael (1979, p. 37).
226 Lev 21:14.
227 Carmichael, 1979, pp. 37-38.
228 Bird, 1997, p. 222.

father. This is dishonourable.[229] However, the reader who ponders their point can only agree up to a point. Shechem did so treat the woman, but he then attempted to legitimise the relation by marriage. His generous offers during the negotiations and his post-coital seeking of her family's consent was a recognition of her status as a daughter and not as זונה (prostitute). The brothers' anger does not allow them to see past the original crime.[230] Of course, as Shechem was a Hivite, the marriage was not possible (or, at least, not ideal), but he had made the appropriate move and we can only imagine that some sympathy is called for. This indicates that although the sons have the last word and a good point that the narrator wants us to take with us, they do not have a good enough point to justify the massacre and this can only rebound to cast doubt on their course of action. Thus it is, in my view, false to conclude that because the sons have the final word the narrator wishes the reader to fully align his or her view with them. West is wrong to describe v. 31 as "Scripture's own justification of their act"[231] and Sarna is wrong to call it "an irresistible argument."[232]

So where is the reader at the end of Genesis 34? It seems that the narrator has induced a sympathetic response to all the characters in one way or another and also a disapproval of all the characters at some point. The reader is never able to see any of the male characters as clear models to imitate. There is a "permanent ambiguity" created by the text.[233]

> The narrative deals with a situation which is not easy to adjudicate. The initial crime is severe and the rape is condemned. Yet, once revenge is sought, it seems to go too far ... How does the narrator judge such a situation? The complexities are carefully shown ... By maintaining these ambiguities and complexities, the narrator challenges the reader to consider both the Israelites and the Hivites as

---

229 Raymond Westbrook has objected to this proposal (in a conversation at Cheltenham and Gloucester College of Higher Education, July, 2000). The sons' argument, according to me, proceeds as follows: Prostitutes are not under the authority of a father or husband; to rape a daughter is to treat her as one not in the father's house; therefore to rape a daughter is to treat her as a prostitute. This, Westbrook rightly notes, is faulty logic because prostitutes are not the only people not under the authority of a father or husband. Orphans and widows falls into the same category. If the point was that Dinah was treated as if she not under her father's authority why not say, "he has treated her like an orphan?" In reply, I would say that given a sexual act was involved the choice of "prostitute" seems sensible and obvious. It also has overtones of dishonour and lack of respect which "widow" or "orphan" did not.

230 Luther,1986, p. 219.

231 West, 1980, p.151.

232 Sarna, 1989, p. 238.

233 Jeansonne, 1990, p. 88.

human beings and not simplistically as caricatures.[234]

Commenting on vv. 30-31 Kidner comments, "The appeaser [Jacob] and the avengers [Simeon and Levi], mutually exasperated, and swayed respectively by fear and fury, were perhaps equidistant from true justice. They exemplify two perennial but sterile reactions to evil." Thus Genesis 34 provokes thought but does not aim to settle all the moral questions prematurely. Chapter Five will show how broader canonical contexts can go some way towards resolving the confusions generated by Genesis 34 over the appropriateness of Simeon and Levi's behaviour.

---

234 Jeansonne, 1990, p. 97.

## Chapter Five

# Genesis 34 in Intertextual Communion with the Canon

The purpose of this chapter is to bring Genesis 34 into conversation with biblical texts outside the Jacob-Cycle.[1] This flows from our discussion in Chapter Two about the importance of reading stories in their place in the metanarrative. We shall move out from the centre looking first at the only other clear[2] biblical reference to the massacre at Shechem - Genesis 49:5-7. This will lead us on to trace the consequences of the actions of Simeon and Levi past Exodus 32 and on to Numbers 25 and 31. Having done this we shall backtrack and ask how Genesis 34, as a story set in the period of the patriarchs, relates more generally to the Mosaic dispensation. Lastly, we shall bring the narrative into conversation with the New Testament period of the super-story in which modern Christians will place themselves in terms of the plot development.[3]

### The Curse on Simeon and Levi: Tracing its Trajectories

#### *Genesis 49:5-7*

It was many years after the incident at Shechem that Jacob returned to the subject of the massacre and, in the midst of "blessing"[4] his sons, he utters a fierce and unequivocal condemnation of their deeds. The death-bed blessings uttered by Jacob serve to push Joseph (in the North) and Judah (in the South) into prominence among the twelve tribes. This mirrors their prominence in the

---

1 Genesis 25:19-36:43

2 There is a possible reference in Genesis 48:22 in which Israel says to Jacob, "I will give you one shoulder (שכם) above your brothers, which I have taken from the hand of the Amorite with my sword and bow." This seems to refer to a piece of the land of Canaan which Jacob captured from the Amorites. The problem is that Genesis records no such event. Although one can see that it may refer to Shechem that is unlikely given that Jacob did nothing to capture Shechem and shortly he will condemn Simeon and Levi for what they did there.

3 For completeness we would need to consider Psalms, Prophets and Wisdom literature but space does not permit.

4 Gen 49:28.

surrounding narratives. 40% of the whole chapter is given over to Judah and Joseph.[5] Vv. 5-7 explain why Simeon and Levi are passed over in favour of their younger brothers. From these observations Longacre concludes that there is a background macro-structure behind the Joseph story and the whole *toledot*: "Among the descendants of Jacob, Joseph and Judah are to be pre-eminent both as individuals and tribes."[6]

It is necessary to give reasons why Reuben, Simeon and Levi, all who were born before Judah and thus, one would think, ought to be prominent over him, are not the central focus of the blessing. Thus Reuben, the firstborn, is demoted for sleeping with his father's concubine[7] and Simeon and Levi are rebuked for the massacre at Shechem.[8] This paves the way for the rich blessing bestowed upon Judah.[9] Contextually then, 49:5-7 is not the focus of chapter 49 but subordinate to broader concerns. Nevertheless, that does not diminish its importance in our reflections on Genesis 34.

The text of 49:5-7 is awkward in several places but the overall impression is clear. With Hamilton we could see the structure of 49:5-7 as follows:[10]

1. Address or heading (v. 5a) - "Simeon and Levi"
2. Accusation (v. 5b-c)
3. Statement of disassociation from the criminals (v. 6a-b)
4. Justification for disassociation (v. 6c-d)
5. Pronouncement of Curse (v. 7a-b)
6. Particulars of the curse (v. 7c-d).

It will be noted that 2-5 all deal with past events whilst 6 deals with future consequences. In what follows our focus in on v. 7. Please refer to Appendix 2 for an analysis of vv. 5-6.

*Pronouncement of the Curse (v. 7a-b)*
The two כִּי could be read as:-

(i) emphatic:[11] "Cursed be their fury *so* fierce, and their rage *so* cruel!"[12] or

---

5 Longacre, 1989, p. 53. "We have a glimpse of the embryonic nation - with the Judah and Joseph tribes destined to have pre-eminence in the south and north respectively. It is, therefore, no accident that the three prominent participants in the *toledot ya'aqob* are Jacob, Joseph and Judah. Nor is it an accident that a chapter like 38 is included, where a vital piece of Judah's family history is told. Nor should it be surprising that Joseph itself has the same three central participants." Ibid., p. 54. cf. Douglas, 1993, p. 177.
6 Longacre, 1989, p. 54.
7 Gen 49:3-4 cf. 35:22.
8 Gen 49:5-7 cf. 34:25-26.
9 Gen 49:8-12.
10 Hamilton, 1995, p. 651.
11 O'Connor, 1980, p. 171.

(ii) causal: "Cursed be their fury *for* it is fierce and their rage *for* it is cruel."

The violent temper of the two sons is stressed very clearly and cursed. Jacob's attitude here seems to be in line with a prevalent Old Testament theme concerning the importance of controlling one's anger.[13] Westermann thinks that it is the anger of the two sons and not they themselves that are cursed.[14] A similar line is taken by Blass.[15] Jacob's curse on their anger rather than on them, claims Blass, indicates that he realises that their anger was "a momentary reaction rather than a durable personality characteristic."[16] It seems to me that Blass is more concerned to vindicate the ancestors of Israel than to exegete the text. V. 7c-d clearly shows the consequences of the curse *on the tribes of Simeon and Levi*. It will not do to say that only their anger is cursed.

*The Particulars of the Curse*
Again v. 7c-d is fairly straight-forward. It reads:

> I will scatter them in Jacob
> and disperse them in Israel

This is the consequence of Simeon and Levi's actions. The fulfilment of the curse can be traced through biblical history. Concerning the tribe of Simeon, Sarna writes,

> The tribe of Simeon completely lost its importance. In the first Israelite census the tribe numbered 59,300 (Num 1:23); for unknown reasons, its population was reduced to 22,200 by the end of the wilderness wanderings (Num 26:14). Neither the blessing of Moses (Deut 33) nor the Song of Deborah (Jud 5) mentions the tribe. From Josh 19:1 and 1 Chr 4:23-24, it is clear that Simeon was largely swallowed up by Judah and remained unsettled until quite late in the monarchy period.[17]

Joshua, in allotting the territories to the tribes, makes no mention of borders for Simeon's territory, only towns. They lived within Judah's borders.[18] "The one tribe, besides Levi, which did not receive a specifically demarked portion of the Promised Land was the tribe of Simeon."[19] The curse was very clearly worked

---

12 Hamilton's translation.
13 See Baloian, 1997.
14 Westermann, 1985, p. 226.
15 Blass, 1982, pp. 55-61.
16 Ibid., p. 57.
17 Sarna, 1989, p. 334.
18 Josh 19:1-8
19 Aalders, 1981, p. 274.

out in the Simeonite tribe.

Things are not so clear in the case of Levi. The Levites had no territory but merely towns in which to live.[20] Even more than Simeon they were "dispersed throughout Israel". This text seems to link that fact to their violent behaviour after the rape of Dinah. However, later texts link their unusual status to their spiritual destiny and privileged position.[21] For this reason many scholars have suggested that we have two rival traditions in the Old Testament which try to account for Levi's lack of land. Genesis 49:7 is taken to be very early because it supposedly reflects a time when the tribe of Levi was not associated with the Temple and its rituals but was merely a "secular" tribe. It terms of the plotline of Genesis-2 Kings it is indeed the case that the Levites are not associated with any special sacred duties at this point and Jacob does not make mention of any in this forecast of the future. However, the claim that this text reflects a lack of awareness of later ritual associations for the tribe on the part of its author is a fragile proposal to say the least. Nevertheless, we still have to give some account of the two explanations for Levi's landlessness. Aalders is most likely correct when he notes that the Levites' special tasks receive no explicit mention at all until Exodus 38:21 when they are given the position of servants.[22] He suggests that it was their zeal for Yahweh after the golden calf incident that turned their curse into blessing. Here, the violence of the Levites is channeled correctly. [23] The curse is still in place but God turns it into a blessing. I shall

---

20 Num 35:1-8.

21 Num 18:20-24; Deut 8:10ff; 18:1ff..

22 Aalders (1981, pp. 273-274. See too Jensen, 1997, pp. 772-773). Mary Douglas when considering why the Levites fare so well given Jacob's curse writes, "In Deuteronomy Moses praises Levi because he denied his father and mother and his brethren (Deuteronomy 9). This is to be taken as a reference to the day when Moses called the Levites to his aid in the matter of the golden calf, and the children of Levi slew three thousand men" (1993, p. 134). This, says Douglas, goes some way to explaining their change in fortunes. Moberly ponders why Levite violence is condemned in Genesis 49 but commended in Exodus 32. He writes, "It is not so much the action performed as the motive underlying it which is of central importance. What distinguishes the Levites' slaying is that it is done out of faithfulness to Yahweh (32:26)... It is loyalty to Yahweh that for this writer is the crucial factor in assessing the worth of an action." (1983, p. 55).

23 The Levites do get a mention in the blessing of Moses (Deut 33:8-11) and are specifically blessed (v. 11). However, Duane Christensen has argued that the "blessing" of Levi in Deuteronomy 33:11 may actually be a curse (1989). He suggests that the use of ברך is amphibolous and is thus really a euphemism for "curse". He proposes reading 33:11 as,

Curse, O YHWH, his strength;
but the work of his hands accept

"The verse would then refer to the tradition of the tribe of Levi taking matters into their own hands. Levi's "strength" in military matters is cursed; whereas the "work" of his hands is to be accepted" (ibid., pp. 278-279). If we accept this interpretation then we

later argue that Numbers 25 and 31 make a deliberate allusion to Genesis 34 but that, yet again, Levite violence is rightly directed in zeal for Yahweh to reverse the situation in Genesis 34.[24]

So Jacob's second rebuke to his sons is even more fierce than the first in Genesis 34:30 despite its being uttered years after the events. The question for our purposes is what role the narrator intended this curse to play in shaping his readers' attitudes to the massacre of the Hivites.

Sternberg argues at length that in Genesis 34 the narrator is trying to lead the audience towards a sympathetic approval of the killings. Thus, commenting on the selfish first rebuke of the sons in 34:30 he adds that

> a moral note in Jacob's rebuke only as late as his death bed dissociation... from the men of violence, whose rage he curses. But Jacob makes that diatribe many years later, in Egypt, when the dangers of the Hivite affair are long past and he can afford to play the moralist.[25] That he adopts no such viewpoint at present - just as he never glances at the despicable but less risky business of looting - suggests that he finds the slaughter reprehensible only in its consequences.[26]

Sternberg argues that 34:7 reflects the narrator's assessment of the sons' anger. The narrator considers the anger rational and justified given its root in their grief at Shechem's shameful behaviour.[27] In effect, Sternberg is claiming that Jacob speaks for himself and not the narrator, putting a moral varnish on his real reasons for the disapproval of the massacre.

There are several reasons to take issue with Sternberg's evaluation here and

---

could see Deuteronomy 33:11 as a part of the transition from curse to blessing for the tribe. However, the only clear amphibolous uses of ברך have God as the object of the verb (Job 1:5,11; 2:5,9; 1 Kg 21:10-13; Ps 10:3). Clearly it was thought impious to "curse God" and thus a euphemism was used. Why one would use ברך in this way of the tribe of Levi is unclear and thus ought to be suspect. It is better to see Deuteronomy 33:11 as Levi on the other side of the transformation of curse into blessing.

24 It is most interesting that Shechem itself was given to the Levites as one of their towns. Calvin writes, "but God mitigates the punishment, by giving them an honourable name in the church, and leaving them their right unimpaired: yea, his incredible goodness unexpectedly shone forth, when that which was the punishment of Levi, became changed into the reward of priesthood. The dispersion of the Levitical tribe had its origin in the crime of their father, lest he should congratulate himself on account of his perverse and lawless spirit of revenge. But God, who in the beginning had produced light out of darkness, found another reason why the Levites should be dispersed abroad among the people, - a reason not only free from disgrace, but highly honourable, - namely, that no corner of the land might be destitute of competent instructors" (1965, p. 448).

25 Cf. Jubilees 30:25.

26 Sternberg, 1987, p. 473.

27 Ibid., p. 453.

to maintain that the narrator wishes his audience to agree with Jacob.

First of all, this is Genesis' last word on the affair. It seems odd to leave Jacob's damning speech as our final impression if the narrator intends the reader to approve of the massacre.

Second, as Paul Noble says, "death bed utterances carry a special weight."[28] We need to pay careful attention to words spoken in such a context.

Third, Longacre identifies Genesis 49 as the peak of the Jacob תלדות. He writes, "This chapter, in that it is poetry, seems intended to be the high point of the *toledot ya'aqob*, if not the whole of Genesis."[29] It is "the didactic peak of the *whole toledot.*"[30] If he is right about this then Jacob's comments about the embryonic nation ought to be taken seriously.

Fourth, we should observe the wording in v. 7. It has been noted by several commentators that v. 7 reads more like a prophetic oracle than Jacob speaking on his own behalf. Von Rad writes,

> Could Jacob have said, "I will divide them in Jacob?" Perhaps one must think of a man of God who, in a situation similar to the summons of the tribes against Benjamin (Jud. 20.1ff) called a ban against the guilty. The "I" in v. 7b is God himself...[31]

Noble thinks that

> the fact that Jacob is foretelling what will subsequently befall his sons (49:1) gives the saying similar status to that of prophecy. Since the narrator presents them without comment or qualification, they should be taken as expressing his own viewpoint.[32]

If we take v.7 b-c as a prophetic oracle then we have *God's* verdict on the massacre and, as the narrator never disagrees with God, we have the narrator's also. This prophetic interpretation of 49:5-7 is strengthened when one considers that the reader is clearly intended to see Jacob's blessing on Judah, for example, in 49:8-12 as prophetic. The reader is intended to agree with Jacob's verdicts on his other sons so why not Simeon and Levi?

Fifth, to reinforce the claim that Jacob speaks prophetically in v. 7c-d we must note that his curse does in fact work itself out in the history of Israel (we shall consider how the book of Numbers contributes to this reflection soon). It would seem odd if God approved of the massacre (as Sternberg thinks 35:5

---

28 Noble, 1996, p. 193, fn. 38.
29 Longacre, 1989, p. 23.
30 Ibid., p. 25.
31 Von Rad, 1972, pp. 423-424.
32 Noble, 1996, p. 193, fn. 38.

makes clear) that he allowed his heroes to be so effectively cursed.[33]

Finally, Leibowitz has suggested that that the temporal distance from danger makes Jacob's second condemnation more considered as the motives of expediency have been removed.[34] This is no less plausible than Sternberg's reading of the situation and it fits with the above considerations.

Thus it seems that both God and the narrator would agree with Jacob in his evaluation of the brothers' deed. This chapter brings a certain amount of moral closure to Genesis 34. The reader has been left pondering the issues for the intervening fourteen chapters without being totally sure what to make of the massacre. This issue is now laid to rest although the question of exactly how the Israelites *should* have responded to Hamor is not answered. Genesis 49 merely closes down the choice that was actually made rather than prescribing that which ought to have been. The reader receives no closure here and must continue to ponder the way of wisdom.[35]

## Numbers 25 and 31

Since the earliest Jewish interpretations of Genesis 34 comparisons have been drawn between Levi in Genesis 34 and Phineas in Numbers 25 (see Chapter Three). Gordon Wenham has produced a list of parallels between Genesis 34 and Numbers 25 and 31 and suggests that the latter texts allude to the former.[36] The action of Phineas the Levite mirrors to some extent the actions of his ancestor Levi in his massacre of the Shechemites. As the former's actions were considered extremely meritorious Wenham suggests that we may read Genesis 34 similarly - a qualified narratorial approval of the massacre *and* the looting.[37] In support of this suggestion Wenham draws attention to the following parallels:-

---

33 One could argue on the theological basis of texts such as John 11:49-52 that perhaps Jacob meant the words as a curse but God meant them as a blessing. In support of this view it could be pointed out that in the rest of the Old Testament the scattering of Levi is an honour bestowed upon them due to their unique status. However, I hope to show below that this argument cannot account for the fate of the tribe of Simeon and that another explanation is available for how the curse on Levi becomes a blessing. Thus, unless we have good reasons to the contrary, it ought to be assumed that what God wanted to say through v. 7c-d is the same as what Jacob wanted to say.

34 Leibowitz, 1981, p. 381.

35 One issue which is raised by this is why the narrator left so long before bringing a measure of closure. What effect did he hope to achieve by leaving the reader so long with these loose ends?

36 Wenham, 1994, p. 316.

37 Wenham's more recent book *Story as Torah* seems to represent a shift in his position. There he argues that the narrator agrees with Jacob in 49:5-7 and does not approve of the massacre at all. He makes no mention of how the allusion to Numbers 25 and 31 is to be dealt with but I hope to do so in what follows.

(a) Genesis 34:2 a pagan, Shechem, seduces Dinah, an Israelite whilst in Numbers 25:1 the Midianite women seduce the Israelite men. In both cases there are sexual relations.

(b) Phineas the Levite kills one especially guilty pair in Numbers 25:6-8 just as his ancestor Levi killed the guilty man, Shechem.[38]

(c) The Israelites take vengeance on Midian by killing every Midianite male[39] including the kings of Midian.[40] In Genesis 34 Simeon and Levi kill all the males of Shechem[41] including the ruler, Hamor and his son.[42]

(d) Phineas the Levite kills the offending couple[43] and then all Israel attacks[44] just as in Genesis 34 Simeon and Levi attack[45] and then the rest of the Israelites.[46]

(e) "Num 31:9 repeats [Gen] 34:29 almost word-for-word in reverse order."[47] This is best seen if we list the elements of each account as follows:

| Genesis 34 | | Numbers 31 | |
|---|---|---|---|
| 1 | sons of Jacob | a | they captured (see 12) |
| 2 | plunder the city which… | b | sons of Israel (see 1) |
| 3 | flock | c | women of Midian (see 11) |
| 4 | cattle | d | their children (see 10) |
| 5 | donkeys | e | all animals (see 3-5) |
| 6 | all in the city | f | all property |
| 7 | whatever in the field | g | all wealth (see 9) |
| 8 | they took | h | they plundered (see 13) |
| 9 | all wealth | i | all their cities and habitations |
| 10 | all children | j | all their towns |
| 11 | all women | k | they burned |
| 12 | they captured | l | they took their spoil to Moses |
| 13 | and they plundered | | |
| 14 | all in the house | | |

We notice the following *verbal* links between Genesis 34 and Numbers 31:
- sons of Jacob/Israel

---

38 Gen 34:26.
39 Num 31:7.
40 Num 31:8.
41 Gen 34:25.
42 Gen 34:26.
43 Num 25:6-8.
44 Num 31:3-8.
45 Gen 34:25-26.
46 Gen 34:27-29.
47 Wenham, 1994, p. 316.

- plunder (בזז)
- wealth (חילם)
- children (טפם)
- women (נשי־מדין/נשיהם)
- they captured (וישבו/שבו). In both texts it is wives and children who are captured.

We also notice the following *thematic* links:

- animals
- property

Finally we observe the *order* links:

| Gen 34 | Num 31 |
|---|---|
| 1 | b. (had to come at start) |
| 2 | h. |
| (3-5) | (e.) |
| 9 | g. |
| 10 | d. |
| 11 | c. |
| 12 | a. |
| 13 | h. (already mentioned in Numbers) |

We can see that, with the exception of the animals put in brackets, the main body of the Numbers 31 list is, as Wenham noted, an exact reverse of Genesis 34 with some omissions (6-8, 14) and additions (f., i-l).

The structure of the Numbers plunder list is also chiastic like the Genesis list. We can set it out as follows:

A. <u>And-captured</u> sons-of Israel women-of Midian and their-children

    B. and-all-their-wealth <u>they-plundered</u>

    B1.and-all-their-cities, their-habitations and all-their-towers, <u>they-burned</u>...

A1. <u>And-they-took</u> all-the-spoil and all-the-prey among-people and among-animals.

The pattern is the same as in Genesis 34:27-29:

A. <u>They looted</u> the city where they [the men of Shechem] had defiled Dinah their sister

    B. sheep, cattle, donkeys - whatever was in city and field <u>they took</u>.

    B1. their wealth, children and wives <u>they captured</u>.

A1. <u>They looted</u> everything which was in the house.

The pattern in both looting texts is:

A.  verb-(subject)-object
   B.  object-verb
   B1.  object-verb
A1.  verb-object

I can find no other Old Testament plunder account that is as close to Genesis 34:29 as Numbers 31:9-10.[48]

    To Wenham's list we can add the following parallels that vary in their significance:

      (a)  The Midianite woman who is a catalyst for Phineas' lethal actions is the daughter of Zur,[49] one of the Midianite kings killed by the Israelites.[50] Shechem, the chief offender in Genesis 34 is the son of Hamor, the Hivite ruler who is killed in the attack on the city.[51] Notice

---

48 We may note that there is a strong parallel of order between Numbers 31 and the plundering instructions in Deuteronomy 20:14 for cities outside of Canaan (of which Num 31 but not Gen 34 forms an example). Here the list is shorter but the order is almost identical with Numbers 31:

|   | Deuteronomy 20:14 |   | Numbers 31 |
|---|---|---|---|
| A | women | c | women of Midian |
| B | children | d | their children |
| C | animals | e | all animals |
| D | all in the city |   |   |
|   |   | f | all property |
|   |   | g | all wealth |
| F | loot | h | they plundered |
|   |   | i | all their cities and habitations |
|   |   | j | all their towns |
|   |   | k | they burned |
| E | all the spoils | l | they took their spoil to Moses |

Only l. (the "spoils") is out of sequence and that is required by the Numbers story. In fact, if we take f. & g. ("all property" and "all wealth") to correspond to D. & E. ("all in the city" and "all spoils") the parallel order between the two accounts is stronger. Now Numbers 31 is a classic Deuteronomy 20 case except that particular circumstances required some of the women to be killed. It could be that Numbers 31 primarily reflects Deuteronomy 20 and only secondarily (or coincidentally?) Genesis 34. The order between Deuteronomy 20 and Numbers 31 is the same and the two passages share some vocabulary links with each other that neither have in common with Genesis 34 ("animals" and "spoils"). Nevertheless, I argue above that we ought to consider the strong possibility that the Numbers 31 list does reflect the Genesis 34 list.
49 Num 25:15.
50 Num 31:8.
51 Gen 34:26.

    the identifications: "Shechem, son of Hamor the Hivite, prince of the land"[52] and "Cozbi, daughter of the prince of Midian."[53]

(b) The Hebrew root זנה is used to describe Dinah in Genesis 34:31 (a "prostitute") and the unfaithful Israelites in Numbers 25:1 (they "fornicated").

(c) In Genesis 34:7 the sons are angry at Hamor (ויחר) for treating Dinah as a prostitute whilst in Numbers 25:3 God is angry at the Israelites (ויחר) for their "fornicating."

(d) Simeon and Levi "took" (ויקחו) swords and "came (ויבאו) upon" the city in Genesis 34:25. In Numbers 25:7b-8 Phineas "took" (ויקח) a javelin and "came (ויבא) after" the man of Israel.

(e) Just possibly the verb sequence ויבאו... ויקח (And he saw... and he took) in Numbers 25:7 echoes the same sequence in Genesis 34:2 although this may be pushing the parallels.

(f) Similarly the deceit theme is found in Genesis 34:13 and Numbers 25:18 (although the Hebrew word for "deceit" is different in each case and the function of the deceit in the narratives is different).

(g) We notice that Dinah is "sister" of the Israelite sons[54] whilst Cozbi is "sister" to the Midianites.[55]

(h) Numbers 31:7b is word for word the same as Genesis 34:25: "and they killed every male" (ויהרגו כל־זכר). Not only that but it is linked chiastically to the slaughter of the enemy rulers in exactly the same way as Genesis 34:25-26. The Genesis text reads:

And they killed    every male

and Hamor and Shechem his son    they killed with the edge of the sword

Line 1 gives the general act in verb-object order and moves in to consider how two particular people were included in the massacre in the object-verb order. Numbers 31:8 is the same. It reads:

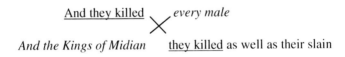

And they killed    every male

And the Kings of Midian    they killed as well as their slain

After the massacre at Shechem and of the Midianites the Israelites must ritually purify themselves and change their clothing.[56] From the above Wenham

---

52 Gen 34:2.
53 Num 25:18.
54 E.g. Gen 34:31.
55 Num 25:18.
56 Gen 35:2; Num 31:21-24.

concludes,

> (T)hese parallels suggest that the brothers' action here [massacre then looting] is
> not viewed as unequivocally evil, for the later action of Phineas is seen as
> extremely meritorious, and the follow up attack by all Israel is expressly
> commanded by God. As Jacob's sons here foreshadow the actions of their
> descendants, this seems to imply the narrators' qualified approval.[57]

Before we can ask how, if at all, Numbers 25 and 31 can function in the
interpretation of Genesis 34 we need to spell out some of the differences. Some
are major and some minor.

(a)  The Midianite women who led Israel astray in Numbers 25 are not
residents of Canaan unlike the Hivites in Genesis 34.

(b)  In Numbers 25 many Israelite men have sex with many Midianite
women. In Genesis 34 one Israelite woman is sexually imposed upon
by one Hivite man.

(c)  The issue in Numbers 25 is idolatry and not primarily extra-marital
sex.[58] The Midianite women lead Israelite men to sacrifice to their
gods.[59] For this the Israelite men are to blame and God's anger against
Israel is kindled. The Israelite leaders are to be executed.[60] There is no
analogue for this in Genesis 34. Idolatry is not mentioned at all,
certainly not in relation to Shechem's crime. At best it is hinted at in
the concern over circumcision. Indeed Dinah receives no blame at all
in Genesis 34 except a possible hint at her naiveté in 34:1.[61]
Shechem alone takes the blame and, in the end, the consequences. No divine
anger rages against Israel. There is no plague and no need to appease
God by punishing Dinah.

(d)  In Numbers 25 Phineas kills the Midianite woman *and* the Israelite
man (in the act it seems). In Genesis 34 no-one is killed in the act and
only the pagan partner (Shechem) is killed.

(e)  Phineas is zealous for Yahweh and atones for Israel's sin by his act.[62]
No such motives are said to drive Simeon and Levi. There is no sin of
Israel atoned for and no zeal for Yahweh: only anger at the
dishonouring of their sister.

(f)  In Genesis 34:25-26 Simeon and Levi join forces in the attack on the

---

57 Wenham, 1994, p. 316.

58  זנה in 25:1 is to be seen as a sexual metaphor for idolatry (as adultery and
prostitution often are in the Old Testament)

59 Num 25:2-3.

60 Num 25:4.

61 See Chapter Six.

62 Num 25:10-13.

pagans. In Numbers 25 Phineas the Levite finds his enemy to be Zimri, a Simeonite.[63]

(g) In Numbers 31:2 God authorises the attack and plundering of the Midianites for leading Israel into idolatry. God does not appear in Genesis 34, being almost conspicuous by his absence. There are no divine commands to kill or plunder. Indeed the motives for the killing and plunder are that Dinah was defiled by Shechem. God only turns up after the deed to protect the family from retribution which, as we have suggested, does not indicate a divine endorsement of the actions.

(h) The Israelite attack on Midian was conducted by 12,000 men with all tribes represented[64] whilst in Genesis 34 only two tribes are represented in the massacre (Simeon and Levi) and nine in the looting (all Israel minus Simeon and Levi and Benjamin, who was not yet born).

(i) In Numbers 31:14-18 the boys taken in plunder are killed as are all the women who led Israel astray.[65] By the nature of the case there are no parallels in Genesis 34.

(j) In Numbers 31 the Levites profit from the plunder whilst it seems that this is not the case in Genesis 34 (at least Simeon and Levi did not take part in the looting).

(k) In Numbers 31:8 *five* Midianite kings are killed whilst in Genesis 34:26 *one* Hivite king is.

(l) Jacob's angry reaction to his sons' actions in Genesis 34:30 and 49:5-7 contrasts sharply with Moses' approval of the massacre and plunder. Indeed Moses is only angry that the massacre is not ruthless enough![66]

(m) The plunder accounts, although very similar, also display differences. Genesis 34 contains the following words and phrases not paralleled in Numbers: "flock", "cattle", "donkey", "all in the city," "whatever in the field," "they took,"[67] "all in the house." Numbers 31 mentions the following unparalleled terms: "animals", "property", "spoil", "burning of towers."

What should we make of all this? Stuart Lasine asks, "how is one to distinguish between "echoes" that are little more than symptoms of synchronic tinnitus and those that should be viewed as rhetorical devices designed by the author or redactor to be heard by a reader in order to make a point...?"[68] To put the

---

63 Num 25:14.

64 Num 31:4-5.

65 Meyers thinks that the capture of the virgins to be wives reflects the importance of population size in the struggle to survive in the hill country of ancient Israel (1988, p. 67-71). I remain unconvinced.

66 Num 31:14-17.

67 Though, cf. the spoil which they "took to Moses".

68 Lasine, 1993, p. 42.

question differently, when is an allusion really an illusion? There is no precise method to determine the answer to such a question so scholars must use their own judgement. One thing which we can safely say is that Numbers 25 and 31 should *not* be determinative for our reading of Genesis 34. If we have no good reasons from Genesis 34 or its closer literary context to look favourably on the brothers, Numbers 25 and 31 could hardly make us view them positively.

The disanalogies between Numbers and Genesis are quite strong. This is especially so of the two situations confronted: Israelite idolatry in Numbers and Shechem's sexual crime in Genesis. Nevertheless, the similarities to which Wenham draws our attention do seem to be more than a coincidence. Indeed his case for an intertextual relation is strengthened if we consider Mary Douglas' somewhat idiosyncratic though insightful study, *In The Wilderness: the Doctrine of Defilement in the Book of Numbers.* She thinks that the death-bed "blessings" of Jacob in Genesis 49 were deeply influential on the shaping of the book of Numbers.

To start with, the order of the Israelite tribes camped around the Tabernacle clearly indicates the effect of the Genesis narrative and especially chapter 49 on Numbers.[69] The birth order[70] and inheritance order[71] of Jacob's sons is adapted by God in Numbers 1:1-17. God demotes the sons of Rachel and Leah's servants (Dan, Naphtali, Asher and Gad) by listing them after Leah and Rachel's sons and by jumbling up their order. Around the tabernacle we find Rachel's sons on the West in birth order (Ephraim, Manasseh, Benjamin) facing Leah's sons on the East in birth order (Judah, Issachar, Zebulun). To the North we find three of the sons of the servants (Dan, Asher, Naphthali - the order is jumbled) whilst in the South we have the son of a servant (Gad) and two of the sons cursed by Jacob in Genesis 49 (Reuben and Simeon). "Thus cursed and low-ranking sons can stand together on the North and South, regardless of their birth place in the family."[72] The key son on the West is Ephraim, destined to be the central tribe in the Northern Kingdom whilst the key son on the East is Judah, the central tribe in the Southern Kingdom. "Judah's position on the diagram is part of the rhetorical strategy for demonstrating that Jacob's curses and blessings came true."[73] The positions of Ephraim and Judah here correspond to the positions of Joseph and Judah in Genesis 49. Levi, due to its now unique status, stands outside this arrangement at the centre. Their positioning is also of interest. The Gershonites (the eldest tribe) are associated with Ephraim on the West, whilst the Aaronites are associated with Judah on the East. This reflects how as Judah supersedes

---

69 Douglas,1993, p. 134.
70 Gen 30 and 35:17-19.
71 Gen 46:8-27.
72 Douglas, 1993, p.177.
73 Ibid., p. 183.

Ephraim historically, so Aaron supersedes Gershon.[74] The Aaronites are on the side of the rising sun - the entrance of the tabernacle. The Merari, linked with the servants' sons on the North have the servants' jobs of carrying the tent frames and the Kohathites are linked with the cursed sons. It may not be a coincidence that the rebellious and cursed Korah was a Kohathite.

Douglas also observes that the named characters in Numbers draw attention to Genesis 49. The hero Caleb was from Judah and Joshua from Ephraim, whilst the rebellious Korah was a Levite, Dathan and Abiram were Reubenites and Zimri was a Simeonite.[75] Thus the three rebels from Genesis 49 are shown to be rebels again and all receive a divine rebuke.

The priestly privileges in Numbers are not an alternative tradition to Genesis 49 - the tribe of Levi survives but

> without either summarily cancelling or ignoring the curse. Instead, the words of the curse are fulfilled. In conformity with Jacob's saying that they shall be "scattered in Israel" the Levites are explicitly not to be heirs to territory of their own in the promised land. In effect, it means they are not to be a political unit... Second, they are taken out of the list of the twelve inheriting tribes and made over to be a new kind of tribe... Third, the guilt of their ancestor Levi is transferred to Korah, the Kohathite; the Levites are purged when he and his followers are destroyed.[76]

Douglas has made a convincing case for the claim that the author/redactor of Numbers wrote with Genesis 49 in mind. This makes a link between Numbers 25 and 31 and Genesis 34 highly likely. So I take it that Wenham is correct in claiming that the massacre and looting in Numbers 31 are a deliberate parallel with Genesis 34. The question now is how exactly Numbers 25 and 31 relate to Genesis 34.

I suggest that we *are* intended to see a parallel between the two events but *not* one that reflects back positively on the ancestor of Phineas (contra Wenham). Levi kills and his act is followed by a rebuke and a curse.[77] When Phineas kills his deed is followed by an outpouring of commendation from Yahweh.[78] Yahweh says that Phineas "became impassioned with my passion among them."[79] Indeed, his descendants are promised an everlasting priesthood

---

74 Ibid., p. 179.
75 Ibid., p. 195.
76 Ibid., pp. 134-135. Douglas does draw attention to parallels between Genesis 34 and Numbers 25, but her arguments seemed rather strained and, in my opinion, she misses the key point of the analogy (ibid, ch. 3).
77 Gen 34:30; 49:5-7.
78 Num 25:11-13.
79 Num 25:11.

because of this act.[80] God commends Phineas for his "zeal for Yahweh" but no such divine commendation comes to Levi. In fact Genesis 49:7, as a divine oracle, is the exact opposite - a curse.

We have seen that in Genesis 49:7 Simeon and Levi are cursed to be "scattered in Israel" for their violence. We have also seen that in Israel's history that curse was turned to a blessing in Levi's case (though not Simeon's). The story of the Levites' zealous and violent response after the Golden Calf[81] was the turning point in that change and the reason for the tribes' service as guardians of, and servers in, the tabernacle. The Phineas story is, I believe, also part of the change. This claim is supported by the clear links between Exodus 32 and Numbers 25.[82]

Now, I have argued that Exodus 32 was the key turning point in the fortunes

---

80 Num 25:12-13. See Milgrom, 1990, pp. 216-217, for a helpful discussion of this promise vis-à-vis the later Zadokites.

81 Ex 32:26-29.

82 Wenham (1981) notes how the stories run in parallel. Both occur at structurally significant places in the narrative that runs from Exodus-Numbers. The golden calf incident occurs by Mount Sinai whilst the Baal Peor incident in on the Plains of Moab. These locations are used as structural divisions within the book (ibid., pp. 14-18). In both there is a highpoint of revelation on the mountain (Ex 20ff.//Num 22-24), followed by rebellious idolatry at the foot of the mountain by Israel (Ex 32:1//Num 25:1-3). Yahweh is angry and threatens to destroy the people (Ex 32:34//Num 25:4) but Levites intervene by slaughtering the guilty Israelites (Ex 32:26-29//Num 25:7-8) (ibid., pp. 14-18 7 p. 184). Milgrom, reflecting on Exodus 32:34b-35, goes as far as to suggest that "Baal-peor is the punishment for the sin and the fulfilment of the sentence for the golden calf" (1990, p. 211). Philip Budd sees Exodus 32 and Numbers 25 as the outer ring of a large scale chiasm that spans between the two chapters (1984, p. 281) and Dennis Olson makes much of the links between Exodus 32 and Numbers 25 (1996, pp. 153-154). He lists the following parallels:

Both stories include sacrifices to other gods (Ex 32:6; Num 25:2).

Both stories involve foreigners indirectly or directly (Ex. 12:35; 32:2-4//Num 25:1-2, 6).

In the aftermath of the golden calf story in Exodus 34:15-16 God warns the Israelites to avoid the very error into which they fell in Numbers 25 - sacrifice to the gods of the land and inter-marriage with their daughters.

The Levites kill 3,000 of the guilty in Exodus 32:28 as the leaders of Israel are commanded to do in Numbers 25:5.

As a consequence of their obedience the Levites are ordained as priests to God (Ex 32:25, 29) just as Phineas is given the covenant of an eternal priesthood for his zeal (Num 25:6-13).

After the golden calf incident Moses makes atonement for Israel (Ex 32:30) whilst Phineas makes atonement for Israel in Num 25:13.

A plague is sent as punishment in both stories (Ex 32:35//Num 25:9)

"The significant parallels between the golden calf and the Baal Peor stories suggests that the older generation of Israelites have made little or no progress on their commitment to God's covenant. They end up where they began - worshipping other gods and breaking the first and most fundamental of the Ten Commandments" (Olson, 1996, p. 154).

of the tribe of Levi vis-à-vis the curse of Jacob. Given its links with Numbers 25 and given the way in which the book of Numbers is shaped to some extent by the "blessings" of Jacob in Genesis 49 it seems highly likely that Numbers 25 was also seen as having some significance in terms of the reversal of the fortunes of the tribe of Levi in the light of Jacob's curse. It would be peculiar, given the seriousness with which Jacob's curse of Simeon and Levi is taken in Numbers, if Numbers 25 were read in such a way as to vindicate Levi's behaviour in Genesis 34. If Phineas' good behaviour indicates approval of Levi's then the foundation of Jacob's curse is undercut. Such a move would be odd to say the least. So it seems preferable, against Wenham, to seek another interpretation.

I suggest that Numbers 25 marks the end of the negative influence of Genesis 34 on the Levites. The golden calf incident marked the turning point but Aaron's behaviour then[83] and later in Numbers[84] casts a shadow over the tribe as does Korah's rebellion.[85] Possibly, we could see Korah's annihilation as atoning for the Levites in which case that incident too plays its role on the road to recovery.[86] The atoning zeal of Phineas legitimates the Aaronite priesthood and fittingly terminates the power of the curse over Levi. The older generation of Israel who worshipped the golden calf are now replaced, so Phineas' act forms an inclusio with that of the Levites in Exodus 32. It is doubly fitting that he should transform the curse of Genesis 49 by enacting an incident very similar to the very one which brought a curse in the first place. Thus Numbers 25 also forms a thematic inclusio with Genesis 34. Olson writes that

> Numbers 25 closes the book on the curses pronounced on an earlier generation in Jacob's blessing of Genesis 49. The slate is clean, and a new generation can now begin again with the warnings of the past and the promises of the future as their guide into the land of promise.[87]

Now an Aaronic, priestly Levite acts again in zeal for Yahweh and against idolatry.[88] His reward is that his descendants are promised an everlasting priesthood. His deed is parallel to his ancestor's and yet strangely different. His deed, I suggest, is *a symbolic undoing of Levi's deed in Shechem*.[89] The violent inclinations of the Levite are turned to serve Yahweh and to incur divine blessing. The landlessness of the Levites is not revoked but is turned into a privilege. Indeed, the town of Shechem itself is given to the tribe as one of its

---

83 Ex 32:1-5.
84 Num 12.
85 Num 16.
86 Douglas, 1993, p. 135.
87 Olson, 1996, p. 156.
88 Cf. Ex 32.
89 And quite possibly also Aaron's deed.

own as a sign of this reversal. It could be that the reversal of the order in the plunder list is also a clue that this plundering by all Israel reverses the one in Genesis 34:27-29. So Genesis 34 is re-enacted with Cozbi playing the role of Shechem, and Zimri playing a role similar to Dinah with one very strategic difference - Zimri, unlike Dinah (or so I have argued), consented to the sin and was thus held responsible for it. Phineas acts in the role of Levi performing a very similar deed to the one which got the tribe cursed in the first place. This new act of violence is transformed by zeal for Yahweh and thus the curse is transformed into a blessing.

The tribe of Simeon, however, were not zealous for the LORD. Indeed, unlike Genesis 34 when Simeon and Levi fought side by side, in Numbers 25 the key idolater is a Simeonite and it is only by killing him that Phineas atones for Israel. Thus the curse over the tribe of Simeon and their landlessness remain. Indeed, in the census figure for the tribe of Simeon in Numbers 26:14 we find that their number has decreased from the first census by 37,100. Given the key role of a Simeonite in the Baal Peor affair of the previous chapter and the plague sent by God which killed 24,000 people[90] one may wonder what role the plague played in the dramatic reduction in numbers.

In summary, my argument has progressed as follows: There are good reasons to think that the reader is expected to agree with Jacob's verdict on Simeon and Levi in Genesis 49:5-7. Exodus 32 seems to be a turning point for the tribe of Levi. After that time their "scattering in Israel" is a sign of their special status rather than the curse. Numbers 25 and 31 are clearly linked with Genesis 34 and Exodus 32. As Exodus 32 reverses the curse of Genesis 34 I suggest that Numbers 25 and 31 function in the same way. Given the interest in the Genesis 49 curses displayed by the redactor of Numbers this suggestion gains in plausibility.

I have tried to bring four biblical texts into dialogue. Genesis 34 records the act which brings down Jacob's curse in Genesis 49:5-7. Exodus 32 is the turning point in the fortunes of the tribe of Levi whilst Numbers 25 is the final act of Levitical zeal for God which transforms and guarantees the new status of the tribe. As the violence is transformed so too is the curse.

## How Does the Patriarchal Story in Genesis 34 Relate to the Mosaic Period?

### *Moberly's* Old Testament of the Old Testament

Having seen how Genesis 34 resonated through the rest of the Old Testament we need to turn our attention to the question of how Genesis 34 fits into the metanarrative. We shall explore how Genesis 34, as a Patriarchal story, relates to the Mosaic era and then, in turn, to the Christian era.

---

90 Num 25:8-9.

The relationship between the Patriarchal period and the Mosaic period has been fruitfully explored by Walter Moberly in his study, *The Old Testament of the Old Testament* (1992). In this section I shall briefly outline part of Moberly's argument and then consider its implications for reading Genesis 34.

Moberly draws a series of contrasts between the Patriarchal religion and Mosaic Yahwism *as presented in the Pentateuchal documents.*[91] As the heart of the difference lies the patriarchal "matter-of-fact worship of one God, with its corresponding absence of a sense of religious choice."[92] That is to say that the call to have no gods but Yahweh, so central to Mosaic Yahwism, is absent from the religion of Abraham, Isaac and Jacob.

On the one hand this leads to a lack of conflict with Canaanite religion. Genesis is surprisingly "open" to Canaanites. Although some are portrayed negatively (most notably Sodom and its king in chs. 14 and 19) the overwhelming impression is that the Canaanites are no worse than the patriarchs. Indeed, at times Canaanites are shown as, or more, positively than Abraham (Abimelek in ch. 20 and Melchizedek in ch. 14).[93]

On the other hand patriarchal religion differs from Mosaic in a number of ways. First, the patriarchs had no cultic centre in contrast with later Yahwistic focus on Shechem, Bethel or Jerusalem.[94] Second, trees and pillars play some role in patriarchal religion[95] whilst they are banned in Mosaic religion.[96] Third, Sabbath and dietary laws, crucial to Mosaic Yahwism, have no role in Genesis 12-50.[97] Fourth, the patriarchs, unlike later Israel, have no need of prophets or priests to mediate between themselves and God. Fifth, in Genesis the

---

91 Moberly, 1992b, ch. 3. What interests us in this study are not the contrasts between the religion of the historical patriarchs and later Yahwism but the contrasts which later biblical authors saw between the two phases in the story. It is reasonable to think that the latter distinctions offer clues to the former but I wish to avoid speculation and controversy about the historical reality behind the patriarchal traditions in the Bible.

92 Ibid., p. 99.

93 Ibid., pp. 88-89.

94 Which is not to say that Jerusalem is not foreshadowed in the final shaping of Gen 14 (Salem) and 22 (Moriah).

95 Gen 12:6-7; 13:18; 21:35; 28:18, 22; 31:45; 35:14.

96 Ex 23:24; 34:13; Lev 26:1; Deut 16:21-22.

97 Moberly thinks that even though circumcision is prominent in the covenant of Genesis 17 it does not have the exclusivist significance that it does in later texts. In support of this claim Moberly draws attention to the fact that Ishmael is the one circumcised for Isaac is not yet born. However, circumcision does mark out Abraham's descendants from those who are not, as Genesis 34 makes clear. Moberly sees Genesis 34 as a special case of anachronism, but what concerns us is the role of circumcision in Genesis 12-50 not the Abraham of history. To this we may add that Mosaic Israel recognised the "special" relationship between themselves and the closely related descendants of Ishmael and Esau. It seems that circumcision is seen as a boundary marker in Genesis 12-50.

Canaanites are regarded as legitimate owners of the land *for the present* with Israelite ownership a thing of the future.[98] Obviously to the Mosaic generation that future was present reality and thus they would have a different attitude towards Cannanite ownership of the land. Sixth, in contrast to Yahwism there is not much emphasis placed upon the moral obedience of the patriarchs. Finally, the central Mosaic notion of holiness has no place in patriarchal religion.

> The concept of holiness, from Exod 3.15 onward, focuses the exclusive, demanding, regulated, mediated and sanctuary-centred relationship between YHWH and Israel, while the absence of holiness in patriarchal religion equally epitomises its open, unstructured, and non-located, unaggressive nature, its "ecumenical bonhomie".[99]

There is a clear discontinuity between the religion of Abraham and that of Moses with the turning point being the revelation of God *as Yahweh* at the burning bush.[100] However, the biblical writers also saw their Mosaic religion as standing in a clear continuity with Abraham's. Moberly very helpfully explores the relation between the "dispensations" by analogy with Christian views on the relationship between Old Testament and New Testament.[101] Christians see that "the religious practices of the Old Testament were entirely proper within their own context, but insofar as Christ has initiated a new period of history, the former requirements no longer necessarily obtain."[102] Nevertheless, there is "a genuinely common underlying dynamic"[103] between the testaments.

The patriarchal stories as we have them have already been shaped under the influence of Mosaic religion, but not so far as to destroy their dispensational distinctiveness. What is very clear is that the Old Testament writers are in no doubt that the El of Abraham *is* the Yahweh of Moses[104] and that the plan being worked out by Yahweh is a new stage in the *same plan* being worked out by El Shaddai. Patriarchal religion may no longer be always authoritative in light of the new revelation, but it was appropriate in its own context. Having said this, the lives of the fathers of the nation, especially Abraham, Jacob and Joseph, are all in some ways paradigmatic for the life of Israel.[105] Abraham's faith and obedience, for example, are a model response to Israel's God for the nation to

---

98 Gen 12:7; 13:15-16; 15:18; 17:8; 28:13-14.

99 Moberly, 1992b., p. 104. This expression is from Wenham: "There is an air of ecumenical bonhomie about the patriarchal religion which contrasts with the sectarian exclusiveness of the Mosaic age." (Wenham, 1980, p. 184). Wenham's article provides still more differences between the patriarchal and the Mosaic ages.

100 Ex 3.

101 Moberly, 1992, ch.4.

102 Ibid., p. 129.

103 Ibid., p. 129.

104 Ibid., p. 131.

105 Ibid., p. 132.

imitate.

Now the continuity between Genesis 12-50 and Exodus 3ff. is marked by (a) promise and fulfilment as well as (b) typology.

(a) The promise given to Abraham of descendants who would live in a covenant relationship with him in the land of Canaan lies at the heart of the stories. It is this promise which is fulfilled in Mosaic Israel living in its promised land. This is a clear continuity.

(b) The two fundamental traditions of Israel, the exodus deliverance and the giving of the torah, are typologically foreshadowed in the story of Abraham. To take just two examples, Abraham's time in Egypt[106] is a type of Israel's time in Egypt and its exodus. Similarly, in Genesis 22, Abraham's acts are clearly set up as a model of torah obedience.[107]

Thus there is both continuity and discontinuity between the Old Testament (Mosaic Yahwism) and the Old Testament of the Old Testament (patriarchal religion). Having examined Moberly's thesis, with which I am in substantial agreement, we can ask how our understanding of Genesis 34 is informed by it.

### *Genesis 34 Within the "Old Testament of the Old Testament"*

First of all, we need to note the continuities between Genesis 34 and Mosaic Yahwism. Most obviously rape was considered wrong by the Jacobites in Genesis 34 just as it was by later Israel. Thus Israelite readers would be expected to agree with the verdict of the brothers. Indeed, it looks as though the story has been shaped and retold in terms of later Israelite categories. This is most notable in the expression "folly in Israel"[108] which seems to be an anachronistic understanding of the ancestral family of Israel representing the whole of the nation-to-come.[109] Thus Shechem offends not just against the standards of Israel the man but also, from a Mosaic perspective, against those of Israel the nation.

Another piece of Yahwistic shaping of the story is evidenced in the description of Dinah's status as "defiled". This is primarily a cultic term belonging to Priestly terminology found nowhere in Genesis apart from Chapter 34, in which it occurs three times.[110] It is out of step with the lack of holiness categories in patriarchal religion noted by Moberly and points strongly to a typological *retelling* of the tale. To this we shall return, but for now we

---

106 Gen 12:10-13:2.
107 Moberly, 1992b, pp. 144-145.
108 Gen 34:7.
109 Here I stand in strong sympathy with the historical critics. See too Sternberg, 1987, p. 455.
110 Gen 34:5, 13, 27.

may simply note the continuity in judgements between the sons (as portrayed in the narrative) and the Mosaic implied readers.

Intermarriage with Canaanites was disapproved of by the patriarchs as well as by Mosaic believers. However, Moberly notes that *in practice* some of Jacob's sons did marry foreigners[111] and adds that "it is striking that with each prohibition on marrying a Canaanite woman no religious reason is given."[112] We recall Steinberg's thesis that in Genesis marriage serves to establish patrilineal descent within the line of Terah. Obviously exogamy is out of order within such kinship structures. This stands in contrast to marriages which are used to establish alliances and thus which encourage exogamy. Hamor and Shechem propose a marriage-alliance and Steinberg sees this as fundamentally objectionable on the patriarchal pattern *but not for explicitly religious reasons.* Nevertheless, in light of the sons' reference to circumcision as a covenant sign in their justification for not allowing the marriage[113] it is better to see the patriarchal objection as having *some* religious foundation – perhaps one which merges with and justifies the anthropological explanation proposed by Steinberg.[114] As I see it, the difference is that the issue of *idolatry* is not an explicit motive for the patriarchs' objection to intermarriage. Mosaic religion develops a *stronger* religious reason to resist intermarriage with Canaanites which majors on idolatry.[115] This dimension seems to be missing from Genesis 34 although it may be hinted at in Jacob's command to his family in 35:2-3 to remove the foreign gods they have, purify themselves and go to Bethel to worship at God's altar. Given that Jacob apparently had no principled objection to a marriage between Dinah and a circumcised Shechem, it seems clear that his reference to idols in 35:2-3 was not connected by him with any objection to intermarriage. What we may have here is another indication of a typological retelling of the story so as to make connections with later readers. Perhaps the story drops clues to prompt the readers to see in the disapproval of intermarriage a *typological precursor* of the later, idolatry objection. This is not to claim that the sons had an idolatry objection themselves but that the idolatry objection brings out the *sensus plenior* of the original objection.

A third continuity is that circumcision is a sign of the covenant between Abraham's descendants and God marking them off from the nations in Canaan. God instituted the covenant in Genesis 17 and Genesis 34:15 quotes directly from that monumental chapter clearly linking the two. Later Israel, especially in the post-exilic period, made circumcision into a defining identity marker for the

---

111 Joseph in Gen 41:50-52; Judah in Gen 38:2; Simeon in Gen 46:10. Though see Chapter Four, fn. 104.

112 Moberly, 1992, p. 90.

113 Gen 34:15 clearly alludes to Gen 17:10 which connects circumcision with the Abrahamic covenant.

114 Or some other explanation such as that of Pitt Rivers, 1977.

115 Deut 7:1-4; Num 25.

nation. Even earlier the Philistines were looked down upon as "uncircumcised"[116] and thus not in a covenant relationship with Yahweh as Israel was. Circumcision may not have had such polemical or exclusivistic overtones in patriarchal religion, but it certainly did serve to mark Abraham's descendants apart from others. This mark in the flesh was a sign of the *same covenant* in both patriarchal and Mosaic religion and the Yahwistic readers of the story can be expected to agree with the brothers of Dinah in their objection to Dinah marrying an uncircumcised man.

Family solidarity is important in Israel with its many laws that protect the centrality of marriage and the family. Jacob's emotional distance from Dinah would be a failure on his part whichever dispensation he lived in and the sons' anger at her rape is likewise proper in both ages.

Finally, the *lex talionis* was central to the torah justice system. The punishment must fit and not exceed the crime. Although it is not certain that the narrator intends us to think that it operated in patriarchal times, he does wish us to see it as pre-Mosaic. God says to Noah after the flood that "whoever sheds the blood of man, by man shall his blood be shed"[117] indicating that the intuition behind the law of the *talion* predates the patriarchs. It seems fairly certain that the response of the sons would have been considered disproportionate in both stages of the plot. Certainly, Jacob saw it as such[118] and, as we have seen, there are good reasons for thinking that the narrator intended us to agree with him.

Having seen some of the continuities we need to direct our gaze to some of the discontinuities which have bearing on Genesis 34.

In Deuteronomy and Joshua the Canaanites are to be totally obliterated.[119] They must not be intermarried with nor must any kind of other alliance be entered into lest they lead Israel into idolatry – annihilation is the only way forward. This stands in contrast to the "ecumenical bonhomie" of Genesis 12-50 where good relations with the Canaanites were the ideal. We have here what Goldingay refers to as a "contextual contradiction."[120] Genesis does not disapprove of the destruction of the Canaanites *under Joshua* but this is seen as a future course of action and *not appropriate for the present*. Genesis affirms that the land of Canaan will be given to Abraham's descendants[121] but *only*

---

116 1 Sam 17:26.
117 Gen 9:6.
118 Gen 49:5-7.
119 The literature on Holy War in Israel is vast. The classic work is Von Rad's *Holy War in Ancient Israel*. The 1991 Eerdmans edition has an especially helpful introduction by Ben Ollenburger setting Von Rad's work in context and a very useful annotated bibliography by Judith Sanderson on selected works dealing with Holy War since Von Rad wrote.
120 See, p. 81.
121 Gen 12:7; 13:14-17; 15:18-20.

when the wickedness of the locals reaches its peak is Israel warranted[122] in dispossessing them.[123] The Canaan of Abraham's day was a place of sin (Sodom and Shechem) but also a place where God is feared (Abimelek and Melchizedek). Consequently, land acquired by patriarchs was legally purchased[124] and not taken by force because, for the time being, the land belonged to its inhabitants. Jacob himself bought some land at Shechem from the sons of Hamor[125] and modelled the proper, peaceful model of Israelite-Canaanite relations. This harmony was shattered by the terrible actions of one of those who had sold land to Jacob.

It seems to me that this discontinuity is of considerable significance. Some commentators have moved from observing that the sack of Shechem serves as a prototype of the later conquest of Canaan to seeing narratorial approval of the attack.[126] What needs to be appreciated is that *in the context of Genesis 12-50* the sack of Shechem is right out of step with the approved paradigm of Israelite-Canaanite relations[127] so it would be surprising to find such violent behaviour approved of. The day for such massacres is not yet and even a later Yahwistic narrator or reader could see that behaviour which would be approved of under Joshua may be wrong in Jacob's day. As argued in the first section of this chapter it was seen as wrong in its context by the redactors of the Pentateuch. Simeon and Levi did *not* act out of zeal for Yahweh as Joshua did, nor at a command from God. When one considers the stereotypical common components of a Yahweh War[128] it is clear that although the action of the sons is an *antitype* of such a war, *it does not itself constitute a Holy War*. Prior to Holy War the will of God is either given[129] or sought;[130] the soldiers prepare spiritually by sacrificing,[131] consecrating themselves,[132] circumcising themselves, if necessary,[133] abstaining from sexual relations[134] and making

---

122 The conquest of Canaan is one of the most difficult themes in the Old Testament for modern readers to find sympathy with. Even among readers who would agree that God did indeed authorise Israel to conquer Canaan there is a feeling of considerable discomfort. It is a difficulty which must be lived with. Some helpful works which try to help modern readers understand the conquest include Craigie, 1978; J. Wenham, 1985.
123 Gen 15:16.
124 Gen 23.
125 Gen 33:19.
126 E.g. West, 1980; Ross, 1996; Geller, 1990.
127 So Wenham, 2000, pp. 118-119.
128 On which see Von Rad, 1991, ch. 1 and Longman and Reid, 1995, Ch. 2. The analysis in the main text is based mainly upon Longman and Reid.
129 E.g. Josh 5:13-15.
130 E.g. 1 Sam 23:1-6.
131 E.g. 1 Sam 13.
132 E.g. Josh 5:5.
133 E.g. Josh 5.
134 E.g. Lev 15:16-18; 2 Sam 11:11.

religious vows.[135] The war camp was also made ritually clean.[136] In Genesis 34 no mention is made of God's will nor any of the above preparations; this makes the actions of Simeon and Levi stand apart from the Holy War traditions.

During a Yahweh War we find elements such as a worship march into battle[137] and the presence of the Ark of the Covenant.[138] It is not surprising to find these elements missing from Genesis 34 and it must be said that the Dinah story *does* include one element central to Holy War stories: the limited number of Israelite warriors and weapons followed by a victory against odds.[139] This enables Genesis 34 to serve as a type but we should not be too quick to see this as a presentation of the massacre *as* a Holy War. The chief reason for the small number of Israelite soldiers in the Holy War tradition is to draw attention to what is the central theme: that *Yahweh himself is the chief warrior of Israel* and that it is he who defeats Israel's foes.[140] It is noticeable that the victory in Genesis 34 is not explicitly[141] attributed to Yahweh, again marking it off from Holy War texts.

After a Yahweh War there is praise,[142] the enemies, if they live within the boundaries of the promised land, are put under the ban (חרם) and the plunder belongs to Yahweh.[143] In Genesis 34 there is no praise to God for the victory,[144] only the men are killed and the plunder seems to belong to the sons, again setting our story apart from Holy Wars.

However, despite seeing the sons' actions as wrong a later Israelite could not help but notice how they do, in some ways, serve to foreshadow the day when such massacres will be "appropriate". All the early Jewish interpretations we investigated in Chapter Three noticed this dimension of the story. The story, as it stands, paradoxically serves as a antitype of the conquest, as well as a model

---

135 Nu 21:2; Jud 11:36; 1 Sam 14:24.

136 Deut 23:9-14.

137 E.g. 2 Chr 20:20-25; Ps 149:6-9; Nu 10:35-36.

138 Josh 5:13-15; 1 Sam 4:4; 2 Sam 11:11.

139 Cf. Jud 7; 1 Sam 17.

140 E.g. Ex 14:21; Josh 10:1-15; Josh 5:19-21.

141 Some think that the protection which God provides for his people in 35:5 implicitly attributes the victory to Yahweh (e.g. Sternberg, 1987). However, I would argue that this merely indicates God's covenant faithfulness to Jacob's family even when they err. It remains the case that even if my arguments fail to convince this is at best a very subtle and indirect attribution of the victory to Yahweh and it contrasts with the usual explicit Holy War attributions.

142 Ex 15:1-8; Jud 5:4-5; Ps 98.

143 Josh 6:24; 7; 1 Sam 30:23-25.

144 The journey to set up an altar for worship at Bethel (Gen 35:1-5) is not so as to worship Yahweh for the victory he has given at Shechem. If it were so Jacob would not maintain his insistence that his sons have done wrong (Gen 49:5-7). The Bethel altar (Gen 35:6-7) is connected with the earlier revelation there (Gen 28:10-22) and the patriarchal promises.

of a wrong response to evil. It may seem very odd that the narrator would take an action of which he *disapproves* and make it a model of the conquest of Canaan of which he *does* approve. I concede that it is strange but not unprecedented. It seems to me that exactly the same kind of thing is found in Genesis 12:10-13:2. There we read of Abraham's shameful behaviour in Egypt. It is most plausible to see narratorial disapproval of Abraham's behaviour there[145] and some qualified approval of Pharaoh.[146] At the same time there is also a clear typology at work. Abraham in Egypt pictures Israel in slavery there many years later.[147] As the earlier Pharaoh suffers plagues at the hand of God, so does the later Pharaoh. As Abraham leaves Egypt with more riches, so Israel leaves Egypt having plundered the Egyptians. Indeed it is partly due to this double function of the massacre in Genesis 34 that readers have been so unclear of whether the narrator sees Simeon and Levi as the "good guys" or the "bad guys". My analysis would indicate that *they are, on balance, "bad guys" but that they are also a partial type of the later "good guys"*. I say *partial* type because the difference is that Joshua acts when the sin of the Amorite had run its course (unlike Simeon and Levi), at the command of Yahweh (unlike Simeon and Levi) and out of zeal for Yahweh (unlike Simeon and Levi).

In conclusion, we may say that the implied readers of Genesis (who were not "living" in the Patriarchal period depicted in the book) would see that certain continuities and discontinuities in dispensation have hermeneutical importance in the ethical reading of Genesis 34. They will agree with the sons' condemnation of Shechem, their disapproval of exogamy and their stress on circumcision. They will also feel uncomfortable with their deception and their use of the covenant sign in that ruse. They will disapprove of the excessive force used in retaliation and despite approving of the virtues of family solidarity which led to their anger they will have to condemn the angry men, as Jacob does, as the time for conquest is still future. They will frown upon Jacob's emotional detachment from Dinah and his initial condemnation, but will sympathise strongly with his more considered response in 49:5-7. Finally, they will see in the massacre *at one and the same time* an ethical model to be avoided *and* a partial type of the conquest which is to be approved of. This, or so I maintain, is how the story was to be appropriated in Act Four.

### Genesis 34 from the Perspective of the New Testament

*The Links between the Old Testament and the New Testament*

The relationship between the two testaments of the Christian Bible is a matter

---

145 Contra Gunkel, 1997. So Von Rad, 1972; Polzin, 1975; Wenham, 1991.
146 Contra Sternberg, 1987, p. 316.
147 So Cassuto, 1964; Pratt, 1973; Wenham, 1991.

of considerable complexity and controversy.[148] There is no single, monolithic New Testament theology on the relation of the church age and the pre-church age but it does seem that strong, common threads run through the entire New Testament such that their distinctive voices can be heard together as a harmony rather than as a discord. The divergent theologies give rise to numerous examples of formal contradictions[149] and many would claim some substantial contradictions. What is clear is that all the New Testament texts share the same worldview and, to a very great extent, the same basic approach to the relationship between the people of God in the pre- and post-Jesus periods. N.T. Wright overviews all four Gospels, Acts, Paul and Hebrews and maintains that they all share the same story world.[150] It seems to me that we could add 1 Peter and other New Testament texts such as Revelation[151] to this list. *All* these texts see the story of Jesus as the climax to which Israel's own story pointed and in which Israel's story is fulfilled. Jesus' story is told *as* the story of Israel writ small. And Israel's story is part of a larger story still, that of the relationship between the creator God and his creation. Essentially Wright's whole New Testament theology project is giving textual support for the claims made in Chapter Two of this thesis about the metanarrative. The various ways in which the story is told in the New Testament could be boiled down to the following: the creator God wishes to bring salvation/blessing to his world through Israel but this becomes impossible because Israel, through her disobedience to the torah, becomes part of the problem standing in need of salvation herself. This is the story presupposed by the Synoptic Gospels and against which those Gospels must be read if they are to make sense. The story of Jesus is then the story of how God brought salvation (and judgement) to Israel through her messiah and brought her exile to an end in his death. The resurrection of Jesus marks the return of Israel from exile and the inauguration of a new age. Now that Israel is healed through the messiah the nations can join in worshipping Israel's God and the Spirit can be given. Jesus thus marks the inauguration of the new age and it is this key thought that lies behind the New Testament appropriation of the Old Testament with its shedding of some aspects of Jewish religion and the retention of others.

This section will briefly outline central features of New Testament appropriations of Israel's faith providing a background for our re-examination of Genesis 34. Naturally, the difficult and contentious nature of many of the issues to be considered means that I will not even be able to survey all the alternatives, let alone defend the line I have taken. It is hoped that at least the main thrust of what I sketch carries some plausibility.

---

148 See Baker, 1991.
149 See Chapter Two. A good example is R. Hays on New Testament teachings on divorce in Hays, 1996a.
150 Wright, 1992, ch. 13.
151 Beale, 1999.

*Abraham and Christ*

We will first address the issue of how New Testament writers saw the relationship between the Abrahamic covenant and the church.[152] Abraham was highly esteemed within the early church as he was in Second Temple Judaism. He was a model of faithful endurance[153] and obedience to God.[154] The promise of covenant blessing to Abraham's descendants was important in Judaism[155] and its fullest treatment in early Christian literature comes from Paul. In Galatians 3-4 we find an extended discussion of the Abrahamic covenant and its relationship with the community of Jesus. The passage is much discussed and difficult in several places but the broad argument, as far as it relates to Abraham, seems to run as follows: God had declared Abraham to be righteous because he believed the divine promise.[156] God had promised Abraham that all nations would be blessed through him[157] and this is exactly what is now happening through the preaching of the gospel. In other words, *Gentiles coming to faith in Christ is how the promise to Abraham is being fulfilled!* Paul then embarks on an important discussion of the torah to which we shall return later. Suffice it to say, Paul argues that torah obedience cannot bring the promise to Abraham to pass and that it is faith that makes one a son of Abraham.[158] This brings to mind the words of John the Baptist in the double tradition that physical descent from Abraham was no guarantee against God's judgement and that God can raise children of Abraham from the very stones.[159] Paul, by opposing "works of law" to the "hearing of faith,"[160] seems to be departing from standard Second Temple readings of Abraham[161] which saw him as living according to Mosaic law thus combining faith[162] and works.[163]

In Romans 3:27-4:25 Paul contends with Jews who saw Abraham as an ideal Jew and one who, as themselves, could boast in his special covenant status.[164] But Abraham has no grounds for such boasting for he was declared righteous by faith and not by any "works of torah."[165] He was "justified" *before* he was

---

152 See Calvert, 1993, On Abraham in Paul see Witherington III, 1994b, ch. 4.

153 Heb 2:14-16; 6:13-20; 11:8-12, 17-19.

154 Jas 2:21-24 cf. Sir. 44:20; 1 Macc 2:52; Jub 17:17-18.

155 Jub 15:9-10; Ps. Phil. Bib. Ant. 7.4; 1 Qap Gen 21:8-14. See Calvert, 1993.

156 Gal 3:6 cf. Gen 15:6.

157 Gal 3:8 cf. Gen 12:3; 18:18; 22:18.

158 Gal 3:6-7.

159 Mt 3:9; Lk 3:8 cf. Isa 51:1-2. See also Jn 8:39 and Rom 9:7.

160 Gal 3:5.

161 So Calvert, 1993.

162 Jub 11:6-17; 12:1-5, 16-21; 20:6-9; Josephus Ant. 1.2.1.154-157.

163 Jub 15:1-2; 16:20; Sir. 44:10; 4 Macc 13:13-18.

164 Rom 2:17, 23; 3:27.

165 The controversy surrounding what Paul means by "works of torah" boils down to whether he refers to the attempt to earn salvation by obedience to the law (the traditional Protestant reading) or whether he refers to boundary markers for the covenant nation

circumcised[166] and is thus the father of both the circumcised (Jews) and the uncircumcised (Gentile believers) with his circumcision being merely a seal of a righteousness he *already* had by faith.[167] Circumcision (which Paul saw as a paradigmatic "work of the torah") added nothing to his covenant status. In 4:16-17 Paul rejects the notion that one must obey the torah to be a descendant of Abraham – that, argued the apostle, has *never* been the case.[168]

So for Paul, Christian believers are children of Abraham from many nations – the fulfilment of that age-old covenant. Here we see fairly simple continuity but it is complicated by the role of the Mosaic torah. To this topic we now turn.

*Jesus and Moses*

What exactly did the early Christians think of the torah?[169] This question is one of the most hotly debated issues in New Testament studies with a small cottage industry growing up around interpreting Paul's view never mind the interest in other texts. There is a growing, though by no means unanimous[170] consensus that the Lutheran view, according to which the Jews used the law to earn a relationship with God, is a misleading anachronism which needs exorcising from New Testament studies.[171]

It seems appropriate to begin our study with the Gospels. Here too there is great controversy but I hope that what follows is broadly correct. Each of the Gospels takes a different angle on the place of the law and we should not lose sight of their distinctives: Mark's Jesus makes certain ritual aspects of the law

---

(primarily circumcision, Sabbath and food laws). On the former see Westerholm, 1988. On the latter see Dunn, 1998.

166 Rom 4:10-12; Gen 15:6 and 17.

167 Rom 4:11.

168 See too Rom 9-11.

169 On Jesus and Moses in Paul see Witherington III, 1994b, pp. 51-72; Dunn, 1998, pp. 128-161.

170 Some have defended a modified but essentially Lutheran reading of Paul for a post-Sanders generation. See especially, S. Westerholm, 1988.

171 The revolution really dates from E.P. Sanders' landmark text, *Paul and Palestinian Judaism* (1977) in which Sanders demonstrated that Jews in the Second Temple period did not think of the torah as a means of earning salvation (contra Luther and his heirs) but rather of maintaining a covenant relationship which had been given by grace (it is increasingly acknowledged that Sanders' work needs some qualifications but he still seems to be essentially correct). Whatever Paul was criticising in the Judaism of his day it could not be legalism of the variety Protestantism had seen there. Since Sanders there has been, and continues to be, a revolution in Pauline studies. Some continue to maintain the traditional view modified to meet Sanders-like objections (e.g. Westerholm), others have used Sanders to totally rethink Paul and the Law along the lines of debate about the boundary markers for the people of God (e.g. J.D.G. Dunn, N.T. Wright, R. Hayes). Some think that Paul is totally inconsistent in his views, others that his views changed over time and others that his views cohere well.

redundant;[172] Matthew sees Jesus as endorsing but surpassing the torah;[173] Luke-Acts is rather conservative about torah observance but sees the torah in a strong salvation-historical framework[174] which renders torah central only until John the Baptist[175] after which its role becomes primarily prophetic; John sees Jesus as replacing the torah not because it was bad but because it had been rendered obsolete now that its fulfilment was here in Jesus.[176] All Gospels are aware that the coming of Jesus changes the place of torah.

Central to Jesus' relationship to torah is his hermeneutic of love. Jesus identifies the heart of the torah as the twin commands to love God[177] and to love one's neighbour.[178] He uses these commands to interpret the intent of the others (not to reject the others[179]) and thus has a humanitarian approach to Sabbath,[180] prefers mercy to sacrifice[181] and clearly saw some commands (justice, mercy and faithfulness) as more important than others.[182] Although Jesus never actually breaks Sabbath rules from Moses, he is somewhat daring with them and claims authority over the Sabbath to interpret, transform or reject it as he sees fit.[183] Indeed Jesus makes little use of the commands of the law in his ethical teaching, preferring to speak on his own authority, even though his teaching stands in continuity with Old Testament demands.[184] The Sermon on the Mount provides some of the most controversial comments by Jesus about the law.[185] It seems safe to say of it that for Matthew *the law is only of abiding*

---

172 Mk 7:14-15.

173 Mt 5:17-48.

174 So Blomberg, 1984, Moo, 1992.

175 Lk 16:16.

176 John 1:16-17. To my mind, the most plausible interpretation of these verses is that of Carson who reads them as follows: "From the fullness of his grace we have all received [lit.] grace [in Christ] after grace [in torah]. *For* the law was given through Moses; grace and truth came through Jesus Christ." On Carson's view the second "grace" is the law of Moses which is replaced by a fuller "grace" in Christ. The point is that this reflects a fundamentally positive view of torah in John even if it is now surpassed.

177 Deut 6:5.

178 Lev 19; Mt 22:34-40 par. Cf. Mt 7:12.

179 So Moo, 1992, p. 452.

180 Mk 2:27.

181 Mt 9:13; 12:7.

182 Mt 23:23.

183 Mt 12:8 par.

184 Mt 5:17; 7:12.

185 The antitheses ("You have heard... but I say to you... Mt 5:17-48) have been seen by some to have Jesus revoking the torah, by others to have him adding to the torah and by still others to have him simply agreeing with the torah! He certainly cannot be rejecting the torah in the light of 5:17 and a study of the antitheses suggests that Jesus transcends the Mosaic commands even if he does not reject them. Jesus is seen to fulfil

*significance when filtered through Christ.*

There was one area in which Jesus seemed to stand in obvious discontinuity with Moses and that is in the area of purity regulations.[186] Mark seems happy to strip away the ritual dimensions of the torah and Matthew, whilst not going that far, sees the ritual aspects as less important than, and worthless without, the weightier matters of justice, mercy and faithfulness.[187] The transformation of the ritual parts of the torah was taken up and developed by other New Testament texts such as Paul's epistles, Acts and the letter to the Hebrews. Paul argued that purity as it relates to food is no longer relevant in the Kingdom of God. All foods, as Mark had noted,[188] are now clean and Jewish food laws no longer bind the Christian[189] although Christians may follow food regulations if their consciences were especially sensitive.[190] It is not that these writers were saying that food laws were wrong. Rather, what is being said is that in the light of the new eschatological transformations brought about in Jesus, food laws are no longer relevant: the plot has moved on. How so?

To begin to see why the arrival of Jesus was seen to initiate these and other changes we need to appreciate the role of torah in Second Temple Judaism. Torah observance was the identity-marker for the covenant nation marking Israel off from the Gentiles.[191] Particular laws stood out as of special significance: circumcision, food laws and Sabbath. Those who observed these were the true people of God. Now the prophets of Israel had seen a day when the nations would join Israel in worship of Yahweh,[192] but in the 1st century Gentile converts had to be circumcised and never had full status as citizens of Israel. Those in the Jesus Movement believed that the eschatological new age had dawned and that the Gentiles were now to join with Israel in a single community. This, however, raised difficult issues about the identity markers of Israel. Did Gentile Christians have to be circumcised or follow food and Sabbath regulations? In Acts, James and Peter seem to agree with Paul that God

---

the law and whatever the exact nuances of this it is clear that it involves some transformation of it.

186 The woman with the flow of blood would make all who touched her unclean (Lev 15:25-30) yet Jesus has no qualms about being touched by her and is not unclean as a result. On the contrary, she is made clean (Mk 5:27). To enter a house with a dead body and to touch a corpse contaminated in a similar way (Num 19:11) yet again when Jesus does this he remains pure and the dead live (Mk 5:41). The same story could be told about touching lepers (Mk 1:44//) and, as far as the Pharisees were concerned, eating with the sinners would pollute and yet Jesus made a habit of doing this (Mk 2:14-17; Mt 11:19; 21:28-32; Lk 15:1-32; 19:1-10).

187 Mt 23:23.

188 Mk 7:14-15.

189 Gal 2:11-19; 1 Cor 8; 10:14-11:1; Rom 14:1-15: see too Acts 10:9-23a.

190 Rom 14:14.

191 Jub 20:6-10; 21:21-24; 22:16-19; Jos. Ant. 1.10.5.192.

192 Isa 2:2-4; Mic 4:1-3; Isa 25:6.

can even accept the uncircumcised[193] but James[194] seems to have remained attached to Mosaic purity regulations[195] leading to the compromise of Acts 15 – a compromise that Paul seems *not* to have enforced.[196] For Paul, Gentile believers are *full* members of the community apart from their observance of Jewish torah rules.[197] Food purity laws mark Israel apart from the Gentiles, but the time has now arrived in which Jew and Gentile are united in Christ. Food laws, according to some New Testament writers, are obviously inappropriate at such a time.[198] Paul now interprets purity in terms of moral intentions and not foods,[199] a move which Chilton describes as "one of the most important theological achievements of the New Testament."[200]

It was not food laws but circumcision which was to become the great dividing issue within the early church and the issue was a live one in some churches well beyond the second century. Circumcision was considered necessary for conversion to Judaism by most first century Jews[201] and it is not surprising that many early Christians assumed that it would be required for conversion to Christianity given that Christians saw themselves as a transformed version of Judaism. The Gospels make no mention of the circumcision issue[202] although in the book of Acts "Luke" clearly sides with Paul's view that circumcision was no longer necessary now that the new age had begun.[203] Paul insisted that circumcision must not be imposed on Gentile converts to Christianity as they had already received the Spirit as a sign that they belong to the family of Abraham by faith[204] and this was without their being circumcised. Paul's discussion of circumcision cannot be separated from his discussion of torah, for to Paul circumcision is a prime example of a work of the law. To discuss Paul's view of the law adequately at this point will be impossible. It seems to me that the best way to proceed is to traverse the books

---

193 Chilton, 1997, p. 993.
194 The letter of James takes a very positive approach to "the perfect law that gives freedom" (1:25) although arguably the law in James is the Mosaic torah transformed for the messianic age (Schreiner, 1997; Bauckham, 1999).
195 Gal 2:1-10.
196 1 Cor 8.
197 See Dunn on justification by faith (1998, pp. 354-359). See Donaldson on faith in Christ rather than torah as a boundary marker for God's people (1997).
198 Acts 10-11; Gal 2.
199 1 Cor 8:7-13; Rom 14:13-23.
200 Chilton, 1997, p. 988.
201 Esther 8:17 LXX; Jdt 14:10; Josephus Ant 13.9.1; Philo Mig Ab 89-93.
202 Which, in passing, indicates their concern not to add sayings of Jesus received prophetically in Christian congregations to their accounts of what Jesus had said in his lifetime. If there was a single issue on which this would have been done circumcision was probably it.
203 Acts 15.
204 Gal 3:1-5.

of Romans and Galatians to sketch the place of torah in the journey of the promise from Abraham to Jesus.[205]

God had promised Abraham that the world would be blessed through Israel and we have seen that Paul sees the gospel as bringing this about. So where does the law fit in? In Galatians 3 the law is presented as a problem, for on the basis of the great covenant chapter Deuteronomy 27 he thinks that "all who rely on observing the torah are under a curse"[206] and Israel was in exactly that position. Wright has argued that the curse Paul's use of Deuteronomy 27 would call to mind would be the curse *of exile* which many Jews still thought was the present experience of the nation.[207] The law seems to have introduced a problem for, with Israel under curse, the blessing of Abraham cannot reach the Gentiles. To understand why the law is problematic we need to glance at Romans. There Paul makes it abundantly clear that the law is holy, righteous and good - reflecting God's perfect will.[208] The law was given to bring life and blessing but it was unable to deliver because of Israel's sinful human nature ("the flesh").[209] Israel's history had shown the nation to be stiff-necked and disobedient and the law did not provide the power to follow its stipulations.[210] Thus the torah, when combined with "the flesh", becomes a "law of sin and death"[211] being able only to condemn. This seems to be the argument in the very controverted Romans 7: that sin used the commandment of the torah to kill Israel.[212] This does not make the law bad but it shows sin in all its "glory".[213] Of course, Israel wants to follow torah but she cannot and sin is now focused in the "self" of Romans 7 which I, following Moo,[214] take to be Paul the Jew thinking as a representative of Israel.[215] Who can rescue from this body of death? It seems as though God's promise to Abraham cannot proceed unless Israel herself is delivered, and that is what Paul's argument in Galatians 3 moves onto:

---

205 The outline which follows is based on N.T. Wright, 1991a, 1995. For an alternative approach, also located within the new perspective on Paul, see Donaldson, 1997 (esp. pp. 153-161 for a critique of Wright on Galatians). For a generally sympathetic critique of Wright on Romans see Hays, 1995.

206 Gal 3:10, cf. Deut 27:26.

207 Wright, 1991a.

208 Rom 7:12.

209 Rom 7:10; 8:3a.

210 Rom 8:7-8.

211 Rom 8:2b (cf. 7:2) taking "law" here to refer to the torah rather than some "principle" of sin and death.

212 Rom 7:7-12.

213 Rom 7:13.

214 Moo, 1996, pp. 423-431.

215 Rom 7:13-20. This is a minority view dating back to Chrysostom (according to Moo, 1996).

Christ [the representative of Israel] has redeemed us [Israel] from the curse of the law [exile] by becoming a curse for us, for it is written, "cursed is everyone who is hung on a tree" [Deut 27:26]. He redeemed us [Israel] in order that the blessing given to Abraham might come to the Gentiles through Christ Jesus so that by faith we [Christian Jews? Christian Jews and Gentiles?] might receive the promise of the Spirit."[216]

Wright thinks that the train of Paul's thinking is as follows: the law was given so as to focus sin onto Israel and then to focus it still further onto Israel's representative Messiah, Jesus. The curse of the law was laid on Jesus and he took the whole of Israel's exilic punishment on his cross. This would make the resurrection a return from exile and the end of Israel's curse. Given this logic we can see why the Gentiles are now included along with Israel in the family of Abraham and why the Spirit can be given for, according to the prophets, both these events belong to the new age on the other side of Israel's exile.[217] So Jesus' death deals with the problem of sin, which torah highlights, by focusing it onto Jesus where it is dealt a death blow. Now the post-exilic Spirit can be given in the Messiah and the believer is set free from the torah of sin and death. In Christ, the torah becomes the "torah of the Spirit of life" for it can at last deliver life.[218]

Thus for Paul, Christ is the *telos* (fulfilment? goal? end?) of the law[219] and the time of law has passed. The torah was a glorious gift that, due to sin, brought death and that is replaced with an even more glorious ministry of the Spirit.[220] The law, in contrast to the Abrahamic promise, was intended only as a temporary provision in place until the Messiah inaugurates the new age.[221] Consequently, food laws, circumcision[222] and Sabbath are no longer relevant boundary markers for the family of God. That family is now composed of Jew and Gentile united by faith and baptism in Christ.[223] The old dividing wall between Jew and Gentile symbolised by the "works of the law" has been

---

216 Gal 3:13-14.

217 A similar argument is seen in Romans 7-8. "For what the torah was powerless to do in that it was weakened by the sinful nature, God did by sending his own Son in the likeness of sinful humanity to be a sin offering. And so he condemned sin in sinful man in order that the righteous verdict of the torah [i.e., life] might be fully met in us, who do not live according to the sinful nature but according to the Spirit" (Rom 8:3-4).

218 Rom 8:2.

219 Rom 10:4.

220 2 Cor 3:7-11. On 2 Corinthians see S.J. Hafemann, *Paul, Moses and the History of Israel*, Massachusetts: Hendrickson, 1995. Hafemann argues in great detail that in 2 Corinthians 3 Paul does not contrast law and gospel but law with and law without the power of the Spirit given in Christ. This fits in well with the approach above.

221 Gal 3:15-4:7. Dunn, 1998, pp. 143-144.

222 Gal 5:13-15; Phil 3:2-4.

223 Gal 3:28.

broken down in this eschatological age.[224]

This is not to deny the ongoing *typological* significance of circumcision for New Testament authors. Picking up the promise in Deuteronomy 30:6 about God circumcising the hearts of the post-exilic Israel, Paul argues that believers are the true circumcision: those who have circumcised hearts.[225] This is another way of saying that eschatological Israel is not delineated by literal circumcision, which was now irrelevant, but by inner circumcision manifest by faith in Christ.[226] The nearest Christian equivalent of circumcision is *perhaps* baptism which marks membership of the community of believers.[227] Baptism divides the world not on the basis of race, but on that of faith, with the Galatians 3:28 baptismal formula as the magna carta of the renewed Israel: neither Jew nor Greek, neither slave nor free, neither male nor female. So the issue of Jew-Gentile exogamy, whilst it was an issue of crucial significance in the Old Testament and first century Israel, for New Testament writers[228] it was an issue of no religious relevance whatsoever.

The eschatological transformation brought in by Christ led to a reinterpretation of all the institutions and stories of Israel. The Temple with its *shekinah* glory was now replaced by Christ himself,[229] who was full of God's glory,[230] and his church[231] with its members.[232] The Jerusalem Temple was destined for judgement[233] and Jerusalem itself was replaced by a *heavenly* Jerusalem.[234] The Jewish feasts of Passover,[235] Tabernacles,[236] Dedication[237] as well as Jewish rituals in general[238] are transformed, fulfilled and replaced in Jesus. Hebrews makes much of the fact that Jesus' death replaces the ritual

---

224 Eph 2:11-22. Cf. Acts 15:11; 10:1-11:38.

225 Rom 2:28-29; Phil 3:3.

226 See this idea also in Justin Dial.Tryph 11:3; 24:1; 34:1; 43:1; 67:9; 118:2.

227 Col 2:11-12 seems to connect circumcision and baptism and Justin makes the connection explicit (Dial Tryp. 43:2). Later the link became established in the tradition.

228 This is not to say that many Christian Jews in the early church would have found it difficult. The transition to the Pauline stance was not quick nor was it uniform. On the contrary it was divisive and painful for many years.

229 Jn 2:19-22. On Jesus as replacing the Temple see especially Motyer, 1997. Motyer argues that John's Gospel was written to a post-70 CE Jewish audience traumatised by the destruction of the Temple. The Gospel responds to this concern by putting Jesus forward as the replacement for the Temple and the festivals associated with the Temple.

230 Jn 1:14.

231 1 Cor 3:16-17.

232 1 Cor 6:19-20.

233 Mark 13 par.

234 Gal 4:25-26; Heb 12:22-23; Rev 21-22. On Jerusalem in the New Testament see Walker, 1996.

235 Jn 6:25ff; 19:31-34; 1 Cor 5:7; 1 Pet 1:19; Rev 5:6, 9, 12. Hays, 1996b, pp. 35-37.

236 Jn 7-8.

237 Jn 10:22-42.

238 Jn 2:1-11.

sacrifices in the Jerusalem Temple rendering all those rituals fulfilled and thus redundant.[239] Similarly the Aaronic priesthood is replaced by the superior priesthood of Melchizedek[240] and, as mentioned earlier, purity regulations are eventually seen in terms of moral purity.[241] Even the land, which was central in Second Temple Judaism, hardly gets a mention in the New Testament nor in early Christian writings.[242] Some early Christians may have held onto Palestine as of continuing religious significance[243] and this *may* explain why Jerusalem became the first centre of the church, but by and large the land of Israel is replaced by the whole earth of which it was probably seen by some as a type[244] or by Jesus himself: the holy man who replaces holy land. I am not suggesting that *all* Christians thought *all* of these things but rather that behind them all lies the same pervasive insight and impulse: that the plot has moved on and that the new age has dawned leading to a transformation of the chrysalis of Jewish institutions into the butterflies they were always intended to become.

### Genesis 34 in the Light of the New Testament

The issue which we need to address is whether this eschatological shift will affect our appropriation of Genesis 34. I maintain that it clearly does. We shall observe discontinuity in the significance of Jew-Gentile intermarriages and of circumcision between Genesis 34 and the New Testament. Within this discontinuity we shall observe certain relevant continuities as well. Amongst these we may mention a continuity in the sexual ethics and the desire for non-violent conflict resolution, although we shall note that the New Testament accentuates the need for non-violence within and without the community of faith.

With regard to Genesis 34, two related issues stand out as discontinuous with the New Testament. First the issue of Jew-Gentile exogamy, whilst it was relevant in Genesis 34, is no longer relevant in the New Testament period. Second, circumcision was a crucial marker of the Abrahamic family in Genesis 34, but it no longer plays that role in the Pauline strand of the New Testament – the strand that eventually prevailed. This is not to say that there is not a typological continuity amidst the discontinuity. The New Testament equivalent of Jacob's family is the church and the New Testament equivalent of circumcision is faith marked by baptism.[245] Although Jew-Gentile intermarriage

---

239 Heb 9-10.

240 Heb 7-8. Hebrews contrasts not a bad and a good covenant but a good though temporary covenant with a better and everlasting one.

241 Rom 1:24-32; Gal 5:19-21; Eph 5:3-5; Col 3:5-6.

242 Allison, 1997, p. 644.

243 Acts 1:6.

244 Mt 5:5; 8:11.

245 Rom 2:28-29; Col 2:11-12.

is obviously no longer an issue on the New Testament scheme believer-unbeliever marriages are a matter of concern. Paul's teaching seems to be that if a person from a non-Christian marriage converts to Christianity they must remain with their unbelieving partner.[246] However, if the person is not married then he or she ought to choose to marry a believer.[247] So one could imagine a New Testament equivalent situation in which a Christian girl was raped by a non-Christian man. Ideally such a marriage is inappropriate, for the man is outside the baptised community of faith.

The typological links discussed earlier open up a Christian way to appropriate the typological dimension of Genesis 34. We have seen that the massacre in Genesis 34 can serve as a type of the conquest under Joshua. We need briefly to consider the New Testament appropriation of the Holy War motif and the general New Testament attitude towards violence.

Arguably, the Gospels present Jesus in the role of the divine warrior fighting the demonic powers which oppress his people and leading them in a new exodus.[248] Ironically he defeats the powers by allowing himself to be crucified and this victory through non-violent suffering left its mark on the early Christian interpretation of the Holy War theme. Both the Gospels and Paul make clear that the victory of Jesus takes place in two phases: the cross[249] and the Day of the Lord.[250] For Paul the church living between these poles is the army of Christ[251] which wears his armour[252] and bears his weapons of righteousness.[253] However, the enemies are no longer "flesh and blood" but are principalities and powers[254] and the Christian's weapons are not worldly weapons but powerful "spiritual" ones.[255] This shift was made possible by at least two things: first, the fact that the eschatological Israel of the church had no physical territory to defend and second, the model of Jesus who fought and triumphed without violence.[256]

---

246 1 Cor 7:10-14; 1 Pet 3:1-7.

247 1 Cor 7:39; 2 Cor 6:14-18 (although not about marriage the text has obvious implications for marriage).

248 Longman and Reid, 1995, chs. 7-8. On the Synoptics and the transformation (continuity and discontinuity) of the Yahweh War traditions, see especially Swartley, 1994, pp. 95-153.

249 Ibid., pp. 146-153.

250 Ibid., pp. 153-154. Developing a theme found in the prophets.

251 2 Tim 2:3-4; Phil 2:25; Phm 2; 1 Cor 9:7.

252 Eph 6:12-17; 1 Thes 5:8; Rom 13:12.

253 Eph 6:12-17; 2 Cor 6:7; 2 Cor 10:3-5.

254 Eph 6:12.

255 2 Cor 10:3-5.

256 Perhaps the Christian transformation of holy war is seen nowhere more clearly than in the book of Revelation (see now Bredin, 2003). The apocalypse is full of gory, violent images from the Yahweh War tradition but they have a radical twist. The central christological metaphor of the book is that of the apocalyptic warrior lamb (found in 1

In the Christian typology the church plays the role of Israel in the conquest. The land of Canaan is replaced by the earth which at present is under the control of principalities and powers but which God will liberate at the return of Christ. The church's battle is not against flesh and blood but rather against power-systems which oppose the Kingdom of God. Thus a Christian could legitimately read the massacre at Shechem as a type of the spiritual "violence" of the church deployed against the real violence and injustice of the world unleashed against the saints. This typological reading of the story makes no claim to be what the narrator of Genesis was getting at, but does claim to be a legitimate *re*appropriation of the story *guided by* the aims of the implied author. It does not deny the real violence of the conquest of Canaan (or the sack of Shechem) but argues that although actual violence was appropriate in Joshua's day, it is no longer appropriate now. To use the conquest story to justify physical or mental violence would be illegitimate as a *Christian* rereading of those texts. It would deny the plot developments which have subsequently taken place.[257]

So *at one level* Genesis 34 can be seen by a Christian reader as a *type of* righteous resistance to evil. Nevertheless, the Christian should, following the logic of my argument in the section on Mosaic Yahwism, refuse to see the sons' actions as *actual* righteous resistance to evil. In fact, it was very wrong and the Christian reader would agree with the implied author of Genesis in

---

Enoch 85-90) who defeats his enemies by being slain (Rev 5:6)! Hayes writes: "Rome [the beast] rules by the power of violence, but the one is the true King of kings and Lord of lords by virtue of his submission to death – precisely the opposite of armed violence against the empire. That is why he alone is worthy" (Hays, 1996a, p. 175). Following in his footsteps his army defeat the demonic trinity of dragon, beast and false prophet by "the blood of the Lamb and the word of their testimony, for they did not cling to life even in the face of death" (Rev 12:10-11). Caird says, "If God allows the monster to wage war on his people and conquer them [as in Rev 13:9-10], what must God's people do? They must allow themselves to be conquered as their Lord had done, so that like their Lord they may win a victory not of this world" (Caird, 1966, pp. 169-170).

257 The reader may feel that I am 'spiritualising' concrete dilemmas and courses of action. I would strongly deny this charge. It should be clear from my argument that Christians face concrete situations analogous to those faced by Jacob's family. It should also be clear that concrete courses of action, namely violent ones, are exposed as wrong. All that I claim is that in the Mosaic phase the sons' sinful actions could serve as a type of legitimate violence by Israel whilst in the Jesus phase it cannot serve as a type of legitimate violence by the church. For the church, it serves as a type of legitimate non-violent "warfare". This is not necessarily to deny a place for legitimate violence by states. That Holy Wars can no longer legitimate actual violence by God's people as God's people need not rule out such a role for the state. However, Old Testament Yahweh War traditions can hardly serve to defend the use of force in the modern world because modern wars are not analogous to Yahweh Wars. At best they can support the claim that sometimes the use of lethal force is not unjustified.

siding with Jacob in Genesis 49:5-7.[258] It is here that it seems appropriate to explore some of the continuities between Genesis 34 and the New Testament church.

One interesting area of relevance to Genesis 34 is that of sexual ethics. Here there seems to be little change from the Old Testament. Paul, like the Old Testament, sees sexual wrongdoing as leading to impurity[259] indicating that purity has not been exorcised from the regulatory system even though it is not a *ritual* impurity anymore.[260] The ancient Mediterranean world was marked by widespread sexual license[261] but all the New Testament documents maintain the Old Testament teachings against sexual immorality,[262] prostitution,[263] adultery[264] and homosexuality.[265] Sex seems to have been reserved for the covenant relationship of marriage and was considered impure outside of that bond. There is no explicit discussion of rape but we may feel certain that Old Testament condemnation of that was also maintained in the early Christian communities. Consequently, the early Christian would have no hesitation agreeing with the narratorial condemnation of Shechem.

We have seen that the preferred Israelite-Canaanite relations in Genesis are peaceful and avoid conflict. This preference for peaceful conflict resolutions is endorsed in Wisdom texts[266] and legal texts even if the latter, given their location in the metanarrative, do not have Canaanites in mind. The New Testament strongly continues, indeed accentuates, the Old Testament stress on non-violent conflict resolution. Anger is portrayed as generally negative[267] and Christians are urged to avoid the destructive force of anger within the community.[268] There may be times when anger is appropriate but one must not

---

258 The earliest critical interpretation of the sons which I could find is that of the Christian Ambrose. Until "recent" times it seems from my soundings in Chapter Three to have been the case that the majority of Christian readers were basically critical of the sons whilst the majority of Jewish readers saw the sons' action as, on balance, right. If my suggestion in the main text is correct, both sets of readers have picked up on some clues in the text and have missed others.

259 E.g. 1 Cor 5, Gal 5:19.

260 Chilton, 1997.

261 D.F. Wright, 1993, 1997.

262 1 Thes 4:3-5; Eph 5:5; 1 Cor 6:9-11; Gal 5:19; Eph 5:3; 2 Cor 12:21; Acts 15:20; 1 Pet 4:3; 2 Pe 2:15.

263 1 Cor 6:9-11; Rev 9:21.

264 Jas 2:11; Heb 13:4; Mt 19:9.

265 Rom 1:18-27; Jude 11.

266 Proverbs displays a strong antipathy towards anger and regular support of peaceful living: Pr 12:10, 16; 14:29; 15:1, 18; 16:7, 29, 32; 17:14; 19:11; 20:3; 22:24; 29:8, 22; 30:33; Ps 37:8; Ecc 7:9.

267 Jas 1:20.

268 Eph 4:31; Col 3:8; 1 Tim 2:8.

be quick to anger[269] and if one is justifiably angry one must deal with it quickly and carefully lest sin is committed.[270] The Christian community is called to be a community which actively strives to live in peace with itself[271] and to strive for peaceful relations with outsiders: "Make every effort to live in peace with *all* men and to be holy; without holiness no-one will see the Lord."[272] "Therefore, as we have opportunity, let us do good to *all* people, especially to those who belong to the family of believers."[273] "If it is possible, as far as it depends on you, *live at peace with everyone*."[274]

The way that Jesus taught the community to deal with insult and injury was radical and non-violent[275] so it is hard to see how a Christian reader could endorse the behaviour of Simeon and Levi even if they could sympathise with their initial anger. For the Christian reader as, so I have argued, for the implied reader, Simeon and Levi are not models to follow but to avoid, at least insofar as their deception and violence are concerned. Their anger could be seen as both legitimate and desirable but from then on they are anti-models.

## Conclusion

In conclusion, a Christian can agree with the Jacob and, I claim, the narrator in condemning the violence of Simeon and Levi. In fact, he or she can agree with the narrator in all his moral positioning. The shift in dispensations affects the typological appropriation more clearly than the literal although even at the surface level of the text certain discontinuities require a shift in application from the issue of Jew-gentile intermarriage to that of Christian-non Christian intermarriage. At that level the story does not provide *the* answer so much as provoke thought.

In this Chapter I hope to have shown how the biblical super-story can set up parameters within which Christian moral readings of Genesis 34 can roam.

---

269 Jas 1:19.
270 Eph 4:26.
271 Rom 14:9; 2 Cor 13:1; Eph 4:3; Jas 3:17; Col 3:12-13; 1 Pet 3:8.
272 Heb 12:14.
273 Gal 6:10.
274 Rom 12:18.
275 Mt 5:38-46; Rom 12:14-20; 1 Pet 3:9.

## Chapter 6

# Can Biblical Stories Be Bad For Us? Feminist Hermeneutics and the Rape of Dinah

*The biblical texts are entangled in a marginalization of women that in different ways and degrees encompasses the past, the present and the foreseeable future.* Francis Watson[1]

*To speak of the Hebrew Bible/Old Testament as "holy scripture" is to accord it an authority and a prestige which ultimately transcends the feminist critique.* Francis Watson[2]

It is traditionally *assumed* by Christian readers of the Bible that the narratives in the Old Testament are ethically beneficial and that a Christian hermeneutic will be primarily a hermeneutic of faith and trust. However, things are not quite as simple as that, and recent feminist critics have been amongst those who have approached the biblical text first and foremost with a hermeneutic of suspicion. They consider the text of the Bible to be both patriarchal and androcentric and thus potentially harmful to women. Many would say that rather than uncritically opening ourselves to be shaped by the stories we ought to expose some of them as oppressive and damaging even if they are, in other ways, liberating. This challenge cuts very deeply and simply cannot be ignored. The present chapter is an attempt to maintain the centrality of the canon in Christian ethics whilst, I hope, trying to take the problems posed by androcentrism and patriarchy within the Bible seriously. The following reflections begin and proceed from within a fairly conservative Christian tradition. This interpretative community and its tradition forms the sedimentation upon which I hope that creative interpretative innovation can take place as that tradition comes into dialogue with feminist scholarship.

The focus will be on Genesis 34 but I shall have to set my reflections on that passage within a broader set of considerations. The first main section gives a

---

1 Watson, 1994, p. 187. This chapter appeared in the *Tyndale Bulletin* 53.1, 2002, pp. 1-28.
2 Ibid., p. 189.

brief introduction to feminist interpretation whilst the second outlines feminist concerns with Genesis 34 in particular. I then move on in the third main section to defend the continuing usefulness of Genesis 34 in Christian ethics whilst attempting to learn important lessons from feminist schools of thought. I believe that although initially a feminist hermeneutics of suspicion seem to undermine the *normative* use of scripture in Christian ethics it can open up fruitful ways of ethically reading stories which the Christian can welcome.

## The Challenge of Feminist Hermeneutics

Feminism is a broad family of related but different positions. Consequently, feminist readers of biblical texts are often at variance with each other both in terms of conclusions and methodology. However, according to Katherine Doob Sakenfeld "the beginning point, shared with all feminists studying the Bible, is appropriately a stance of *radical suspicion*."[3] This is because women's experiences have been excluded from (a) the official interpretations of the Bible often (b) from the Bible itself making the Bible a powerful tool in the oppression of women. Letty Russell writes that, "it has become abundantly clear that the scriptures need liberation, not only from existing interpretations but also from the *patriarchal* bias of the texts themselves."[4] Similarly, Fiorenza thinks that the Bible is "authored by men, written in androcentric language,[5] reflective of male experience, selected and transmitted by male religious leadership. Without question the Bible is a male book."[6]

Feminist interpreters have been keenly aware of the uses to which the Bible

---

3 Sakenfeld, 1985, p. 55.
4 Russell, 1985, p. 11.
5 Patriarchy is a surprisingly difficult notion to pin down but it is usually seen as a dominance of men over women in the power relations of a society as reflected in public institutions such as government, marriage, the law, religion, education, labour and so on. This is seen by feminists as oppressive for women and a necessary evil in that it is a primary structure of human alienation and exploitation. Androcentrism is the claim that texts are written from the perspective of men. Clearly one could have texts which reflect patriarchal structures but which do so from women's' perspectives. However, biblical texts usually discuss issues of war or the royal court or the Temple which are the domain of men and it is not surprising to find that such texts are both patriarchal and androcentric. Thus the biblical text gives the impression that Ancient Israel was far more oppressive of women than it actually was (so C. Meyers, 1988). Even when women come into the frame they are often seen from a male perspective and this poses perhaps more of a problem than the patriarchal social structures themselves. My comments shall thus focus on androcentrism and only make passing reference to the problem of patriarchy.
6 Quoted in Thistleton, 1992, pp. 442-43. The claim is not that the Bible sets out to consciously exclude women but simply that it reflects "a culturally inherited and deep-rooted gender bias" (C. Exum, 1990, p. 59).

has been put and the problem of biblical authority has always been never far from the surface. Ruether says:

> The Bible was shaped by males in a patriarchal culture, so many of its revelatory experiences were interpreted by men from a patriarchal perspective. The ongoing interpretation of these revelatory experiences and their canonisation further this patriarchal bias by eliminating traces of female experience or interpreting them in an androcentric way. *The Bible, in turn, becomes an authoritative source for the justification of patriarchy in Jewish and Christian society.*[7]

How can a text like *this* be authoritative? Christian and Jewish feminists have been forced to struggle with this question because the Bible is the foundational document for both faiths and cannot simply be dismissed.

Sakenfeld[8] presents a typology of the views of feminist biblical scholars on biblical authority. At one end of the spectrum she places Fiorenza who argues that the maleness of the Bible makes it impossible for it to form the basis for a transcontextual critical principle. That honour belongs to the experience of oppressed women according to which biblical texts are interpreted and evaluated. The Bible stands and falls as measured against this standard and cannot itself be considered authoritative.[9] At the other end of the spectrum are the evangelical feminists who wish to maintain as much of a traditional view of the Bible's authoritative status as possible.

Between the poles one could place Letty Russell,[10] Mary Ann Tolbert[11] and Phyllis Bird[12] who see scripture as authoritative *in so far as* it makes sense of their experience or mediates God's liberating word for the oppressed. Farley similarly argues that the truth claims of the biblical witness simply cannot be believed unless they "ring true" to the experience of women.[13] The authority of scripture is redefined by Russell, as the "authority to evoke consent" rather than as an extrinsic authority[14] thus the locus of authority shifts from text to reader.[15] David Clines has even suggested that the notion of authority should be abandoned by feminists altogether because he sees it as a male notion ill fitted to feminist perspectives.[16] This would be a dramatic shift away from the Christian tradition and is going unnecessarily far for some Christian feminists.[17]

---

7 Ruether, 1985, p. 116 (italics mine).
8 Sakenfeld, 1988, pp. 5-18.
9 See Thistleton, 1992, pp. 442-450 for a critique of Fiorenza.
10 See Russell, 1985.
11 See Tolbert, 1990, pp. 5-23.
12 See Bird, 1997.
13 Farley, 1985, p. 43.
14 Russell, 1985, p. 141.
15 Ibid., p. 141.
16 Clines, 1990, pp. 45-48.
17 E.g. Bird, 1997, pp. 260-261.

Perhaps the most useful typology of feminist responses to the Bible is that of Carolyn Osiek[18] who discerns five basic stances:[19]

- *The Rejectionist.* The Bible is rejected as authoritative perhaps along with Christianity itself (if the Christian tradition is seen as irredeemable).[20]

- *The Loyalist.* The Bible cannot be rejected under any circumstances. Two possibilities open up for the loyalist: one can reinterpret "oppressive" texts in non-oppressive ways, seeing the problem not with the text but with its readers,[21] or one could opt for the complementarian position which, strictly speaking, is not a feminist position.[22]

- *The Revisionist.* The Bible and the Christian tradition, it is argued, have been stamped by the patriarchal culture in which they arose but they are not *essentially* patriarchal and can be reformed. The "submerged female voices" of women hidden behind text and tradition can be recovered from scraps of linguistic, rhetorical and narrative evidence. The intention is to reconstruct, as far as is possible, the lives of ordinary Israelite women at different periods of the nation's history.[23] One may also try to bring to the surface often ignored texts which present women in a more positive light.[24] The revisionist, along with the rejectionist and the liberationist, may also highlight the androcentric and patriarchal dimensions of biblical texts in order to show how women are often ignored or, if they are included, are presented from men's perspectives.[25] Some try to put biblical texts under the critical eye of psychoanalytic theory with the aim of uncovering subconscious themes.[26] The aim of such studies is often to

---

18 Osiek, 1985, pp. 99-100.

19 For a different typology see Sakenfeld, 1985.

20 Osiek, 1985, pp. 97-99. Mary Daly is the most obvious writer in this category.

21 This is the main strategy of evangelical feminists. For non-evangelical examples, see Meyers on Gen 3:16 (1988, ch. 5); Trible on Gen 2 (Trible, 1978).

22 Osiek, 1985, pp. 99-100.

23 Carol Meyers' magnificent study, *Discovering Eve* (1988) is a classic example of this approach. See too Phyllis Bird's, 'The Place of Women in the Israelite Cultus' in Bird, 1997 and now Bauckham's brilliant *Gospel Women*, 2002.

24 For example, Exum, 1983, pp. 63-82. Exum still thinks that Exodus 1-2 has a very positive portrayal of women yet she now thinks that this too supports patriarchy for the message sent out is: "Stay in your place in the domestic sphere; you can achieve important things there. The public arena belongs to men; you do not need to look beyond motherhood for fulfillment" (Exum, 1994, pp. 75-87). Exum goes too far here. The text does not strongly subvert patriarchy but neither does it set out to reinforce it. I simply cannot hear what Exum thinks she hears in the story.

25 Bach (ed.), 1999, pp. xiv-xv.

26 See for instance, Rashkow, 1993 and Exum, 1999.

at least partially subvert such texts and undermine their authority. Such studies may then "playfully" reimagine the story from the perspective of the women.[27]

- *The Sublimationist.* The "feminine principle" of life-giving and nurturing are glorified and the tradition is scoured for feminine symbols of God and the church.[28]
- *The Liberationist.* To consider the Bible generally looking for theological perspectives which can be used to critique patriarchy (e.g., new creation, *shalom*, prophetic critique of oppression, *koinonia*). The central message of the Bible is seen to be that of human liberation motivated by eschatological hope. Letty Russell finds a biblical basis and motivation for her liberationist message "in God's intention for the mending of all creation"[29] and Ruether seeks strands of cultural critique from Israel's prophets with which to attack patriarchy.[30] Both, however, take the starting point as a feminist ideology which comes from beyond the text and is brought to it with the hope of correlating the feminist critical principle with one internal to scripture.[31]

Clearly these strategies, or at least b)-e), need not be seen as in conflict and one could embrace some combination of each. I shall make use of selected strategies from the loyalist, the revisionist and the liberationist arguing that they not only contribute to reading the Bible ethically but that they are consistent with a high view of scripture.

### Feminist Readings of Genesis 34: Restoring Dinah's Honour

Feminists can read *with* the biblical text and against androcentric interpreters and/or against the biblical text itself. Both strategies have been used to attempt to restore both Dinah and her honour in recent work.

#### *Reading with the Text but Against the Classical Interpreters*

On reading the history of the interpretation of Genesis 34 one is struck by the fact that an element of only minor interest to the narrator of the story, Dinah's "going out to see the daughters of the land", becomes a matter of central

---

27 See for instance Alice Bach's, "With a Song in her Heart: Listening to Scholars Listening for Miriam" in Bach (ed.), 1999, pp. 419-27.
28 Osiek, 1985, pp. 101-02. Gray's, 1989, seeks for feminine metaphors of atonement in the tradition to replace dominant "male" ones and could be seen as "sublimationist".
29 Russell, 1985, p. 138. A recent collection of essays in honour of Letty Russell picks up this new creation theme: Farley and Jones (eds.), 1999. See also my review of this book in *European Journal of Theology*, X (2001):1, pp. 76-77.
30 Ruether, 1983.
31 Ruether, 1985.

concern to both Jewish and Christian interpreters. Without doubt past interpretations of Genesis 34 have reflected the perspectives of the male interpreters for "classical" readings of the story often blame Dinah for the massacre.[32] Consider Aalders' Christian commentary on Genesis where we read:

> We can surmise that [Dinah] also had some natural desires to be seen by the young men of the city as well... It was disturbing that Dinah would so flippantly expose herself to the men of this pagan city... As a matter of fact, *Dinah was far more at fault for what had happened than anyone else in the City of Shechem.*[33]

All interpreters agree that Dinah was a young woman who went out alone in a dangerous place and that, at very least, this was unwise. Beyond that there is divergence. Some see Dinah as "asking for it" by being deliberately provocative[34] whilst others are more sympathetic towards her.[35] Some see Dinah's act as a rebellion against her parents[36] whilst others see her acting with parental permission.[37] Still others see her sin as enjoyment of the illicit sexual encounter with Shechem.[38] The morals drawn from the story are simple: First, that parents should ensure that daughters stay in the home in safety.[39] Second, that women should avoid both curiosity and allowing men to see them.[40]

Two recent studies helpfully exemplify contrasting feminist attempts to read Genesis 34 *with* the text but *against* androcentric interpreters. The first is that of Dana Nolan Fewell and David Gunn whilst the second is that of Susanne Scholz.

Fewell and Gunn criticise Meir Sternberg[41] for reading the story through

---

32 So *Genesis Rabbah* LXXX:II h-i and III f-g; Bernard of Clairvaux, 1987, p. 124; *Ancrene Wisse*, 1991, p. 68; Calvin, 1965, p. 218.

33 Aalders, 1981, pp.154, 159 (italics mine).

34 So *Genesis Rabbah* LXXX:I; LXXX:IV.4-5; St Gregory's Pastoral Rule XXIX; *Ancrene Wisse*, p. 17, pp. 67-68; Matthew Henry, 1725, p. 112, 114.

35 Luther, 1986, pp. 187-88, 192, 194. On Luther see especially J.A. Schroeder, 1997, pp. 775-91.

36 So Luther, 1986, pp. 192-94.

37 *Genesis Rabbah* blames Jacob for letting Dinah go.

38 So *Glossa Ordinaria* (Schroeder, 1997, pp. 779-80); *Genesis Rabbah* LXXX:XI; Richard of Saint Victor (Schroeder,1997, p. 780); *Ancrene Wisse*, p. 68; Matthew Henry implies it (1725, p. 112). Luther took the opposite view – that the rape was not pleasurable for Dinah but was a crime against her.

39 So Jerome, Letter CVII. 6; XXII. 25; Luther, 1986, p. 93; Calvin, 1965, p. 218; Gervase Babbington, 1615, pp. 139-140; Matthew Henry, 1725, p. 112.

40 St Bernard, pp. 124-25; Ancrene Wisse, pp. 68-69.

41 To follow the whole debate one needs to read Meir Sternberg original chapter in *The Poetics of Biblical Narrative: Ideological Literature and the Drama of Reading*, 1987, ch. 12; D. Fewell and D. Gunn's response, "Tipping the Balance: Sternberg's Reader

androcentric, "action-man" glasses. He fails to see that the ideology of the reader plays a critical role in the sense that is made of a text.[42] Against Sternberg they propose a feminist reading of the text which makes as much, if not more, sense of it as his.[43] As far as Dinah is concerned they argue that the narrator in v. 2 may be storing up sympathy for her, the victim, rather than her brothers, as Sternberg thinks.[44] At the very least, as readers with a horror at the crime of rape, we cannot help but feel for Dinah.[45] However, Shechem in v. 3 calms her fears and, out of genuine love for her, he promises to take care of her. This is a surprising sequel to the rape and it complicates our response as the narrator "tips the balance in Shechem's favour".[46] Dinah herself, according to Fewell and Gunn, sees a marriage as the best way forward and that is what Shechem offers.[47] She chooses to remain in his house until the wedding.[48] The narrator is calling for a "compromised, but realistic, resolution".[49] In contrast to the reformed rapist we see the aggressive brothers of Dinah who care only for *their* honour (not hers). In mindless revenge they murder, plunder and rape a whole city[50] – an act that is grossly disproportionate - and they cannot see that Shechem is trying to make restitution for his crime.[51] Having no concern about what is best for Dinah they take her *against her will* from the house of Shechem and kill the reformed fiancé, the only person who will allow her a voice.[52] Dinah must be seen as a young woman with her own choices but the brothers only see a helpless girl needing to be rescued from herself and her fiancé.[53]

---

and the Rape of Dinah", 1991; Sternberg's reply, "Biblical Poetics and Sexual Politics: From Reading to Counter Reading", 1992, and Paul Noble's assessment, "A 'Balanced' Reading of the Rape of Dinah: Some Exegetical and Methodological Observations", 1996.

42 Fewell and Gunn, 1991, p. 194.

43 Ibid., p. 194.

44 Ibid., p. 195.

45 Ibid., p. 195.

46 Ibid., pp. 196-97.

47 Ibid., p. 210 and S.P. Jeansonne, 1990, p. 95, use Deuteronomy 22:28-29 to support Dinah's right to marry Shechem. There are, however, three problems with this. For a start, Deuteronomy 22:28-29 may not even refer to a rape case (so Hugenberger, 1994, pp. 225-260). Second, the negotiations in Genesis 34 presuppose that the family of Dinah can refuse the marriage which indicates that a law more like Exodus 22:15-16 than Deut 22:28-29 was at work. Finally, as Sternberg has shown (1992, pp. 482-83), even if Deuteronomy 22 is about rape it would not, from a Mosaic perspective at least, be applicable to a Hivite.

48 Fewell and Gunn, 1991, p. 200.

49 Ibid., p. 197.

50 Ibid., p. 205.

51 Ibid., pp. 200-01.

52 Ibid., p. 211.

53 Ibid., p. 211.

Scholz[54] argues that Fewell and Gunn's approval of the marriage of the
rapist to the rape-victim makes the status of their interpretation as a *feminist*
reading of Genesis 34 suspect.[55] She claims that biblical texts are always read
from some non-neutral perspective and that true feminist readings must be
"from the perspective of the subjugated, that is the rape victim-survivor".[56] To
illustrate how Genesis 34 has not been read from that perspective she argues
that 19th Century German commentaries on Genesis 34 paralleled contemporary
German medical attitudes towards rape. They marginalized it, distrusted and
condemned the victim, and claimed that love can make rape "not so bad".[57]
Thus the "commentaries of Genesis 34 were not developed from the
perspective of Dinah. They reflected the perspective of the powerful."[58] She
then re-reads Genesis 34:1-3 from Dinah's perspective[59] in such a way as to
make the horror of rape the key focus. V. 2, she argues, emphasises Shechem's
increasing use of violence against Dinah so that v. 2b describes the action of
rape.[60] Her treatment of v. 3 is her most original contribution to the study of the
chapter.[61] She argues that it is *not* intended to reflect positively upon Shechem.
She reads it as follows: "His (sexual) desire (נפשו) stayed close to (בדינה)
Dinah." The context then requires us to read the second line as "and he lusted
after (ויאהב) the young woman." Following Fischer[62] she reads the final line as,
"and he attempted to soothe (וידבר על-לב הנער) the young woman." In other
words, he has to calm her because she does not consent.

> This interpretation of Gen. 34:1-3 indicates that several verbs describe the
> selfishness and the disregard Shechem held for Dinah. The interpretation confirms
> the notion of the Women's Movement that rape is *primarily* an act of violence
> rather than a sexual act. When rape is accentuated, love talk is not involved.[63]

Despite their stark differences, both these studies argue that the story must be
read from the woman's perspective and that one can, to some extent at least,
read *with* the text to restore Dinah's honour as a person with value and choices.

### Reading Against the Biblical Text

Within Genesis 34 both patriarchy and androcentrism are issues of concern to

54 Scholz, 1998, pp. 150-71.
55 Ibid., p. 151.
56 Ibid., p. 151.
57 Ibid., pp. 154-60.
58 Ibid., pp. 159-60.
59 Ibid., pp. 164-71.
60 Ibid., pp. 165-68.
61 Ibid., pp. 168-71.
62 Fischer, 1984, pp. 244-50.
63 Scholz, 1998, p. 171.

feminist readers. The problem with patriarchy is seen most clearly in the way in which marriages in Israel are arranged without any reference to the wishes of the girl involved. Genesis 34 reflects this widespread custom. Naomi Segal complains that

> Dinah is an object of exchange so blank that to violate her is to enter nothing but instead to "take" something - from whom? not from her. The text is singularly clear in exposing the discursive economics of male sexuality, with its exchange of object-females among subject-males ... The shared norm of all the men is expressed in the narrowly ambiguous pronoun that defines the crime as "a disgrace to *us*".[64]

Perhaps more worrying seems to be the clear androcentrism of a story which, although it involves the rape[65] of a woman, is all about men and their reactions. The silence of Dinah is the central issue of concern for most feminist readers. Why is her view not directly represented? Why is she never consulted about what she would like to happen vis-à-vis marriage? The worry is that it is not simply biblical interpreters who ignore her perspective, but *the biblical narrator himself.*

Rashkow[66] objects to the androcentrism reflected in the way that Dinah is defined in relation to men. She is Jacob's daughter. She is the brothers' sister. Why is she never simply Dinah – a woman with her own identity?[67] As I do not think this a particularly strong objection I shall deal with it now rather than later. Rashkow is very individualistic in her assumptions and seems to presuppose that people are only seen most fully as people when they are considered as isolated individuals who are fully "themselves" on their own. This notion of the solitary self has been subjected to sustained criticism by philosophers and theologians in recent years. The self is a self-in-relation: part of what it is for me to be me is to be someone's son, someone's brother, someone's father. Feminism itself has played an important role in rediscovering the crucial place of relationality in identity.[68] Thus Genesis 34 does not demean Dinah by referring to her as "Jacob's daughter" or "their sister". On top of that,

---

64 Segal, 1988, pp. 247-48.
65 Bechtel, 1994, pp. 19-36 is the only feminist scholar I have come across who challenges this consensus. I critique her view in Chapter Four.
66 Rashkow, 1993, pp. 250-65.
67 Ibid., pp. 104-06. See too Segal, 1988, p. 248.
68 Margaret Kock (1993, pp. 70-113) argues that Western feminism has often made the mistake, among other things, of assuming that Western views of individual autonomy are essential to the liberation of women. Feminists from non-western cultures have rightly objected and refused to see the necessity of the abstracting women from the network of social relations within which they find their sense of identity. Western feminists have usually taken these criticisms seriously. It seems to me that Rashkow is stuck in an Enlightenment-Feminist mode of thought in her criticisms here.

the men are described as *"her* father" and *"her* brothers" indicating that their identity is formed, in part, by their relation to her. Also she is related to Leah in v. 1 who is a female and thus it seems to me that this criticism really misses the mark. In fact, all the relational participant references Dinah receives reinforce her value. She is not just another woman to the Israelites but a *sister* and *that* is why they are so angry at the rape.

Rashkow raises another objection to the narrator in Genesis 34 claiming that

> a repeated theme in biblical narratives is the daughter's transgression against her father and subsequent departure from the closure of the house. For example, Dinah "goes out", is raped (Gen 34:1-2), and is then narratively banished from the text.[69]

Rashkow here seems to accept the "classical" reading of Dinah's "going out" as an excursion condemned by the narrator. My first task in the next section will be to question this view but it seems appropriate, at this point, to make a preliminary criticism of Rashkow's argument, for she only gives two examples of this supposedly "repeated theme": the first is Genesis 34 and the second is Jephthah's daughter in Judges 11. Apart from the fact that two examples would not be enough to establish the claim, it seems to me that neither of the examples provides any evidence for the proposal. Jephthah's daughter does not transgress against her father in any straightforward sense and the text of Genesis 34 says nothing of Dinah's rebellion against Jacob. Nevertheless, Rashkow, in line with the classical interpreters, clearly thinks that Dinah's "going out" is condemned by the narrator and she subjects that condemnation to a feminist-psychoanalytic critique.[70]

## Dinah's Honour: Some Reflections

### *Does the Narrator Disapprove of Dinah's "Going Out"?*

Given the agreement between *some* feminist readers such as Rashkow and "classical" readers it is appropriate to begin with a reassessment of the view that the narrator condemns Dinah for "going out".

---

69 Rashkow, 1993, p. 67

70 Another complaint about Genesis 34 is the way in which insult is added to injury by using Dinah's violation as an excuse for victimising Canaanites (Laffey, 1988, pp. 41-44). Men typically use the rapes of women to justify wars and Genesis 34 is no exception (Keefe, 1993, pp. 79-94). I do not intend to take up this challenge in what follows for I argue in chs 4-5 that the narrator is not trying to defend the massacre.

Does אצי Indicate a Narratorial Disapproval of Dinah?

The first thing to refute is Sarna's claim that the verbal stem אצי can connote "coquettish or promiscuous conduct".[71] Jacob Neusner also comments that, "the verb 'go out' when associated with a woman carries the sense of 'awhoring'."[72] Neither Sarna nor Neusner provide any evidence for this assertion. Wenham tentatively provides some support for the claim by observing that in the Laws of Hamurabi 141 the cognate Akkadian verb *watsu* "describes a housewife who conducts herself improperly outside her home, and the targums translate 'cult prostitute' as 'one who goes out into the countryside'."[73] However, that one example of a cognate verb can be produced in which a woman "goes out" in a dubious fashion is very weak grounds for the claim that the Hebrew verb itself carries bad connotations. For a start, we cannot make a simple transfer from Akkadian to Hebrew. Secondly, that a verb *in some contexts* can carry negative overtones does not suggest that the verb carries those connotations inherently. We shall see below at least one "whorish going out" from the Hebrew Bible but this simply does not show that all women "going out" were viewed negatively. That the later Jewish targums spoke of cult prostitutes as women who "go out into the countryside" does not establish that women "going out" carried sexual overtones *whatever* the context nor even that the sexual usage of אצי goes back to the time when Genesis was written. We need to study the "goings out" of women in the Hebrew Bible itself. On inspection the Emperor's new prostitute vanishes into thin air. All the Qal uses of אצי predicated of females can be categorised as follows:

- Genesis 24 is full of women who "go out" to collect water (vv. 11, 13, 15, 43, 45. See also 1 Sam 9:11) yet it certainly cannot be said that "coquettish or promiscuous conduct" is connoted.
- It seems to have been quite common for groups of women to "go out" in worship.[74] In none of these cases does the verb אצי imply improper behaviour (Ex 15:20; Jud 11:34; 21:21; 1 Sam 18:6; Jer. 31:4).
- Most of the 1,068 uses of the אצי stem simply denote someone moving from one place to another. It is not surprising that it is used of women in this way (Ruth 1:7; 2:22; 2 Kg. 4:21, 37; 8:3).
- The Old Testament often describes women who "go out" to meet people. This category includes Leah (Gen 30:16), Dinah (34:1), Jael (Jud 4:18, 22) and Michal (2 Sam 6:20). The only case in which a woman "goes out" as a prostitute is Proverbs 7:10, 15.
- Some miscellaneous examples of the verb אצי predicated of females include "going out" in divorce (Deut 24:2) and "going out" in

---

71 Sarna, 1989, p. 233.
72 Neusner, 1985, p. 146.
73 Wenham, 1994, p. 310.
74 See Meyers, 1994, pp. 207-30.

approved romantic contexts (Cant 1:8; 3:11).[75]

- Women can also be freed ("go out") from slavery (Ex. 21:3, 7, 11).

What we can say with certainty is that when the verb יצא is used of women it does not carry any automatic negative connotations. The vast majority of the above women who "go out" are not being implicitly condemned for having done so. It all depends on what the women "go out" to do, thus Sarna and Neusner are simply wrong. The closest we get to support for the traditional view if Proverbs 7:10, 15[76] where a prostitute comes out to seduce a man. Clearly *her* "going out" is morally suspect but let us remember that Dinah did *not* go out to seduce men. She went out to see the *women* of the land and was raped!

The rabbis in *Genesis Rabbah* and later commentators such as Rashi saw a connection between Leah's "going out" to have sex with Jacob and Dinah's "going out": As Leah went awhoring so did Dinah.[77] The connection is less than convincing. Firstly, it is not fair to describe Leah's act as one of prostitution: she was *married* to Jacob.[78] Second, there is nothing sexual about the *verb* יצא in Genesis 30:16. The proposal Leah made was sexual but her "going out" was merely a pre-requisite for the making this proposal. Third, apart from the parallel phrases ("and Leah went out"// "and Dinah went out") the two events do not parallel at all. Leah went out to persuade her husband to impregnate her whilst Dinah went out to see the local women and was raped. One simply cannot read off a negative assessment of Dinah from this parallel. This strategy having failed another rears its head.

Hamilton translates v. 1 as "she went out *to be seen* [implied – 'by the men'] among the daughters of the land."[79] As we have seen the idea that Dinah went out to get "picked up" by some dishy young bloke traces its roots way back into the history of interpretation. His reasoning is that the construction ראה (to see) in the infinitive + ב is unique and thus he prefers to translate as a passive rather than an active form. However, out of 111 uses of the Qal infinitive construct of ראה in the Old Testament there is no clear example of a passive use ("be seen"). Every occurrence is most naturally read as active ("to see"). If the narrator had wanted to say that Dinah had gone to "be seen" he would have used the Niphal

---

75 Other miscellaneous uses include Zech 5:9; Jer 29:2; 38:20-23; Mic 4:10 (the last three refer to going out into exile).

76 Possibly also Judg 4:18 as the account of Jael's "going out" to welcome Sisera seems to make use of sexual innuendoes (see Niditch, 1999, pp. 305-315). However, her later "going out" to meet Barak does not seem to have such overtones.

77 *Genesis Rabbah,* LXXX:I.Y.

78 And unlike a prostitute Leah paid Rachel in mandrakes for the privilege of sleeping with Jacob rather than seeking payment from her "client".

79 Hamilton, 1995, p. 351; so too Aalders, 1981, p. 154 and Kass, 1992, p. 31.

infinite construct which always bears that sense.[80] Hamilton does add that "the active sense is possible only if one understands $b^e$ partitavely, that is, 'to see *some* of the women'."[81] The weight of evidence would support *this* reading.

Perhaps, the traditionalist may reply, women could "go out" acceptably in groups but to go out alone was seen as wrong. This is more plausible but unpersuasive. We note that Rebecca is not frowned upon in Genesis 24 for "going out" alone before all the other women to collect water. Similarly, Rachel kept her father's sheep, apparently alone, yet there is not obvious condemnation for that.[82] Having said this, I do think that it would have been considered unwise for a woman to go out alone into territory not her own. This is put very well by Naomi in Ruth 2:22, "It will be good for you, my daughter, to *go* with the girls, because in someone else's field you might be harmed." It is not that Ruth would have been seen as *immoral* in going out to someone else's field. Rather she would have put herself in possible danger and would be wise to find security in a group. The Dinah situation finds its most comfortable parallel with Ruth 2:22. Dinah was going out into dangerous territory – the land of the Canaanites. In doing so alone she may well have been considered to have acted naively but not necessarily promiscuously.

### Does the Narrator Blame Dinah?

Given the mountains of blame heaped upon Dinah by classical interpreters, one is struck by the fact that at *no* point in the chapter is Dinah blamed for what has happened. Blame is always placed squarely on Shechem's shoulders. Shechem saw her, took her, lay her and shamed her (v. 2). Shechem "defiled" her (v. 5, v. 13, v. 27[83]) and "did folly in Israel" (v. 7). Now it was perfectly possible for a woman to "do folly" by engaging in illicit sexual relations[84] but no mention is made of Dinah "doing folly". Shechem treated her as a prostitute (v. 31). No mention is made of Dinah *acting* like a prostitute and thus sharing in the blame. This is because in Israel, women were not held responsible in cases of rape.[85]

Did Dinah know what would happen to her? Did she know that she would (or may) be raped? Could she have known how her rapist would react? Could she have anticipated her brothers' response? The only action for which she is responsible is her own "going out" and the only blame is any that may attach to

---

80 There is some textual support for a Niphal in the Samaritan Pentateuch (followed by some of the Jewish Midrashim – see Salkin, 1986) but the MT and LXX (which uses an aorist infinitive clearly meaning she went "to understand" and not "to be understood") support the Qal reading (as does Hamilton himself).

81 Hamilton, 1995, p. 353.

82 Gen 29:6-12.

83 V. 27 actually says that "they (i.e., the now deceased men of Shechem) defiled Dinah". Nevertheless, no blame is attached to Dinah here.

84 Deut 22:21.

85 Deut 22:25-27.

her lack of wisdom.

### *Does Genesis 34 Support Locking up our Daughters?*

Interpretation is underdetermined by the text with regard to the restriction of daughters to the home. It could be used, as argued above, for Dinah's lack of wisdom in going out alone given the dangers. However, beyond that it cannot direct us. If one is already committed to the idea that women are vulnerable and best kept safe in the security of the home, as the classical readers were, then Genesis 34 certainly could be used to reinforce such a belief. Alternatively, if one was a feminist who was angered at the fact that women are preyed upon, one could equally use the text to support a "Claim Back the Night" kind of campaign. The narrator is not especially concerned to address such issues. We may be, and we may use the text to inspire us in our reflections but we cannot use it to settle the issue either way. Either readers' response could be a legitimate one *as far as doing justice to the text goes.*

### The Problem of Patriarchy in Genesis 34

Patriarchy is simply *assumed* in Genesis 34 as in the rest of the Hebrew Bible where it is was neither justified nor critiqued. Does the fact that Israel was a patriarchal society make patriarchy a biblical norm for all cultures at all times?[86] Not obviously. Let me make a few brief remarks in an attempt to set the problem posed by Israel's apparently male dominated social structures in some perspective.

First, Carol Meyers has urged great caution in this area. She argues that the concept of patriarchy needs to be nuanced to deal with differences across time and culture, maintaining that in Ancient Israel, as in some contemporary peasant societies, women had a great deal of power even if they had little authority[87] and would not have (usually) found their place in society as harsh or oppressive. Biblical societies were strongly patrilinear[88] but "male dominance [was]... a public attitude of deference or of theoretical control but not a valid description of social reality."[89] Thus care ought to be taken when criticising Ancient Israelite society for it may not have been nearly *as* oppressive for

---

86 The best discussion of culture and hermeneutics is now Webb, 2001.

87 Authority is a hierarchical arrangement that may be expressed in formal legal or juridical traditions (Meyers, 1988, p. 41).

88 Patrilineality refers to the tracing of group membership through the father's line. The inheritance of property is also through this line. Patrilineality has been explored by Naomi Steinberg in the Genesis stories (1993).

89 Meyers, 1988, p. 42.

women as it may at first look.[90] It remains the case that Israel's laws and social structures are dominated by men and can be termed patriarchal so long as care is taken when so doing.

Second, the biblical metanarrative of creation, fall and restoration could provide the ground for a biblical critique of patriarchy.[91] In creation men and women are equally in God's image[92] and equally commissioned to fill and subdue the earth.[93] Francis Watson believes that "the Hebrew narrators [in Genesis 1-3] were somehow able to transcend the all-embracing, self-evident patriarchal context in which they no doubt lived and worked, in order to assert that 'in the beginning it was not so'."[94] Genesis 3:16 seems to be a watershed in gender relations as sin could be seen as the origin of men ruling over their women.[95] If this is correct, then oppressive patriarchy could be rooted not in the creative intentions of God but in the fallenness of the world. Redemption then restores men and women equally[96] enabling men and women to receive both the Spirit and his gifts.[97] One could see the patriarchy of Israel along the same lines as the divorce laws – not God's intention, but allowed due to sin-hardened hearts.[98] However, now that the new age has dawned such social structures are passing away.[99] This basic hermeneutic is that adopted by the majority of so-

---

90 Similar warnings are made by Schroer in Schottroff, Schroer and Wacker, 1998, pp. 89-91. Schroer writes that "one must warn against comparing ancient Israelite patriarchy with that of today's industrialised, technological, and individual-orientated societies. In an agrarian culture where they are part of the process of production, women are often in positions of equal power to men even when they are excluded, for example, from politics and public activities' (ibid., pp. 90-91).

91 See 'Living Between The Times: Bad News and Good News About Gender Relations' in (ed.) M.S. Van Leeuwen, 1993, pp. 1-16; Walsh and Middleton, 1995; F. Watson, 1994, ch. 11.

92 Gen 1:26. There are many and diverse feminist interpretations of this crucial text. For an excellent introduction to the range of Feminist readings of all the key texts in Genesis 1-3 plus a generous but critical analysis of then see now Abraham, 2003.

93 Gen 1:28.

94 Watson, 1994, p. 194.

95 Gen 3:16 has generated many feminist studies among which are P. Bird, 'Genesis 3 in Modern Biblical Scholarship' in Bird, 1997, pp.174-93; A. Bledstein, 'Are Women Cursed in Genesis 3:16?' in A. Brenner (ed.), 1993a, pp. 142-145; C. Meyers, 'Gender Roles in Genesis 3:16 Revisited' in A. Brenner (ed.), 1993a, pp. 118-41 (see too Meyers, 1988); Trible, 1978, pp. 126-28. On Feminism and Gen 3 see now especially Alexander, 2003.

96 Gal 3:28.

97 Acts 2:16-17; 1 Cor. 11:3ff..

98 Mt 19:4-9 pars.

99 The persistence of patriarchy in the New Testament could be seen in terms of the tension between the now and the not yet which marks the present experience of the Christian. The patriarchy of the New Testament is a radically Christianised and subversive form of patriarchy but it is patriarchy none the less. The question is, "was the

called evangelical feminists as well as by many non-evangelical, Christian feminists. It has the benefit of allowing one to recognise the patriarchy of Israel without seeing it as normative. It also seeks out a critical principle with which to critique patriarchy that has genuine claims to be Christian and *internal* to the biblical canon rather than an alien principle rooted in secular ideology.[100]

## The Problem of Androcentrism in Genesis 34

It is true that there is no *direct* indication of Dinah's perspective on the crime in Genesis 34. Before commenting on this it is worth pointing to some *indirect* indicators of how she felt.

First, we are told in 34:3 that Shechem "spoke to her heart" which clearly indicates that she was distressed and Shechem consequently took steps to calm her.[101]

Second, the sons (and Jacob?) saw the rape as an act which treats Dinah as a prostitute (v. 31) and thus "defiles her" (v. 5, v. 13, v. 27). It is "folly in Israel" (v. 7). It is sometimes assumed that this is merely the men's view on the crime and not Dinah's. The marriage, we are told by the sons, is "a disgrace to us" and both Fewell and Gunn and Segal take the "us" here to refer to the sons *in contrast to* Dinah. Segal thinks that we ought to see the rape from Dinah's perspective - as her autonomy being cruelly violated.[102] However, it is most unlikely that Dinah would see her rape as modern western women would.[103] For us, rape is primarily a violation of a woman's autonomy and bodily integrity, but that is no reason to imagine that Dinah would see a violation of her autonomy as primary. It may be the case that the sons *imagine* that Dinah will see the rape from the same perspective as themselves and they cannot see that

---

patriarchy of the New Testament merely a concession to culture or a norm for all Christians?"

100 Thistleton criticises Fiorenza and Daly for finding their critical principle outside the biblical text and not being open to a dialogue with the text from which one can learn. Instead one approaches the text with all the answers and simply measures the text against them (1992, pp. 442-50). Francis Watson finds the redemption of an otherwise oppressive Bible in the claim that the elements in the canon which resist oppression are not mere "scattered fragments" but belong to the "fundamental structure" of that very canon (1994, chs. 9-11). Thus the critical principle used to subvert many biblical narratives is not merely secular and external to the Bible but also religious and internal to it (ibid., p. 190).

101 Rightly, Scholz, 1998. Incidentally, Fewell and Gunn are quite wrong to take Shechem's speaking to Dinah's heart as a perlocutionary act which wins her over to his cause (1991, p. 196). Sternberg has clearly demonstrated that it indicates nothing about Dinah's response to Shechem's soothing words (1992, pp. 476-78). Thus the text does not indicate that Dinah came to love Shechem.

102 Segal, 1988, p. 247.

103 Rightly Keefe, 1993, p. 79.

even if this is so it would be much more than that to her. They do fail to perceive *fully* her perspective and this is a weakness on their part. Nevertheless, I would imagine that she would perceive her rape in much the same categories as her family: as "folly" and as "defiling".[104] Now they *are* presuming on Dinah here, for they have not actually consulted her (she was inaccessible at Shechem's house), but presumably she shares the basic Israelite perspectives on rape and exogamy – the same one her brothers would have.[105]

The considerations above suggest that if it is legitimate to re-imagine the story from Dinah's perspective, then care ought to be taken to avoid anachronism – to imagine that Dinah is a modern western woman with modern western values. We need to try to understand how the rape would be seen *within an Israelite worldview*. Attempts to restore Dinah's voice must ring true to the ancient cultural context.

However, we are still left with the problem that the story, quite clearly, does not take Dinah's perspective into consideration and this raises the legitimate concern that the person most affected by the crime is silenced, not only by the men who negotiate over her fate, but also by the narrator himself. What can we say about this?

Let us first note that every story is told from some perspective. Any incident can be told from the perspective of any of the parties directly or indirectly involved. The Genesis 34 events could be narrated from the perspective of the Hivite town dwellers, Jacob, the sons, Shechem, Dinah, or from any number of other perspectives. Each version would be, to some extent, a different story. Every story is told for some reason. This leads to a selection and organisation of the material so as to make the desired point. Every telling of a story has to marginalise some characters and events so as to focus on whatever it is the story teller wishes to focus on. That Dinah is marginalized in the plot need not imply that she is not morally relevant but only that *in the telling of this story* the rape is not the main focus of the plot. Unless one believes that every story which *includes* a rape must be a story *about* rape there is no *prima facie* problem with the narrator's strategy here. Nobody would suggest that the rape is not taken seriously in Genesis 34 – it leads to a massacre.

Nevertheless, even though the rape is taken seriously it is done so *from a male angle*. Is Dinah's view of the crime seen to be irrelevant? To some extent it depends on whether one feels that the lack of a certain perspective in the biblical narrator's telling of a story rules out the legitimacy of that perspective. In this case, we could ask, "Does the fact that the narrator's chosen function for this story makes no use of Dinah's perspective rule out the legitimacy or relevance of Dinah's perspective?" Clearly that depends on what we mean by

---

104 One could argue that Dinah had internalised a male perspective on rape but even if that were so it would still remain her perspective.
105 Incidentally, to imagine, as some have, that Dinah would enjoy the rape owes more to male fantasising than to textual evidence or studies of actual rape cases.

relevance. Dinah's perspective is not relevant to the point our narrator wants to draw attention to in his telling of story. This, however, is not to say that it is not relevant to *any* legitimate telling of the story. Stories may be open to the possibility of a range of uses of, and perspectives on, the events so long as those perspectives cohere with their overall worldview. From the fact that Dinah's view is not found in Genesis 34 one cannot infer that Dinah's view does not matter, nor even that Dinah's view does not matter to the author.[106] One can only infer that Dinah's view is not relevant to the point that the narrator wants to make in his use of the story here.

It could be argued that the narrator *should* have set out to see her side of things. Her view may not suit his purposes but that is merely because his purposes are androcentric and so the feminist critique still has bite. However, although the task of presenting Dinah's view would be very worthwhile why *must* the narrator do this? If the narrative somehow made Dinah's perspective illegitimate or irrelevant in a broader sense (rather than simply for the purposes in mind for his particular use of a story) then we have strong grounds for deep concern. However, as I've already said, we cannot infer from Dinah's silence that the views of the victims of rape do not matter.[107]

A deeper concern is that Dinah's silence is a manifestation of "the androcentric values and the androcentric worldview of the biblical narrative"[108] in which rape was considered a crime against men (husbands and fathers) and not women.[109] Consider Thistlethwaite's definition of rape in Israel: "Biblical rape is theft of sexual property."[110] Rape, on this analysis, has nothing to do

---

106 I hesitate to say "narrator" as it seems to me that a narrator has no existence beyond the text and consequently one cannot talk of their holding views which are not expressed in the text (as authors can).

107 There are possible explanations for Dinah's silence which do not reflect the view that her perspective is irrelevant because it is female. For instance, Sternberg (1992) has suggested that Israelite rules on exogamy would rule the marriage out of court and that, consequently, Dinah's views for or against the marriage were really irrelevant, but then so too were those of any of the male characters. It is not only Dinah's views but also Jacob's which are absent from the story. A fascinating alternative view on Dinah's silence is that of feminist scholar Alice Keefe (1993).

108 Exum, 1999, p. 145.

109 See for instance, Pressler, 1994. Pressler argues that behind the laws on violence against women lies the assumption that "female sexuality is male property" (p. 112).

110 Thistlethwaite, 1993, p. 59. Rashkow similarly writes, "And as the Genesis 34 narrative of Jacob's daughter Dinah makes clear, rape is not considered a violation of the daughter so much as a theft of property that deprives the father and necessitates compensation to him" (1993, p. 70). Besides my comment above to the effect that rape was also a crime against women in Israel, I think that it is dubious to claim that there is any form of compensation to Jacob in Genesis 34. Shechem offers a generous but standard payment of a *mohar* for the marriage. There is no obvious compensation mentioned except the generous amount but that is presented as Shechem's desperate attempt to persuade Jacob to allow the marriage and not a compensation.

with a crime against the woman herself. Thistlethwaite is correct, in my view, that rape in Israel was seen as a crime against the father (if the girl was unmarried) or the husband. Children were under the authority of their fathers and one was not allowed to engage in sexual relations with a daughter unless the father had given permission for marriage. However, she is, I suspect, wrong if she intends to imply that rape in Israel was *only* an offence against the father or the husband. Rape was also seen as wronging a woman herself. Consider the words of Tamar to Amnon in 2 Samuel 13:12-13 before the rape: "Don't force me... What about me? Where could I get rid of my disgrace?" Consider her words after he rapes her and then casts her out in v. 16: "Sending me away would be a greater wrong than what you have already done to me." Notice, the crime is, from her perspective, primarily against her and not her father.[111] Furthermore, it is misleading, in my view, to talk of wives in Israel as sexual property.[112] Nevertheless, in spite of all that I have said, it remains the case that Genesis 34, along with most Old Testament narrative, is androcentric. As I consider Dinah and Leah's views to be valuable it is at least an inadequacy *in some sense* that they are not presented.

The outcome of this discussion seems to me threefold. First, the fact that Genesis 34 is told from a male perspective does not, in and of itself, make it illegitimate for such perspectives are surely relevant. Second, the androcentricity need not even make it problematic in *a strong sense* for such perspectives are not necessarily inconsistent with female ones and do not rule out the latter's legitimacy. Third, if we grant the legitimacy of a female perspective then we grant *that there is more to be said about the incident at Shechem than is said by Genesis 34*. This need not be a threat to Genesis 34 but it may point towards the legitimacy of some kind of re-imagining the story from the perspective of the women involved (Leah, Dinah and the Hivite women). This leads me on to a recent hermeneutical proposal by Richard Bauckham.[113]

Bauckham argues that the Bible contains several narratives, or parts of narratives, which are gynocentric (seen from a female perspective). He pays

---

111 It could be argued in response that 2 Samuel 13 presents Tamar's personal female perceptions of her rape and not the public male perceptions embodied in law codes such as those Pressler discusses. This distinction is too sharp. Tamar's perceptions would reflect the social attitudes of ancient Israelite society which were broader than the law codes but which played an important role in Israelite personal and social ethics (on the complex and obscure relations between Old Testament laws and social norms see Rodd, 2001). Such social attitudes were admittedly shaped by Israelite patriarchy so that the crime against the woman was not primarily one of violence against her autonomy but a crime against her honour and her chances of marriage. Nevertheless, rape was still seen as an offence against the woman as well as her father or husband (contra Rodd, 2001, pp. 263-69).
112 Hugenberger, 1994, ch. 6; C.J.H. Wright, 1990, ch. 6.
113 Bauckham, 1996; 1997, pp. 29-45.

special attention to the book of Ruth demonstrating how it reflects female perspectives on its subject matter.[114] "The value of Ruth as women's literature is precisely that it renders visible what is usually invisible."[115] Now that a book such as Ruth is included within the canon serves as a corrective to the majority of androcentric texts. But it does more than that:

> By revealing the Israelite women's world which is elsewhere invisible in biblical narrative it makes readers aware of the lack of women's perspectives elsewhere and it also authorises them to supply just such a women's perspective elsewhere, expanding the hints and filling in the gaps which they can now see to be left by the narratives written purely or largely from a male perspective'.[116]

He concludes, "Even though the majority of biblical narratives are androcentric, there are enough authentically gynocentric narratives to counteract this dominant androcentricity, provided we allow them to do so."[117] Bauckham is saying that the *biblical canon itself* could legitimate such an imaginative approach to its androcentric narratives.[118]

A traditional Christian will need to ask what the connection is between the voice of the narrative and the voice of God. Perhaps it would be better to speak of the *voices* of a narrative for biblical narratives draw in different voices and different perspectives. Genesis 34 is a case in point, for we have already clearly distinguished the perspectives of Jacob, his sons, Shechem, Hamor and the Hivite men. Sternberg has shown how the narrator skilfully brings all the divergent voices of the characters into play, mediating between them and leading the reader towards certain evaluations of those characters. That is to say that the narrator too has a perspective and a voice and he aims to lead the reader

---

114 Which is not to claim that it was written by a female (Bauckham, 1996, pp. 6-7, 1997a, pp. 29-31) nor is it to claim that Ruth subverts the patriarchal structures of Old Testament society for it does not. "Ruth is the paradigmatic upholder of patriarchal ideology" (Fuchs, 1999, p. 78). Fuchs sees the book of Ruth as a book from a man's world and for a man's world but, although she is correct in seeing the book as one which operates within the norms of patriarchy, she fails to appreciate the degree of gynocentrism observed by Bauckham and others. See (ed.) A. Brenner, 1993b for various essays highlighting the book of Ruth as "a female text" (p. 14), "a collective creation of women's culture" (p. 139) and "an expression of women's culture and women's concerns" (p. 143).

115 Bauckham, 1996, p. 14.

116 Ibid., p. 17.

117 Ibid., p. 23.

118 And, of course, a male reimagining of the gynocentric sections of Ruth is also legitimated.

to share this view. Should we identify the narrator's perspective with God's?[119] Sternberg thinks that the narratorial voice is actually presented as a prophetic voice identified with God's.[120] However, this is questionable[121] and, from a canonical perspective, it seems that it is too simplistic to *identify* a narratorial perspective with God's for a narratorial perspective does not exhaust God's perspective even if it captures an element of it. The canon of the Hebrew Bible and the New Testament both endorse multiple, authorised perspectives on the same events indicating that no single telling of the event claims to pick out *every* morally and theologically salient feature, and numerous different perspectives can stand side by side in harmony. What, for instance, is God's perspective on Jesus? That of some particular Gospel writer? Of Paul? Of Peter? Of Revelation? God's view cannot be exhausted by any one of their perspectives nor by their cumulative totality.

Nevertheless, for the traditional Christian, all the biblical narrators' perspectives are divinely authorised as appropriate ones and together they shape and inform readerly perspectives. None of them would be seen to *conflict* with divine perspectives[122] and God speaks through them to his people recommending ways of seeing situations. However, we should not infer from the authorised nature of biblical narratives that the narrator says all that is worth saying or exhausts the divine perspective. This seems to me to make imaginative retellings of Dinah's feelings unthreatening to the canonical account – at least in principle. So long as they are not thought by the Christian community to have the status of the canonical telling the enterprise seems perfectly legitimate.

Some reflections on biblical authority may be in order here. One cannot move without thought from the claim that a particular biblical text was inspired by God to the claim that it is normative or authoritative. Classical Christian views of the Bible have seen divine authority mediated through *the canon as a whole* rather than its individual parts in isolation.[123] The Bible is not authoritative because it is composed of authoritative parts as if normativity is

---

119 The notion that a God's-Eye view is neutral in some way is not a Christian one. A God's-Eye view would be one in full possession of the facts and pure in its moral judgements.

120 Sternberg, 1987, ch. 2.

121 Wolterstorff, 1995, pp. 245-52.

122 Perhaps Wolterstorff would nuance this to suggest that God would be saying what the narrator is saying unless we have good grounds for thinking that God would not be saying that (ibid., ch. 12). Exactly what would count as good reasons is then a crucial question as the door could be open to anybody to reject illocutionary stances of biblical narrators on the grounds that they think that God would never take such a stance. The whole notion that God appropriates human illocutionary stances could be ultimately undermined in this way.

123 Some feminists see the canon itself as a patriarchal construction. For a brief but helpful critique see Bauckham, 1997a, pp. 44-45.

found as much in those parts in isolation. Nor is normativity something which supervenes upon the complex inter-textual links of the completed canon as if at some point the collection "went critical" and suddenly, as if by magic, the authority appeared. Rather, I suggest, each part of the whole is inspired and, in its original contexts, mediated some mode[124] of divine authority. However, when incorporated within the canon the way in which they are normative is modified by interactions with fellow texts. Thus any part of the Bible can *only* function authoritatively for the Church *when seen within the context of the whole*. Clearly, as the canon has grown and the plot line has moved on, the way in which different texts function normatively changes.

So, returning to feminist concerns, even if a biblical narrative sets out models for appropriate wifely behaviour (say) one cannot simply *assume* that those models are still normative today in the same way as they were when the texts were originally redacted. It seems to me that the very nature of the canon invites a certain kind of relativising of texts in light of the whole. Biblical narratives can, in principle, be supplemented and relativised by other biblical texts[125] and by archaeological finds without threatening their inspiration or their authority. In the context of gender issues the kind of relativising that I am proposing does not relativise the androcentric texts *in every respect* but simply in their androcentrism.[126]

Let me bring these reflections to Genesis 34 and briefly explore the limits and legitimacy of restoring the female perspectives. Genesis 34 simply does not provide the information from which to construct Dinah's viewpoint, let alone those of Leah or the Hivite women. In the story her view is not a gap that needs to be filled in order to make sense of the narrative but a blank – an information gap to which the narrator does not draw attention.[127] Herein lies the potential danger of "authoring the secret diaries of Dinah"[128] – "Anyone who wanted answers to these questions [about Dinah's view] would have no option but to invent their own."[129] One could invent a range of totally contradictory perspectives for Dinah and none of them could claim to be anything more than the imaginative reconstructions of the reader. This is only a problem if one

---

124 Clearly different genres mediate divine authority in different ways (compare the Ten Commandments with Proverbs) and thus I speak of modes of authority. Further clarification is obviously required here. It may be that the notion of authority is not elastic enough to cover all the biblical texts and should be abandoned in some cases.

125 I suggest that the biblical plot-line itself prioritises certain key texts and themes theologically over others. For instance, Genesis 1-2 has long been recognised as carrying a priority over Esther (say) or Deuteronomy in theological considerations of gender relations. This is because Genesis 1-2 reflects the way God set things up in the beginning prior to sin's distortions (see Mt 19:1-8).

126 With Bauckham, 1997a, p. 44.

127 On gaps and blanks see Sternberg, 1987, pp. 235-58.

128 Noble, 1996, p. 200.

129 Ibid., p. 198.

thinks that one is finding the "right" answer given by the text rather than supplementing the text with informed yet *imaginative* stories. Some reflections are in order.

An *exegesis* of Genesis 34 should make no reference to Dinah's views as they are simply irrelevant to the story-telling of the chapter.[130] This does little for issues of women's justice or dignity but, I have attempted to argue that it need do nothing to harm them either *so long as* it does not legitimate the broader claim that Dinah's view does not matter *at all*.

If we grant, as we must, that the female views are not irrelevant, then we open up the legitimacy and possibility for imaginative, Midrashic reflections on how Dinah, Leah or the Hivite women may have felt. Such reflections will not make the pretence to exegesis, but will simply claim the status of readerly reflections using the text as a springboard and not explanations of the narrator's interests.

Such readerly reflections must be grounded upon the text and a careful reading of it and they will never replace the text. Genesis 34 will be the basis for every fresh readerly reflection. Any reflection which misreads the actual text would thereby falsify itself. The biblical narrator may not share our concerns or interests but that need not stop us reading a text from the perspective of those concerns and interests. The narrator may say things which have a bearing on our concerns and provide fuel for our own reflections. Reflections on Dinah's view on her rape could draw on the story of the rape of Tamar in 2 Samuel 13 which, I would argue, deliberately alludes to Genesis 34. The narrator in 2 Samuel sees the importance of the view of the rape victim and a reader could thus claim scriptural support for reflecting on the Shechem incident from an imaginative reconstruction of Dinah's view. Schroer comments on 2 Samuel 13 that

> a woman reading this text will note that the narrators of the story are on Tamar's side. They declare her to be free from any guilt, stress her wisdom and thoughtfulness, and feel sympathy for her. And this is how the story of a sexual assault at the royal court is at least snatched from the jaws of the final injustice, that of being silenced. In Israel, the victims of violence are remembered.[131]

Perhaps a text like Psalm 55 could also be brought into intertextual relationship

---

130 Rightly Noble, Ibid..

131 Schottroff, Schroer and Wacker, 1998, p. 55. Judges 19 is often seen as a text which dehumanises women in the grotesque brutality dealt to the Levites concubine. However, the text very clearly presents the rape and murder of the woman as a dreadful deed indicating how serious the decline of Israel has become. In no way is the deed presented as legitimate nor is the Levite's shocking behaviour in throwing her out to be abused excused. Her story is told and must be retold in memoriam of women victims of violence.

with our texts also. Ulrike Bail has argued that it is a woman's complaint to God about a sexual assault by a man close to her.[132] Even if this is not correct the text could be *re*appropriated in such a way. Such can only enrich one's reading scripture.

Third, for readers who consider the biblical text inspired, readerly reflections will not be able to reject the narrator's perspective as false. This is not likely to impress some feminist readers. Alice Bach argues that feminist readers must suspect and resist the biblical narrator. Clearly, such a method *can* and *has been* applied to the Bible as to many texts but *prioritising* an orientation of suspicion as opposed to one of trust in approaching the Christian scriptures is alien to the Christian tradition.[133] Feminists may often read the Bible in this way but to do so is not to read with a traditional Christian hermeneutic. Christian *Midrash* on Old Testament narratives may see the women's view as either running along the grain of the text (in line with the narrator) or perpendicular to the text (neither with nor against the narrator[134]) or against the text.[135] However, if a woman's re-imagined perspective does run against the grain the text it is subverted by the narrator who, for the Christian community, retains his "authorised perspective" which, though not complete, will not be seen to be wrong. It may be felt that this hamstrings some important feminist critiques of the Bible and I am forced to agree. Nevertheless, I believe that to surrender the fundamental biblical hermeneutic of faith for one of suspicion is to pay a price too high.

---

132 Bail, 1994, pp. 67-84.

133 I do not want to suggest that a feminist hermeneutic is one of suspicion as opposed to one of faith. It should be obvious from my first section that many feminists seek to combine both. My point is that a feminist hermeneutic will usually begin with suspicion and then see what is left for faith whilst a Christian hermeneutic will begin with faith and suspicion will play a role subsidiary to it. Alternatively one may tone this down and argue that any critique of the biblical narrators must be done by means of a critical principle rooted in the biblical metanarrative itself rather than one imposed from the outside (Watson, 1994, ch. 11; Middleton and Walsh, 1995, ch. 8). However, pitting the whole against its parts seems at very least problematic as a method in conservative Christian hermeneutics. I can see that the whole can complement or relativise the parts but I am very cautious about the idea that it can be used to reject the parts.

134 Much of Stephen Spielberg's cartoon *The Prince of Egypt* would be what I call reading perpendicular to the text.

135 One could imagine that "Telling Queen Jezebel's Story", say, would involve reading against the narrator. However, the traditional Christian will not want to subvert the narrator's condemnation of Jezebel even if they may seek to understand her in a more rounded way. The biblical narrator may not tell the whole truth about Jezebel but they do tell the truth.

# Conclusions

In Chapter One it was argued that the narrative shape of individual and communal identity helps us to see why stories have the ethically transforming power that they do. Identity is constructed in dialogue with stories and our ethical values are embodied in such narratives. In particular, stories can model virtues and vices, highlight the importance of particularity in moral judgements, shape a reader's emotional profile, and even explicate the grammar of virtues and moral rules. Our study of Genesis 34 has not sought to offer a full-blown reappropriation but rather to offer boundaries *within which* Christian ethical readings will operate. Nevertheless, we have seen in Chapter Four that the Dinah story does exemplify most of these points:

Shechem's rape of Dinah is clearly set forth as an evil action which readers should condemn. The sons' actions are also seen as *over*reactions and not as models to be imitated.

Particularity is important in Genesis 34. The reader's judgement is complicated by the narrator's attempts to get him or her to sympathise with the sons' anger. The dilemma faced by the Jacobites can be felt intensely and the reader struggles to play with different potential solutions. The actual solution of the sons must be seriously considered by the reader before being rejected. The best way forward is never disclosed, and the reader is left to wrestle with the situation. How should the family have acted in *this* situation?

Emotional perception is *illustrated* well by the text. Jacob perceives the danger to his family and feels the weight of his responsibility to them. However, he does not perceive the ethical import of the crime against Dinah. Shechem and Hamor treat the family with a certain amount of respect and are eager to please. However, they fail to see the seriousness of Shechem's offence. Jacob's sons, unlike the other characters, do perceive the depth of the crime committed against their family (and, to some extent, that against Dinah herself) but close their eyes to the horrors that their own action bring about. All of the male characters have partial, emotionally informed, ethical insight and partial blindness. Precisely how the story will shape the emotionality of the *reader* will vary from one reader to another.

Genesis 34 does not contribute to the grammar of any virtues or moral rules.

Chapter One maintained that the reception history of a *particular text* ought to be considered as one seeks to read it afresh. In Chapter Three we did just this by taking samples from Jewish and Christian ethical interpretations of Genesis 34 over two millennia. We discovered an amazing diversity in the moral evaluations of the different participants and this became the background to our fresh attempt to interpret the story in Chapter Four.

Our first chapter also argued that all readers employ interpretative

*methodologies* that are situated within reading traditions. Chapter Two sets out
the contours of a *Christian* hermeneutic grounded in the biblical metanarrative.
Such a hermeneutic begins with the overall plot of the Bible and seeks to relate
specific texts to their place in the whole and to the reader's location in that
same plot. We saw that even the non-narrative parts of biblical ethics find their
home in this large story that stretches from creation to new creation. This
chapter thus revealed the centrality of story for Old Testament ethics in both its
narrative and its non-narrative forms.

Chapter Five sought to see how the theological hermeneutic proposed in
Chapter Two would guide Christian ethical appropriations of Genesis 34. It was
argued that for a Mosaic audience the sons' action would be seen as wrong.
This conclusion was defended on the basis of Genesis 34 and strengthened by a
detailed study of Old Testament texts which seem to allude to that text (Gen 49,
Num 25, 31). We argued that, paradoxically, to a Mosaic audience the story
could *also* function as a type of the *legitimate* conquest of Canaan under
Joshua. It is this double-function of the story that has generated what, at first
sight, seem to be conflicting hints concerning the narrator's assessments of the
sons' action in Genesis 34 (explored in Chapter Four). I suggest that, to some
extent, the positive hints are there to enable the typological function to come
into play.

The story can be appropriated by a Christian audience in much the same way
as by a Mosaic audience with the following differences. First, the issue of
circumcision and Jewish exclusivism is not relevant for the Christian for whom
the dividing wall between Jew and Gentile has been broken down in Christ.
However, the analogous issue of faith, baptism and Christian exclusivism
makes it easy to find Christian partial parallels. Even here, the parallels will not
be simple as Genesis 34 embodies clear cultural elements, such as patriarchal
marriage conventions, which are not universal and which resist attempts to
draw *simplistic* parallels. The particularity of the situation needs to be respected
in one's attempts to find a model morality. The drawing of parallels is more an
art than a science requiring acts of moral imagination. Second, at the
typological level the story *cannot* serve as a type of legitimate violence by the
church in the way that it did for Israel. The Yahweh War tradition was modified
in the New Testament such that it was interpreted in a *non-violent* way. A
Christian *typological* interpretation will be non-violent. So the Christian reader
can ethically explore the story within these limits.

Chapter Six looked at the challenge of feminist scholarship which
problematises a hermeneutic that simply *assumes* Old Testament narratives to
be ethically beneficial. It is argued that one could maintain that the patriarchy
of Israelite society is not legitimated by the metanarrative but reflects the
structures of a fallen world. This makes various aspects of Genesis 34 culturally
relative and able to be appropriated in different cultures in different ways. More
particularly, I suggested that the silence of Dinah need not be seen as
problematic in a *strong* sense so long as it does not entail the objectionable

view that her perspective is irrelevant. The metanarrative itself, and other parts of the canon, can legitimise Midrashic reconstructions of the missing perspectives (Dinah's, Leah's, the Hivite women's). Such imaginative reconstructions cannot be authoritative for the church in the same way that the text is but they can be good for the emotional formation of the ethical imagination. Such explorations need not subvert the authoritative narratorial perspectives but can complement them and bring out the necessary limitations of any particular telling of a story.

# Appendices

# Appendix 1: A Discourse Analysis of Genesis 34

## The Discourse Analysis of Robert Longacre

In this Appendix I aim to bring to bear the resources of modern discourse analysis to provide the foundation for a sensitive hearing of the Dinah story. "Discourse grammarians have emphasised that explicit linguistic criteria are indispensable as proof of the validity of analysis."[1] My intention is neither to further the development of modern linguistics nor to evaluate specific linguistic theories. Rather I intend to take one prominent theory in the field, that of Robert Longacre, "off the peg" and try it out for size on Genesis 34. My justification for this is that this book is about Genesis 34 and *not* about discourse analysis. After setting Robert Longacre's method of discourse analysis within the broader context of Hebrew linguistics, I will explain key elements of his method to enable the reader to better understand Chapter Four of this book.

### Surveying the Surroundings

First, we shall to seek to locate Longacre's method on the broader map of discourse analysis. Discourse analysis is an umbrella term for contextual approaches that relate syntactic form to "conversational etiquette, presuppositions, intentions, cognitive processes, world view, and even personal values."[2] Peter MacDonald, in his survey of the varieties of discourse analysis, draws attention to grammatical discourse analysis; sociolinguistics with its focus on everyday conversational speech in which the context is the *social setting* of the speaker and listener; ethnography with its attempt to uncover the worldviews of homogeneous groups by analysis of language; psycholinguistics where the mental processes governing the reception or perception of discourse are scrutinised; cognitive linguistics with its attempt to model the mental processes involved in the production and reception of discourse and pragmatics, the child of speech-act theory. "The approaches to discourse are so many because the object of analysis - human discourse - is so complex."[3] This Appendix focuses on grammatical and sociolinguistic discourse analysis.

Since the 1970s many Biblical Hebrew grammarians have, under the influence of modern linguistic theory, shifted away from the traditional

---

1 Winther-Nielsen, 1995, p. 10.
2 MacDonald, 1992, pp. 153-154.
3 Ibid., p. 161.

sentence-based approach to grammar. H. Weinrich writes that "a grammar which does not accept units beyond the sentence can never even notice, let alone resolve the most interesting problems in linguistics."[4] Christo van der Merwe identifies three main lines of thought since the pioneering work in the early seventies.

*The Form-To-Function Approach*[5]

These approaches "favour an entire revaluation of existing grammatical knowledge in terms of a new look at all the Biblical Hebrew data."[6] The formal data at the lower levels (ie., morphology, morphosyntax, sentence syntax) are treated exhaustively prior to any higher level phenomena. Van der Merwe identifies Hoftijzer, Richter and Talstra as major players in this approach.

*The Functional Approach*[7]

These are "those approaches that treat specific problem areas in the description of Biblical Hebrew in terms of one modern linguistic or discourse theory."[8] These begin with a hypothesis on specific linguistic notions and attempt to explain awkward Biblical Hebrew data in terms of it. Van der Merwe thinks that we ought to consider the Form-to-Function and the Functional approaches as complementary. The tendency of the latter approach is to focus on levels between the sentence and the text.[9] Some of these methods are "bottom up" (eg. Dik, Andersen) whilst others are "top down" (eg. Longacre).

Francis Andersen is the father of the functional approach in Biblical Hebrew. His work on the verbless clause[10] and the sentence[11] broke new ground by the application of tagmemic theory. It is this particular theory which I use in the analysis of Genesis 34. Another key name in the Functional approach is Muraoka whose work on particles and word order[12] was ground breaking. Van der Merwe himself has built upon and advanced Muraoka's work. However, I have been primarily inspired by the "top down" approach of Robert Longacre. Presently I shall return to explain the theory in question.

---

4 Quoted in Niccacci, 1990, p. 19.
5 Van der Merwe, 1994, pp. 16-17.
6 Ibid., p. 15.
7 Ibid., pp. 17-21.
8 Ibid., p. 15.
9 We shall see that Longacre's approach has a strong focus on the paragraph. Winther-Nielsen writes that "the paragraph... is the most important unit of interclausal coherence in the information flow of a discourse" (Winther-Nielsen, 1995, p. 82).
10 Andersen, 1970.
11 Andersen, 1974.
12 Muraoka, 1985.

*The Traditional Approaches Revised[13]*

Strictly speaking traditional approaches are not discourse analysis at all. Van der Merwe singles out Waltke and O'Conner's massive 1990 work on Biblical Hebrew syntax and Muraoka's reworking of Jouon's 1927 classic *Biblical Hebrew Grammar* for specific attention. Waltke and O'Conner resist the move towards text linguistics as they feel that the discipline is still in its infancy and thus of little help to many of the problems of grammar.[14] Their resistance to discourse grammar is a great shame because this infant offers such promise in the task of interpreting Hebrew texts.[15] Van der Merwe sums up well:

> Studying Biblical Hebrew from a discourse perspective is part of a greater movement in the study of Biblical Hebrew. Most scholars now would concede that Biblical Hebrew needs to be studied beyond the level of the sentence. But they differ as to the appropriate stage in research for beginning these studies. Some prefer to concentrate first of all on problems within the safe boundaries of the sentence. Others insist that if a higher level description is investigated, it must always be determined, as far as humanly possible whether, and to what extent, the hierarchically structured lower levels can serve as a foundation for the higher levels. Others are more adventurous and are prepared to apply theories based on data in other languages to Biblical Hebrew constructions beyond the sentence: However, a feature of even these more adventurous approaches is the prominent role that the Biblical Hebrew data play in the scrutiny of hypotheses postulated.[16]

This latter point is of major importance to discourse grammarians. Dawson makes the first item of the discourse analysis *Credo* the "primacy of the data."[17] Analysts must always allow the data to modify their presuppositions. Emending the data to fit a theory will always be the last resort.[18]

Having surveyed the terrain we now can see how the thesis of Robert Longacre fits into the spectrum of approaches. He is one of van der Merwe's adventurous linguists who applies theories drawn from various languages to Hebrew. He is an exponent of a top down Functional approach.

## *Longacre and Tagmemic Linguistic Theory*

David Dawson considers Longacre's 1989 book, *Joseph: a Story of Divine Providence,* to be "the most significant advancement in Hebrew textlinguistics seen to date; it contains much of near-revolutionary value to the student of

---

13 Van der Merwe, 1994, p. 21.
14 Waltke and O'Conner, 1990, p. 55.
15 For a critique of Waltke and O'Conner see Dawson, 1994, pp. 24-28.
16 Van der Merwe, 1994, p. 22.
17 Dawson, 1994, p. 108.
18 Ibid., p. 113.

Classical Hebrew syntax."[19] Not everybody is as uncritical of Longacre as Dawson, but all would agree that his work is of major importance. I am not interested in *evaluating* Longacre so much as *using* his approach to see what light it may shed on Genesis 34. In the explanations which follow I am primarily indebted to Dawson's book, *Text-Linguistics and Biblical Hebrew*.

Longacre is a "member" of the Tagmemic school of linguistics. Tagmemics was born in the Fifties out of the work of K.L. Pike and it has developed with an ongoing openness to the data of real live languages around the world. Longacre himself has worked for many years in the field with indigenous languages in Mexico, the Pacific, North America and Africa. He has "long been at the forefront of this development, and is without doubt the text-linguist with the greatest exposure to the breadth of the world's language data, of anyone in print today."[20]

*Language Universals*

Longacre and others of the Tagmemic school have observed certain features that occur regularly in the world's languages which are often labelled "language universals".[21] One such language universal is that languages linguistically mark significant events in a story (so called "peak events") so as to make them stand out from the rest of the story. Also languages normally make distinctions between foreground and background information.[22] Such "language universals" play an important role in Tagmemic approaches to Biblical Hebrew. They indicate the kind of things which we may expect to find in the Hebrew text and, given the limited Biblical Hebrew data-base and the lack of living speakers, such ideas are helpful.[23] Of course, any application of a language universal to Biblical Hebrew must be open to being modified or rejected if the data does not fit - the particular language always has priority in the spiral from hypothesis to data and back to hypothesis.

Language is a part of human behaviour[24] and the setting in which language is used is reflected in linguistic features. Central to human behaviour is "patterning" and "it follows that we should require that a linguistic theory give centrality to linguistic patterns."[25] The discourse grammarian is concerned to describe the patterns that occur at *text* level. It is here that Longacre's work helps us to get a more text-sensitive appreciation of Genesis 34 than has often been the case in the past.

---

19 Ibid., p. 56.

20 Ibid., p. 58.

21 Ibid., p. 18. We should understand the word universal to mean no more than that most languages display the feature in question.

22 Ibid., p. 18.

23 Ibid., p. 20.

24 Ibid., p. 76.

25 Longacre, quoted in ibid., p. 77.

*Key Elements in Longacre's System*

In the appendix of *Joseph* Longacre mentions three elements which he considers central to tagmemics. These are tagmeme, syntagmeme and hierarchical linguistic structures. It is simpler to begin with the third of these.

(a) Hierarchical Linguistic Structures
Hierarchical linguistic structure simply refers to a series of levels of language from morpheme to word to phrase to clause to sentence to paragraph to discourse. Typically each level is composed of units from a lower level. Thus words are built from morphemes, phrases from words and so on. Constituent structure analysis is the taking apart of a linguistic unit and breaking it down into its component parts. This allows for patterns to emerge.

(b) The Slot-Filler Distinction (Tagmeme and Syntagmeme)
The next step is to grasp the slot-filler distinction.[26] Dawson helpfully illustrates this concept as follows:

> A man gets dressed and goes to work in a bank in Edinburgh, Scotland. There are certain things he must wear, of course: shoes, socks, trousers, shirt, tie and jacket being the basics. Now he has a choice of which shirt to wear..., and he can choose from among several dark suits, or combinations of trousers and jackets; he has a fairly wide variety of socks, and more than a few ties. He has a choice between three different pairs of black shoes. Yet the ensemble is more or less dictated by custom. There is a typical "slot-filler" relationship involved here. In each case, a required piece of clothing is supplied from a collection of suitable options: the man undoubtedly has... many pairs of socks..., but it would be socially unacceptable for him to wear one of these in place of the required neck tie. In the same way, grammatical (and other) relations can be described as "slot" into which an item is fitted; the item is chosen from among a set of acceptable "fillers".[27]

We are now in a position to make sense of Longacre's other two keys to Tagmemics: syntagmeme and tagmeme. *A syntagmeme is a language unit composed of sub-units called tagmemes.* If we look at a sentence as a syntagmeme it will be composed of clause tagmemes. If we consider a clause as a syntagmeme the tagmemes will be words and phrases. Thus one could consider Dawson's banker illustration as follows:[28] "Male Banker's Uniform" is the syntagmeme which is composed of the following tagmemes (slots) - "shirt", "suit", "tie", "socks", "shoes". Each slot/tagmeme can be filled in various ways. Alternatively we could consider "Suit" as the syntagmeme and

26 Dawson, 1994, pp. 82-84. Longacre himself referers to this distinction as the 'function-set' distinction (1989, p. 311).
27 Dawson, 1994, p. 83.
28 Ibid., p. 86.

"dark jacket" and "trousers" as the tagmemes to be filled.

A linguistic example considered by Dawson is the "intransitive-clause" syntagmeme.[29] It is composed of an obligatory subject tagmeme and an obligatory predicate tagmeme. The subject slot could be filled with a noun phrase, a pronoun, a proper name etc.. The predicate slot could be filled with an intransitive verb phrase. Typically a slot is filled by a syntagmeme from the next lower level in the language hierarchy. Thus a subject slot in an intransitive clause syntagmeme could be filled by a noun phrase - a syntagmeme from a lower level.[30] This is what Longacre calls "primary exponence". There are other types of exponence. There is "recursive exponence" when "a unit fills a slot in a syntagmeme of that same level."[31] For example, a phrase within a phrase. There is "back-looping exponence" is when a higher level unit fills a slot in a lower level. For example, a sentence within a phrase or a clause within a phrase.[32] Finally, there is "level-skipping exponence". Here a slot is filled not from the next layer in a linguistic hierarchy but from one below that. "A shorthand term for both recursive exponence and back-looping exponence is "embedding"."[33] My analysis of Genesis 34 is primarily concerned with recursive exponence when one paragraph fills a slot in another. I simply refer to this as "embedding".

(c) Text Types

Central to Longacre's system is the notion of "text-types". He writes, "I must posit here that (a) every language has a system of discourse types (eg., Narrative, Predictive, Hortatory, Procedural, Expository and others); (b) each discourse type has its own characteristic constellation of verb forms that figure in that type; (c) that uses of given tense/aspect/mood form are most surely and concretely described in relation to a given discourse type."[34] He sets up three parameters that form a grid to enable him to identify different such text-types.

*(i) Agent Orientation*

First of all Agent-Orientation.[35] This is the aspect of a text where participants are highlighted (or not). A text can thus be +Agent Orientation or -Agent Orientation. For example, a narrative is +A.O. and a "How to assemble your model car" set of instructions is -A.O. as the activities to be performed are highlighted rather than the person who does them.

*(ii) Contingent Temporal Succession*

Secondly, there is Contingent Temporal Succession. Dawson explains the issue

---

29 Ibid., p. 87.
30 Ibid., pp. 89-90.
31 Ibid., p. 90.
32 Ibid., p. 92.
33 Ibid., p. 92.
34 Longacre, 1989, p. 39.
35 Dawson, 1994, p. 94.

as one of "whether or not events or doings in a text are related to (or 'contingent upon') prior events or doings."[36] Thus narrative has chronological linkage and is thus +CTS whereas an explanation as to why red wine ought not to be chilled before consumption is -CTS.

### (iii) Projection
Thirdly, there is Projection.

> If a text is "plus Projection", it looks towards the future in some way; if it is "minus Projection", it does not. For example, a set of instructions about how to turn lead into gold will be "plus Projection"; a lab report about how lead was turned into gold will be "minus Projection".[37]

These three combine to form a matrix of the following eight text-types each of which is illustrated by Dawson.[38]

|  | + Agent Orientation | - Agent Orientation |  |
|---|---|---|---|
| + Contingent Temporal Succession | 1. NARRATIVE | 2. PROCEDURAL |  |
|  | Prediction[39] | How-to-do-it | + Projection |
|  | Story | How-it-was-done | - Projection |
| - Contingent Temporal Succession | 3. BEHAVIOURAL | 4. EXPOSITORY |  |
|  | Exhortation | Budget proposal | + Projection |
|  | Promisory Speech | Futuristic essay |  |
|  | Eulogy | Scientific paper | - Projection |

Each quadrant of this matrix represents one of the four major types of discourse identified by Longacre in his work on Philippine languages.[40] It is central to the method which I use that there are different text-types and that the syntactic features of a language function differently in these different text-types. Traditional Hebraists have erred by looking at how particular elements of Hebrew, verbs for example, work without paying attention to differences in discourse type.[41] Thus all the uses of the Qal infinitive, say, may be investigated but, because its different functions in different text types are not

---

36 Ibid., p. 94.

37 Ibid., p. 97.

38 Ibid., pp. 98-99.

39 It needs to be made clear that Longacre himself sees prediction as a text type with its own cline. Dawson points out, by means of this diagram, that we may think of prediction of a subtype of narrative.

40 Niccacci affirms only two narrative text-types: narrative and discourse. I think that such a distinction is critical but inadequate (on Niccacci see Dawson, 1994, pp. 28-39).

41 See Longacre, 1992a, p. 177.

distinguished, the results are distorted.

### (d) "Main-Line" verses "Off-Line"

Every text-type in a language has a clause-type it "prefers".[42] Such clauses are the "back-bone" of that text-type and carry the text forward. For example, it is widely agreed by scholars that the back-bone of narrative is the WAYYIQTOL or preterite.[43] This clause-type moves the plot forward. Similarly, the volitive is the back-bone of the Hortatory text-type. We refer to such clause types as the "Main-Line" for a particular text-type.[44] Any other type of clause is "Off-Line". It does not carry the text forward but performs some other function.[45] For example, it may fill in background information. Thus, if we found a simple nominal clause (ie., a verbless one) in Narrative it is Off-Line. Such a clause is, however, Main-Line in Exposition. Main-Line and Off-Line are syntactic surface-structure features that mark the notional distinction between "foreground" (marked by the Main-Line) and "background" (marked by the Off-Line[46]).[47] Now there is not a simple binary opposition between foreground and background as some suggest (eg., Eskhult). For Longacre "the simple distinction between 'foreground' and 'background' is not nuanced enough to cope with the subtleties of story telling."[48] Clauses can have *varying degrees* of backgrounding.[49] That is to say that some clauses are closer to the Main-Line than others. It is on the basis of this suggestion that Longacre proposes his clines.

---

42 Longacre, 1989, p. 64.

43 See GKC 326; Longacre, 1989, pp. 65-66; Niccacci, 1990, pp. 175-180; Eskhult, 1990, pp. 34-36. However, Endo has some reservations and qualifications, 1996, pp. 244 ff..

44 The Main-Line is actually part of a text's cohesion (Longacre, 1989, pp. 17-18). It runs like a strand through a text holding it together. Another cohesive strand that runs vertically through a text is participant reference (ibid., p. 18). This cohesion along with coherence (lexical and referential continuity) constitute the "texture" of a text. The texture of a text is essential for the realisation of the macro-structure (the germinal idea that acts as an overall plan in the development of the discourse. Ibid., p. 17).

45 As a matter of fact the perfect or noun + perfect can carry the story forward in a secondary story-line sense. See now Longacre, 1992b, p. 215.

46 Endo thinks (contra Longacre et al) that the foreground-background distinction "seems not to be the determining factor for the choice of verbal forms" but is "a by-product of a certain determining factor" (1996, pp. 27-28). The real factor, in Endo's view, is sequentiality and non-sequesntiality (ibid., p. 324).

47 Dawson, 1994, p. 102.

48 Andersen in Endo, 1996, p. 25.

49 Longacre, 1989, p.59. Longacre, claims to have tried out this notion of degrees of backgrounding on some forty languages (1992b, p. 215).

*The Scheme*

*Longacre's Clines*

Dawson describes Longacre's verbal rank schemes as "one of the most immediately accessible - and revolutionary - contributions of the [*Joseph*] book."[50] A cline is "a scheme symbolising degrees of departure from the storyline."[51] For three of the four major discourse types Longacre proposes a verb rank scheme. The clines can now be set out as follows.[52]

*Diagram 1. Biblical Hebrew Narrative Discourse*[53]

| | |
|---|---|
| **Band 1: Storyline** | 1.1 Preterite: primary |
| **Band 2a: secondary** | 2.1 Perfect: secondary |
| **storyline** | 2.2 Noun + perfect: secondary (with noun in focus). |
| **Band 3: Background** | 3.1 Noun + imperfect: implicitly durative/ |
| **Activities.** | repetitive |
| | 3.2 הנה + participle |
| | 3.3 Participle (explicitly durative) |
| | 3.4 Noun + participle |
| **Band 4: Setting** | 4.1 Preterite of היה (to be) |
| | 4.2 Perfect of היה (to be) |
| | 4.3 Nominal clause (verbless) |
| | 4.4 Existential clause with יש |
| **Band 5: Irrealis** | 5 Negation of any verb |
| | (in any band). |
| | (n.b., a momentous negation |
| | promotes 5 to 2) |
| **Band 6: (optional ויהי** | 6.1 General reference |

---

50 Dawson, 1994, p. 63.

51 Longacre, 1989, p. .82, fn. 6.

52 In *Joseph* Longacre places the perfect and the noun + perfect in a Band 2 which he lables "Background Actions". However, in a footnote on p. 82 he argues that there is a compatible but different way to conceive of the way that these constructions function in narrative. The alternative way is set out in an essay written about the same time as Joseph (Longacre, 1992a). Subsequent thought has led Longacre to prefer the alternative (Longacre 1992b) and thus I shall use that cline, rather than the one in Joseph, even though the differences are minor. Essentially Longacre now refers to N + QATAL as "Secondary storyline". This would "allow that the great majority of N + QTL clauses are 'background actions'... but would allow a minority of cases where the secondary storyline functionally extends up towards the primary storyline" (1992b, p. 216).

53 This cline is my combination of features from the clines in Longacre 1989, p. 81 and 1992a, p. 180.

**+ temporal phrase -**                          6.2  Script predictable
**cohesion)**
                                                 6.3 Repetitive


*Diagram 2.  Biblical Hebrew Predictive Discourse*

**Band 1: Line of prediction**     1. ו (consecutive) perfect
**Band 2:  Background/**            2.1 Imperfect
**secondary predictions**          2.2 Noun + imperfect (with noun in focus).
**Band 3:  Background**             3.1 הנה + perfect
**Activities**                      3.2 Participle
                                    3.3 Noun + participle
**Band 4: Setting**                 4.1 ו (consecutive) perfect of היה (to be)
                                       4.2  Imperfect of היה (to be)
                                          4.3  Nominal clause (verbless)
                                          4.4  Existential clause with יש


*Diagram 3.  Biblical Hebrew Hortatory Discourse*

**Band 1: Primary line of**         1.1 Imperative (2nd person)
**exhortation**                     1.2 Cohortative (1st person)
                                    1.3 Jussive (3rd person)
**Band 2: Secondary line of**       2.1 על + jussive/imperative
**exhortation**                     2.2 Modal imperfect
**Band 3: Results/**                3.1 ו (consecutive) perfect
**consequences**                    3.2 פן /לא + imperfect
**(motiviation)**                   3.3 (Future) perfect
**Band 4: Setting**                    4.1 Perfect (of past events)
                                       4.2 Participles
                                       4.3 Nominal clauses


Longacre maintains that

> we must approach a paragraph as follows: Is it N[arrative], P[redictive],
> H[ortatory], or E[xpository]? Resorting to the correct verb ranking scheme, we
> can ask of each sentence: What is the relative rank of the main verb? Then
> analysing the internal structure of the paragraph, we give highest relative rank in
> the paragraph to the sentence(s) with the highest ranking verb according to [the
> idea that] relative height in the rank scheme determines relative salience in the
> local span.[54]

Clearly then how we categorise a text (N, P, H or E) determines the analysis.

---
54 Longacre, 1989, p. 60.

*Paragraph Types*

Longacre also distinguishes different types of paragraph that can manifest themselves in the different text-types. By a paragraph Longacre refers to that linguistic unit between a sentence and a discourse. It is a structural and not a visual notion (i.e., one to break the monotony of a solid page) and thus such paragraphs are "not necessarily co-extensive with orthographic indentation-bound paragraphs."[55] They are as follows:

Sequence Paragraphs[56]

These are paragraphs in which each sentence (with the possible exception of the setting and terminus) is a top ranking one. Thus we have a sequence of top-band sentences. In Narrative this would be a sequence of WAYYIQTOLs; in Prediction it is a sequence of WEQATALs; in Hortatory, a sequence of volitives and so on. Scene One in Genesis 34 provides an example of a Narrative Sequence Paragraph.

Simple Paragraphs

Such a paragraph is "a specialised instance of the... sequence paragraph."[57] It is a Main-Line paragraph that consists of one sentence, thus the sequential nature of the sequence paragraph is missing. An example of such a paragraph is found in Genesis 34:4 where there is a Hortatory Simple Paragraph that consists of:

Setting: "And Shechem spoke to Hamor his father saying..."
BUn: "Take this child as a wife for me."

Reason Paragraphs

One of these paragraphs "features an action/event or situation as its Text,[58] then proceeds to give in the Reason the cause or reason that underlies the action/event or situation."[59] For example Genesis 34:14 is an Expository Reason Paragraph with:

Text: "We are not able to do this thing - to give our sister to a man who has a foreskin"
Reason: "for he is a disgrace to us."

Similarly 34:7 is a Narrative Reason Paragraph with:

---

55 Ibid., pp. 60-61.
56 Ibid., pp. 85-89.
57 Ibid., p. 89.
58 By "Text", in this context, Longacre refers to the dominant tagmeme in the paragraph syntagmeme (Longacre, 1989, p. 61).
59 Ibid., p. 92.

Text: "the men were grieved and very angry" and
Reason: "for he had done folly in Israel by laying with Jacob's daughter - a thing which should not be done."

Result Paragraphs
Such a paragraph "features in its Text an action/event or situation, then proceeds to give in the Result the outworking of the action/event or situation."[60] For example, 34:23 is a Hortatory Results Paragraph (in 34:23 the Text is highlighted over the Result even though it follows it for rhetorical reasons[61]).

Result: "Will not their property, possessions and all their cattle be ours?"
Text: "Only let us agree to them and let them live with us."

Comment Paragraphs
These are opportunities for the narrator or a character to comment on or explain some event or situation on the Main Line. In narrative such comments serve to "enhance great moments of the story or the crescendo to a great moment." 34:7 is a Comment embedded within the reason sentence of a narrative reason paragraph.

Text: "For he had done folly in Israel..."
Comment: "a thing not done."

This is all part of the tension building prior to the negotiations. Normally the Text would be a preterite,[62] but here this is overridden by the fact the Text is a subordinate clause.

Amplification Paragraphs
"Amplification paragraphs are paragraphs that consist of a Text and an Amplification, with the latter adding new information not contained in the former, while at the same time essentially incorporating the material found in it."[63] 34:18 is a Narrative Amplification Paragraph

Text: "And their words were good in the eyes of Hamor and in the eyes of his son Shechem."
Amplification: "And the lad did not delay to do the thing for he loved Jacob's daughter."

34:27 is another Narrative Amplification Paragraph.

60 Ibid., p. 92.
61 Ibid., p. 92.
62 Ibid., p. 95.
63 Ibid., p. 97

Text: "and they plundered the city where they (i.e., the Hivites) had defiled their sister"
Amplification: "their flocks, cattle, donkeys and whatever was in the city and in the field they took."

This latter is also a chiasm. Many chiasms are Narrative Amplification Paragraphs.[64] In both of the above examples the Text is a Main Line preterite clause and the Amplification is ranked lower in the cline. This, however, need not be the case.[65]

### Paraphrase Paragraphs

"In the Paraphrase Paragraphs the Paraphrase adds little or no new information to the Text."[66] Such paragraphs are very infrequent. Longacre finds only one example in Joseph (40:23). Genesis 34:11 is such a paragraph. As in 40:23, the Paraphrase precedes the Text and is, by definition, lower ranking than the Text

Paraphrase: "May I find favour in your eyes and whatever you say to me I'll give."
Text: "Impose on me a very great *mohar* and gift and I will give whatever you say to me."

### Co-ordinate Paragraphs

In co-ordinate paragraphs two clauses are equally ranked but sequence is not a focus. "Also" (גם) frequently occurs in the second sentence.[67] 34:10 has what I consider to be a Predictive Co-ordinate Paragraph with two components:

"you will dwell with us"
"and the land will be before you"

### Antithetical Paragraphs

Here the "component parts of the paragraph either have equal rank or the first member outranks the second."[68] The components stand in an antithetical (contrasting) relationship. Such paragraphs often occur towards the end of a unit. 34:15-17 is a large Hortatory Antithetical Paragraph.

Thesis: "Only in this will we agree to you - if you will be as we are by circumcising every male, then..."
Antithesis: "But if you will not listen to us by getting circumcised then..."

This is not only the climactic speech in Scene Two but the pivotal section of the

---

64 Ibid., p. 97.
65 Ibid., p. 98.
66 Ibid., p. 97.
67 Ibid., pp. 100-101.
68 Ibid., p. 100.

chapter.

*The "Peak" Section of a Narrative*

Another important aspect of Longacre's work is his notion of the peak of a story. This feature, as noted earlier, is claimed by Longacre to be a "language universal".

> Essentially, *peak* is a kind of zone of turbulence... in which predictable discourse features are skewed so that certain typical features are removed or partially surpressed, while other features are introduced. It represents a kind of gear-shift in the dynamic flow of a discourse.[69]

Obviously such a feature exists at a discourse level - we have moved beyond the level of the tagmemes in the paragraph syntagmeme to a tagmeme in the discourse syntagmeme. Little work has been done at this level so we need to be tentative in our thinking. Essentially Longacre is claiming that the key part of the story can be marked in various ways. There is no simple formula here. One must look for combinations of the kinds of features mentioned below as syntactic clues:[70] Episode introduced by *wayehi*, repetition of participant name, greater descriptive detail to build suspense, chiastic structures often follow peaks (Longacre gives numerous examples from Joseph), multiple tellings of the same story, a crowded action line is typical - "Peak is marked essentially by a change in pace or character of a narrative."[71] In Chapter Four I suggested that the peak of the Dinah story is 34:25-27 whilst 34:28-29 and 30-31 are post-peak episodes 1 and 2.

*Longacre on Dialogue*

Here we must be brief. Longacre argues that quotation formulas give important clues about the social dynamics of the discourse situation. I shall simply set out his results in a table. All that is required to understand the table is that "Sp." means "speaker", "Add" means "Addressee", "Pr" means "pronoun", "N' means "noun" and 0 means that the dialogue participant is not explicitly referred to. Thus Sp:N + Add:N means that the direct speech is introduced by a quotation formula in which the speaker and the addressee are named, eg., "Simon spoke to John, saying..."

69 Ibid., p. 18.
70 Ibid., pp. 30-35.
71 Ibid., p. 39.

Summary Table of Variations in Formulas of Quotation[72]

| A | *Dialogue Initiation:* | Any way that is contextually adequate to identify Sp and Add; very often N + N or 0 + pr/N, but even here N + pr may be according to D3. |
|---|---|---|
| B | *Dialogue Continuance (normal and uncomplicated):* | between peers: 0 + pr<br>emphasis on social gap (often sizable): 0 + 0. |
| C | *Dialogue Redirection (fresh beginning, whether or not Sp/Add is changed):* | N + N |
| D | *Mid Dialogue Dynamics* | 1.   N + N (other than C): balance/tension/confrontation between Sp and Add; often = "important interview of two important people."<br>2.   0 + 0 (possibly overlapping somewhat with B2): plays down tension and confrontation between Sp and Add; no struggle; stalemate, civilities, working out details of already accepted plan; compliance at end of dialogue.<br>3.   N + pr: speaker-dominant (or trying to be); rank/rank-pulling; decisive utterance; attempt to gain control of dialogue.<br>4.   N + 0: speaker centred; emotional outburst; strong assertion of point of view; often attempted finality.<br>5.   0 + N: addressee dominant. |

Then Longacre sets out the different types of dialogue. These are as follows:

---

72 Ibid., p. 184. For a critical analysis of this schema see de Regt, 1991-92, pp. 157-161.

| *Simple Resolved Dialogues* | I.U. (initiating utterance) | a) Q (question)<br>b) PROP (proposal)<br>c) REM (remark) |
|---|---|---|
| | R.U. (resolving utterance) | a) A (answer)<br>b) RES (response)<br>c) EVAL (evaluation) |
| *Simple Unresolved Dialogues* | In these dialogues there is an I.U. but no R.U.. Genesis 34:4 is an example in which Shechem makes a PROP but Hamor's reply is not recorded. | |
| *Complex Dialogue Paragraph* | I.U. | (see *Simple Resolved Dialogue*) |
| | C.U. (complicating utterance) | a) Q (a counter question)<br>b) REM ( a counter-remark)<br>c) PROP (a counter-proposal) |

For example 34:30-31 is a complex dialogue. The I.U. is a rebuke in the form of a REM to the effect that "we're in big trouble". The C.U. fires back a biting rhetorical counter-question (Q): "should he have treated our sister as a prostitute?

## Genesis 34: Scene 1 (34:1-4)

| Band 6 | Band 5 | Band 4 | Band 3 | Band 2 | Band 1 | |
|--------|--------|--------|--------|--------|--------|---|
| | | | | Narrative Sequence Paragraph | | |
| וַתֵּצֵא דִינָה בַּת־לֵאָה אֲשֶׁר יָלְדָה לְיַעֲקֹב לִרְאוֹת בִּבְנוֹת הָאָרֶץ: | | | | | | **v. 1**<br>Setting |
| | | וַיַּרְא אֹתָהּ שְׁכֶם בֶּן־חֲמוֹר הַחִוִּי נְשִׂיא הָאָרֶץ | | | | **v. 2**<br>BU 1 |
| | | | | וַיִּקַּח אֹתָהּ | | BU 2 |
| | | (Narrative Result Paragraph) | | | | BU 3 |
| | | | | וַיִּשְׁכַּב אֹתָהּ | | (Text) |
| | | | | וַיְעַנֶּהָ: | | (Result) |
| | | (Narrative Paraphrase Paragraph) | | | | **v. 3**<br>BU 4 |
| | | | | וַתִּדְבַּק נַפְשׁוֹ בְּדִינָה בַּת־יַעֲקֹב | | (Text) |
| | | | | וַיֶּאֱהַב אֶת־הַנַּעֲרָ | | (Para.) |
| | | | | וַיְדַבֵּר עַל־לֵב הַנַּעֲרָ: | | BUn |
| | | Unmitigated Hortatory Simple Paragraph | | | | |
| | | | וַיֹּאמֶר שְׁכֶם אֶל־חֲמוֹר אָבִיו לֵאמֹר | | | **v. 4**<br>QF |
| | | | | קַח־לִי אֶת־הַיַּלְדָּה הַזֹּאת לְאִשָּׁה: | | BUn |

V. 1 is a Setting for the Narrative Sequence which follows. It is not usual to begin a story with a WAYYIQTOL but if that preterite is a verb of motion (as here) it can be done.[73] So I take v. 1 as a Setting and not as on the Main Line. The Scene is set - "Dinah went out to see the daughters of the land."

V. 1b is a subordinate clause which interrupts the sentence in mid-flow. This construction[74] is used to signify a flashback - an event out of chronological sequence. The subject changes from v. 1a (Dinah) to v. 1b (Leah with Dinah as object). The sub-clause identifies Dinah as Jacob's daughter - a relationship that is central to the story. It is thus significant that in v. 1a Dinah is identified as *Leah's* daughter rather than as Jacob's, as she is in the rest of the story.

The action proper begins with Shechem seeing Dinah (v. 2a). We have a straightforward On-Line sequence of events marked by a chain of preterites. Each clause takes the action a step further. The clauses are short and add to the pace of the action. "He saw her (then a lavish participant reference)... he took her, he lay with her, he shamed her." We could regard וַיְעַנֶּהָ as part of the chronological sequence (BU4) but this would be, in my view, a category

---

73 Longacre, 1989, p. 87.

74 On אֲשֶׁר + QATAL see ibid., p. 79.

mistake. "He shamed her" is not *another* act in a sequence (he took her *then* he lay with her *then* he shamed her), but rather describes the result of his "laying (with)" her. That is to say, he shamed her *by* laying (with) her. The WAYYIQTOL usually encodes a temporal advancement but can function as an unmarked, non-sequential overlay.[75] The WAYYIQTOL may be used to avoid demoting non-sequential information off the Main-Line.[76] Buth has flash-backs in mind when he discusses unmarked, non-sequential overlay but I suggest that here we have, perhaps, a logical but *not a temporal* advance in the sequence of thought.[77]

I have taken the aftermath of the crime to be a continuance of the Narrative Sequence Paragraph. One could see a chain of three BUs (BU4, BU5, BUn) but I have chosen to take וַיֶּאֱהַב as a paraphrase of BU4 as it does not seem to advance the action but merely redescribes it. The two verbs in BU4 are verbs describing mental state (his soul clung, he loved) and, according to Longacre,[78] they ought to rank lower than action verbs, like those which describe the crime. The logic behind this is that they are more static.[79] Be that as it may, I have ranked BU4 as band 1 as it seems clear to me that a surprising new advance is occurring in the plot. The three clauses really labour the point about Shechem's love for Dinah[80] and do so with very positive terminology.[81]

Suddenly we find Shechem speaking with his father. We assume a change of scene although no mention is made of one.[82]

The quotation formula (QF) is Speaker:Noun + Addressee:Noun (Sp:N + Add:N). According to Longacre this serves as a dialogue initiation (clearly the case here). Shechem is mentioned by name for the second time in the narrative, as is Hamor, thus integrating both men as major participants. Given that the proper noun "Shechem" could be replaced by a pronoun ("he") in this context, the repetition of his name may serve to keep the protagonist central and focused,[83] or perhaps it emphasises just how important the words that follow are to him.[84] From this point on Shechem and Hamor function almost as a

---

75 See Buth (1994) and on Buth see C. Collins (1995).
76 So Buth, 1994, p. 148.
77 In lines 1 and 2 we have fronted predicates which, according to Shimasaki (1999), means that they are informationally prominent. It is odd in these cases because neither Dinah nor Shechem are already activated referents in the readers' minds and this clause structure normally presupposes referents activated in previous texts (ibid., ch. 5). To deal with problem both referents are "anchored" by linking them to other referents (i.e. their parents) (ibid., pp. 106-108).
78 Longacre, 1989, p. 94.
79 See Endo, 1996.
80 Andersen, 1974, p. 42.
81 On which see Fewell and Gunn (1991) and Brooke (1997).
82 See too the shift from v. 29 to v. 30.
83 Shimasaki, 1999, pp. 98-99.
84 de Regt, 1991-92, pp. 168-169.

single unit. The speech act is actually a top ranking hortatory appeal in which the speaker urges an item on the hearer by the use of an imperative verb.[85] As there is only one verb the paragraph is a Simple Paragraph.[86]

Shechem's speech is a Simple Unresolved Dialogue - there is no responding utterance from Hamor.[87] The reader is left in suspense not knowing Hamor's reply. Will he rebuke his son? Will he support him? Indeed the speech is a suspended execution paragraph where a plan is put forward but the execution delayed whilst we find out what is going on with the Jacobites.

As a son speaking to his father one would expect Shechem to speak with some deference. He does not. He starts with a single imperative verb. There is no mitigation at all.[88] This communicates Shechem's intense sense of urgency and passion. It is also more than a little rude.

Scene One, as far as the story development goes, has the Exposition introducing Dinah (v. 1) and the Inciting Incident, which sets up the problem that needs resolving (vv. 2-4) as well as a clear indication as to how Shechem wishes to resolve it. As will become clear, that potential solution is itself part of the inciting incident - part of the problem itself.

### Genesis 34 Scene Two: Hivite-Israelite Negotiations

### *Discourse Analysis of vv. 5-7*

Vv. 5-7 set the scene for what follows. Jacob has heard of the crime but passively waits for his sons' return. Hamor and Shechem set out to see Jacob. In the meantime Dinah's brothers return and are furious about Shechem's deed.

The main section of the Scene is composed of three speeches. First, Hamor proposes a marriage between Shechem and Dinah as well as a close relationship between Israelites and Hivites. Second, Shechem urges the family to allow him to marry Dinah. Third, the brothers set the terms according to which a deal can be done - the Hivites must be circumcised. The scene closes with Hamor and Shechem accepting the conditions. Our discourse analysis will take these five sections one at a time.

---

85 Longacre, 1989, pp. 120-123.

86 See Endo, 1996, chapter 2 for a discussion of one-clause verbal utterances in Hebrew direct discourse.

87 Miller identifies this type of QF as a לאמר frame. In a לאמר frame we find one finite verb plus לאמר. The finite verb identifies the nature of the speech act and the לאמר merely introduces what is said (Longacre, 1989, p. 71). In this case we have ויאמר as the speech act. Miller comments, "The verb אמר is the most semantically bare word with respect to metapragmatic content; only the fact of the speech event is indexed" (C.L. Miller, 1994, p. 217).

88 e.g. נא (if that is mitigatory - see later) or even, "Father, get this girl..."

*Old Testament Story and Christian Ethics*

| Band 6 | Band 5 | Band 4 | Band 3 | Band 2 | Band 1 | |
|---|---|---|---|---|---|---|
| | | | | | | Setting |
| | | | וַיַּעֲקֹב שָׁמַע כִּי טִמֵּא אֶת־דִּינָה בִּתּוֹ | | | **v. 5**<br>item i |
| | | וּבָנָיו הָיוּ אֶת־מִקְנֵהוּ בַּשָּׂדֶה | | | | Item ii |
| | | | וְהֶחֱרִשׁ יַעֲקֹב עַד־בֹּאָם: | | | Item iii |
| | | | וַיֵּצֵא חֲמוֹר אֲבִי־שְׁכֶם אֶל־יַעֲקֹב לְדַבֵּר אִתּוֹ: | | | **v. 6**<br>item iv |
| | | | | | Narrative Reason Paragraph | |
| | | וּבְנֵי יַעֲקֹב בָּאוּ מִן־הַשָּׂדֶה כְּשָׁמְעָם | | | | **v. 7**<br>Setting |
| | | | | (Narrative Paraphrase Paragraph) Text | | |
| | | | וַיִּתְעַצְּבוּ הָאֲנָשִׁים | | | (Text) |
| | | | וַיִּחַר לָהֶם מְאֹד | | | (Para) |
| | | | | (Narrative Comment Paragraph) Reason | | |
| | | | כִּי־נְבָלָה עָשָׂה בְיִשְׂרָאֵל לִשְׁכַּב אֶת־בַּת־יַעֲקֹב | | | (Text) |
| | | וְכֵן לֹא יֵעָשֶׂה: | | | | (Comment) |

The sequence is not perspicuous and one could set up the detailed relationships in more than one way. To complicate matters further one of the QATAL verbs is היה which Longacre and others argue does not rank like normal QATALs (band 4), two of the WAYYIQTOLs are verbs of mental state and these too do not rank like normal WAYYIQTOLs. Finally one of the WAYYIQTOLs is a verb of motion which also ranks unusually.

One central problem is line 4. All the other lines concern the actions, circumstances and reactions of Dinah's family but set right in the midst of this is a WAYYIQTOL about Hamor setting out to see Jacob. One would normally expect X-V word order.[89] The verb of motion *may* account for this like in v. 1. It is possible to treat lines 1-4 as a Narrative Simple Paragraph. Lines 1-3 would form the Setting and line 4 the BUn - a Main Line action.[90] Then lines 5-9 would form a Narrative Reason Paragraph with line 5 as the Setting, lines 6 & 7 as the Text and lines 8 and 9 as the Reason. Against this, however, are the following considerations:-

- WAYYIQTOL (item iv) preceded by WEQATAL (item iii) can continue the sense of the preceding construction.[91] Niccacci thinks that

---

89 Or, to put it in Shimasaki's categories, the clause has a Px (predicate focus) structure rather than an Xp (argument focus) or XP (clause focus) structure. Hamor is "anchored" to Shechem to "get around" the unusual word order which would ordinarily presuppose that he is a referent already activated in the readers' minds.

90 cf. Longacre, 1989, p. 88.

91 Niccacci, 1990, pp. 177-8. See also Endo, 1996, pp. 282-285.

non-initial WAYYIQTOLs which are subordinate to a WAW-X-QATAL in the Setting are an exception to the rule that the WAYYIQTOL is Main Line. They should be translated in the same way as the WAW-X-QATAL (pluperfect).[92] We could consider them a short narrative part of the prelude.[93]

- The verb is a verb of motion (וַיֵּצֵא) and, as already mentioned, such verbs can be considered part of the Setting rather than the Main Line.[94]
- The line is placed within the Setting for the Scene.

These considerations incline me to treat line 4 as simply item 4 in a Setting.

Line 1: Francis Andersen points out that it is common to begin an episode with a string of circumstantial clauses.[95] The use of the perfect in narrative indicates background actions and events. Contrary to Niccacci, for whom we-x-שָׁמַע is an answer to the question, "*Who* heard?" rather then, "*What* did Jacob do?, Shimasaki has argued that this word order (what he calls a 'clause focus structure') makes *both* the predicate ('heard') and the noun ('Jacob') informationally prominent.[96] So *her own father had found out*! Given the cultural assumptions shared by sender and receiver about the relationship between fathers and daughters the reader is bound to wonder what his reaction will be.

The actual response is delayed until line 3 which is chiastically linked to line 1

| WE -X | QATAL | and-Jacob | heard |
|-------|-------|-----------|-------|
| WE QATAL | X[97] | and-was-silent | Jacob |

The repetition of Jacob's name and the reversal of word order plus the obvious thematic connection conspire to indicate a chiastic link. The verb הֶחֱרִשׁ, being in the perfect, is part of the backdrop to the following. Muraoka sees the word order V-S as normal and thus lacking focus, but Longacre thinks that in intransitive V-S clauses a preliminary action is presented with a focus on what is done - in this case nothing.[98] So possibly Jacob's inactivity is highlighted.

Now that we see how lines 1 and 3 are connected we need to return to line 1 again. כִּי טִמֵּא אֶת־דִּינָה בִתּוֹ. One *could* see this as a temporal use of כִּי.[99] If the

---

92 Contra Goldfajn (1998), for whom wayyiqtol describes past sequential events.
93 Niccacci, 1990, p. 48.
94 Longacre, 1989, pp. 87-88.
95 Andersen, 1974, pp. 79 and 87; Bandstra, 1990, p. 120. Contra Goldfajn (1998, p. 147) who thinks it unusual to start a narrative sequence with qatal.
96 Shimasaki, 1999, ch. 7.
97 Jouon (1991) sees this use of WEQATAL as abnormal and reflecting a pre-classical usage (p. 405).
98 Longacre, 1989, p. 75. So too Shimasaki, 1999, ch. 5.
99 Waltke and O'Connor, 1990, p. 643.

subordinate clause ("כִּי he had defiled Dinah, his daughter") is contemporary
with the main clause ("and Jacob heard") כִּי can mean "when". More likely we
should read כִּי as "that."[100] This is common after verbs of perception as we have
here. So Jacob heard[101] *that* he (Shechem) had defiled Dinah his daughter.

The readers must await Jacob's response as line 2 interrupts the chiasm.[102]

Line 2 is consecutive on the previous line (Jacob heard...*whilst* his sons...).
The perfect of היה puts this clause into band 4 of the Narrative Rank Scheme. It
functions as a Setting for the previous clause and *possibly* as a *reason* for line
3. Niccacci[103] claims that on rare occasions WEQATAL is a continuation of the
emphatic construction X-QATAL. Thus we may link the first three lines as
follows: "Now *Jacob* had heard... *whilst* his sons were... *so* he kept silent until
they returned."

The perspective now shifts in line 4 to Hamor setting off to see Jacob who
silently waits for his sons to return. The reader knows that the Jacob they will
encounter is one who already knows what has happened and they will be keen
to know how the father will respond when his silence breaks. As already
mentioned, we could see line 4 as a Main Line sentence but I prefer to translate
it as a pluperfect (Now Hamor, father of Shechem, *had set out*...). However, the
use of WAYYIQTOL does serve to mark it out from the information on Jacob's
sons and may add to the pace of the text.

The shift from the WAYYIQTOL in line 4 to WE-X-QATAL in line 5 is a
discontinuing construction[104] even though the events recorded do continue the
narrative. "The function of this marked X-V construction is apparently to create
a dramatic pause."[105] *The sons* have now *returned*[106] (presumably whilst Hamor
and Shechem are still on their way as there is no indication that negotiations
have started). As line 5 has a verb of motion I have demoted it from band 2. It
forms the Setting for what I take to be a Narrative Reason Paragraph the Text in
which is an embedded Narrative Paraphrase Paragraph (Text = "the men were
grieved", Paraphrase = "and they were very angry"). The reason for their anger
is given in the Reason which is an embedded Narrative Comment Paragraph
(Text = "for he had done folly in Israel by lying with the daughter of Jacob".
The expository Comment = "and this ought not to be done"). The actual

100 Ibid., p. 645.
101 On the pluperfect here see Goldfajn (1998) on qatal.
102 See Andersen, 1974, p. 32 for an example of an interrupted chiasm.
103 Niccacci, 1990, p. 185.
104 Muraoka finds the fronting of the subject inexplicable and is forced to argue that the
verb of movement has affected the word order (1985, p. 36). This is unnecessary as
there is a perfectly good explanation of the shift (see main text).
105 Van der Merwe, 1994, p. 39. It may also serve to reintroduce the sons (Shimasaki,
1999, p. 146).
106 This is a clause focus structure in which both the sons and their action are marked
(Shimasaki, 1999). Goldfajn (1998) thinks that v. 7a is anterior to the previous sentence
and therefore pluperfect ("had returned").

response of the sons is fronted for comment and underlined by having two parallel WAYYIQTOLS in the Text, a lavish explanation (Reason) and very strong verbs and adverbs. To complicate matters these are both verbs of mental state and are thus fairly static. Longacre[107] prefers to see such verbs as a Setting, although he admits that they could rank higher than band 4. In this case the result of placing the two mental-state verbs (grieved, angry) in band 4 is that the subordinate clause ("for[108] he did folly in Israel...") now ranks higher than the clauses to which it is subordinate! For this reason I have placed the two clauses in band 2 as secondary storyline.

This fierce anger is set out clearly in the Setting to build up tensions for the negotiations. The anger plays a crucial role in the unfolding story and the narrator wants the reader to be in no doubt about the sons' feelings. The final comment ("and this ought not to be done") seems to be part of the narrator's explication of the sons' thinking but also a comment expressing his own view.

*Discourse Analysis of vv. 8-10*

| Band 6 | Band 5 | Band 4 | Band 3 | Band 2 | Band 1 | |
|---|---|---|---|---|---|---|
| Unmitigated Hortatory Sequence Paragraph | | | | | | |
| | | | | וַיְדַבֵּר חֲמוֹר אִתָּם לֵאמֹר | | v. 8 QF |
| | שְׁכֶם בְּנִי חָשְׁקָה נַפְשׁוֹ בְּבִתְּכֶם | | | | | Setting |
| Predictive Results Paragraph (Text) | | | | | | |
| | | | | תְּנוּ נָא אֹתָהּ לוֹ לְאִשָּׁה: | | BU 1 |
| [Amplification Paragraph] BU 2 | | | | | | |
| | | | | וְהִתְחַתְּנוּ אֹתָנוּ | | v. 9 [Text] |
| {Predictive Antithetical Paragraph} [Amplification] | | | | | | |
| | | | | בְּנֹתֵיכֶם תִּתְּנוּ־לָנוּ | | {Thesis} |
| | | | | וְאֶת־בְּנֹתֵינוּ תִּקְחוּ לָכֶם: | | {Antith} |
| [Predictive Co-ordinate Paragraph] (Results) | | | | | | |
| | | | | וְאִתָּנוּ תֵּשֵׁבוּ | | v. 10 [item I] |
| | | | | וְהָאָרֶץ תִּהְיֶה לִפְנֵיכֶם | | [item ii] Setting |
| | | | | | שְׁבוּ | BU 3 |
| | | | | | וּסְחָרוּהָ | BU 4 |
| | | | | | וְהֵאָחֲזוּ בָהּ: | BUn |

---

107 Longacre, 1989, pp. 87-88.

108 כִּי + perfect in a subordinate clause is pluperfect (i.e. out of chronological sequence - a flashback to an earlier event). On כִּי see van der Merwe, 1993, pp. 38-41.

I read the whole of Hamor's speech as essentially an unmitigated Hortatory Sequence[109] Paragraph with an embedded Prediction Results sequence which in turn is composed of a Predictive Antithetical Paragraph and a Predictive Co-ordinate Paragraph.

The QF is a לֵאמֹר frame. The Sp:N + Add:Pr is especially used in "initiating a dialogue... (it) clearly indicates a social dominance of the speaker."[110] This is the case here for Hamor has already been identified as "the chief of the land" (v. 2). The speech he gives is essentially an unmitigated hortatory discourse which is fitting given his social status.[111] Hamor begins his speech with a Setting:[112]שְׁכֶם בְּנִי חָשְׁקָה נַפְשׁוֹ בְּבִתְּכֶם. The use of the perfect makes this clause a Setting for the following Hortatory Sequence. This clause is a classic example of the so-called *casus pendens* where the nominal construction ("Shechem my son") is in extra-position (i.e. outside) at the head of the clause. It is thus "syntactically independent"[113] and functions not for emphasis but to mark off the topic for consideration – Shechem.[114]

So the situation is that Shechem loves Dinah. The terminology is very strong and positive. חָשְׁקָה "does not suggest a sudden surge of emotion; it presupposes not just an unconditional erotic attraction but also a reasoned and unconditional decision."[115]

Hot on the heels of the Setting comes the first imperative:

תְּנוּ נָא אֹתָהּ לוֹ לְאִשָּׁה

Fitting Hamor's social standing vis-à-vis Jacob and sons, the speech is unmitigated. It is possible, however, to take the particle נָא as a slight mitigation.[116] In this case Hamor asks politely for Dinah as a wife for his son. On the other hand, it is not obvious that we ought to take the word in this way.

---

109 Though see Endo who believes that volitives are not, strictly speaking, sequential (1996, p. 230).

110 Longacre, 1989, p. 179.

111 On the other hand, de Regt would say that Jacob and sons are major participants already identified by the context and thus they only need a pronoun whilst Hamor needs a proper noun to reintroduce him (1991-92, pp. 158). De Regt does not think that the social implications which Longacre sees in the QF are there.

112 Speaking to the family Hamor talks of Dinah as "your (plural) daughter". For an explanation of why she is talked of as her brothers' daughter see Parry, 2000b, pp. 134-135.

113 Muraoka, 1985, p. 94

114 See Niccacci, 1990, p. 148; Bergen, 1994, p. 123; Muraoka, 1985, pp. 94-95; Jouon, 1991, pp. 586; Waltke and O'Connor, 1990, p. 76.

115 TDOT 5:263.

116 E.g. Longacre 1989, p. 121 following Gesenius.

Lambdin,[117] followed by Waltke and O'Connor,[118] sees נָא as a logical particle. In other words - "*as a logical consequence of his love* - give her to him." If the particle is merely highlighting the connection between Setting and BU1 then even here there is no mitigation.

BU2 is, I think, better pointed as אִתָּנוּ ('*with* us') rather than the MT's אֹתָנוּ ('us'). Thus we have a main Text, "give in marriage with us." How does this link with the previous sentence? Niccacci suggests that a chain of WAYYIQTOL + WAYYIQTOL in which both are taken as volitives can be either co-ordinated (i.e., "Give her in to him... *and* intermarry") or a dependent construction of purpose (i.e., "Give her to him... and *thus* intermarry with us").[119] On this latter view the marriage of Dinah and Shechem is the opening for a far wider inter-relationship between the two groups. The development of this speech inclines me to accept the latter reading.

F. Andersen suggests that there is a chiasmus linking[120]

which is interrupted by the Antithetical Paragraph about swapping daughters. This could support the emended pointing of אִתָּנוּ Thus on this view the "intermarrying" is the other side of the coin to the dwelling together. However, I prefer not to see a chiasmus here. The word order of the second clause is better explained by the fact that if we had a WAYYIQTOL here it would be volitive[121] rather than a result. The grammatical convention required a reversal of word order. Also I prefer to tie all the Result clauses together. If one tied this clause back chiastically to BU2 it makes the relation of the others more complex and awkward.

I take line 4 (intermarry with us) to be the Text for an Amplification Paragraph (exchange of daughters - itself an embedded Predictive Antithetical Paragraph) and BU2 as a whole is a Text for a Predictive Results Paragraph with two items as results (dwelling together and the freedom of the land).

---

117 Lambdin, 1973, p. 170.

118 Waltke and O'Connor, 1990, pp. 578-579.

119 Niccacci, 1990, p. 94.

120 Andersen, 1974, p. 132.

121 See Niccacci, 1990, pp.181 and 187. Niccacci's rule is that a fronted YIQTOL in discourse is a volitive though Endo (1996, p. 46), following Talstra, questions this rule and refers to Genesis 43:29 as a possible counter-example. The effect of Endo's critique, if successful, is merely to suggest that Niccacci's rule is not exceptionless, not that it is mistaken.

Now lines v-vi are an embedded Predictive Antithetical Paragraph. It is best conceived as an amplification of what Hamor means by "intermarry with us" ("your daughters give to us and our daughters take for yourselves") rather than the *result* of the intermarriage.

The O.V. word order in the Thesis and Antithesis of the exchange of daughters speech serves to effect and emphasise a contrast.[122] It is also worth noting that Hamor, the rhetorical master, puts the emphasis on the Israelite initiative in the exchange - "*you* give... *you* take."

Having spelled out the details of the intermarriage proposal he gives the results of the deal in an embedded Predictive Co-Ordinate Paragraph with two components:

you will dwell with us.
the land will be before you.

The OV word order here makes the objects and predicates informationally prominent.[123] It may serve to set the scene for what follows[124] or as a climax.[125] The final Result forms the Setting for the final chain of three volitives (note that the pronoun in BU5 and BUn refer back to "the land" in this clause).

Having laid out the great mutual benefits of such an alliance (with the focus on benefits to the Israelites) Hamor ends his appeal as he began it - with top ranking appeals designed to sway his audience. These appeals follow on from the results.

A chain of IMPV (BU3) + IMPV (BU4) + IMPV (BUn) *can* be a chain of purpose.[126] Thus we would have, "Dwell *so that* you can travel about in it *so that* you can acquire possessions in it."[127] אחז in the Niphal is a technical term for occupation or possession of property in the sense of a settler or inhabitant. It

---

122 Bandstra, 1990, p. 120; Muraoka, 1985, p. 39; Shimasaki, 1999, pp. 150-153.

123 Shimasaki's clause focus structure. Alternatively, if the implicit questions, "Who will you dwell with? Where will you stay?" are presupposed then these sentences have an argument focus structure and they draw attention to "us" and "the land" (Muraoka, 1985, p. 38).

124 Shimasaki, 1999, p. 174.

125 Ibid., p. 178-180.

126 Niccacci, 1990, p. 94.

127 Alternatively Endo argues that volitives never occur in units of more than two members (1996, p. 230). Faced with this counter-example he argues that my BU3 and BU4 are semantically tighter than BU4 and BUn (ibid., p. 200). BUn is semantically independent of the preceding two member chain. In support of such a [IMPV + IMPV] + IMPV construction he notes that each of his units ends with a pronominal suffix (BU4 + BUn) and also that BU3 in unit one is a verb of movement and Endo thinks that one common type of two member volitive unit is that in which a movement verb is in the first clause (ibid., pp. 196-197). Endo may well be right here but we should not take this to mean that BUn is not closely linked to BU4 and BU5.

is generally associated with the term יש‍ב.[128] Thus the acquisition of possessions (BUn) is closely linked to the "dwelling" (BU4) and the "travelling about" (BU5) even if סחר means "travel about" rather than "trade".[129] So as not to miss the wood for the trees we could paraphrase Shechem's words to highlight the aforementioned relations as follows:

My son Shechem - he is strongly attracted to your daughter
*so* (please?) give her to him as a wife
*and by doing that* intermarry with us (give your daughters to us, take our daughters to yourselves)
*The result of such an alliance would be* that you would live with us *and* the land would be an open expanse before you.
*So take advantage of the benefits* - dwell *and* travel about in it
*and* acquire possessions in it.

Notice that the second chain of volitives is not put in the direct form of an urge to sign up to the deal. Rather it is the more rhetorically effective urge to enjoy the results of the deal with the obviously *implied but unstated* call to sign up.

*Discourse Analysis of vv. 11-12*

| Band 6 | Band 5 | Band 4 | Band 3 | Band 2 | Band 1 | |
|---|---|---|---|---|---|---|
| | | | | Hortatory Amplification Paragraph | | |
| | | | וַיֹּאמֶר שְׁכֶם אֶל־אָבִיהָ וְאֶל־אַחֶיהָ | | | **v. 11** QF |
| | | | | (Hortatory Amplification Paragraph) Text | | |
| | | | אֶמְצָא־חֵן בְּעֵינֵיכֶם | | | (Text) |
| | | | וַאֲשֶׁר תֹּאמְרוּ אֵלַי אֶתֵּן: | | | (Amp) |
| | | | (Hortatory Antithetical Paragraph) Amplification | | | |
| | | | הַרְבּוּ עָלַי מְאֹד מֹהַר וּמַתָּן | | | **v. 12** (Thesis) |
| | | | וְאֶתְּנָה כַּאֲשֶׁר תֹּאמְרוּ אֵלָי | | | (Antith) |
| | | | וּתְנוּ־לִי אֶת־הַנַּעֲרָ לְאִשָּׁה: | | | Climax |

Before Jacob can respond to Hamor, Shechem joins his father in the appeal. There are some interesting differences between the two speeches. Hamor's chief focus is on the benefits of the alliance - the marriage of his son to Dinah is passed over quickly as merely a preliminary and entrance to what really interests him. Shechem, by contrast, is solely interested in Dinah. He makes no

128 Kanke, 1997.
129 Cornelius, 1997, p. 243.

mention of an alliance. That, at best, is an enticement to the Israelites to agree to his marrying Dinah.

Secondly, as son of Hamor, Shechem does not talk to the Israelites as his father had. In fact he speaks rather deferentially to begin with ("May I find favour in your eyes") with the focus on what he is willing to give them for Dinah - as much as they ask for! The climax is the bluntest part of the speech where his passion flows out - "Now give me the girl as a wife!" Though even here he refers to Dinah as הַנַּעֲרָ (as does the narrator in v. 3) rather than by the *possibly* more derogatory term הַיַּלְדָּה he uses when talking to his father.

The Quotation Formula ("Shechem spoke to her father and her brothers") is a case of Sp:N + Add:N. According to Longacre this single verb frame tells us that an "important interview/debate/confrontation is afoot."[130] There is a "balance/tension/confrontation between Sp and Add. Often the implication is 'balance with a mild tension'."[131] Such a confrontation can occur even across a social gap.[132] Shechem's speech is partially mitigated, unlike his father's unmitigated speech. As his interest is in Dinah, the QF gives his perspective on his audience - they are not Jacob and his sons, but *her* father and *her* brothers.

Shechem's speech is essentially an appeal to the Jacobites to set a bride price with a climactic imperative - "Give me the girl as a wife!"

First of all we encounter a Hortatory Amplification Paragraph.

Text: "May I find favour in your eyes"
Amplification: "and whatever you will say to me I will give".

Here the Amplification explains *how* Shechem can be shown favour. Then we encounter a Hortatory Antithetical Paragraph.

Thesis: "Impose on me a large *mohar* and gift"
Antithesis: "and I will give whatever you say to me"

With regard to the latter Endo points out that the sequence imperative + cohortative in a two member chain *can* mean that the second member is purposive.[133] Thus "Impose... *so that* I can give..." In 34:12 it may be better to simply see an injunctive sense in both members with the focus on Shechem's reliability. Thus "Impose... and I *will* give..."

Closer attention to the speech reveals that lines 2 and 4[134] are related chiastically.[135]

---

130 Longacre, 1989, p. 177.
131 Ibid., p. 175.
132 As with Jacob and Laban in Genesis 31, ibid., p. 175.
133 Endo, 1996, p. 226.
134 My numbering is of lines within the speech and does not include the QF.
135 Andersen, 1974, pp. 121-22.

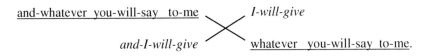

and-whatever you-will-say to-me          *I-will-give*

        *and-I-will-give*          whatever you-will-say to-me.

There is a single point being made with these two clauses although the first clause, simply due to the place of the verb, is ranked slightly lower than the second. It is unusual to have the first member of the chiasmus with the reversed word order, but the rhetorical effect of the move here is that it allows the speech to end with a chain of volitives. Another *possible* effect of the change in word order is that it makes the object in line 2 informationally prominent - "*whatever* you ask for I will give". Line 4, however, has the focus on Shechem's reliability - "*I will* give whatever you ask of me." I say that this is a possible effect because the change in word order is required by the chiasmus and thus the OV word order in line 2 does not *necessarily* mark (and perhaps put an emphasis[136] on) the object.[137]

Given this chiasmus we clearly need to indicate how the Hortatory Amplification Paragraph (lines 1 and 2) and the Hortatory Antithetical Paragraph are related. We have noticed that line 2 and line 4 parallel each other and line 1 ("May I find favour in your eyes") may parallel line 3 ("impose on me a very large bride price"). But what is the nature of the parallel? I suggest that lines 1-4 are a Hortatory Amplification Paragraph with the predicates in lines 3 and 5 marked for prominence.[138]

The climax of Shechem's speech is his impassioned appeal for Dinah's hand in marriage. Like his father, Shechem too builds up to a climax.

---

136 On emphasis see Shimasaki, 1999, ch. 2.
137 So Muraoka (1985) & Andersen (1974, p.121). However, both authors feel that chiasmus usually over-rides the normal effect of the word order. This is, rightly in my view, disputed by Shimasaki who argues that it can do but usually does not (1999, pp. 225-227).
138 Shimasaki, 1999, ch. 5.

### Discourse Analysis of vv. 13-17

| Band 6 | Band 5 | Band 4 | Band 3 | Band 2 | Band 1 | |
|---|---|---|---|---|---|---|
| | | וַיַּעֲנוּ בְנֵי־יַעֲקֹב אֶת־שְׁכֶם וְאֶת־חֲמוֹר אָבִיו בְּמִרְמָה | | | | **v. 13** QFa |
| | | | וַיְדַבֵּרוּ אֲשֶׁר טִמֵּא אֵת דִּינָה אֲחֹתָם: | | | QFb |
| | | | | וַיֹּאמְרוּ אֲלֵיהֶם | | **v. 14** QFc |
| | | | | Expository Reason Paragraph | | |
| | | לֹא נוּכַל לַעֲשׂוֹת הַדָּבָר הַזֶּה לָתֵת אֶת־אֲחֹתֵנוּ לְאִישׁ אֲשֶׁר־לוֹ עָרְלָה | | | | Text |
| | | | | כִּי־חֶרְפָּה הִוא לָנוּ: | | Reason |
| | | | Hortatory Antithetical Paragraph | | | |
| | | | (Predictive Results Paragraph) **Thesis** | | | |
| | | [Hortatory Amplification Paragraph] (Text) **v. 15** | | | | |
| | | | | אַךְ־בְּזֹאת נֵאוֹת לָכֶם | | [Text] |
| | | | | אִם תִּהְיוּ כָמֹנוּ לְהִמֹּל לָכֶם כָּל־זָכָר: | | [Amp] |
| | | | | (Results) | | |
| | | | [Predictive Antithetical Paragraph] (item i) | | | |
| | | | | וְנָתַנּוּ אֶת־בְּנֹתֵינוּ לָכֶם | | **v. 16** [Thesis] |
| | | | | וְאֶת־בְּנֹתֵיכֶם נִקַּח־לָנוּ | | [Antith] |
| | | | | וְיָשַׁבְנוּ אִתְּכֶם | | (item i) |
| | | | | וְהָיִינוּ לְעַם אֶחָד: | | (item ii) |
| | | | Predictive Results Paragraph) **Antithesis** | | | |
| | וְאִם־לֹא תִשְׁמְעוּ אֵלֵינוּ לְהִמּוֹל | | | | | **v. 17** (Text) |
| | | | | (Results) | | |
| | וְלָקַחְנוּ אֶת־בִּתֵּנוּ | | | | | (item i) |
| | וְהָלָכְנוּ: | | | | | (item ii) |

Given that Hamor went to see Jacob (v. 6) and spoke to him (v. 8) and given that the reader has been wondering since v. 5 what Jacob's response will be, we are surprised to find that it is not Jacob but his sons who respond. The reader is in no doubt about the sons' feelings on the matter and the lavish multiple-verb-frame (MVF) that introduces the speech reinforces this. However, MVFs with more than two verbs are rare.[139] This very lavish extended quotation formula[140]

---

139 Miller, 1994, p. 233, fn. 20. Miller explains a multiple verb frame as being when we have a combination of more than one finite, metapragmatic verb. Each verb refers to the same speech event and the speech participants in each clause are identical and play identical roles. Each verb is inflected identically with respect to gender, number and

is the narrator's way of saying that the speech to follow is of critical importance in the plot.

Now Longacre's scheme for dealing with quotation formulas may not really help us to deal with a three-fold QF that breaks down as follows:

Sp:N + Add:N

Sp: 0 + Add:Pr (?)

Sp:0 + Add:Pr

According to him a) alerts us to the confrontational nature of the negotiations whilst b) and c), if we take אֲשֶׁר in b) as functioning as a pronoun, would identify a dialogue between peers. However, line 1 supplies the nouns for speaker and addressee and these are assumed in b) and c). This being the case we probably ought to read little into their omission in b) and c). Be that as it may, line a) does let the reader know that what follows is deceitful (though how it is so remains unclear until v. 25). It is worth noting also a possible pun on the word ענה (to answer). There is homonym in Hebrew – ענה (to afflict). In v. 2 Shechem 'afflicted/shamed' Dinah (וַיְעַנֶּהָ) and now in v. 13 her brothers answer (וַיַּעֲנוּ) Shechem in deceit. The reader will see that they also afflict (וַיְעַנּוּ) him by means of the deceit.

Now line b) is tricky. Strictly speaking there is no pronoun here to identify the addressee but Sternberg thinks that אֲשֶׁר can function as a pronoun.[141] This is, to my mind, questionable. Out of twenty-one occasions when דבר takes a direct object without a preposition (as here) there are no examples where אֲשֶׁר is the object of דבר and this makes it unlikely that we ought to translate line 2 as "and they spoke to *him who* defiled their sister."[142] אֲשֶׁר, when the direct object of a verb, can mean "whom" *if* we have the object marker (אֶת) present. This is not the case in v. 13 so it is better to read אֲשֶׁר as "because". This is how Shoshan[143] and BDB[144] take the text and Sternberg agrees that it is one intended

---

tense (ibid., pp. 204-205). The first verb usually indexes the speaker and other features of the speech event (e.g. in our case that it is a response). Multiple verb frames only occur in dialogue (ibid., p. 230) which explains why some verbs never occur in them whilst others are very common. For example ענה is the most comment verb in the MVF occurring some seventy times. דבר occurs thirty two times and אמר seven times (ibid., pp. 210-211). When אמר does occur in a MVF it is usually in final position (ibid., p. 205). This final clause of the MVF conveys the least information (ibid., p. 205). When ענה does occur it is usually followed by דבר (ibid., p. 205. e.g. Josh 22:21-29; 2 Kg 1:10, 11b, 12). So our combination of ענה and דבר followed by אמר is a mixture of common combinations.

140 Miller thinks that Longacre's term "Extended Quotation Formula" is too broad to be very useful (ibid., p. 233, fn. 21). I am happy to use Longacre's terms for my purposes.

141 Sternberg, 1987, pp. 459-460.

142 My thanks to Professor Gordon Wenham for pointing me in the direction of this critique of Sternberg.

143 Shoshan, RVA # 4019.

meaning. Consequently, line 2 explains *why* the sons spoke deceitfully (*because* he defiled their sister) and does not say who it was they addressed.

What is interesting now is, following the huge build up in anticipation resulting from v. 7 and v. 13 which alert us to the hostility of the sons, we have a speech that is completely mitigated. The deceit that the reader, but not Jacob or the Hivites, is aware of manifests itself in a speech that gives the impression that the sons are happy to go along with the negotiations if they can set the requirements.

I suggest that the sons' speech opens with an Expository Reason Paragraph - it explains the state of affairs in a main Text ("We are not able to do this thing - to give our daughter to a man who has a foreskin") and then provides the Reason ("for he is contemptible[145] to us").

Longacre does not provide a cline for Expository texts but on pp. 111 ff. of *Joseph* he argues that it would be the opposite of Narrative, Procedural or Hortatory. For want of anything better to go on, if we invert the Narrative cline then the Text is band 1 Exposition and the Reason is band 2.[146] It would appear that this is a high ranking Exposition in which the request is flatly refused. However, this is immediately modified by the words אַךְ־בְּזֹאת נֵאוֹת לָכֶם. Van der Merwe describes אַךְ as a focus inducing particle[147] - "a proposition is constrained by the restriction posed by a second, that is the one preceded by אַךְ..."[148] In this case the flat refusal to give Dinah (or any Israelite woman) to an uncircumcised man is restricted by the following exception - if a man be circumcised. Muraoka thinks that the words following אַךְ may be prominent.[149] Thus the sons may be putting the words "in this" in focus to say that, "there is a way - only one - around this refusal, so listen carefully."

The main body of the speech forms a large Antithetical Paragraph with the Thesis being "if you, like us, circumcise every male then..." and the Antithesis being "but if not then..."

Both the Thesis and the Antithesis are embedded Results Paragraphs. The Thesis has its Text as "only in this will we agree to you - if you will circumcise..." and the Results are three items (exchange of daughters, we will dwell with you, we will be one people). The Antithesis has as its Text "if you will not listen to us to get circumcised" and its Results are two items (we will take our sister and go).[150] These two Result Paragraphs are embedded in the

---

144 BDB, 834.8c.

145 See J. Hartley, 1997, on חרפה

146 Contra Dawson (1994, p. 116) who tentatively suggests putting the verbless clause in band 1. That would rank my Text lower than its subordinate Reason which, by definition, cannot happen.

147 Van der Merwe, 1993, pp. 35-38. The quotation is from p. 30.

148 Ibid., p. 37.

149 Muraoka, 1985, p. 130.

150 Using Goldfajn's (1998) analysis the thesis and antithesis use YIQTOL to indicate a future time future whilst the consequent items in vv. 16-17 are WEQATALS (which,

large Antithetical Paragraph. But it is more complex yet. The Text of the Results Paragraph in the Thesis is an embedded Amplification Paragraph where "if you will be as we are in circumcising to yourselves every male" amplifies "in this" from the previous clause. Similarly we have an embedded Predictive Antithetical Paragraph as item i of the Results in the Thesis (exchange of daughters). Thus there are two cases of embedding within embedding in this speech.

In essence the brothers' speech says - "No marriages unless our conditions are met. If they are then all the benefits can be enjoyed but if not then we are unable to do a deal."

I am not certain how to categorise the speech in terms of text type. Is it Expository explaining the state of affairs or making a proposal? Yet the hints that Longacre gives for a cline would come asunder if this were the case as the text would rank far too low. Is it Predictive? In a sense it is but not in any straightforward sense - the predictions are conditional. Is it Hortatory? Are the sons seeking to persuade Hamor to accept the deal on their terms in order to set them up for retribution? It is not clear. All of this shows that further work is required to refine the notion of text-types. I would suggest the speech is essentially Hortatory and I have ranked it accordingly. It is clear that no volitives are used in the speech as the sons conceal their wrath and address the Hivites in an uncompromising yet polite way. The complete mitigation is in keeping with their social position vis-à-vis the Hivite ruler. So well do they hide their anger that Hamor and Shechem suspect nothing.

It is worth commenting on the Predictive Antithetical Paragraph in v. 16 as the sons have turned it into a chiasm.

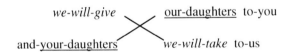

Andersen writes that "in a chiastic sentence, a chiastic clause combines with the lead clause to give a single picture of two simultaneously occurring aspects of the same situation or event."[151] On the exchange of daughters speeches in Genesis 34 he notes that in Hamor's proposal (v. 9) the two clauses are conjoined. In the Israelite counter-proposal (v. 16) they are chiastic, whilst in Hamor's speech to the townsmen there is a conjunctive sentence (v. 21). He then says, "there may be very little difference between the two patterns. But, if we are right, the Shechemites are proposing a mutual agreement in conjunctive sentences, whilst the Israelites are proposing a reciprocal arrangement in a

---

she says, only occur in reported speech) to describe events which succeed each other in the future of the Speech time (the results of the future agreement). The WAYYIQTOL in v. 18 shifts the temporal perspective back again.

151 Andersen, 1974, p. 121.

chiastic sentence. The Israelites are thinking in terms of complete integration, *to become a single people.*[152] Although Hamor repeats this phrase in v. 22 it is clear from v. 23 that he expects the Shechemites to preserve their identity and absorb the Israelites. The Shechemite proposal is not entirely one-sided. There is a chiasmus in the pronouns:

$$-kem \diagdown -nu \qquad\qquad -am \diagdown -nu$$
$$-nu \diagup -kem \text{ (v. 9)} \qquad -nu \diagup -hem \text{ (v. 21)}$$

This was not obligatory. They could have said, 'and you will take our womenfolk from us', rather then 'for yourselves'."[153]

This explanation *may* well be correct. Both the chiasm and the OV, OV patterns emphasise the contrast. The difference is that the chiasmus ties the two clauses closer together.[154] Andersen *may* have indicated a reason for the sons' use of the chiasm. Nevertheless, it is worth remembering that the sons are *not* really thinking "in terms of complete integration" - they are lying through their teeth.

Finally, it is important to note the veiled threat in the Antithesis of the sons' speech. "If you will not agree... we will take our sister and go." This is the first indication that the reader has that Dinah is not, in fact, at home but is with the Shechemites.[155] As it happens, the sons planned all along to "take their sister and go" *whatever* the Hivites did.[156]

### Discourse Analysis of vv. 18-19

| Band 6 | Band 5 | Band 4 | Band 3 | Band 2 | Band 1 | |
|---|---|---|---|---|---|---|
| | | | Narrative Result | | Paragraph | |
| | | וַיִּיטְבוּ דִבְרֵיהֶם בְּעֵינֵי חֲמוֹר וּבְעֵינֵי שְׁכֶם בֶּן־חֲמוֹר׃ | | | | **v. 18** |
| | | | | | | Text |
| | | (Narrative Reason Paragraph) | | | Result | |
| | | וְלֹא־אֵחַר הַנַּעַר לַעֲשׂוֹת הַדָּבָר | | | | **v. 19** |
| | | | | | | (Text) |
| | | כִּי חָפֵץ בְּבַת־יַעֲקֹב | | | | (Reason) |
| | | וְהוּא נִכְבָּד מִכֹּל בֵּית אָבִיו׃ | | | | Comment |

---

152 Gen 34:16.
153 Ibid., pp. 132-133.
154 Gibson, 1994, p. 171.
155 Unless my earlier suggestion on the distortion of the type-scene is correct in which case it is the second indication.
156 Gen 34:26.

The Scene closes with a Narrative Result Paragraph which informs us of the success of the brothers' modified deal. In the Text we see that the Hivite ruler and his son find this condition good. The result is that the lad does not delay to do the thing.[157] The Result part of the paragraph is an embedded Narrative Reason Paragraph where the reason given for the haste on Shechem's part is his love for Dinah. This love is what drove him to accept the deal that leads to his downfall.

The terminus[158] of the Scene is a comment on Shechem. There is a non-fronted verb with a redundant pronoun at the head. The word order when the subject is a personal pronoun is irrelevant but the personal pronoun gives emphasis to the subject anyway.[159]

So we have a comparative superlative in which Shechem is shown as the most honoured in all his father's house.[160] It is an episode final circumstantial clause.[161] It is not clear why the narrator should choose to impart this information to his readers at all, even less clear why he should do so here. Perhaps he wishes to indicate that Shechem truly loves Dinah and will indeed keep his part of the agreement because he is such an honourable chap. Alternatively, though unlikely, the narrator may be saying that this worthless lad is the best that the Hivites can produce so imagine how bad the others are. Most likely, the information is conveyed to set us up for the next scene when Hamor and Shechem speak to the Shechemites. Shechem was honoured by this audience and that may encourage us to expect positive results from those negotiations.[162] If so, then we are not disappointed.

157 AL + QATAL can sometimes be a "momentous negation" which moves the story forward. This is the case here and that is why I rank the clause so high (see Longacre, 1994, p. 68)
158 Longacre, 1989, p. 88 notes that termini are of a lower rank.
159 Muraoka, 1985, p. 31.
160 See Waltke and O'Connor, 1990, pp. 267-270.
161 On which see Andersen, 1974, pp. 80-82.
162 Calvin, 1965, p. 223.

## Scene Three: Genesis 34:20-24

| Band 6 | Band 5 | Band 4 | Band 3 | Band 2 | Band 1 | |
|---|---|---|---|---|---|---|
| | | | | Narrative Simple Paragraph | | |
| | | | | וַיָּבֹא חֲמוֹר וּשְׁכֶם בְּנוֹ אֶל־שַׁעַר עִירָם | | v. 20 Setting |
| | | | | וַיְדַבְּרוּ אֶל־אַנְשֵׁי עִירָם לֵאמֹר: | | BUn (QF) |
| | | | Hortatory Comment Paragraph | | | |
| | | | (Expository Simple Paragraph) Setting | | | |
| | הָאֲנָשִׁים הָאֵלֶּה שְׁלֵמִים הֵם אִתָּנוּ | | | | | v. 21 (item n) |
| | | Hortatory Amplification Paragraph] (Text) Text | | | | |
| | | | | וְיֵשְׁבוּ בָאָרֶץ | | [Text] |
| | | | | וְיִסְחֲרוּ אֹתָהּ | | [Amp] |
| | וְהָאָרֶץ הִנֵּה רַחֲבַת־יָדַיִם לִפְנֵיהֶם | | | | | Comment |
| | | | Predictive Antithetical Paragraph | | | |
| | | | | אֶת־בְּנֹתָם נִקַּח־לָנוּ לְנָשִׁים | | Thesis |
| | | | | וְאֶת־בְּנֹתֵינוּ נִתֵּן לָהֶם: | | Antithesis |
| | | | Expository Amplification Paragraph | | | |
| | אַךְ־בְּזֹאת יֵאֹתוּ לָנוּ הָאֲנָשִׁים לָשֶׁבֶת אִתָּנוּ לִהְיוֹת לְעַם אֶחָד | | | | | v. 22 Text |
| | בְּהִמּוֹל לָנוּ כָּל־זָכָר כַּאֲשֶׁר הֵם נִמֹּלִים: | | | | | Amp |
| | | | Hortatory Results Paragraph | | | |
| | מִקְנֵהֶם וְקִנְיָנָם וְכָל־בְּהֶמְתָּם הֲלוֹא לָנוּ הֵם | | | | | v. 23 Results |
| | | | (Hortatory Sequence Paragraph) Text | | | |
| | | | | אַךְ נֵאוֹתָה לָהֶם | | (item i) |
| | | | | וְיֵשְׁבוּ אִתָּנוּ: | | (item ii) |
| | | | Narrative Sequence Paragraph | | | |
| | | וַיִּשְׁמְעוּ אֶל־חֲמוֹר וְאֶל־שְׁכֶם בְּנוֹ כָּל־יֹצְאֵי שַׁעַר עִירוֹ | | | | v. 24 BU 1 |
| | | | | וַיִּמֹּלוּ כָּל־זָכָר כָּל־יֹצְאֵי שַׁעַר עִירוֹ: | | BU 2 |

In Scene Three the narrator follows Hamor and Shechem back to their city so that we can overhear their attempts to sell the alliance to the Hivites. As with Scene Two, the whole scene, with the exception of the Setting and Closure is direct speech.

The Setting is a short Narrative Simple Paragraph that has a Setting ("And

Hamor and Shechem his son came to the gate of their city") and a BUn which
is a לֵאמֹר frame quotation formula.

Of interest is that the verb of motion (וַיָּבֹא) is in the singular ("and *he* came")
even though the subject is plural (Hamor and Shechem). *Possibly* it indicates
that father and son are united as a single unit.[163] The reason that I have down-
ranked the first WAYYIQTOL is that it is a motion verb as in 34:1.

The men open with a Hortatory Comment Paragraph the beginning and end
of which are marked by circumstantial clauses.

The Setting is a band 1 Expository Simple Paragraph. I have ranked it in
band 4 as it forms part of a Hortatory Paragraph and have graded it on that
cline. In my analysis I have taken the overarching text type as the cline by
which to rank any embedded paragraphs. So we have a simple nominal clause
in which Hamor exhorts no one but simply expounds the state of affairs vis-à-
vis the Israelites - "They are peaceful men". This forms the springboard for the
following exhortations.[164]

The main Text of the paragraph is composed of two, top ranking, volitive
appeals.[165] "Let them dwell in the land and travel about in it." I suggest that the
second clause amplifies the first. Then follows the Comment, "The land - look -
it extends out before them!"[166] As with the first nominal clause, this one is
intended to calm the fears his audience may have. The two volitives are
sandwiched between two reassuring, simple nominal clauses - a good rhetorical
strategy. Hamor has just urged his fellow townsfolk to allow the Israelites
freedom to travel in the land. He immediately draws their attention to just how
large the land is. The use of a simple noun clause and הִנֵּה[167] expresses a present

---

163 Or, perhaps the ו was lost in transmission.

164 This particular nominal clause is probably another example of the so called casus
pendens. The words "These men" stand outside the clause and introduce the topic. The
clause then reads הָאֲנָשִׁים הָאֵלֶּה שְׁלֵמִים הֵם אִתָּנוּ with the predicate-subject word order - an
unusual word order in a nominal clause with a participle predicate (Andersen, 1970).
However, Muraoka argues that the word order has no relevance to the question of
emphasis when the predicate is a participle (pp. 22-23). The subject is not identifying,
i.e. the question is not, "Who comes in peace?" but, "In what way do these men come to
us?" and the answer is, "In peace." (Muraoka, 1985, pp. 19-23, 75. See also Bandstra,
1990, pp. 122-123, Jouon, 1991, p. 574, Waltke and O'Connor, 1990, pp. 130-13; Van
der Merwe, Naude and Kroeze, 1999, pp. 339-340).

165 See Endo, 1996, pp. 204-206 on jussive-jussive units.

166 Sarna thinks that "the city-state of Shechem in pre-Israelite times extended its
control over a vast area that at one time included the central hill country as far as the
borders of Jerusalem and Gezer in the south and Megiddo in the north, a domain of
about 1,000 square miles" (1989, p. 233).

167 On הנה see Niccacci 1990, pp. 96-101; van der Merwe, 1994, p. 38; Muraoka, 1985,
p. 138; Waltke and O'Connor, 1990, p. 627. Van der Merwe says that "It is the most
salient information in the context typically marking information that runs counter to
expectations." Muraoka writes that, "the primary function of these particles lies in

tense.[168] The הִנֵּה draws attention to the preposition - the largeness of the land.

Having calmed fears Hamor goes on to spell out some benefits. We have a Predictive Antithetical Paragraph (with obvious hortatory intent) in which, for the third time, we have the exchange-of-daughters speech. As in the first, the OV+OV word order emphasises the antithesis. What is of interest is the rhetorical strategy employed. Now that the audience has changed the emphasis changes. In v. 9, when addressing the Israelites, Hamor focuses on Israelite primacy in the exchange of daughters - *they* give and take. Here, with the Hivite audience, it is the Canaanites who do the giving and taking.

Having whetted the men's appetites Hamor proceeds to introduce the tough conditions with the words אַךְ־בְּזֹאת יֵאֹתוּ לָנוּ הָאֲנָשִׁים לָשֶׁבֶת אִתָּנוּ לִהְיוֹת לְעַם אֶחָד. The אַךְ serves to restrict the enjoyment of the blessing to those who comply with the following conditions. Hamor spells out at length the desired results (dwelling together in an alliance) between explaining *that* there is a condition (only in this...) and *what* that condition is (circumcision of all males as[169] they are circumcised). Given the difficult pill Hamor has to persuade the men to swallow, one can understand his rhetorical strategy - Hamor is doing what he can to help it go down. The paragraph in which the condition is reported is an Expository Amplification Paragraph with hortatory intent.

Immediately after speaking these difficult words Hamor pulls out his trump card[170] to focus his audience once again on the glittering prize to be had. We have a Hortatory Results Paragraph with the Results placed first for the rhetorical purpose of keeping the benefits, rather than the cost, at the front of the audience's mind. The Results sentence is a simple nominal clause which is in the present tense[171] - "the Israelite property is ours now," says Hamor. Obviously this is not strictly true but it is an effective method of persuasion - their property is *as good as* ours (through the trade that an alliance would open up). The Predicate-Subject word order marks the predicate for focus and, in this context, is probably emphatic. The Text begins with a restrictive use of אַךְ. The clause that follows lays down the conditions for the enjoyment of the benefits of the previous clause - "The Israelite property will be available to us if only we agree to them." The two clauses of the Text are linked chiastically in terms of the subjects

indicating that the speaker... wants to draw the special attention of the hearer... to the fact... which can be said to be important, new, unexpected".
168 Niccacci, 1990, p. 151.
169 On the comparative use of כַּאֲשֶׁר see Waltke and O'Conner, 1990, pp. 641-642.
170 Bandstra, 1990, p. 121.
171 Niccacci, 1990, p. 151.

Agreeing to the Israelite conditions and letting them dwell in the land are two sides of the same attitude. Hamor, as before, ends as he began - with a burst of hortatory speech.

Closure

The Execution of the proposal is a Narrative Simple Paragraph in which the townsfolk listen to Hamor and Shechem and then circumcise themselves, bringing their doom one step closer. Two things are worthy of note here. Firstly, the fact that the subject of the two sentences is "those who go out of the gate of the city."[172] However, unusually, instead of naming the subject in the first sentence and using the pronoun in the second the subjects are *named* in both sentences. Why? Francis Andersen suggests that this marks the two sentences not as two sides of the same event but as clearly sequential in time.[173] On this view the narrator is stressing that *first* they listened positively and *then* they were circumcised. I am not convinced that temporal sequentially is what is being marked in this case but I have little by way of alternative suggestions.[174] Other than that an explicit reference with a proper noun (and, I assume, a nominal phrase) can mark the end of a paragraph.[175] This however, does not explain the repetition of the nominal phrase. More interesting is that this scene, unlike the previous one, ends with a sequential WAYYIQTOL. Endo suggests that this is a way of setting up "literary reverberations".[176] It hints that something else will follow.[177] One could describe it as a "cliff hanger."[178] And this is exactly what it is, because in the next scene we hit the peak of the story!

---

172 "Those who go out of the gate of the city" are the able bodied men who were potential defenders of the city (Speiser, 1967; 1969, p. 265; Sarna, 1989, p. 237).
173 Andersen, 1994, pp. 106-107.
174 Shimasaki (1999, pp. 88-99) argues that the use of a noun instead of a pronoun can serve several purposes including the following: (a) to resolve ambiguity; (b) to narrow down the topic (e.g. He came in a car, in a Ford Fiesta); (c) literary rephrasing (same entity referred to by different nouns as a literary device); (d) theme announcement at the start of a subsection; (e) participant referencing resources to keep the protagonist central. Out of these (e) is just possibly relevant.
175 de Regt, 1991-92, p. 156.
176 Endo, 1996, pp. 260-264.
177 Ibid., p. 261.
178 Ibid., p. 263.

## Scene Four: Genesis 34:25-31

| Band 6 | Band 5 | Band 4 | Band 3 | Band 2 | Band 1 | |
|---|---|---|---|---|---|---|
| | | | | | Narrative Sequence Paragraph | |
| וַיְהִי בַיּוֹם הַשְּׁלִישִׁי בִּהְיוֹתָם כֹּאֲבִים | | | | | | v. 25 Setting |
| | | וַיִּקְחוּ שְׁנֵי־בְנֵי־יַעֲקֹב שִׁמְעוֹן וְלֵוִי אֲחֵי דִינָה אִישׁ חַרְבּוֹ | | | | BU 1 |
| | | | | וַיָּבֹאוּ עַל־הָעִיר בֶּטַח | | BU 2 |
| | | | (Narrative Amplification Paragraph) BU 3 | | | |
| | | | | | וַיַּהַרְגוּ כָּל־זָכָר: | (Text) |
| | | וְאֶת־חֲמוֹר וְאֶת־שְׁכֶם בְּנוֹ הָרְגוּ לְפִי־חָרֶב | | | | v. 26 (Amp) |
| | | | וַיִּקְחוּ אֶת־דִּינָה מִבֵּית שְׁכֶם | | | BU 4 |
| | | | | | וַיֵּצֵאוּ: | BU n |
| | | | Narrative Sequence Paragraph | | | |
| | | בְּנֵי יַעֲקֹב בָּאוּ עַל־הַחֲלָלִים | | | | v. 27 Setting |
| | | (Narrative Amplification Paragraph) BU 1 | | | | |
| | | | | וַיָּבֹזּוּ הָעִיר אֲשֶׁר טִמְּאוּ אֲחוֹתָם: | | (Text) |
| | אֶת־צֹאנָם וְאֶת־בְּקָרָם וְאֶת־חֲמֹרֵיהֶם וְאֵת אֲשֶׁר־בָּעִיר וְאֶת־אֲשֶׁר בַּשָּׂדֶה לָקָחוּ: | | | | | v. 28 (Amp) |
| | | (Narrative Amplification Paragraph) BU n | | | | |
| | | וְאֶת־כָּל־חֵילָם וְאֶת־כָּל־טַפָּם וְאֶת־נְשֵׁיהֶם שָׁבוּ | | | | v. 29 (Amp) |
| | | | | וַיָּבֹזּוּ וְאֵת כָּל־אֲשֶׁר בַּבָּיִת: | | (Text) |
| | | Narrative Comment Paragraph | | | | |
| | | | וַיֹּאמֶר יַעֲקֹב אֶל־שִׁמְעוֹן וְאֶל־לֵוִי | | | v. 30 QF |
| | עֲכַרְתֶּם אֹתִי לְהַבְאִישֵׁנִי בְּיֹשֵׁב הָאָרֶץ בַּכְּנַעֲנִי וּבַפְּרִזִּי | | | | | Text |
| | | וַאֲנִי מְתֵי מִסְפָּר | | | | Comment |
| | | Predictive Sequence Paragraph | | | | |
| | | | | | וְנֶאֶסְפוּ עָלַי | BU 1 |
| | | | | | וְהִכּוּנִי | BU 2 |
| | | | | וְנִשְׁמַדְתִּי אֲנִי וּבֵיתִי: | | BU n |
| | | Hortatory Simple Paragraph | | | | |
| | | | | | וַיֹּאמְרוּ | v. 31 QF |
| | | | | הַכְזוֹנָה יַעֲשֶׂה אֶת־אֲחוֹתֵנוּ: | | BU n |

Scene Four opens with a וַיְהִי.[179] Niccacci argues that וַיְהִי is not to signal a break in the narrative but to connect what follows with the main thread. It actually *avoids* a break in communication.[180] That all depends what one means by "break in communication". It seems clear that a break of *some sorts* occurs here, even if the start of Scene Four follows on directly from the end of Scene Three (as Niccacci's comments would lead us to expect). וַיְהִי is common before a temporal phrase as part of the Setting of a scene. It also serves to mark this episode as a peak episode. The subject of וַיְהִי is the complete paragraph it introduces[181] - it does not function like a normal WAYYIQTOL.[182]

The Setting is a temporal phrase. The fronting of such a phrase indicates a new stage in the action.[183] It is three days later and the local men are in pain from their recent surgical procedure. The brothers of Dinah have them where they want them.

We move straight into a Narrative Sequence - "and they took... and they came... and they killed... and they took... and they went..." - the peak of the story.[184]

In BU1 Simeon and Levi take their swords. In BU2 they "come upon" the city. BU3 is an embedded Narrative Amplification Paragraph. In the Text we read "and they killed every male" whilst the Amplification focuses in on two men in particular - "and Hamor and Shechem his son they killed with the edge of the sword". The Text and Amplification are linked chiastically.[185]

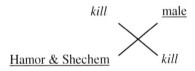

The chiasm ties in Hamor and Shechem's killing as part of the general massacre.[186] In the Text the killing is focused, whilst in the Amplification

---

179 On ויהי see Longacre, 1989, pp. 66-67; Niccacci, 1990, pp. 48-62, 156-162; Bandstra, 1990, p. 117; Endo, 1996, pp. 273-274.

180 Niccacci, 1990, p. 57.

181 Ibid., p. 160.

182 Ibid., p. 159.

183 Bandstra, 1990, p. 117.

184 Line 1 has a predicate focus structure with the predicate domain divided around the subjects. However, the whole predicate ('they took... their swords') is marked as new information (Shimasaki, 1999, pp. 103-105).

185 Longacre writes "when the perfect occurs paragraph medial, a preterite clause and a perfect clause constitute a chiastic sentence when the two verb forms are from the same or synonymous verbs and there is not an intervening we - 'and'." (1989, p. 77)

186 The reverse of word order may make them informationally marked in their clause (Muraoka, 1985, pp. 38-40). However, it may not be as the word order is required by the chiasm.

Hamor and Shechem are. In BU4 and BU5 the brothers carry out their earlier veiled threat to "take" Dinah and "go".

The tension lessens as the narrative proceeds into a post-peak episode. We now hit a very elaborate chiasm which is introduced by an X-QATAL secondary storyline sentence to mark a change in subject (Simeon and Levi have left[187] but the other brothers now attack). The chiasmus is as follows:

A - They *looted the city* where they [the men of Shechem] had defiled Dinah
  their sister
  B - sheep, cattle, donkeys - whatever was in city and field *they took*.
  B1 - their wealth, children and wives *they captured*.[188]
A1 - *They looted* everything which was in the house.

Now A and B are linked chiastically

as are B1 and A1

      Object      Verb
           ✕
      Verb       Object

When combined A-B chiastically mirrors B1-A1

      V   O   O   V
       ✕       ✕
      O   V   V   O

Clearly B1-A1 do not paraphrase A-B or amplify them. I see a progression in action (thus a Sequence Paragraph). *First* they loot field and city and *then* they loot the house. I suggest that BU1 (A-B) and BUn (A1-B1) are embedded Amplification Paragraphs. A and A1 focus the sons for comment informing us of what they did whilst B and B1 focus what was plundered.

The second post-peak episode comes in vv. 30-31. It is a complex dialogue in which Jacob rebukes Simeon and Levi for putting the family in peril. The sons respond by turning a fierce rhetorical question on Jacob. The QF is a single verb frame Sp:N + Add:N. Jacob and Simeon and Levi are reinstated into the story after an absence by the use of their names. The N + N formula

---

187 So Sternberg, 1987, pp. 469-470.
188 B and B1 both have a clause focus structure and run in parallel for the purpose of itemizing (Shimasaki, 1999, pp. 185-190).

may alert us to the confrontational nature of the exchange[189] or it may merely serve to reintroduce the participants.[190] Jacob's only words in the story are words of rebuke to his violent sons.

First we have a Narrative Comment Paragraph in which Jacob describes the situation as he sees it (Initiating Utterance = Remark).

> Text: You have brought ruin on me by making me stink among the inhabitants of the land: the Canaanites and Perizites.
> Comment: and (yet) I am only a small number.

The Comment, a simple nominal clause, is an implied antithesis induced by the word order (Subject-Predicate) - "I, contrary to the hostile majority."[191]

Given this scenario Jacob now prognosticates in a Predictive Sequence Paragraph. There is a clear build up in a sequence of ever more frightful consequences.

> BU1 - "and they will band together against me"
> BU2 - "and attack me"
> BUn - "and I shall be destroyed - *I* and my house."

With regard to the use of the redundant pronoun in italics in BUn Muraoka argues that

> the personal pronoun with the *verbum finitum* serves to express an intense concern with, special interest in, or concentrated, focused consciousness of, the object referred to by the pronoun on the part of the speaker or writer. And moreover, sometimes the speaker or writer wants a listener or reader to share his concern, interest, or consciousness, which derives from the very nature of the linguistic activity.[192]

The sons' reply (Concluding Utterance = Question) is a Hortatory Simple Paragraph.[193] Simeon and Levi's top ranking rhetorical question is an angry,

189 So Longacre, 1989.

190 de Regt, 1991-92, p. 157.

191 Muraoka, 1985, pp. 11-12; Waltke and O'Connor, 1990, p. 133; Andersen, 1970, p. 42.

192 Muraoka, 1985, p. 48, see p. 5 for more.

193 The QF is Sp:0 + Add:0. Longacre's account begins to look very tenuous here. 0 + 0 in a dialogue continuance indicates "emphasis on a social gap (often sizeable)" (1989, p. 184). In mid-dialogue it "plays down tension between Sp and Add; no struggle; stalemate; civilities; working out details of already accepted plan; compliance at end of dialogue." (ibid., p. 184). The first of these is possible but the rest are clearly inapplicable. Two things could reduce this problem. First of all, the QF in v. 30 has already possibly set up the confrontational nature of the dialogue. Secondly, Longacre

rude, unmitigated rebuke to their father. The fronting of the adverb topicalises and, in this context, puts emphasis on it.[194] Thus the focus is on the words "as a prostitute."

To end the story with such a powerful rhetorical question ringing in the ears of Jacob and the reader is almost unique in Hebrew story telling. The book of Jonah ends similarly and the narrator's sympathy lies with the asker of the question (God). Is that so here? Is this the narrator's way of saying that Simeon and Levi were in the right? I argue in Chapter Four that things are not quite as simple as this. What can be said is that this ending is not a simple tying up of strands from the story. The crisis created by Shechem's crime has been resolved, but the method of resolution has now generated two more crises: dangerous animosity between Canaanites and Israelites and tension within the Israelite family itself. The abrupt ending leaves the reader with a sense of unfinished business. One problem has been replaced by another but like the Hydra, the removal of the head of the first problem has led to a new two-headed beast.

---

notes that 0 + 0 can introduce a "speech act that marks a stalemate in an argument (before someone or something breaks the stalemate)... perhaps marking thereby the relative... ineffectiveness of the speech act thus introduced" (ibid., p. 169). He mentions three examples. 42:13 which marks the stalemate between Joseph and his brothers before he breaks it (42:14-16). 42:38 where the argument between Jacob and his sons "reaches a stalemate after Reuben's ineffectual attempt to get consent to take Benjamin with them. Here Jacob... proves to be utterly recalcitrant: 'and he said not shall go down my son with you because....'(T)he dialogue is not over, only discontinued and is quickly renewed in chapter 43" (ibid., pp. 171-172). Finally 43:7 is another stalemate over the sending of Benjamin. Could it be that 34:31 is not the end of the debate but a stalemate that awaits a resolution? If so when is it resolved? Chapter 49 - Jacob's final words on the subject is a curse on the violence of Simeon and Levi. Nevertheless, the huge gap between 34 and 49 plus the small data base just examined makes this a tenuous suggestion to base on a QF. De Regt (1991-92) notes that the shift from first to second speaker is often of the form Sp:0 + Add:0 and it "may serve to enliven the dialogue" (ibid., pp. 160-161). Jacob's response is not recorded in this story (there is no R.U., cf. the end of the parallel episode in Scene One). Perhaps one is not required - the sons are not asking for a reply but making a statement. Indeed "a rhetorical question is really more than an emphatic statement; it includes the implication that the audience know the answer, and not only the answer, but also that the audience will be full cognisant of this implication" (de Regt, 1992, p. 362).
194 Muraoka, 1985, p. 43.

# Appendix 2: Genesis 49:5-6

It is possible, along with Francis Andersen to construe v. 5 as follows:[1]

v. 5a    שִׁמְעוֹן וְלֵוִי

v. 5b    אַחִים כְּלוּ[2]

v. 5c    חָמָס מְכֵרֹתֵיהֶם

This has the effect of making the words "Simeon and Levi" into a title (cf., Deut 33 and later Oracles against the nations).

## The Accusation (v. 5)

If we set out v. 5 in the way in which it is usually done, then we read, "Simeon and Levi are brothers." "Brothers" in more than a physical sense would be implied.[3] Speiser translates it as "Simeon and Levi are a pair" and Wenham claims that the meaning is of an associate.[4] We could say that they are partners in crime. The negative connotations of the term "brothers" is provided by the context.

The second part of the accusation, on the traditional view, has two difficulties. Firstly, the word כלי[5] qualifies חמס and could be read as:

(i)      *vessels* of (כלי) violence (MT).

(ii)      *instruments* (*weapons*) of (כלי) violence (MT).

(iii)      *they completed* (from כלל - 'to complete/perfect') (in) violence (Sam Pent).

(iv)      *they destroyed* (from כלה - 'to destroy') (by) violence (LXX).

On (i) and (ii) the *hapax legomenon* מכרתיהם is the subject of the phrase "vessels of violence." Thus we read "The instruments of their violence are מכרתיהם." Alternatively, with (iii) and (iv), it could be the object of the phrase. Thus, "they destroyed (with) violence מכרתיהם." Not knowing what מכרתיהם means does not help here.

The meaning of the hapax is the second problem in the verse and it has prompted many suggestions.

(i)      כרת ("to cut") root?[6]

---

1 Andersen, 1966, pp. 106-107.

2 This inclines us to read כלו with the Sam. Pent. instead of כלי with the MT.

3 Aalders,1981, p. 271.

4 Speiser, 1969, p. 473; Wenham, 1994.

5 כלו Sam Pent.

6 Dahood argued for the meaning, "circumcision blades" from this root and its use in Exodus 4:25 (Dahood, 1961) "What the poet in Gen 49,5 is alluding to is the fact that Simeon and Levi, in persuading the Shechemites to submit to circumcision, lent them their circumcision blades to perform the operation... By slaying all the males of

(ii)    כרר ("round") root?[7]

(iii)   מכר ("to sell/trade") root?[8]

(iv)    *mkr* (Ethiopic - "to plan/advise") root?[9]

(v)     כרה ("to dig") root?[10]

(vi)    μαχαιρα root?[11]

(vii)   *kirru* (Sumero-Akkadian) root?[12]

---

Shechem on the third day when the pain was most acute, Simeon and Levi may be said to have turned the circumcision-knives, which were meant to be instruments of peace and union, into tools of violence" (ibid., pp. 55-56). Rashi thought that "swords" is most likely. In this he has been followed by many (e.g., Westermann, 1985, p. 225), often for want of any better suggestions. Delitzsch opts for "murderous weapons" (1889, p. 371), perhaps weapons which bore a round gaping wound. Probably, "instruments of piercing." Thus, "their swords are weapons of violence." Francis Andersen (1966, pp. 106-107) suggests that the word is a piel participle of כרה (as in "cut a covenant"). He sees מכרתיהם as a noun meaning "covenanters" (i.e. the Hivites).

7 Dillmann sees it as a curved instrument like a sabre from the word כרר (Dillmann, 1892, p. 453). Thus, "their instruments of violence are sabres" or "their sabres are instruments of violence."

8 Speiser (1969, p. 365) tentatively suggested "wares" from the verb מכר "to sell." This seems to lie behind Cross and Freedman's translation "stock in trade" (1975, pp. 78-79). Thus, "their stock in trade is in weapons/instruments of violence"

9 Ullendorf (1956, p. 194) suggests "counsels" from this root as does Barr (1968, pp. 57, 270). Thus we read, "weapons of violence are their counsels."

10 Sarna (1989, p. 334), following an earlier proposal by Aquila,  proposes a link with כרה "to dig." Thus a tool which is a digging or piercing instrument. Aalders takes a similar line and says "at the slightest pretence they would be apt to take a tool that they were using for their regular work and turn it into a vicious weapon against another person." (1981, p. 272).

11 Genesis Rabbah argues that the Greek word μαχαιρα "knives" is the root of the word. Cyrus Gordon (1955) and O. Margalith (1981) defend the notion that the MT uses a Greek loan word with the meaning "knives". This is rejected by Delitzsch (1889, p. 371) and most who have followed him (Dillmann, 1892, p. 459; Cohen, 1981, pp. 472-477; Young, 1981, p. 335).

12 Dwight Young (1981) has made an interesting recent proposal. He suggests that the initial מ was originally suffixed to the previous word. If we remove the suffix and the מ we get the word כרת - a feminine plural noun reflecting a prior כרה. There was a word in international usage during the latter half of the second millennium - *kirru/kiru*. It denoted a container of liquids. He suggest translating line 2. as follows, "their kirru-vessels are implements (כלי) of lawlessness/injustice (חמס)" (ibid., p. 337). Young sees a pun in v. 5. "If we are right, כלי is a prismatic device, a pregnant pun. Save for the modifying חמס the connotation would be "vessels", in agreement with the meaning of כרה presented above. But the poet knows full well a particular type of implement, "swords", will be understood, yea, recognised at once because of (1) the initial position accorded the construct phrase כלי חמס and (2) the audience's familiarity with the story about Simeon and Levi in Gen 34:25-26 where swords play a conspicuous role" (ibid., p. 339). But why does the poet mention kirru-vessels at all? Young shows that they

Many of these suggestions see מכרתיהם as the implements used to carry out the massacre. Some see it as a lethal weapon (a knife, sword or sabre). Others see it as a non-lethal weapon turned to violent use (a digging implement). Other suggestions see it as an indirect allusion to the massacre in that covenant ceremonies (circumcision knives, *kirru* vessels) are turned into an opportunity to kill. Only Andersen sees the hapax as a reference to those who were killed.

Andersen sees v. 5 as follows:

v. 5a   שִׁמְעוֹן וְלֵוִי

v. 5b   אַחִים כִּלּוּ

v. 5c   חָמָס מְכֵרֹתֵיהֶם

Thus כלו is a verb[13] modifying "brothers" and not a noun in construct with חמס. Thus we read the line as, "Simeon and Levi: brothers they destroyed..." The "brothers" are thus not Simeon and Levi but the Hivites. The Hivites are considered "brothers" to the Israelites as a consequence of the covenant they had entered into.[14] Andersen then takes חמס to mean "they were violent to..." One would expect to read חמסו in this case but Andersen says that the final vowel would not be shown on the old orthography,[15] hence the MT. The second line (if we forget the title for now) is chiastically related to the first and so we are looking for a noun to parallel "brothers" as the victims of the Israelite violence. Anderson proposes "covenanters" based on the root כרת and its association with covenant ceremonies. Thus we read,

v. 5a       Simeon and Levi:

v. 5b       Brothers they destroyed;

v. 5c       They were violent to their covenant partners

This approach has the advantage of bringing the first two lines into the same pattern as the rest of the poem which is all in clear parallelism.[16]

We can no longer be certain of the exact nature of Jacob's accusation against his sons. What is clear is that it is a rebuke on their violent behaviour and probably their actions at Shechem are what he has in mind.[17]

## Statement of Disassociation from the Criminals (v. 6a-b)

V. 6a-b also has some complex difficulties. Jacob says, "Let my soul/self not

---

were used in marriage ceremonies in Mesopotamia and argues that this fits with the marriage context in Genesis 34 (ibid., pp. 340-341). The brothers used what was intended to symbolise the unity of the two families as an opportunity for slaughter - they turn a scene of solemn ritual into a massacre. Their kirru-vessels were implements of injustice.

13 כלה - to destroy.

14 Cf. Amos 1:9, ברית אחים.

15 Andersen, 1966, p. 107.

16 "Five well-nigh perfect bicola." Ibid., p. 107.

17 Contra Zakovitch, 1985, pp. 190-191. In the final redaction of Genesis no other option makes sense.

enter into their council." Then follow two points over which interpretations differ.

(i)      תחד. If this is a 3fs impf Qal of יחד then it means "be united". Thus, "in their company may my glory/liver (see later) not be *united.*" This parallels the previous line perfectly. Dahood, however, suggests that the root is חזה (cognate with Ugaritic *hdy*), to see.[18] This is thus a Niphal jussive and we read, "Let my glory/liver not be seen in their company." Alternatively, the root may be חדה (Akkadian cognate - *hdu* - to be happy), to rejoice.[19] In support of this the Akkadian *hadu* often occurs with *kabattu*, liver. This may be the case in v. 6b. Thus we read, "May my liver not rejoice in their company." Gary Rendsburg suggests that this "problem" is deliberate on the author's part.[20] We have, he suggests, an example of double polysemy. The line can be read *both* as "Let my spirit not *rejoice* in their company" *and* "Let my spirit not be *united* with their company." Similarly, the previous line can be read both as "in their council my soul has no *pleasure*" and "in their council *come* not my soul." Thus, "the original reader did not have to choose between the double meanings. The poet intended that two meanings be inherent in תחד."[21]

(ii)     כבדי. Does this mean "my glory" as MT or should it be repointed to mean "my liver" as the LXX seems to require?[22] In fact, little of any consequence hangs on this. Whether we read "liver" or "glory" it is clear that a self-reference to the inner aspect of a person is referred to. Jacob is strongly disassociating himself from his violent sons.

### Justification for Disassociation (v. 6d-e)

The כי indicates that Jacob is now giving the reasons for his not wanting to associate with Simeon and Levi. Line 5. reads, "for in their anger they killed a

---

18 Dahood, 1955, p. 229 quoted in Hamilton, 1995, p. 649.

19 Watson, 1981, pp. 92-95.

20 Rendsburg, 1982, pp. 49-51.

21 Ibid., p. 50.

22 In support of the latter suggestion we note that in Akkadian texts hadu is often constructed with either *kabatta* (liver) or *libbu* (heart) with the liver being seen as the seat of the emotions. In 49:6a-b we read אל־תחד כבדי which could be read as "may my liver not rejoice." Some resist this suggestion (Rendsburg, Speiser, Collins) and argue that although כבד does parallel נפש as a means of self reference, the MT "my glory" is best retained as it can mean the inner aspect of a person (so too BDB).

man" and line 6. "and at will[23] (ובדצנם) they hamstrung an ox."

The main problem with this verse is not translational but interpretational. What, or who, is the object of the violence in line 5. and in line 6.? Who is the "man"? Is it Hamor or Shechem? Is it any man? Is it another man unconnected to the Shechem incident? And what of the ox? Genesis 34 makes no mention of any oxen being hamstrung. Some commentators take the reference literally and suggest that in fact the sons did literally hamstring oxen at Shechem even though Genesis 34 made no mention of it.[24] If we take the "ox" to be a metaphor rather than a literal ox to what does it refer? Vawter suggests, following Ugaritic parallels, that "men" or "princes" could be referred to as "bulls".[25] This suggestion is made more likely when we note that "ox" in line 6 parallels "man" in line 5. Perhaps in v. 5 we are to think that Simeon and Levi were violent towards a group (the Hivites) whilst in v. 6c-d they are violent towards an individual (Hamor? Shechem?). Possibly "man" refers to Shechem and "ox" to Hamor. The word Hamor means "donkey" (although hardly an ox) and, being the leader, he may best be seen in terms of an ox. It could be objected that to hamstring an ox is not to kill it. This is indeed so. Much depends on how the metaphor is intended to function. We are not, in my view, to think of a literal ox nor of a literal hamstringing. To hamstring an ox is to make it useless for work and defenceless. It is an act of great cruelty. By killing Hamor the sons have made the great ox useless. They have humiliated him. Just possibly there is a reference to the use of circumcision to render Hamor defenceless. The circumcision was the means by which they hamstrung the ox so that they could kill the man. Others think that the "ox" is Jacob whose peaceful existence in the land has been shattered by the killing of Hamor and Shechem.[26]

---

23 The main uncertainty in translation terms is ובדצנם. Dahood ("Northwest Semitic Notes on Genesis" *Bib* 55, 1974, p. 81; quoted in Hamilton, 1995, p. 650) repoints to בְּרָצֻנם (inf. cons. of רוצ + plural suffix - to hurry). Thus, "in a rush they hamstrung an ox." רצה can refer to a negative pleasure (so Fretheim, 1997, p. 1186, who refers to Dan 11:3 as an example). Thus, J. Kugel (quoted in Hamilton, 1995, p. 650) translates the line as "in a good humor they hough an ox". In other words they laugh in the midst of their violence. Walker (1962) argues that רצן can refer to "pleasure" or "will". Thus Hamilton translates the line as, "at will they hamstrung an ox."
24 Aalders takes this line and argues that the word עקר in the Piel proves the point (1981, pp. 225-226) as it refers to the literal hamstringing of oxen. This, however, hardly closes the case. If the "ox" is a metaphor then the use of the verb עקר is an appropriate extension of the metaphor and need not be taken literally.
25 Vawter, 1955, p. 4.
26 Carmichael, 1969. One could circumnavigate the whole problem with oxen if we repoint the word to read שׁור – "wall". The verb translated as "hamstrung"; is twice used to mean "uproot" (Ecc 3:2; Zeph 2:4). Thus we may be permitted to see a poetic reference to the sacking of the city - "they uproot a wall." Final certainty in this matter is impossible given our present state of knowledge.

# Bibliography

Aalders, G.C.. 1981. *Genesis*, Vol. 2 (tr. From Dutch by J. Vriend). Bible Students Commentary, Grand Rapids: Zondervan.

Abraham, J.. 2003. *Eve: Accused or Acquitted? A Reconsideration of Feminist Readings of the Creation Narrative Texts in Genesis 1-3*, Carlisle: Paternoster Press.

Adams, R. 1979. "Divine Command Metaethics Modified Again", *Journal of Religious Ethics* 7, pp. 66-79.

Adar, Z.. 1990. *The Book of Genesis: An Introduction to the Biblical World*, Jerusalem: Magnes Press.

Alexander, T.D.. 1997. *Abraham in the Negev: A Source Critical Investigation of Genesis 20:1-22:19*, Carlisle: Paternoster Press.

Allison Jr., D.C.. 1997a. "Land in Early Christianity" in (eds.) R. Martin and P. Davids, *Dictionary of the Later New Testament and its Developments*, Downers Grove and Leicester: IVP, pp. 642-644.

—— 1997b. "Moses" in (eds.) R. Martin and P. Davids, *Dictionary of the Later New Testament and its Developments*, Downers Grove and Leicester: IVP, pp. 777-782.

Alonso-Schökel. 1976. "Sapiential and Covenant Themes in Genesis 2-3" in J. Crenshaw (ed.), *Studies in Ancient Israelite Wisdom*, New York: KTAV Publishing House, pp. 468-480.

Alston, W.. 1989. "Some Suggestions for Divine Command Theorists" in W. Alston, *Divine Nature and Human Language*, Itaca: Cornell University Press, pp. 253-273.

Alter, R.. 1981. *The Art of Biblical Narrative*, Hemel Hempstead: George Allen and Unwin.

—— 1996, *Genesis: Translation and Commentary*, New York: W.W. Norton and Co.

Amir, Y.. "Philo Judaeus" in *Encyclopedia Judaica*, Vol. 13, Jerusalem: Enclyclopedia Judaica, pp. 409ff.

Andersen, F.I.. 1966. "Moabite Syntax" in *Orientalia*, pp. 106-107.

—— 1970. *The Hebrew Verbless Clause in the Pentateuch*, JBL monograph XIV, Nashville: Abingdon Press.

—— 1974. *The Sentence in Biblical Hebrew*, The Hague: Mouton.

———1994. "Salience, Implicature, Ambiguity and Redundancy in Clause-Clause Relationships in Biblical Hebrew" in Bergen (ed.), *Biblical Hebrew and Discourse Linguistics*, Summer Institute of Linguistics, Indiana: Eisenbrauns, pp. 99-116.

Andersen, F.I. and Freedman, D.N.. 1989. *Amos: A New Translation With Introduction and Commentary*. Anchor Bible Commentary, New York: Doubleday.

Anderson, T.D.. 1994. "Genealogical Prominence and the Structure of Genesis" in Bergen (ed.), *Biblical Hebrew and Discourse Linguistics*, Summer Institute of Linguistics, Indiana: Eisenbrauns, pp. 242-266.

Auerbach, M. and Grossfeld, B.. 1982. *Targum Onkelos to Genesis*, New York: KTAV.

Babbington, G.. 1615. *Workes Containing Comfortable Notes Upon the Five Bookes of Moses*, London, pp. 139-140.

Bach, A. (ed.). 1990. *The Pleasure of Her Text: Feminist Readings of Biblical and Historical Texts*, Philedelphia: Trinity Press International.

——— 1999a. "Signs of the Flesh" in A. Bach (ed.), *Women in the Hebrew Bible: A Reader*, London: Routledge, pp. 351-365.

——— 1999b. "With a Song in her Heart: Listening to Scholars Listening for Miriam" in A. Bach (ed.), *Women in the Hebrew Bible: A Reader*, London: Routledge, pp. 419-427.

Bail, U. 1994. "Vernimm, Gott, Mein Geber: Psalm 55 und Gewalt gegen Frauen" in H. Jahnaw (*et al*, eds.), *Feministische Hermeneutik und Erstes Testament*, Stuttgart: W. Kohlhammer Verlag, pp. 67-84.

Baker, D.L.. 1991 *Two Testaments, One Bible: A Study of the Theological Relationship Between the Old and New Testaments* (2nd edition), Leicester: Apollos.

Bal, M.. 1987. *Lethal Love: Feminist Literary Readings of Biblical Love Stories*, Bloomington: Indiana University Press.

Baloian, B.E.. 1997. "Anger" in W.A. VanGemeren (ed.), *New International Dictionary of Old Testament Theology and Exegesis*, Vol.4, Grand Rapids: Zondervan/Carlisle: Paternoster Press, pp. 337-385.

Bandstra, B.L.. 1990. "Word Order and Emphasis in Biblical Hebrew Narrative: Syntactic Observations on Genesis 22 From a Discourse Perspective" in W. Bodine (ed.), *Linguistics and Biblical Hebrew*, Indiana: Eisenbrauns, pp. 109-124.

Bar Efrat, S.. 1997. *Narrative Art in the Bible*, JSOTS 70 (2nd edition), Sheffield: Sheffield Academic Press.

——— 1983a. *Comparative Philology and the Text of the Old Testament*, London: SCM

Press.

Barr, J.. 1983b. *Holy Scripture: Canon, Authority, Criticism*, Philadelphia: Westminster.

Bartholomew, C.. 1999. *Reading Ecclesiastes: Old Testament Exegesis and Hermeneutical Theory*, Analecta Biblica 139, Rome: Editrice Pontificio Istituto Biblico.

—— 2000. "Consuming God's Word: Biblical Interpretation and Consumerism" in C. Bartholomew and T. Moritz (eds.), *Christ and Consumerism*, Carlisle: Paternoster Press, pp. 81-99.

—— no date. "A God is for Life, and Not Just for Christmas," un-published paper.

—— forthcoming, "Old Testament Wisdom Books" in *New Dictionary of Biblical Theology*, S. Ferguson, D. Wright, J.I. Packer (eds.), Leicester: IVP.

Barton, J.. 1978. "Understanding Old Testament Ethics," *Journal For The Study of The Old Testament* 9, pp. 44-64.

—— 1980. *Amos' Oracles Against the Nations*, Society for Old Testament Monographs Series 6: Cambridge: Cambridge University Press.

—— 1983. "Approaches to Ethics in the Old Testament" in J. Rogerson (ed.), *Beginning Old Testament Study*, London: SPCK, pp. 113-130.

—— 1984. *Reading the Old Testament: Method in Biblical Study*, London: Darton, Longman and Todd.

—— 1994. "The Basis of Ethics in the Hebrew Bible" in *Semia* 66, pp. 11-22.

—— 1996. "Reading For Life: The Use of the Bible in Ethics and the Work of Martha Nussbaum" in *The Bible and Ethics*, J. Rogerson *et al* (eds.), Sheffield: Sheffield University Press, pp. 66-76.

—— 1998. *Ethics and the Old Testament*, London: SCM.

—— 1999 "Virtue in the Bible," *Studies in Christian Ethics*, Vol. 12, No. 1.

Bauckham, R.. 1993. *The Theology of the Book of Revelation*, Cambridge: Cambridge University Press.

—— 1996. *Is The Bible Male? The Book of Ruth and Biblical Narrative*, Cambridge: Grove Books Ltd.

—— 1997a. "The Book of Ruth and the Possibility of a Feminist Canonical Hermeneutic," *Biblical Interpretation* Vol. 5, No. 1, pp. 29-45.

—— 1997b. "Egalitarianism and Hierarchy in the Biblical Traditions" in A. Lane (ed.), *Interpreting the Bible: Historical and Theological Studies in Honour of David F Wright*, Leicester: Apollos, pp. 259-273.

—— 1999a. *James*, London: Routledge.

—— 1999b. *Scripture and Authority Today*, Cambridge: Grove Books Ltd..

——— 2002, *Gospel Women: Studies of Named Women in the Gospels*, Edinburgh: T and T Clark.

Beale, G.K.. 1989. "Did Jesus and His Followers Preach the Right Doctrines From the Wrong Texts?" *Themelios* Vol. 14, no. 3, pp. 89-96.

—— 1999. *The Book of Revelation*, New International Greek Testament Commentary, Grand Rapids: Eerdmans/Carlisle: Paternoster Press.

Bechtel, L.. 1991. "Shame as a Sanction of Social Control in Biblical Israel: Judicial, Political, and Social Shaming" in *Journal for the Study of the Old Testament* 49, pp. 47-76.

—— 1994. "What if Dinah was not raped (Genesis 34)?" in *Journal for the Study of Old Testament* 62, pp. 19-36.

Bergen, R.D. (ed.). 1994a. *Biblical Hebrew and Discourse Linguistics,* Summer Institute of Linguistics, Winona Lake: Eisenbrauns.

—— 1994b. "Evil Spirits and Eccentric Grammar" in Bergen (ed.), *Biblical Hebrew and Discourse Linguistics,* Summer Institute of Linguistics, Winona Lake: Eisenbrauns, pp. 138-154.

Berlin, A.. 1983. *Poetics and Interpretation of Biblical Narrative*. Sheffield: Sheffield Academic Press (Almond), pp. 75-78.

Bernard of Clairvaux. 1987. "On the Steps of Humility and Pride" in *Selected Works*, tr. G.R. Evans, New York: Paulist Press.

Birch, B.. 1988. "Old Testament Narrative and Moral Address" in *Canon, Theology and Old Testament Interpretation: Essays in Honour of Brevard Childs,* Tucker, Peterson and Wilson (eds.), Minneapolis: Fortress Press, pp. 75-91.

—— 1994. "Moral Agency, Community, and the Character of God in the Hebrew Bible," *Semeia* 66, pp. 23-41.

Birch, B.C and Rasmussen, L.L.. 1989. *Bible and Ethics in the Christian Life*, Minneapolis: Augsburg.

Bird, P.. 1997. *Missing Persons and Mistaken Identities: Women and Gender in Ancient*

*Israel*, Minneapolis: Fortress Press.

Blamey, K.. 1995. "From the Ego to the Self: A Philosophical Itinerary" in L.E. Hahn (ed.), *The Philosophy of Paul Ricoeur*, Illinois: Open Court, pp. 571-600.

Blass, T.. 1982. "The Tenacity of Impressions and Jacob's Rebuke of Simeon and Levi", *Journal of Psychology and Judaism*, Vol. 7, pp. 55-61.

Blenkinsopp, J.. 1995. *Wisdom and Law in the Old Testament: the Ordering of Life in Israel and Early Judaism*, Oxford: Oxford University Press.

Blomberg, C.. 1984. "The Law in Luke-Acts," *Journal for the Study of the New Testament* 22, pp. 53-80.

Blue, B.B.. 1997. "Food, Food Laws, Table Fellowship" in R. Martin and P. Davids (eds.), *Dictionary of the Later New Testament and its Developments*, Downers Grove and Leicester: IVP, pp. 376-379.

Blum, L.. 1994. *Moral Perception and Particularity*, Cambridge: Cambridge University Press.

Bodine, W.R. (ed.). 1992. *Linguistics and Biblical Hebrew*, Winona Lake: Eisenbrauns.

Booth, W.. 1988. *The Company We Keep: An Ethics of Fiction*, Berkley: University of California.

Bredin, M. 2003. *Jesus, Revolutionary of Peace: A Nonviolent Christology in the Book of Revelation*, Carlisle: Paternoster Press.

Brenner, A.. 1985. *The Israelite Women: Social Role and Literary Type in Biblical Narrative*, Sheffield: Sheffield Academic Press.

—— (ed.). 1993a. *A Feminist Companion to Genesis*, Sheffield: Sheffield Academic Press.

—— (ed.). 1993b. *A Feminist Companion to Ruth*, Sheffield: Sheffield Academic Press.

—— (ed.). 1994. *A Feminist Companion to Exodus to Deuteronomy*, Sheffield: Sheffield Academic Press.

—— (ed.). 1998. *A Feminist Companion to Genesis: Second Series*, Sheffield: Sheffield Academic Press.

Brooke, G.. 1997. "יחד" in W.A. Van Gemeren (ed.), *New International Dictionary of Old Testament Theology and Exegesis*, Vol. 2, Grand Rapids: Zondervan/Carlisle: Paternoster Press, pp. 433-435.

Brown, W.P.. 1996. *Character in Crisis – A Fresh Approach To The Wisdom Literature*

*Of The Old Testament*, Grand Rapids: Eerdmans.

—— 1999. *The Ethos of the Cosmos: The Genesis of Moral Imagination in the Bible*, Grand Rapids: Eerdmans

Bruce, F.F.. 1976. *This is That* (2nd edition), Exeter: Paternoster Press.

—— 1988. *The Canon of Scripture*, Glasgow: Chapter House.

Brueggemann, W.. 1982. *Genesis*, Interpretation Commentary. Atlanta: John Knox Press.

—— 1997. *Theology of the Old Testament: Testimony, Dispute, Advocacy*, Minneapolis: Fortress Press.

Bruns, G.L.. 1989. "Tragic Thoughts at the End of Philosophy," *Soundings* 72, pp. 693-721.

Budd, M.. 1989. *Wittgenstein's Philosophy of Psychology*, London: Routledge.

Budd, P.. 1984. *Numbers*, Word Biblical Commentary, Dallas: Word, 1984.

Bull, R.J.. 1967. "A Note on Theodotus' Description of Shechem," *Harvard Theological Review* 60, pp. 221-228.

Burge, G. 2003. *Whose Land? Whose Promise? What Christians Are Not Being Told About Israel and the Palestinians*, Carlisle: Paternoster.

Buth, R.. 1994. "Methodological Collision Between Source Criticism and Discourse Analysis" in Bergen (ed.), *Biblical Hebrew and Discourse Linguistics*, Winona Lake: Eisenbrauns, pp. 138-154.

Caird, G.B.. 1966. *The Revelation of Saint John the Divine*, New York: Harper and Row.

Calvert, N.L.. 1993. "Abraham" in G. Hawthorne, R. Martin and D. Reid (eds.), *Dictionary of Paul and his Letters*, Downers Grove and Leicester: IVP, pp. 1-9.

Calvert-Koyzis, N.. 1997a. "Abraham" in R. Martin and P. Davids (eds.), *Dictionary of the Later New Testament and its Developments*, Downers Grove and Leicester: IVP, pp. 1-6.

—— 1997b. "Ancestors" in R. Martin and P. Davids (eds.), *Dictionary of the Later New Testament and its Developments*, Downers Grove and Leicester: IVP, pp. 37-44.

Calvin, J.. 1965. *A Commentary on Genesis*, (tr. J. King, 1847), London: Banner of Truth.

Campbell, E.F. and Ross, J.F.. 1963. "The Excavation at Shechem and the Biblical Tradition," *Biblical Archaeologist* 26, pp. 2-27.

Campbell, W.S.. 1993. "Covenant and New Covenant" in G. Hawthorne, R. Martin and D. Reid (eds.), *Dictionary of Paul and his Letters*, Downers Grove and Leicester: IVP, pp. 179-183.

_____ 1997. "Church as Israel, People of God" in R. Martin and P. Davids (eds.), *Dictionary of the Later New Testament and its Developments*, Downers Grove and Leicester: IVP, pp. 204-219.

Carmichael, C.C.. 1969. "Some sayings in Genesis 49," *Journal of Biblical Literature* 88, pp. 435-444.

—— 1979. *Women, Law and the Genesis Traditions*, Edinburgh: Edinburgh University Press.

—— 1985. *Law and Narrative in the Bible*. Ithaca: Cornell University Press.

—— 1992. *The Origins of Biblical Law: the Decalogue and the Book of the Covenant*, Ithaca: Cornell University Press.

—— 1996. *The Spirit of Biblical Law*, Athens, Ga: University of Georgia Press.

Carpenter, E.. 1997. "קהל" in W.A. Van Gemeren (ed.), *New International Dictionary of Old Testament Theology and Exegesis*, Vol. 3, Grand Rapids: Zondervan/Carlisle: Paternoster Press, pp. 888-892.

Carroll, M.. 1985. "One More Time: Leviticus Revisited" in B. Lang (ed.), *Anthropological Approaches to the Old Testament*, London: SPCK, pp. 117-126 (original article published in 1978).

Carson, D.A.. 1983. "Unity and Diversity in the New Testament" in D. Carson and J. Woodbridge (eds.), *Scripture and Truth*, Leicester: Inter Varsity Press, pp. 65-95.

—— 1996. *The Gagging of God*, Grand Rapids: Zondervan/Leicester: Apollos.

Caspi, M.M.. 1985a. "'And His Soul Clave Unto Dinah' (Gen 34): The Story of the Rape of Dinah: the Narrator and the Reader." *Annual of the Japanese Biblical Institute* 11, pp. 16-53.

—— 1985b. "The Story of the Rape of Dinah: The Narrator and the Reader", *Hebrew Studies* 26, pp. 25-45.

Cassuto, U.. 1964. *A Commentary on the Book of Genesis – Part II: From Noah to Abraham (Genesis VI-XI)*, tr. I. Abrahams, Jerusalem: The Magner Press, (Hebrew original, 1949).

Caws, M.A.. 1983. "Moral Reading, or Self-Containment with a Flaw" in *New Literary History* 15.

Chapman, C.. 1983. *Whose Promised Land?* Tring: Lion Publishing.

Charles, R.H.. 1908. *The Greek Versions of the Testaments of the Twelve Patriarchs*, Oxford: Clarendon Press.

—— 1913. *The Apocrypha and Pseudopigrapha of the Old Testament in English with Introductions and Critical and Explanatory Notes to the Several Books*, London: Oxford University Press.

Chawkat Moucarry, G.. 1988. "The Alien According to the Torah," *Themelios* Vol. 14, No. 1, pp. 17-20.

Childs, B.. 1979. *Introduction to the Old Testament as Scripture*, London: SCM Press.

—— 1985. *Old Testament Theology in a Canonical Context*, London: SCM Press.

Chilton, B.. 1997. "Purity and Impurity" in R. Martin and P. Davids (eds.), *Dictionary of the Later New Testament and its Developments*, Downers Grove and Leicester: IVP, pp. 988-996.

Chisholm, R.. 1997. "כבד" in W.A. Van Gemeren (ed.), *New International Dictionary of Old Testament Theology and Exegesis*, Vol. 2, Grand Rapids: Zondervan/Carlisle, Paternoster Press, pp. 587-588.

Christensen, D.. 1989. "Dtn 33,11 - A Curse in the 'Blessing of Moses'?" in *Zeitschrift für die alttestamentliche Wissenschaft* 101, pp. 278-282.

Clark, J.K.. no date. "The Storied Self," unpublished paper.

Clemens, D.. 1994. "The Law of Sin and Death: Ecclesiastes and Genesis 1-3," *Themelios*, Vol. 19, No. 3, pp. 5-8.

Clines, D.J.A.. 1990. "What Does Eve Do To Help? And Other Irredeemably Androcentric Orientations in Genesis 1-3" in D. Clines, *What Does Eve Do To Help?*, Sheffield: Sheffield Academic Press, pp. 25-48.

—— 1995. *Interested Parties: The Ideology of Writers and Readers of the Hebrew Bible*, Sheffield: Sheffield Academic Press.

—— 1997. *The Theme of the Pentateuch* (2nd edition), Sheffield: Sheffield Academic Press.

Clouser, R.. 1991. *The Myth of Religious Neutrality: An Essay of the Hidden Role of Religious Belief in Theories*, Indiana: University of Notre Dame Press.

—— 1999. *Knowing With the Heart: Religious Experience and Belief in God*, Illinois: IVP.

Coats, G.W.. 1979. "Strife Without Reconciliation - a Narrative Theme in the Jacob Traditions" in *Werden and Wirken des Alten Testaments*, R. Albertz, *et al.* (eds.), Göttingen: Vandenhoek and Ruprecht, pp. 82-106.

—— 1983. *Genesis With An Introduction to Narrative Literature*. FOTL 1. Grand Rapids: Eerdmans.

Cohen, M.. 1981. "MeKEROTEHEM (Genese XLIX.5)", in *Vetus Testamentum* XXXI, No. 4, pp. 472-477.

Cohen, S.M.. 1990. "Luck and Happiness in the Nicomachean Ethics," *Soundings* 73, pp. 209-218.

Collins, A.Y. (ed.). 1985. *Feminist Perspectives on Biblical Scholarship*, USA: Society of Biblical Literature Centennial Publications.

Collins, C.J.. 1995. "The WAYYIQTOL as 'Pluperfect' When and Why?" *Tyndale Bulletin* Vol. 46, No. 1, pp. 117-140.

Collins, J.J.. 1980. "The Epic of Theodotus and the Hellenism of the Hasmoneans" in *Harvard Theological Review* 73, pp. 91-104.

—— 1997. "כבד" in W.A. VanGemeren (ed.), *New International Dictionary of Old Testament Theology and Exegesis*, Vol. 2, Grand Rapids: Zondervan/Carlisle: Paternoster Press, pp. 577-587.

Colson, F.H and Whitaker, G.H.. 1968. *Philo, Vols IV-V* (5th edition), Loeb Classical Library, London: Heinemann.

Comstock, G.. 1986. "Truth or Meaning. Ricoeur Versus Frei on Biblical Narrative," *Journal of Religion* 66, pp. 117-140.

Cook, F.C.. 1871. *Genesis-Exodus*. Speaker's Bible. London: Murray.

Coote, R.B. and Ord, D.R.. 1989. *The Bible's First History*, Minneapolis: Fortress Press, pp. 167-171.

Cornelius, I.. 1997. "סחר" in W.A. Van Gemeren (ed.), *New International Dictionary of Old Testament Theology and Exegesis*, Vol. 3, Grand Rapids: Zondervan/Carlisle: Paternoster Press, pp. 242-243.

Cotterel, P. and Turner, M.. 1989. *Linguistics and Biblical Interpretation*, London: SPCK.

Cotterel, P.. 1997. "Linguistics, Meaning, Semantics and Discourse Analysis" in W.A.

Van Gemeren (ed.), *New International Dictionary of Old Testament Theology and Exegesis*, Vol. 1, Grand Rapids: Zondervan/Carlisle: Paternoster Press, pp. 134-166.

Craigie, P.C.. 1976. *The Book of Deuteronomy*, Grand Rapids: Eerdmans.

—— 1978. *The Problem of War in the Old Testament*, Grand Rapids: Eerdmans.

Crenshaw, J. (ed.). 1976a. *Studies in Israelite Wisdom*, New York: KTAV.

—— 1976b. "Method in Determining Wisdom Influences Upon 'Historical' Literature" in J. Crenshaw (ed.), *Studies in Israelite Wisdom*, New York: KTAV.

Cross, F.M. and Freedman, D.. 1975. *Studies in Ancient Yahwistic Poetry*, SBLDS 21, Atlanta: Scholars Press.

Crüsemann, F.. 1994. "Dominion, Guilt, and Reconciliation: The Contribution of the Jacob Narrative in Genesis to Political Ethics", *Semeia* 66, pp. 41-67.

Dahood, M.. 1955. "A New Translation of Gen.49.6a" *Biblica* 36, p. 229.

—— 1961. "MKRTYHM in Gen 49:5" *Catholic Biblical Quarterly* 23, pp. 54-56.

—— 1974. "Northwest Semitic Notes on Genesis", *Biblica* 55.

Danto, A.. 1984. "Philosophy And/As/Of Literature," *Proceedings and Addresses of the American Philosophical Association* 58, pp. 5-20.

Davidson, R.. 1979. *Genesis 12-50*. Cambridge Bible Commentaries. Cambridge: Cambridge University Press.

Dawson, D.A.. 1994. *Text Linguistics and Biblical Hebrew*, JSOTS Supplement 177, Sheffield: Sheffield Academic Press.

Day, P.. 1989. *Gender and Difference in Ancient Israel*, Minneapolis: Fortress Press.

Delitzsch, F.. 1889. *A New Commentary on Genesis, Volume 2*, (tr. S. Taylor), Edinburgh: T and T Clark.

De Lacey, D.R.. 1997. "circumcision" in R. Martin and P. Davids (eds.), *Dictionary of the Later New Testament and its Developments*, Grand Rapids and Leicester: IVP, pp. 226-230.

De Regt, L.J.. 1991-1992. "Devices of Participant Reference in Some Biblical Hebrew Texts: Their Importance in Translation," *Jaarbericht "Ex Oriente Lux"* 32, pp. 150-171.

—— 1994. "Functions and Implications of Rhetorical Questions in the Book of Job" in R. Bergen (ed.), *Biblical Hebrew and Discourse Linguistics*, Winona Lake:

Eisenbrauns, pp. 361-373.

De Sousa, R. 1994. "Emotion" in S. Guttenplan (ed.), *A Companion to the Philosophy of Mind*, Oxford: Blackwells, pp. 270-276.

De Waard, J. 1977. "The Chiastic Structure of Amos V:1-17" *Vetus Testamentum* 27, pp. 170-77

Diamond, C.. 1983. "Having a Rough Story About What Moral Philosophy Is," *New Literary History* 15, pp. 155-170.

Dillmann, A.. 1892. *Die Genesis* (6$^{th}$ edition), Kurzgefasstes exegetisches Handbuch, Leipzig: Hirzel.

Donaldson, T.. 1997. *Paul and the Gentiles: Remapping the Apostle's Convictional World*, Minneapolis: Fortress Press, 1997.

Douglas, M.. 1985. "The Abominations of Leviticus" in B. Lang (ed.), *Anthropological Approaches to the Old Testament*, London: SPCK, pp. 100-116 (originally published in 1966).

—— 1993. *In The Wilderness: The Doctrine of Defilement in the Book of Numbers*, Sheffield: Sheffield University Press.

Douma, J.. 1992. "The Use of Scripture in Ethics," *European Journal of Theology*, no. 2, pp. 97-112.

Downing, C.. 1989. "Diotima and Alicibiades: An Alternative Reading of the *Symposium*," *Soundings* 72, pp. 631-655.

Driver, S.R.. 1904. *The Book of Genesis* (3$^{rd}$ edition), Westminster Commentary. London: Methuen.

Dumbrell, W.J.. 1984. *Covenant and Creation: An Old Testament Covenantal Theology*, Carlisle: Paternoster Press.

Dunn, A.. 1989. "Tragedy and the Ethical Sublime in 'The Fragility of Goodness'," *Soundings* 72, pp. 657-673.

Dunn, J.D.G.. 1996. "'The Law of Faith', 'the Law of the Spirit' and 'the Law of Christ'" in H. Lovering jr. and J. Sumney (eds.), *Theology and Ethics in Paul and his Interpreters*, Nashville: Abingdon Press.

—— 1998. *The Theology of Paul the Apostle*, Grand Rapids: Eerdmans.

Dunne, J.. 1996. "Beyond Sovereignty and Deconstruction: the Storied Self" in R. Kearney, (ed.), *Paul Ricoeur: The Hermeneutics of Action*, London: Sage pp. 137-158.

Eaglestone, R.. 1997. *Ethical Criticism: Reading After Levinas*, Edinburgh: Edinburgh University Press.

Eichrodt, W.. 1967. *Theology of the Old Testament*, (tr. J. Baker), London: SCM.

Endo, Y.. 1996. *The Verbal System of Classical Hebrew in the Joseph Story: An Approach From Discourse Analysis*, Studia Semitica Neerlandica, Netherlands: Van Gorcum and Co..

Epsztein, L. 1986., *Social Justice in the Ancient Near East and the People of the Book*, London: SCM.

Eskhult, M.. 1990. *Studies in Verbal Aspect and Narrative Technique in Biblical Hebrew Prose*, Uppsala: Almquist and Wiksell International.

Evans, C.S.. 1996. *The Historical Christ and the Jesus of Faith: The Incarnational Narrative as History*, Oxford: Oxford University Press.

Evans, G.. 1958. "'Coming' and 'Going' at the City Gate - a discussion of Prof. Speiser's Paper" in *Bulletin of the American School of Oriental Research* 150.

Exum, C.. 1983. "'You Shall Let Every Daughter Live': A Study of Ex 1:8-2:10," *Semeia* 28, pp. 63-82.

—— 1990. "Murder They Wrote: Ideology and Manipulation of Female Presence in Biblical Narrative" in A. Bach (ed.), *The Pleasure of Her Text*, Philadelphia: Trinity Press International.

—— 1994. "Second Thoughts About Secondary Characters: Women in Exodus 1:8-2:10" in A. Brenner (ed.), *A Feminist Companion to Exodus to Deuteronomy*, Sheffield: Sheffield Academic Press, pp. 75-87.

—— 1999 "Who's Afraid of 'The Endangered Ancestress?'?" in A. Bach (ed.), *Women in the Hebrew Bible: A Reader*, London: Routledge, pp. 141-156.

Farley, B.W.. 1995. *In Praise of Virtue: An Exploration of the Biblical Virtues In a Christian Context*, Grand Rapids: Eerdmans.

Farley, M.. 1985. "Feminist Consciousness and the Interpretation of Scripture" in L. Russell (ed.), *Feminist Interpretation of the Bible*, Philadelphia: Westminster Press, pp. 41-51.

Farley, M. and Jones, S. (eds.). 1999. *Liberating Eschatology: Essays in Honour of Letty Russell*, Louisville: Westminster/John Knox Press.

Fensham, F.C.. 1975. "Gen 34 and Mari," *Journal of Northwest Semitic Languages* 4, pp. 87-90.

Fewell, D.N. and Gunn, D.M.. 1991. "Tipping the Balance: Sternberg's Reader and the Rape of Dinah," *Journal of Biblical Literature* 110, pp. 193-211.

Fichtner, J.. 1976. "Isaiah Among the Wise" in J. Crenshaw (ed.), *Studies in Israelite Wisdom*, New York: KTAV, pp. 429-438 (original published in 1949).

Fiorenza, E.S., "Jesus – Messenger of Divine Wisdom," *Studia Theologica* 49, 1995, pp. 231-252.

Fischer, G.. 1984. "Die Redewendung דבר על־לב im AT: Ein Beitrag zum Verständnis von Jes 40:2," *Biblica* 65, pp. 244-250.

Fishbane, M.. 1998. *Biblical Text and Texture: A Literary Reading of Selected Texts*, Oxford: One World.

Fokkelmann, J.P.. 1975. *Narrative Art in Genesis: Specimens of Stylistic and Structural Analysis*, Amsterdam: Van Gorcum, Assen.

Fowl, S.. 1988. "Some Uses of Story in Moral Discourse: Reflections on Paul's Moral Discourse and Our Own," *Modern Theology* 44, pp. 293-308.

—— 1995. "Texts Don't Have Ideologies," *Biblical Interpretation*, Vol. 3, No. 1, pp. 15-33.

—— 1999. "Learning to Narrate Our Lives in Christ" in Seitz, C. and Greene-McCreight, K. (eds.), *Theological Exegesis: Essays in Honour of Brevard S. Childs*, Grand Rapids: Eerdmans, pp. 339-354.

Fowl, S. and Jones, L.G.. 1981. *Reading in Communion: Scripture and Ethics in Christian Life*, London: SPCK.

Fox, M.. 1999. *A Time to Tear Down and a Time to Build Up: A Rereading of Ecclesiastes*, Grand Rapids: Eerdmans.

Fretheim, T.. 1997a. "ידע" in W.A. Van Gemeren (ed.), *New International Dictionary of Old Testament Theology and Exegesis*, Grand Rapids: Zondervan/Carlisle: Paternoster Press, Vol. 2, pp. 409-414.

—— 1997b. "רצה" in W.A. Van Gemeren (ed.), *New International Dictionary of Old Testament Theology and Exegesis*, Vol. 3, Grand Rapids: Zondervan/Carlisle: Paternoster Press, p. 1186.

Fretheim, T. and Froelich, K.. 1998. *The Bible as God's Word in a Postmodern Age*, Minneapolis: Fortress Press.

Friedmann, D. 2002. *To Kill and Take Possession: Law, Morality and Society in Biblical Stories*, Peabody: Hendrickson.

Frontain, R.J.. 1991. "Dinah and the Comedy of Castration in Sterne's Tristram Shandy" in R. Frontain and J. Wojcik (eds.), *Old Testament Women in Western Literature*, UCA Press, pp. 175-203.

Fuchs, E.. 1999. "Status and Role of Female Heroines in the Biblical Narrative" in A. Bach (ed.), *Women in the Hebrew Bible: A Reader*, London: Routledge, pp. 77-84.

Gardiner, P.. 1983. "Professor Nussbaum on *The Golden Bowl*," *New Literary History* 15, pp. 179-191.

Geller, S.A.. 1990. "The Sack of Shechem: The Use of Typology in Biblical Covenant Religion," *Prooftexts* 10, pp. 1-15.

Gibson, J.C.L.. 1982. *Genesis II*, Edinburgh: St. Andrews Press.

—— 1994. *Davidson's Introductory Hebrew Grammar*, Edinburgh: T and T Clark.

Gilman, J.E.. 1994. "Reenfranchising the Heart: Narrative Emotions and Contemporary Theology," *Journal of Religion* 74, pp. 218-239.

Ginzberg, L.. 1937. *The Legends of the Jews*, Vol. 1, Philadelphia: Jewish Publication Society (original 1909).

Goldjajn, T.. 1998. *Word Order and Time in Biblical Hebrew Narrative*, Oxford: Clarendon.

Goldingay, J.. 1993. "How Far Do Readers Make Sense? Interpreting Biblical Narrative," *Themelios* Vol. 18, no. 2, pp. 5-10.

—— 1994. *Models For Scripture*, Carlisle: Paternoster Press.

—— 1995a. *Models For Interpretation of Scripture*, Carlisle: Paternoster Press.

—— 1995b. *Theological Diversity and the Authority of the Old Testament*, Carlisle: Paternoster Press (first published 1987).

Gottwald, N.. 1979. *The Tribes of Yahweh: A Sociology of the Religion of Liberated Israel 1250 – 1050 BCE*, London: SCM.

Graetz, N.. 1993. "Dinah the Daughter" in A. Brenner (ed.), *A Feminist Companion to Genesis,* Sheffield: Sheffield Academic Press, pp. 306-317.

Graves, R. and Patai, R.. 1963. *Hebrew Myths: The Book of Genesis*, London: Cassell, pp. 235-240.

Green, J.B.. 2000. "Scripture and Theology: Uniting the Two so Long Divided" in J.B. Green and M. Turner (eds.), *Between Two Horizons: Spanning New Testament*

*Studies and Systematic Theology*, Grand Rapids: Eerdmans, pp. 23-43.

Grenz, S.J.. 1997. *The Moral Quest: Foundations of Christian Ethics*, Leicester: Apollos.

Gray, G.. 1976. *Numbers*, ICC, Edinburgh: T and T Clark.

Grey, M.. 1989. *Redeeming the Dream: Feminism, Redemption and the Christian Tradition*, London: SPCK.

Gunkel, H.. 1997. *Genesis* (tr. M.E. Biddle), Macon: Mercer University Press, (based on 3$^{rd}$ German edition, Göttingen: Vandenhoeck and Ruprecht, 1910).

Gunn, D.N.. 1990. "Reading Right: Reliable and Omniscient Narrator, Omniscient God, and Foolproof Composition in the Hebrew Bible" in D.J.A. Clines, S. Fowl and S. Porter (eds.), *The Bible in Three Dimensions: Essays in Celebration of Forty Years of Biblical Studies in the University of Sheffield*, JSOTS 87, Sheffield: Sheffield Academic Press.

Gunn, D.N. and Fewell, D.N.. 1993. *Narrative in the Hebrew Bible*, Oxford: Oxford University Press.

Hafemann, S.J.. 1995. *Paul, Moses and the History of Israel*, Peabody: Hendrickson.

Hahn, L.E. (ed.). 1995. *The Philosophy of Paul Ricoeur*, Illinois: Open Court,.

Hamilton, V.P.. 1990. *The Book of Genesis Chapters 1-17*, NICOT, Grand Rapids: Eerdmans.

—— 1992. "Marriage" in *Anchor Bible Dictionary*, (ed.) D. N. Freedman, New York: Doubleday, Vol. 14, pp. 559-569.

—— 1995. *The Book of Genesis. Chapters 18-50*, NICOT, Grand Rapids: Eerdmans.

Harrisville, R.A.. 1999. "What I Believe My Old Schoolmate Is Up To" in Seitz, C. and Greene-McCreight, K. (eds.), *Theological Exegesis: Essays in Honour of Brevard S. Childs*, Grand Rapids: Eerdmans, pp. 7-25.

Hartley, J.. 1992. *Leviticus*, Word Biblical Commentary, Dallas: Word.

—— 1997. "חרד" in W.A. Van Gemeren (ed.), *New International Dictionary of Old Testament Theology and Exegesis*, Vol. 2, Grand Rapids: Zondervan/Carlisle: Paternoster Press, pp. 280-283.

Hart, T.. 2000. "Tradition, Authority and a Christian Approach to the Bible as Scripture" in J.B. Green and M. Turner (eds.), *Between Two Testaments: Spanning New Testament Studies and Systematic Theology*, Grand Rapids: Eerdmans, pp. 183-204.

Hasel, G.F.. 1991. *Understanding the Book of Amos: Basic Issues in Current Interpretations*, Grand Rapids: Baker Book House.

Hauerwas, S.. 1989. "Can Aristotle be a Liberal? Nussbaum on Luck," *Soundings* 72, pp. 675-691.

Hauerwas, S. and Pinches, C.. 1997. *Christians Among the Virtues: Theological Conversations with Ancient and Modern Ethics*, Indiana: University of Notre Dame Press.

Hayes, J.. 1988. *Amos the Eighth Century Prophet: His Times and Preaching*, Nashville: Abingdon Press.

Hayes, J. and Prussner, F.. 1985. *Old Testament Theology: Its History and Development*, London: SCM.

Hayes, N.. 1994. *Foundations of Psychology: An Introductory Text*, London: Routledge.

Hays, R.. 1989. *Echoes of Scripture in the Letters of Paul*, New Haven: Yale University Press.

—— 1996a. *The Moral Vision of the New Testament*, Edinburgh: T and T Clark.

—— 1996b. "The Role of Scripture in Paul's Ethics" in E. Lovering and J. Sumney (eds.), *Theology and Ethics in Paul and his Interpreters*, Nashville: Abingdon Press, pp. 30-47.

Helm, P. 1981. *Divine Commands and Morality*, Oxford: Oxford University Press.

Henry, M.. 1725. *An Exposition of the Five Books of Moses*, London.

Hettema, T.L.. 1996. *Reading For Good: Narrative Theology and Ethics in the Joseph Story from the Perspective of Ricoeur's Hermeneutics*, Netherlands: Kok Pharos.

Hoffner, H.A.. 1973. "Hittites and Hurrians" in D.J. Wiseman (ed.), *Peoples of Old Testament Times*, Oxford: Clarendon Press, pp. 197-228, 221-295.

Hostetter, E.C.. 1995. *Nations Mightier and More Numerous: The Biblical View of Palestine's Pre-Israelite Peoples*, Texas: Bibal Press.

Hugenberger, G.P.. 1994. *Marriage as Covenant: A Study of Biblical Law and Ethics Concerning Marriage Developed From The Perspective of Malachi*, Leiden: E.J. Brill.

Hurst, L.D.. 1992. "Ethics of Jesus" in J. Green, S. McKnight, I.H. Marshall (eds.), *Dictionary of Jesus and the Gospels*, Downers Grove and Leicester: IVP, pp. 210-222.

Jacobs, A., "Martha Nussbaum, Poets' Defender", *First Things*, 66, 1996, pp. 37-41.

Janzen, W.. 1994. *Old Testament Ethics: A Paradigmatic Approach*, Louisville: John Knox Press.

Jasper, D. (ed.). 1995. *Readings in the Canon of Scripture: Written for our Learning*, London: Macmillan Press.

Jeansonne, S.P.. 1990. *The Women of Genesis: From Sarah to Potiphar's Wife*, Minneapolis: Fortress Press, pp. 87-97.

Jensen, P.. 1997. "לול" in W.A. Van Gemeren (ed.), *New International Dictionary of Old Testament Theology and Exegesis*, Vol. 2, Grand Rapids: Zondervan/Carlisle: Paternoster Press, pp. 772-778.

Josephus. 1943. *Antiquities Vol I*. Loeb Classical Library, London: Heinemann.

Jouon, D. and Muraoka, T.. 1991. *A Grammar of Biblical Hebrew*, 2 Vols., Subsidia Biblica, Rome: Pontificico Istituto Biblico.

Joy, M.. 1988. "Derrida and Ricoeur. A Case of Mistaken Identity (and Difference)," *Journal of Religion* 68, pp. 508-526.

Kaiser, W.. 1983. *Towards Old Testament Ethics*, Grand Rapids: Zondervan,.

Kalin, J.. 1992. "Knowing Novels: Nussbaum on Fiction and Moral Theory," *Ethics* 103, pp. 135-151.

Kalsbeek, L.. 1975. *Contours of a Christian Philosophy: An Introduction to Herman Dooyeweerd's Thought*, Toronto: Wedge Publishing.

Kass, L.R.. 1992. "Regarding Daughters and Sisters: The Rape of Dinah" *Commentary* 93, pp. 29-38.

Kearney, R.. 1989. "Paul Ricoeur and the Hermeneutic Imagination" in Kemp, P.T. and Rasmussen, D. (eds), *The Narrative Path: The Later Works of Paul Ricoeur*, Cambridge, MA: MIT Press, pp. 115-145.

—— 1996a. "Narrative and Ethics" in *The Aristotelian Society*. Supp. Vol. LXX, pp. 29-45.

—— (ed.). 1996b. *Paul Ricoeur: The Hermeneutics of Action*, London: Sage.

—— 1996c "Narrative Imagination: Between Ethics and Poetics" in R. Kearney (ed.), *Paul Ricoeur: The Hermeneutics of Action*, London: Sage, pp. 173-190.

—— 1998. *Poetics of Imagining: Modern to Postmodern* (2$^{nd}$ Edition), Edinburgh: Edinburgh University Press.

Keefe, A.. 1993. "Rapes of Women/Wars of Men", *Semeia* 61, pp. 79-94.

Keevers, P.. 1980. "Etude Litteraire de Gen 34", *Revue Biblique* 87, pp. 38-86.

Keil, C.F. and Delitzsche, F.. 1973. *Commentary on the Old Testament*, 10 vols. Vol. 1: *The Pentateuch* (tr. J. Martin). Repr. 3 vols. in 1. Grand Rapids: Eerdmans.

Kemp, P.T.. 1989. "Towards a Narrative on Ethics: a Bridge Between Ethics and the Narrative Reflection of Ricoeur" in P. Kemp and D. Rasmussen (eds.), *The Narrative Path: The Later Works of Paul Ricoeur*, Cambridge, MA: MIT Press, pp. 179-201.

—— 1995. "Ethics and Narrativity" in L. Hahn (ed.), *The Philosophy of Paul Ricoeur*, Illinois: Open Court, pp. 371-394.

Kemp, P.T. andand Rasmussen, D. (eds). 1989. *The Narrative Path: The Later Works of Paul Ricoeur*, Cambridge, MA: MIT Press.

Kerr, F.. 1997. *Immortal Longings Versions of Transcending Humanity*, London: SPCK.

Kessler, M.. 1965/66. "Gen 34: An Interpretation," *Reformed Review* 19, pp. 3-8.

Kevers, P.. 1980. "Etude Littéraire de Gen 34." *Revue Biblique* 87, pp. 38-86.

Kidner, D.. 1967. *Genesis: An Introduction and Commentary*. Tyndale OT commentaries. London: Tyndale.

Klassen, W.. 1986. "Jesus and Phineas: A Rejected Role Model" in *Seminar Paper Series* - Society of Biblical Literature, pp. 490-500.

Klein, T.. 1995. "The Idea of a Hermeneutical Ethics" in L. Hahn (ed.), *The Philosophy of Paul Ricoeur*, Illinois: Open Court, pp. 349-366.

Kock, M.. 1993. "A Cross Cultural Critique of Western Feminism" in M.S. van Leeuwen (ed.), *After Eden: Facing the Challenge of Gender Reconciliation*, Grand Rapids: Eerdmans, pp. 70-113.

König, E.. 1919. *Die Genesis Eingeleitet, übersetzt, Erklärt*. Gutersloh: Bertelsman.

Konkel, A.. 1997. "אזח" in W.A. Van Gemeren (ed.), *New International Dictionary of Old Testament Theology and Exegesis*, Vol. 1, Grand Rapids: Zondervan/Carlisle: Paternoster Press, pp. 354-358.

Kraut, R.. 1995. "Soul Doctors," *Ethics* 105, pp. 613-625.

Kugel, J.. 1981. *The Idea of Biblical Poetry*, New Haven, London: Yale University Press.

Laffey, A.L.. 1988a. *An Introduction to the Old Testament: A Feminist Perspective*, Minneapolis: Fortress Press, pp. 41-44.

—— 1988b. *Wives, Harlots and Concubines*, London: SPCK.

Lambdin, T.O.. 1973. *Introduction to Biblical Hebrew*, London: DLT.

Lang, B. (ed.). 1985. *Anthropological Approaches to the Old Testament*, London: SPCK.

Lasine, S. 1993. "The Ups and Downs of Monarchial Justice: Solomon and Jehoram in an Intertextual World," *Journal for the Study of the Old Testament* 59, pp. 37-53.

Leclercq, J.. 1989. *Women and Saint Bernard of Clairvaux*, Kalamazoo: Cistercian Publications.

Leeuwen, M.S. van (ed.). 1993. *After Eden: Facing the Challenge of Gender Reconciliation*, Grand Rapids: Eerdmans and Carlisle: Paternoster.

Leeuwen, R. van. 1990. "Liminality and Worldview in Proverbs 1-9," *Semeia* 50, pp. 111-144.

—— 1992. "Wealth and Poverty: System and Contradiction in Proverbs," *Hebrew Studies* 33, pp. 25-36.

Leibowitz, N.. 1981. *Studies in Bereshit*. (4th edition), Jerusalem: World Zionist Organisation.

Lilley, J.P.U.. 1997. "The Judgement of God: The Problem of the Canaanites," *Themelios* Vol. 22, no. 2, pp. 3-12.

Lindbeck, G.A.. 1999. "Postcritical Canonical Interpretation: Three Models of Retrieval" in C. Seitz and K. Greene-McCreight (eds.), *Theological Exegesis: Essays in Honour of Brevard S. Childs*, Grand Rapids: Eerdmans, pp. 26-51.

Lisska, A.J.. 1997. *Aquinas's Theory of Natural Law: An Analytic Reconstruction*, Oxford: Oxford University Press.

Long, V.P.. 1994. *The Art of Biblical History*, Leicester: Apollos.

Longacre, R.. 1989. *Joseph: A Story of Divine Providence: A Text Theoretical and Textlinguistic Analysis of Genesis 37 and 39-48*, Winona Lake: Eisenbrauns.

—— 1992a. "Discourse Perspective on the Hebrew Verb: Affirmation and Restatement" in W. Bodine (ed.), *Linguistics and Biblical Hebrew*, Winona Lake: Eisenbrauns, pp. 177-190

—— 1992b. "The Analysis of Preverbal Nouns in Biblical Hebrew Narrative: Some

Overriding Concerns," *Journal of Translátion and Text Linguistics* Vol. 5, pp. 208-224.

―――― 1994. "Weqatal Forms in Biblical Hebrew Prose: a Discourse Modular Approach" in R. Bergen (ed.), *Biblical Hebrew and Discourse Linguistics*, Winona Lake: Eisenbrauns, pp. 50-98.

Longman, T. and Reid, G.. 1995. *God is a Warrior*, Grand Rapids: Zondervan/Carlisle: Paternoster Press.

Luther, M.. 1986. *Luther's Works* Vol. 6, St Louis: Concordia and Philedelphia: Fortress.

MacDonald, J.. 1976. "The Status and Role of the *na'ar* in Israelite Society," *Journal of Near Eastern Studies* 35, pp. 147-170.

MacDonald, P.. 1992. "Discourse Analysis and Biblical Interpretation" in W. Bodine (ed.), *Linguistics and Biblical Hebrew*, Winona Lake: Eisenbrauns, pp. 153-176.

MacIntyre, A.. 1996. *After Virtue: A Study in Moral Theory,* (2nd edition) London: Duckworth.

Madison, G.B.. 1995. "Ricoeur and the Hermeneutics of the Subject" in L. Hahn (ed.), *The Philosophy of Paul Ricoeur*, Illinois: Open Court, pp. 75-92.

Margalith, O.. 1981. "*mekerotehem* [Gen xlix.5]" *Vetus Testamentum* 31, pp. 472-482.

―――― 1988. "The Hivites," *Zeitschrift für die Alttestamentliche Wissenschaft* 100, pp. 60-70.

Marshall, I.H.. 1988. "An Evangelical Approach to Theological Criticism," *Themelios* Vol. 13, No. 3, pp. 79-85.

Mayes, A.D.H.. 1979. *Deuteronomy*, New Century Bible, London: Marshall, Mogan and Scott.

Mays, J.L.. 1969. *Amos*, London: SCM.

McConville, G.. 1993. *Grace in the End: A Study in Deuteronomic Theology*, Grand Rapids: Zondervan/Carlisle: Paternoster Press.

McFague, S.. 1983. *Metaphorical Theology: Models of God in Religious Language*, London: SCM.

McFall, L.. 1982. *The Enigma of the Hebrew Verbal System,* Sheffield: Sheffield Academic Press.

McKnight, S.. 1992. "Gentiles" in J. Green, S. McKnight, I.H. Marshall (ed.),

*Dictionary of Jesus and the Gospels*, Downers Grove and Leicester: IVP, pp. 259-265.

McMylor, P.. 1994. *Alasdair MacIntyre: Critic of Modernity*, London: Routledge.

Meitinger, S.. 1989. "Between 'Plot' and 'Metaphor': Ricoeur's Poetics Applied to the Specificity of the Poem" in P. Kemp and D. Rasmussen (eds.), *The Narrative Path: The Later Works of Paul Ricoeur*, Cambridge, MA: MIT Press, pp. 161-178.

Meyers, C.. 1988. *Discovering Eve: Ancient Israelite Women in Context*, Oxford: Oxford University Press.

—— 1994. "Miriam the Musician" in A. Brenner (ed.), *A Feminist Companion to Exodus to Deuteronomy*, Sheffield: Sheffield Academic Press, pp. 207-230.

Middleton, R and Walsh, B.. 1995. *Truth is Stranger Than it Used to Be: Biblical Faith in a Postmodern Age*, London: SPCK.

Milgrom, J.. 1990. *Numbers*, JPS Torah Commentary, Philadelphia: *Jewish Publication Society*.

Millar, J.G.. 1998. *Now Choose Life: Theology and Ethics in Deuteronomy*, Leicester: Apollos.

Miller, C.. 1999. "Creation, Redemption, and Virtue," *Faith and Philosophy*, Vol. 16, No. 3, pp. 368-377.

Miller, C.L.. 1994. "Introducing Direct Discourse in Biblical Hebrew Narrative" in R. Bergen (ed.), *Biblical Hebrew and Discourse Linguistics*, Winona Lake: Eisenbrauns, pp. 199-241.

Miller, P.D.. 1990. *Deuteronomy*, Louisville: John Knox Press.

Mills, M.E. 2001. *Biblical Morality: Moral Perspectives in Old Testament Narratives*, Aldershot: Ashgate.

Moberly, R.W.L.. 1983. *At the Mountain of God: Story and Theology in Exodus 32-34*, JSOTS 22, Sheffield: Sheffield Academic Press.

—— 1992a. *Old Testament Guides: Genesis 12-50*, Sheffield: Sheffield Academic Press.

—— 1992b. *The Old Testament of the Old Testament: Patriarchal Narratives and Mosaic Yahwism*, Minneapolis: Fortress Press.

—— 1995. "Christ as the Key to Scripture: Genesis 22 Reconsidered" in R.S. Hess, G.J. Wenham and P.E. Satterthwaite (eds.), *He Swore An Oath: Biblical Themes From Genesis 12-50*, Carlisle: Paternoster Press.

Moo, D.. 1992. "Law" in J. Green, S. McKnight, I.H. Marshall (eds.), *Dictionary of Jesus and the Gospels*, Downers Grove and Leicester: IVP, pp. 450-461.

—— 1996. *The Epistle to the Romans*, NICNT, Grand Rapids: Eerdmans.

Morgan, D.. 1981. *Wisdom in the Old Testament Traditions*, Atlanta: John Knox Press.

Mott, S.. 1993. "Ethics" in G. Hawthorne, R. Martin and D. Reid (eds.), *Dictionary of Paul and his Letters*, Downers Grove and Leicester: IVP, pp. 269-275.

Motyer, S.. 1997. *Your Father the Devil*, Carlisle: Paternoster Press.

—— 2000. "Two Testaments, One Biblical Theology," in J.B. Green and M. Turner (eds.), *Between Two Horizons*, Grand Rapids: Eerdmans.

Moucary, C.C.. 1988. "The Alien According to the Torah," *Themelios*, vol. 14, no. 1, pp. 17-20.

Muraoka, T.. 1985. *Emphatic Words and Structures in Biblical Hebrew*, Leiden, E.J. Brill.

Murphey, M. 1998. "Divine Commands, Divine Will and Moral Obligation", *Faith and Philosophy*, 15.1, pp. 3-27.

Murphey, N.. 1999. "Non-Reductive Physicalism: Philosophical Issues," in N. Murphey and N. Maloney, *Whatever Happened to the Soul? Scientific and Theological Portraits of Human Nature*, Minneapolis: Fortress Press, pp. 127-148.

Murphy, R.E.. 1987. "Religious Dimensions of Israelite Wisdom," in P. Miller, P. Hanson and S. McBride (eds.), *Ancient Israelite Religion*, Minneapolis: Fortress Press, pp. 449-458.

—— 1992. *Ecclesiastes*, Word Biblical Commentary, Dallas: Word.

Naude, J.. 1997. "Sexual Ordinances" in W.A. Van Gemeren (ed.), *New International Dictionary of Old Testament Theology and Exegesis*, Vol. 4, Grand Rapids: Zondervan/Carlisle: Paternoster Press, pp. 1198-1211.

Nelson, P.. 1987. *Narrative and Morality: A Theological Inquiry*, University Park: Pennsylvania State University Press.

Neusner, J.. 1985. *Genesis Rabbah: The Judaic Commentary to the Book of Genesis*. 3 vols. Atlanta: Scholars Press.

Newman, C.C.. 1997. "Covenant, New Covenant" in R. Martin and P. Davids (eds.), *Dictionary of the Later New Testament and its Developments*, Downers Grove and Leicester: IVP, pp. 245-250.

Niccacci, A.. 1990. *The Syntax of the Verb in Classical Hebrew Prose* (trans. W. Watson), JSOTS 86, Sheffield: Sheffield Academic Press.

—— 1994a. "On the Hebrew Verbal System" in R. Bergen (ed.), *Biblical Hebrew and Discourse Linguistics*, Winona Lake: Eisenbrauns, pp. 117-137.

—— 1994b. "Analysis of Biblical Narrative" in R. Bergen (ed.), *Biblical Hebrew and Discourse Linguistics*, Winona Lake: Eisenbrauns, pp. 175-198.

Niditch, S.. 1993. "War, Women and Defilement in Numbers 31," *Semeia* 61, pp. 39-57.

—— 1999. "Eroticism and Death in the Tale of Jael" in A. Bach (ed.), *Women in the Hebrew Bible: A Reader*, London: Routledge, pp. 305-315.

Noble, P.. 1996. "A 'Balanced' Reading of the Rape of Dinah: Some Exegetical and Methodological Considerations," *Biblical Interpretation* Vol. IV, No. 2, pp. 173-203.

Noordtzij, A.. 1983. *Numbers*, BSC, Grand Rapids: Zondervan.

Norman, R. and Reynolds, C.. 1989. "A Symposium on *The Fragility of Goodness*," *Soundings* 72.4, pp. 571-587.

Noth, M.. 1972. *A History of Pentateuchal Traditions* (tr. B. Anderson), Englewood Cliffs, New Jersey: Prentice Hall (from German original, 1948).

Nunnally, W.E.. 1997. "כלל" in W.A. Van Gemeren (ed.), *New International Dictionary of Old Testament Theology and Exegesis*, Vol. 3, Grand Rapids: Zondervan/Carlisle: Paternoster Press, p. 198.

Nussbaum, M.. 1983. "Reply to Richard Wollheim, Patrick Gardiner, and Hilary Putnam", *New Literary History* 15.

—— 1986. *The Fragility of Goodness: Luck and Ethics in Greek Tragedy and Philosophy*, Cambridge: Cambridge University Press.

—— 1987. "Aristotle" in *The Great Philosophers*, B. Magee, London: BBC.

—— 1989. "A Reply," *Soundings* 72, pp. 725-781.

—— 1990. *Love's Knowledge: Essays on Philosophy and Literature*, Oxford: Oxford University Press.

—— 1993a. "Comparing Virtues," *Journal of Religious Ethics* 21, No. 2, pp. 345-367.

—— 1993b. "Non-Relative Virtues: An Aristotelian Approach" in M. Nussbaum and A. Sen (eds.), *The Quality of Life*, Oxford: Oxford University Press.

—— 1994a. "Skepticism About Practical Reason in Literature and the Law," *Harvard Law Review* 107, No. 3, pp. 714-744.

—— 1994b. *The Therapy of Desire: Theory and Practice in Hellenistic Ethics*, New Jersey: Princeton University Press.

—— 1995. "Aristotle on Human Nature and the Foundations of Ethics" in J. Altham and R. Harrison (eds.), *World, Mind and Ethics: Essays on the Ethical Philosophy of Bernard Williams*, Cambridge: Cambridge University Press, pp. 86-131.

O'Connor, M.. 1980. *Hebrew Verse Structure*, Winona Lake: Eisenbrauns,.

O'Day, G.. 1999. "Intertextuality" in J. Hayes (ed.), *Dictionary of Biblical Interpretation*, Nashville: Abingdon Press, pp. 546-548.

O'Donovan, O.. 1994. *Resurrection and Moral Order: An Outline for Evangelical Ethics* (2$^{nd}$ edition), Leicester: Apollos.

Okri, B.. 1996. *Birds of Heaven*, London: Phoenix.

Olson, D.T.. 1996. *Numbers*, Louisville: John Knox Press.

Osiek, C.. 1985. "The Feminist and the Bible: Hermeneutical Alternatives" in A.Y. Collins (ed.), *Feminist Perspectives on Biblical Scholarship*, Society of Biblical Literature Centennial Publications, Atlanta: Scholars Press, pp. 93-106.

Ostriker, A.S.. 1993. *Feminist Revision and the Bible*, Oxford: Blackwells,.

Otwell, J.. 1977. *And Sarah Laughed: The Status of Woman in the Old Testament*, Louisville: Westminster Press.

Otto, E. 1994. *Theologische Ethik des Alten Testaments*, Stuttgart: Kohlhammer.

Pan, C. W.. 1997. "נבל" in W.A. Van Gemeren (ed.), *New International Dictionary of Old Testament Theology and Exegesis*, Vol. 3, Grand Rapids: Zondervan/Carlisle, Paternoster Press, pp. 11-13.

Parkinson, B.. 1996. "What Makes Emotions Emotional?" *Psychology Review*, pp. 2-5.

Parris, D. 1999. *Reception Theory: Philosophical Hermeneutics, Literary Theory, and Biblical Interpretation*. Unpublished PhD from Nottingham University.

Parry, R.. 2000a "Greeks Bearing Gifts? Appropriating Nussbaum (Appropriating Aristotle) For A Christian Approach to Old Testament Ethics," *European Journal of Theology* IX: 1, pp. 61-73.

—— 2000b. "Source Criticism and Genesis 34," *Tyndale Bulletin*, 51.1, pp. 121-138.

——— 2002, "Feminist Hermeneutics and Evangelical Concerns", *Tyndale Bulletin* 53.1, pp. 1-28.

——— 2003a. "Evangelicalism and Ethics" in C. Bartholomew, R. Parry and A. West (eds.), *The Futures of Evangelicalism: Issues and Prospects*, Leicester: IVP, pp. 164-193.

_____ 2003b, "Review of Mary E. Mills' *Biblical Morality: Moral Perspectives in Old Testament Narratives*" *Themelios* 28.3, pp. 70-71

——— (forthcoming a) "Ideological Criticism" in *Dictionary of the Theological Interpretation of Scripture*, K. Vanhoozer, N.T. Wright, C. Bartholomew and D. Treier (eds.), Grand Rapids: Baker Book House.

——— (forthcoming b) "Narrative Criticism" in *Dictionary of the Theological Interpretation of Scripture*, K. Vanhoozer, N.T. Wright, C. Bartholomew and D. Treier (eds.), Grand Rapids: Baker Book House.

——— (forthcoming c) "Reader Response Theory" in *Dictionary of the Theological Interpretation of Scripture*, K. Vanhoozer, N.T. Wright, C. Bartholomew and D. Treier (eds.), Grand Rapids: Baker Book House.

Patrick, D.. 1985. *Old Testament Law*, London: SCM Press.

Perwitt, T.. 1990. *The Elusive Covenant*, Bloomington: Indiana University Press.

Petit, M.V.. 1989. "Thinking History: Methodology and Epistemology in Paul Ricoeur's Reflections on History from *History and Truth* and *Time and Narrative*" in P. Kemp and D. Rasmussen (eds.), *The Narrative Path: The Later Works of Paul Ricoeur*, Cambridge, MA: MIT Press.

Phillips, A.. 1975. "Nebalah," *Vetus Testamentum* 25, pp. 237-241.

Philo, J.. 1968a. *Migration of Abraham* (5th edition), Loeb Classical Library: Philo Vol. IV, (tr. F.H. Colson and G.H. Whitaker), London: Heinemann.

——— 1968b. *On the Change of Names* (4th edition), Loeb Classical Library: Philo Vol. V, (tr. F.H. Colson and G.H. Whitaker), London: Heinemann,.

Pinches, C.R.. 1990. "Friendship and Tragedy: the Fragility of Goodness," *First Things* 3, pp. 38-45.

Pitt-Rivers, J.. 1977. *The Fate of Shechem or the Politics of Sex: Essays in the Anthropology of the Mediterranean.* Cambridge: Cambridge University Press,.

Plantinga, A.. 2000. *Warranted Christian Belief*, Oxford: Oxford University Press.

Plaut, W.G.. 1974. *The Torah: A Modern Commentary: Genesis*, New York: Union of

Hebrew Congregations.

Poidevin, R. le. 1996. *Arguing For Atheism: An Introduction to the Philosophy of Religion*, London: Routledge.

Polzin, R.. 1975. "'The Ancestress of Israel in Danger' in Danger," *Semeia* 3, pp. 81-97.

Powell, M.A. 2001. *Chasing the Eastern Star: Adventures in Reader-Response Criticism*, Louisville: Westminster John Knox Press.

Pratt, R.L.. 1973. "Pictures, Windows, and Mirrors in Old Testament Exegesis," *Westminster Journal of Theology* 85, pp. 143-156.

—— 1993. *He Gave us Stories: The Bible Student's Guide to Interpeting Old Testament Narratives*, New Jersey: Presbyterian and Reformed Publishing Company.

Prentice, P.. 1995. "Rational-Emotive Therapy," *Psychology Review*, pp. 28-31.

Pressler, C.. 1994. "Sexual Violence and Deuteronomic Law" in A. Brenner (ed.), *Feminist Companion to Exodus to Deuteronomy*, Sheffield: Sheffield Academic Press, pp. 102-112.

Prewitt, T.. 1990. *The Elusive Covenant*, Bloomington: Indiana University Press.

Price. M.. 1983. *Forms of Life: Character and Moral Imagination in the Novel*, New Haven, London: Yale University Press.

Proudfoot, W.. 1977. "Religious Experience, Emotion and Belief," *Harvard Theological Review* 70:3-4, pp. 343-367.

Pucci, E.. 1996. "History and the Question of Identity: Kant, Arendt, Ricoeur" in R. Kearney (ed.), *Paul Ricoeur: The Hermeneutics of Action*, London: Sage pp. 125-136

Pummer, R.. 1982. "Gen 34 in Jewish Writings of the Hellenistic and Roman Periods," *Harvard Theological Review* 75, pp. 177-188.

Pury, A. de. 1969. "Gen 34 et l'historie", *Revue Biblique* 87, pp. 5-49.

Putnam, H.. 1983. "Taking Rules Seriously: A Response to Martha Nussbaum," *New Literary History* 15, pp. 193-200.

Quinn, P.. 1978. *Divine Commands and Moral Requirements*, Oxford: Oxford University Press.

—— 1990. "Agamemnon and Abraham: The Tragic Dilemma of Kierkegaard's Knight of Faith," *Literature and Theology* 4, pp. 181-193.

—— 1998. "The Virtue of Obedience," *Faith and Philosophy* Vol. 15, No. 4, pp. 445-

461.

Rad, G. von. 1972. *Genesis.* (2nd ed.), tr. J.H. Marks and J. Bowden. London: SCM Press.

—— 1976. "The Joseph Narrative and Ancient Wisdom" in J. Crenshaw (ed.), *Studies in Ancient Israelite Wisdom*, New York: KTAV, pp. 439-447 (original article published in 1953).

—— 1991. *Holy War in Ancient Israel*, (tr. M. Dawn), Grand Rapids: Eerdmans (translated from 3$^{rd}$ German edition, 1958).

Rainwater, M.. 1996. "Refiguring Ricoeur: Narrative Force and Communicative Ethics" in R. Kearney (ed.), *Paul Ricoeur: The Hermeneutics of Action*, London: Sage.

Ramras-Rauch, G.. 1990. "Fathers and Daughters: Two Biblical Narratives" in V. Tollers (ed.), *Mappings of the Biblical Terrain*, pp. 158-169.

Raphael, D.D.. 1983a. "Can Literature Be Moral Philosophy?" *New Literary History* 15, pp. 1-12.

—— 1983b. "Philosophy and Rationality: A Response to Cora Diamond," *New Literary History* 15, pp. 171-177.

Rashi. no date. *Pentateuch with Rashi's Commentary,* (tr. M. Rosenbaum and A.M. Silberman), New York: Hebrew Publishing Company.

Rashkow, I.M.. 1990. "Hebrew Bible Translation and the Fear of Judaization," *Sixteenth Century Journal* 21, No. 2, pp. 217-233.

—— 1991 *Upon Dark Places: Anti-Semitism and Sexism in English Renaissance Biblical Translation*, Sheffield: Almond Press.

—— 1993a. "Daughters and Fathers in Genesis... or, What is Wrong With This Picture?" in D. Clines and C. Exum (eds.), *The New Literary Criticism of the Hebrew Bible,* JSOTS 43, Sheffield: Sheffield Academic Press, pp. 250-265.

—— 1993b. *The Phallacy of Genesis: A Feminist-Psychoanalytic Approach*, Louisville: Westminster/John Know Press.

Rasmussen, D.. 1996. "Rethinking Subjectivity: Narrative Identity and the Self" in R. Kearney (ed.), *Paul Ricoeur: The Hermeneutics of Action*, London: Sage, pp. 159-190.

Reagan, C.. 1995. "Words and Deeds: The Semantics of Action" in L. Hahn (ed.), *The Philosophy of Paul Ricoeur*, Illinois: Open Court, pp. 331-345.

Reasoner, M.. 1993. "Purity and Impurity" in G. Hawthorne, R. Martin and D. Reid (eds.), *Dictionary of Paul and his Letters*, Downers Grove and Leicester: IVP, pp. 775-776.

Rendsburg, G.. 1982. "Double Polysemy in Gen 49:6 and Job 3:6," *Catholic Biblical Quarterly* 44, pp. 48-50.

—— 1986. *The Redaction of Genesis*, Winona Lake: Eisenbrauns.

Rendtorff, R.. 1993. *Canon and Theology: Overtures to an Old Testament Theology*, Edinburgh: T and T Clark.

Reventlow, H.G.. 1985. *Problems of Old Testament Theology in the Twentieth Century*, (tr. J. Bowden), London: SCM Press (German original, 1982).

Ricoeur, P.. 1967. *The Symbolism of Evil*, New York: Harper Row.

—— 1970. *Freud and Philosophy: An Essay on Interpretation*, New Haven: Yale University Press.

—— 1978. *The Rule of Metaphor*, London: Routledge and Kegan Paul, 1978.

—— 1981a. "Phenomenology and Hermeneutics" in *Hermeneutics and the Human Sciences: Essays on Language, Action and Interpretation*, J. Thompson (ed.), Cambridge: Cambridge University Press, pp. 101-128.

—— 1981b. "The Narrative Function" in *Hermeneutics and the Human Sciences: Essays on Language, Action and Interpretation*, J. Thompson (ed.), Cambridge: Cambridge University Press, pp. 274-296.

—— 1984. *Time and Narrative* Vol. 1, (tr. K. Blamey and D. Pellauer), Chicago: Univesity of Chicago Press.

—— 1985. *Time and Narrative* Vol. 2, (tr. K. Blamey and D. Pellauer), Chicago: Univesity of Chicago Press.

—— 1988. *Time and Narrative* Vol. 3, (tr. K. Blamey and D. Pellauer), Chicago: Univesity of Chicago Press.

—— 1989. "The Human Being as the Subject Matter of Philosophy" in P. Kemp and D. Rasmussen (eds.), *The Narrative Path: The Later Works of Paul Ricoeur*, Cambridge, MA: MIT Press, pp. 203-215.

—— 1991a. "What is a Text? Explanation and Understanding" (originally published in 1970) in M. Valdes (ed.), *A Ricoeur Reader: Reflection and Imagination*, New York/London: Harvester Wheatsheaf, pp. 43-64.

—— 1991b. "Appropriation" (originally published in 1972) in M. Valdes (ed.), *A Ricoeur Reader: Reflection and Imagination*, New York/London: Harvester

Wheatsheaf, pp. 86-98.

—— 1991c. "The Human Experience of Time and Narrative" (original 1978) in M. Valdes (ed.), *A Ricoeur Reader: Reflection and Imagination*, New York/London: Harvester Wheatsheaf, pp. 99-116.

—— 1991d. "The Function of Fiction in Shaping Reality" (original 1979) in M. Valdes (ed.), *A Ricoeur Reader: Reflection and Imagination*, New York/London: Harvester Wheatsheaf, pp. 117-136.

—— 1991e. "Mimesis and Representation" (original 1980) in M. Valdes (ed.) , *A Ricoeur Reader: Reflection and Imagination*, New York/London: Harvester Wheatsheaf, pp. 137-155.

—— 1991f. "Life – A Story in Search of a Narrator" (original 1987) in M. Valdes (ed.), *A Ricoeur Reader: Reflection and Imagination*, New York/London: Harvester Wheatsheaf, pp. 425-437.

—— 1992. *Oneself as Another*, (tr. K. Blamey), Chicago: University of Chicago Press.

—— 1995a. "Reply to G.B. Madison" in L. Hahn (ed.), *The Philosophy of Paul Ricoeur*, Illinois: Open Court, pp. 93-95.

—— 1995b. "Reply to Charles E. Reagan" in (ed.) L. Hahn, *The Philosophy of Paul Ricoeur*, Illinois: Open Court, 1995, pp. 346-347.

—— 1995c. "Reply to Ted Klein" in L. Hahn (ed.), *The Philosophy of Paul Ricoeur*, Illinois: Open Court, pp. 367-370.

—— 1995d. "Reply to Peter Kemp" in L. Hahn (ed.), *The Philosophy of Paul Ricoeur*, Illinois: Open Court, pp. 395-398.

—— 1998a. *Critique and Conviction: Conversations with Francois Azouvi and Mark de Launay*, (tr. K. Blamey), Polity Press.

—— 1998b. *Figuring the Sacred: Religion, Narrative and Imagination*, Minneapolis: Fortress Press.

—— 1998c. "The 'Sacred Text' and the Community" in P. Ricoeur, *Figuring the Sacred: Religion, Narrative and Imagination*, Minneapolis: Fortress Press, pp. 68-74.

—— 1998d. "The Bible and the Imagination" in P. Ricoeur, *Figuring the Sacred: Religion, Narrative and Imagination*, Minneapolis: Fortress Press, pp. 144-166.

—— 1998e. "Biblical Time" in P. Ricoeur, *Figuring the Sacred: Religion, Narrative and Imagination*, Minneapolis: Fortress Press, pp. 167-180.

—— 1998f. "Towards a Narrative Theology: Its Necessity, Its Resources, Its

Difficulties" in P. Ricoeur, *Figuring the Sacred: Religion, Narrative and Imagination*, Minneapolis: Fortress Press, pp. 236-248

—— 1998g. "Ethical and Theological Considerations on the Golden Rule" in P. Ricoeur, *Figuring the Sacred: Religion, Narrative and Imagination*, Minneapolis: Fortress Press, pp. 293-302.

—— 1998h. "Pastoral Praxaeology, Hermeneutics, and Identity" in P. Ricoeur, *Figuring the Sacred: Religion, Narrative and Imagination*, Minneaplolis: Fortress Press, pp. 303-314.

Ricoeur, P and LaCocque, A.. 1998. *Thinking Biblically: Exegetical and Hermeneutical Studies*, (tr. D. Pellauer), Chicago: University of Chicago Press,.

Ridderbos, J.. 1984. *Deuteronomy*, Grand Rapids: Zondervan.

Roberts, A. and Donaldson, J.. 1979. *The Ante-Nicene Fathers: Translations of the Writings of the Fathers Down to A.D. 325*, 10 volumes, Grand Rapids: Eerdmans.

Roberts, R.C.. 1988. "What an Emotion is: A Sketch," *The Philosophical Review*, Vol. XCVII, No. 2, pp. 183-209.

—— 1991a. "What is Wrong With Wicked Feelings?" *American Philosophical Quarterly*, Vol. 28, No. 1, pp. 13-25.

—— 1991b. "Virtues and Rules," *Philosophy and Phenomenological Research*, Vol. LI, No. 2, pp. 325-343.

—— 1992. "Emotions Among the Virtues of the Christian Life," *Journal of Religious Ethics*, Vol. 20, No. 1, pp. 37-68.

—— 1995. "Kierkegaard, Wittgenstein, and a Method of 'Virtue Ethics'" in M. Matustik and M. Westphal (eds.), *Kierkegaard in Post/Modernity*, Indiana: Indiana Press, pp. 142-166.

—— 1998. "Christian Ethics and Moral Wisdom," *Faith and Philosophy* Vol. 15, No. 4, pp. 478-499.

—— 1999. "Narrative Ethics" in P.L. Quinn and C. Taliaferro (eds.), *A Companion to the Philosophy of Religion*, Blackwells, pp. 473-480.

_____ 2003. *Emotions: An Essay in Aid of Moral Psychology*, Cambridge: Cambridge University Press.

Rodd, C.S.. 2001. *Glimpses of a Strange Land: Studies in Old Testament Ethics*, Edinburgh: T and T Clark.

Ross, A.P.. 1996. *Creation and Blessing: A Guide to the Study and Exposition of*

*Genesis*, Grand Rapids: Baker.

Ross, E.M.. 1990. "Human Persons as Images of the Divine: A Reconsideration" in A. Bach (ed.), *The Pleasure of Her Text*, Philadelphia: Trinity Press International, pp. 97-116.

Roth, W.M.W.. 1960. "NBL" in *Vetus Testamentum* 10, pp. 394-409.

Ruether, R.. 1983. *Sexism and God-Talk: Toward a Feminist Theology*, London: SCM.

——— 1995. "Feminist Interpretation: A Method of Correlation" in L. Russell (ed.), *Feminist Interpretation of the Bible*, Philadelphia: Westminster, pp. 111-124.

Ruprecht, L.A.. 1989. "Nussbaum on Tragedy and the Modern Ethos," *Soundings* 72, pp. 589-603.

——— 1992. "A Funny Thing Happened on the Way to Mantineia: Diotima and Martha Nussbaum on Love's Knowledge," *Soundings* 75, pp. 97-127.

Russell, L.M.. 1985. "Authority and the Challenge of Feminist Interpretation" in L. Russell (ed.), *Feminist Interpretation of the Bible*, Oxford: Blackwells, pp. 137-148.

Sailhammer, J.. 1992. *The Pentateuch as Narrative: Genesis*, Library of Biblical Interpretation, Grand Rapids: Zondervan.

Sakenfeld, K.D.. 1984. "Feminist Biblical Interpretation," *Theology Today*, pp. 154-168.

——— 1985. "Feminist Uses of Biblical Materials" in L. Russell (ed.), *Feminist Interpretation of the Bible*, Philadelphia: Westminster, pp. 55-64.

——— 1988. "Feminist Perspectives on the Bible and Theology: An Introduction to Selected Isues and Literature," *Interpretation* 42, pp. 5-18.

Salkin, J.K.. 1986. "Dinah, the Torah's Forgotten Woman", *Judaism* 35, pp. 284-289.

Sanders, E.P.. 1977. *Paul and Palestinian Judaism*, Philadelphia: Fortress Press.

Sarna, N.M.. 1989. *Genesis*, JPS Torah Commentary. Philedelphia: Jewish Publication Society.

Satterthwaite, P., Wenham, G., and Hess R. (eds.). 1995. *The Lord's Anointed*, Carlisle: Paternoster.

Savage, A. and Watson, N.. 1991. *Anchoritic Spirituality*, New York: Paulist Press.

Scalese, C.J.. 1994. *Hermeneutics as Theological Prolegomena: A Canonical Approach*, Georgia: Mercer University Press.

Schaff, P. (ed.). 1979. *A Selected Library of the Nicene and Post-Nicene Fathers of the Christian Church*, Grand Rapids: Eerdmans, 13 vols. and 2$^{nd}$ Series, 14 vols.

Scholz, S.. 1998. "Through Whose Eyes? A 'Right' Reading of Genesis 34" in A. Brenner (ed.), *Genesis: A Feminist Companion to the Bible* (2$^{nd}$ Series), Sheffield: Sheffield Academic Press, pp. 150-171.

Schottroff, L.. 1990. "The Creation Narrative: Genesis 1:1-2:4a" in A Brenner (ed.), *A Feminist Companion to Genesis*, Sheffield: Sheffield Academic Press, pp. 24-38.

Schottroff, L., Schroer, S., and Wacker, M.T.. 1998. *Feminist Interpretation: The Bible in Women's Perspective*, Minneapolis: Fortress Press.

Schreiner, T.R.. 1993a. "Law of Christ" in G. Hawthorne, R. Martin and D. Reid (eds.), *Dictionary of Paul and his Letters*, Downers Grove and Leicester: IVP, pp. 542-544.

——— 1993b. "Circumcision" in G. Hawthorne, R. Martin and D. Reid (eds.), *Dictionary of Paul and his Letters*, Dpwners Grove and Leicester: IVP, pp. 137-139.

——— 1997. "Law" in R. Martin and P. Davids (eds.), *Dictionary of the Later New Testament and its Developments*, Downers Grove and Leicester: IVP, pp. 644-649.

Schroeder, J.A.. 1997. "The Rape of Dinah: Luther's Interpretation of a Biblical Narrative," *Sixteenth Century Journal* XXVIII/3, pp. 775-791.

Schuurman, D.. 1993. "God, Humanity, and the World in Reformed and Feminist Perspectives" in M.S. van Leuwen (ed.), *After Eden*, Grand Rapids: Eerdmans, pp. 147-183.

Seebas, H.. 1986. "סחר" in G.J. Botterweck *et al* (eds.), *Theological Dictionary of the Old Testament*, Grand Rapids: Eerdmans, Vol. X, pp. 211-215.

Segal, N.. 1988. "Review of *The Poetics of Biblical Narrative*, by N. Sternberg," *Vetus Testamentum* 38, pp. 243-249.

Seger, J.D.. 1997. "Shechem" in E.M. Meyers (ed.), *The Oxford Encyclopaedia of Archaeology in the Near East*, Oxford: Oxford University Press, Vol. 5, pp. 19-23.

Seitz, C.. 1998. *Word Without End: The Old Testament as Abiding Theological Witness*, Grand Rapids: Eerdmans.

Seitz, C. and Greene-McCreight, K. (eds.). 1999. *Theological Exegesis: Essays in Honour of Brevard S. Childs*, Grand Rapids: Eerdmans.

Shimasaki, K.. 1999. *Focus Structure in Biblical Hebrew: A Study of Word Order and Information Structure With Special Reference to Deuteronomy*, PhD Thesis, Cheltenham and Gloucester College of Higher Education.

Siebers, T.. 1992. *Morals and Stories*, New York: Colombia University Press.

Silva, M.. 1983. *Biblical Words and their Meaning: An Introduction to Lexical Semantics*, Grand Rapids: Zondervan.

Skinner, J.. 1930. *A Critical and Exegetical Commentary on Genesis*. ICC. (2nd ed.) Edinburgh: T and T Clark.

Sonsino, R.. 1975. *Motive Clauses in Hebrew Law*, California: Scholars Press.

Speiser, E.A.. 1967. "'Coming' and 'going' at the City Gate," *Oriental and Biblical Studies*, J.J. Finkelstein and M. Greenberg (eds.), Philadelphia: University of Pensylvania, pp. 83-88.

―― 1969. *Genesis*. Anchor Bible. New York: Doubleday.

Spiegelberg, H.. 1969. *The Phenomenological Movement: A Historical Introduction* (2 vols), The Hague: Martinus Nijhoff.

Spurrell, G.J.. 1896. *Notes on the Text of the Book of Genesis,* (2$^{nd}$ edition), Oxford: Clarendon Press.

Spykman, G.. 1992. *Reformational Theology: A New Paradigm for Doing Dogmatics*, Grand Rapids: Eerdmans.

Stahl, N.. 1995. *Law and Liminality in the Bible,* Sheffield: Sheffield Academic Press.

Statman, D. (ed.). 1997. *Virtue Ethics: A Critical Reader*, Edinburgh: Edinburgh Univrsity Press.

Steinberg, N.. 1984. "Gender Roles in the Rebakah Cycle," *Union Seminary Quarterly Review* 39, pp. 175-188.

―― 1991. "Alliance or Descent? The Function of Marriage in Genesis," *Journal for the Study of Old Testament* 51, pp. 45-55.

―― 1993. *Kinship and Marriage in Genesis: A Household Economics Perspective*, Minneapolis: Fortress Press.

Sterk, H.. 1993. "Gender Relations and Narrative in a Reformed Church Seting" in M.S. van Leeuwen (ed.), *After Eden*, Grand Rapids: Eerdmans, pp. 184-221.

Sternberg, M.. 1987. *The Poetics of Biblical Narrative: Ideological Literature and the Drama of Reading*, Bloomington: Indiana University Press.

―― 1992. "Biblical Poetics and Sexual Politics: From Reading to Counter-Reading", *Journal of Biblical Literature* 111, pp. 463-488.

Stiver, D.R. 2001. *Theology After Ricoeur: New Directions in Hermeneutical Theology*, Louisville: Westminster John Knox Press.

Stone, K.. 1996. *Sex, Honour and Power in the Deuteronomistic History*, Sheffield: Sheffield Academic Press.

Storkey, E.. 1986. *What's Right With Feminism?* London: SPCK.

Stroup, G.W.. 1981. *The Promise of Narrative Theology*, London: SCM.

Struthers, G.. 1997. "עבר" in W.A. Van Gemeren (ed.), *New International Dictionary of Old Testament Theology and Exegesis*, Vol. 3, Grand Rapids: Zondervan/Carlisle: Paternoster Press, pp. 316-317.

Swart, I and Van Dam, C.. 1997. "חמס" in W.A. Van Gemeren (ed.), *New International Dictionary of Old Testament Theology and Exegesis*, Vol. 2, Grand Rapids: Zondervan/Carlisle: Paternoster Press, pp. 177-180.

Swartley, W.M.. 1994. *Israel's Scripture Traditions and the Synoptic Gospels: Story Shaping Story*, Massachusetts: Hendrickson Publishers.

Talmon, S.. 1963. "Wisdom in the Book of Esther," *Vetus Testamentum* 13, pp. 419-455.

Tanner, M.. 1994. "Morals in Fiction and Fictional Morality," *The Aristotelian Society* Supp Vol. LXVIII, pp. 27-50.

Terrien, S.. 1976. "Amos and Wisdom" in J. Crenshaw (ed.), *Studies in Ancient Israelite Wisdom*, New York: KTAV, pp. 448-455 (original article published in 1910).

Thielman, F.. 1993. "Law" in G. Hawthorne, R. Martin and D. Reid (eds.), *Dictionary of Paul and his Letters*, Downers Grove and Leicester: IVP, pp. 529-542.

Thiselton, A.. 1980. *The Two Horizons: New Testament Hermeneutics and Philosophical Description with Special Reference to Heidegger, Bultmann, Gadamer and Wittgenstein*, Exeter: Paternoster Press.

—— 1992. *New Horizons in Hermeneutics: The Theory and Practice of Transforming Biblical Reading.* London: Marshall Pickering.

—— 1999. "Communicative Action and Promise in Interdisciplinary, Biblical, and Theological Hermeneutics" in R. Lundin, C. Walhout, A. Thistleton, *The Promise of Hermeneutics*, Grand Rapids: Eerdmans/Carlisle: Paternoster Press, pp. 133-239.

Thistlethwaite, S.B.. 1993. "'You May Enjoy the Spoil of Your Enemies' – Rape as a Biblical Metaphor for War," *Semeia* 61, pp. 59-75.

Thomas, W.H.G.. 1958. *Genesis: A Devotional Commentary*, repr. Grand Rapids:

Eerdmans.

Thompson, J. (ed.). 1981. *Hermeneutics and the Human Sciences: Essays on Language, Action and Interpretation*, Cambridge: Cambridge University Press.

Tolbert, M.A.. 1990. "Protestant Feminists and the Bible: On the Horns of a Dilemma" in A. Bach (ed.), *The Pleasure of Her Text: Feminist Readings of Biblical and Historical Texts*, Philedelphia: Trinity Press International, pp. 5-23.

Trible, P.. 1978. *God and the Rhetoric of Sexuality*, London: SCM Press.

—— 1984. *Texts of Terror: Literary-Feminist Readings of Biblical Narratives*, Philadelphia: Fortress Press.

Ullendorf, E.. 1956. "The Contributions of South Semitics to Hebrew Lexicography," *Vetus Testamentum* 6, p. 194 ff.

Umansky, E.. 1990. "Beyond Androcentrism: Feminist Challenges to Judaism," *Journal of Reform Judaism*, pp. 25-35.

Valdés, M.. 1991. *A Ricoeur Reader: Reflection and Imagination*, New York/London: Harvester Wheatsheaf.

Vanderkam, J.C.. 1992. "Jubilees, Book of" in D.N. Freedman (ed.), *Anchor Bible Dictionary* Vol. 3, New York: Doubleday, pp. 1030-1032.

Van der Merwe, C.H.J.. 1993. "Old Hebrew Particles and the Interpretation of Old Testament Texts," *Journal for the Study of Old Testament*, 60, pp. 27-44.

—— 1994. "Discourse Linguistics and Biblical Hebrew Grammar" in R. Bergen (ed.), *Biblical Hebrew and Discourse Linguistics*, Winona Lake: Eisenbrauns, pp. 13-49.

Van der Merwe, C., Naude, J., Kroeze, J.. 1999. *A Biblical Hebrew Reference Grammar*, Sheffield: Sheffield Academic Press.

Vanhoozer, K.. 1990. *Biblical Narrative in the Philosophy of Paul Ricoeur: A Study in hermeneutics and Theology*, Cambridge: Cambridge University Press.

—— 1998. *Is There a Meaning in This Text? The Bible, The Reader and the Morality of Literary Knowledge*, Grand Rapids: Zondervan/Leicester: Apollos.

Vawter, B.. 1955. "The Caananite Background of Genesis 49," *Catholic Biblical Quarterly* 17, pp. 1-18.

—— 1977. *On Genesis: A New Reading*, Garden City: Doubleday.

Verhay, A.. 1997. "Ethics" in R. Martin and P.Davids (eds.), *Dictionary of the Later New Testament and its Developments*, Downers Grove and Leicester: IVP, pp. 347-

353.

Waard, J. de. 1977. "The Chiastic Structure of Amos V 1-17", *Vetus Testamentum* 27, pp. 170-177.

Wade, C. and Travis, C.. 1993. *Psychology*, London: Harper Collins.

Walhout, C.. 1999. "Narrative Hermeneutics" in R. Lundin, C. Walhout, A. Thiselton, *The Promise of Hermeneutics*, Grand Rapids: Eerdmans, pp. 65-131.

Walker, N.. 1962 "The Renderings of *ratson*," *Journal of Biblical Literature* 81, p. 184 ff..

Walker, P.. 1996. *Jesus and the Holy City: New Testament Perspectives on Jerusalem*, Grand Rapids: Eerdmans.

Wall, R.W.. 2000a. "Reading the Bible From Within Our Traditions: The 'Rule of Faith' in Theological Hermeneutics" in J.B. Green and M. Turner (eds.), *Between Two Horizons*, Grand Rapids: Eerdmans, pp. 88-107.

—— 2000b. "Canonical Context and Canonical Conversations" in J.B. Green and M. Turner (eds.), *Between Two Horizons*, Grand Rapids: Eerdmans, pp. 165-182.

Walsh, B. and Middleton, R.. 1995. *Truth is Stranger Than it Used to Be: Biblical Faith in a Postmodern Age*, London: SPCK.

Waltke, B. and O'Connor, M.. 1990. *Introduction to Biblical Hebrew Syntax*, Winona Lake: Eisenbrauns.

Walton, J.H.. 1989. *Ancient Israelite Literature in its Cultural Context*, Grand Rapids: Zondervan.

—— 2002. "A New Equation: (Narrative + Law) x Covenant = Torah", unpublished paper delivered at the Evangelical Theological Society in Toronto.

Walton, K.. 1994. "Morals in Fiction and Fictional Morality," *The Aristotelian Society* Supp Vol. LXVIII, pp. 27-50.

Watson, F.. 1994. *Text, Chruch and World: Biblical Interpretation in Theological Perspective*, Edinburgh: T and T Clark.

Watson, W.. 1981. "Hebrew 'to be Happy' - An Idiom Identified," *Vetus Testamentum* 31, pp. 92-95.

Weavers, J.. 1974. *Genesis*. Septuaginta: Vetus Testamentum Graecum. Göttingen: Vandenhoek and Ruprect.

Webb, W.J. 2001. *Slaves, Women and Homosexuals: Exploring the Hermeneutics of*

*Cultural Analysis*, Downers Grove: IVP.

Weinfeld, M.. 1975. *Sefer Bereshit*, Tel-Aviv: Gordon.

Wells, S.. 1998. *Transforming Fate into Destiny: The Theological Ethics of Stanley Hauerwas*, Carlisle: Paternoster Press.

Wenham, G.J.. 1978. "Grace and Law in the Old Testament" in B. Kaye and G. Wenham (eds.), *Law, Morality and the Bible: a Symposium*, Leicester: IVP, pp. 3-23.

——— 1980. "The Religion of the Patriarchs" in A.R. Millard and D.J. Wiseman (eds.), *Essays in the Patriarchal Narratives*, Leicester: IVP, pp. 157-188.

——— 1981. *Numbers*, Tyndale OT Commentaries, Leicester: IVP.

——— 1983. "Why Does Sexual Intercourse Defile (Lev. 15.18)?" *Zeitschrift für die alttestamentliche Wissenschaft* 95, pp. 432-434.

——— 1991. *Genesis 1-15*, Word Biblical Commentary, Dallas: Word.

——— 1994. *Genesis 16-50*, Word Biblical Commentary, Dallas: Word.

——— 1995. "The Akedah: A Paradigm of Sacrifice" in D. Wright, D. Freedman and A Hurvitz (eds.), *Pomegranates and Golden Bells: Studies in Biblical, Jewish, and Near Eastern Ritual, Law, and Literature in Honour of Jacob Milgrom.*, Winona Lake: Eisenbrauns.

——— 1997. "The Gap Between Law and Ethics in the Bible," *Journal of Jewish Studies*, Vol. XLVIII, No. 1, pp. 17-29.

——— 2000. *Story as Torah: Reading the Old Testament Ethically*, Edinburgh: T and T Clark.

Wenham, J.. 1985. *The Enigma of Evil*, Leicester: IVP.

West, S.A.. 1980. "The Rape of Dinah and the Conquest of Shechem," *Dor le Dor* 7, pp. 144-151.

Westbrook, R.. 1992. "Punishments and Crimes" in D.N. Freedman (ed.), *Anchor Bible Dictionary*, Vol.5, New York: Doubleday.

Westerholm, S.. 1988. *Israel's Law and the Church's Faith: Paul and his Recent Interpreters*, Grand Rapids: Eerdmans.

——— 1992. "Clean and Unclean" in J. Green, S. McKnight, I.H. Marshall (eds.), *Dictionary of Jesus and the Gospels*, Leicester: IVP, pp. 125-132.

Westermann, C.. 1985. *Genesis 12-36*. (tr. J.J. Scullio), Minneapolis: Augsburg

Publishing House.

White, V.. 1996. *Paying Attention to People*, London: SPCK.

Whitekettle, R.. 1996. "Leviticus 15.18 Reconsidered: Chiasm, Spatial Structure and the Body" in J. Rogerson (ed.), *The Pentateuch: A Sheffield Reader*, Sheffield: Sheffield Academic Press, pp. 172-185 (original article published in 1991).

Whybray, R.N. 1968. *The Succession Narrative*, London: SCM.

Wilson, L.. forthcoming. *Joseph, Wise and Otherwise: The Intersection of Wisdom and Covenant in Genesis 37-50*, Carlisle: Paternoster Press.

Williams, J.. 1996. "Narrative and Ethics," *The Aristotelian Society* Supp Vol. LXX,, pp. 47-61.

Williams, W.. 1997. "שׁכב" in W.A. Van Gemeren (ed.), *New International Dictionary of Old Testament Theology and Exegesis*, Vol. 4, Grand Rapids: Zondervan/Carlisle: Paternoster Press.

Wilson, F.M.. 1987. "Sacred or Profane? The Yahwistic Redaction of Proverbs Reconsidered" in K. Hoglund et al (eds.), *The Listening Heart: Essays in Honour of R.E. Murphy*, Sheffield: Sheffield Academic Press, pp. 313-334.

Wilson, R.R.. 1988. "Approaches to Old Testament Ethics" in Tucker, Petersen and Wilson (eds.), *Canon, Theology and Old Testament Interpretation: Essays in Honour of Brevard S. Childs,* Minneapolis: Fortress Press, pp. 62-74.

Winston, D.. 1981. *Philo of Alexandria: The Contemplative Life, The Giants, and Selections.* The Classics of Western Spirituality, London: SPCK.

Winther-Nielsen, N.. 1995. *A Functional Discourse Grammar of Joshua: A Computer Assisted Rhetorical Structure Analysis,* Coniectanea Biblica OT Series 40, Stockholm: Almquist and Wiksell Int..

Wise, M.O.. 1992. "Feasts" in J. Green, S. McKnight, I.H. Marshall (eds.), *Dictionary of Jesus and the Gospels*, Downers Grove and Leicester: IVP, pp. 234-241.

Witherington III, B.. 1994a. *Jesus the Sage: The Pilgrimage of Wisdom*, Edinburgh: T and T Clark.

—— 1994b. *Paul's Narrative Thought World: The Tapestry of Tragedy and Triumph*, Louiseville: Westminster/John Knox Press.

Wolters, A.. 1996. *Creation Regained: Biblical Basics for a Reformational Worldview*, repr. Carlisle: Paternoster Press.

Wolterstorff, N.. 1995. *Divine Discourse: Philosophical Reflections on the Claim that*

*God Speaks*, Cambridge: Cambridge University Press.

——— 1997. *Art in Action: Towards a Christian Aesthetic*, repr. Carlisle: Paternoster Press, 1997.

Wright, C.J.H.. 1983. *Living as the People of God: the Relevance of Old Testament Ethics*, Leicester: IVP.

——— 1990. *God's People in God's Land: Family, Land and Property in the Old Testament*, Grand Rapids: Eerdmans and Carlisle: Paternoster Press.

——— 1992. "Ethical Decisions in the Old Testament," *European Journal of Theology* 1:2, pp. 123-140.

——— 1995. *Walking in the Ways of the LORD: The Ethical Authority of the Old Testament*, Leicester: Apollos.

——— 1996. *Deuteronomy*, NIBC, Carlisle: Paternoster Press.

——— 1997. "Ethics" in W. Van Gemeren (ed.), *New International Dictionary of Old Testament Theology and Exegesis*, Grand Rapids: Zondervan/Carlisle: Paternoster Press, Vol. 4., pp. 585-594.

Wright, D.. 1993. "Sexuality, Sexual Ethics" in G. Hawthorne, R. Martin and D. Reid (eds.), *Dictionary of Paul and his Letters*, Downers Grove and Leicester: IVP, pp. 871-875.

——— 1997. "Sexuality, Sexual Ethics" in R. Martin and P. Davids (eds.), *Dictionary of the Later New Testament and its Developments*, Downers Grove and Leicester: IVP, pp. 1088-1090.

Wright, G.E.. 1964. *Shechem: The Biography of a Biblical City*, London: Gerald Duckworth and Co..

Wright, N.T.. 1991a. *The Climax of the Covenant: Christ and the Law in Pauline Theology*, Edinburgh: T and T Clark.

——— 1991b. "How Can the Bible be Authoritative?" *Vox Evangelica* Vol. XXI., pp. 7-32.

——— 1992. *The New Testament and the People of God*, London: SPCK.

——— 1996. *Jesus and the Victory of God*, London: SPCK.

——— 1999. *The Myth of the Millennium*, London: Azure.

Wyatt, N.. 1990. "The Story of Dinah and Shechem," *Ugarit-Forschungen* 22, pp. 433-458.

Yack, B.. 1989. "How Good is the Aristotelian Good Life?" *Soundings* 72, pp. 607-629

Yearly, L.. 1993. "The Author Replies: 3. Response to Martha Nussbaum," *Journal of Religious Ethics* 21, No. 2, pp. 389-395.

Yoder, J.H.. 1994. *The Politics of Jesus*, (2nd edition), Grand Rapids: Eerdmans.

Young, D.W.. 1981. "A Ghost Word in the Testament of Jacob (Gen 49:5)," *Journal of Biblical LIterature* 100/3, pp. 335-342.

Zabzebski, L.. 1998. "The Virtues of God and the Foundations of Ethics," *Faith and Philosophy* Vol. 15, No. 4, pp. 538-553.

Zakovitch, Y.. 1985. "Assimilation in Biblical Narratives" in J. Tigay (ed.), *Empirical Models for Biblical Criticism*, Philedelphia: University of Pennsylvania, pp. 185-192.

Zimmerli, W.. 1976. "The Place and Limits of Wisdom in the Framework of Old Testament Theology" in J. Crenshaw (ed.), *Studies in Ancient Israelite Wisdom*, New York: KTAV, pp. 314-326 (original article published in 1964).

# General Index

# Scripture Index

346

*Scripture Index*

32–34 xix
34 171
34:6-7 51
34:13 197
34:15-16 194
34:22 64
38:21 182

**Leviticus**
11 50
15:16-18 202
15:18 138, 139
15:24 138
15:25-30 209
18 139, 144, 145
18:15 139
18:18 64
18:24 139, 144
19 208
19:2 50
20:11 138
20:11-13 139
20:12 138
20:13 138, 145
20:18 138, 139, 145
20:2 65
21:14 176
23:6 64
23:34 64
25:42 64
26:1 197

**Numbers**
1:23 181
5:11-31 138, 139
10:35-36 203
12 195
16
18:20-24 182
19:11 209
21:2 203
22–24 194
25 xix, 30, 33, 88,
   146, 179, 183,
   185-96, 244
25:1 186, 189, 190
25:1-2 194
25:1-3 194

25:1-13 190
25:11 193
25:11-13 193
25:12-13 194
25:13 194
25:14 191
25:15 188
25:18 189
25:2 194
25:2-3 190
25:3 189
25:4 190, 194
25:5 194
25:6 194
25:6-8 186
25:6-8 186
25:6-13 194
25:7 189
25:7-8 194
25:7b-8 189
25:8-9 196
25:9 194
26:14 181, 196
27:1-11 67
29:12-38 64
31 xix, 113, 179,
   183, 185-96, 244
31:1 186
31:2 191
31:3-5 186
31:3-8 186
31:4-5 191
31:7 186
31:7b 189
31:8 186, 188, 189,
   191
31:9 186
31:9-10 188
31:10 186
31:11 186
31:12 186
31:13 186
31:14-17 191
31:14-18 191
31:21-24 190
35:1-8 182
36:1-13 67

**Deuteronomy**
4:4 98
4:6 59
4:6-7 60
6:5 208
7:1-3 149
7:1-4 147, 200
7:7 98
8:10ff 182
9 182
10:17-19 50
15:15 64
16:1-8 64
16:13 64
16:21-22 197
18:1ff 182
20 188
20:14 188
21:10-14 147
21:15-17 68
22 225
22:21 144, 231
22:23 144
22:23-24 139, 140,
   142
22:25-27 139, 140,
   142, 143, 231
22:28-29 139, 140,
   142, 143, 169,
   225
23:7-8 147, 149
23:9-14 203
24:2 229
25:15-16 60
27 211
27:20-23 138
27:26 211, 212
30:6 213
30:11-14 60
32:28-29 60
33 181, 293
33:8-11 182
33:11 182, 183

**Joshua**
2:11 164
5 202
5:1 164

# Paternoster Biblical Monographs
*(All titles uniform with this volume)*

Joseph Abraham
**Eve: Accused or Acquitted?**
*A Reconsideration of Feminist Readings of the Creation Narrative Texts in Genesis 1–3*
Two contrary views dominate contemporary feminist biblical scholarship. One finds in the Bible an unequivocal equality between the sexes from the very creation of humanity, whilst the other sees the biblical text as irredeemably patriarchal and androcentric. Dr. Abraham enters into dialogue with both camps as well as introducing his own method of approach. An invaluable tool for anyone who is interested in this contemporary debate.
*2002 / ISBN 0-85364-971-5 / xxiv + 272pp*

Paul Barker
**The Triumph of Grace in Deuteronomy**
This book is a textual and theological analysis of the interaction between the sin and faithlessness of Israel and the grace of Yahweh in response, looking especially at Deuteronomy chapters 1–3, 8–10 and 29–30. The author argues that the grace of Yahweh is determinative for the ongoing relationship between Yahweh and Israel and that Deuteronomy anticipates and fully expects Israel to be faithless.
*2004 / ISBN 1-84227-226-8 / xxii + 270pp*

Jonathan F. Bayes
**The Weakness of the Law**
*God's Law and the Christian in New Testament Perspective*
A study of the four New Testament books which refer to the law as weak (Acts, Romans, Galatians, Hebrews) leads to a defence of the third use in the Reformed debate about the law in the life of the believer.
*2000 / ISBN 0-85364-957-X / xii + 244pp*

Mark Bonnington
**The Antioch Episode of Galatians 2:11-14 in Historical and Cultural Context**
The Galatians 2 'incident' in Antioch over table-fellowship suggests significant disagreement between the leading apostles. This book analyses the background to the disagreement by locating the incident within the dynamics of social interaction between Jews and Gentiles. It proposes a new way of understanding the relationship between the individuals and issues involved.
*2004 / ISBN 1-84227-050-8 / approx. 350pp*

May 2004

Mark Bredin
**Jesus, Revolutionary of Peace**
*A Nonviolent Christology in the Book of Revelation*
This book aims to demonstrate that the figure of Jesus in the Book of Revelation can best be understood as an active nonviolent revolutionary.
*2003 / ISBN 1-84227-153-9 / xviii + 262pp*

Daniel J-S Chae
**Paul as Apostle to the Gentiles**
*His Apostolic Self-awareness and its Influence on the Soteriological Argument in Romans*
Opposing 'the post-Holocaust interpretation of Romans', Daniel Chae competently demonstrates that Paul argues for the equality of Jew and Gentile in Romans. Chae's fresh exegetical interpretation is academically outstanding and spiritually encouraging.
*1997 / ISBN 0-85364-829-8 / xiv + 378pp*

Luke L. Cheung
**The Genre, Composition and Hermeneutics of the Epistle of James**
The present work examines the employment of the wisdom genre with a certain compositional structure and the interpretation of the law through the Jesus' tradition of the double love command by the author of the Epistle of James to serve his purpose in promoting perfection and warning against doubleness among the eschatologically renewed people of God in the Diaspora.
*2003 / ISBN 1-84227-062-1 / xvi + 372pp*

Andrew C. Clark
**Parallel Lives**
*The Relation of Paul to the Apostles in the Lucan Perspective*
This study of the Peter-Paul parallels in Acts argues that their purpose was to emphasize the themes of continuity in salvation history and the unity of the Jewish and Gentile missions. New light is shed on Luke's literary techniques, partly through a comparison with Plutarch.
*2001 / 1-84227-035-4 / xviii + 386pp*

May 2004

Andrew D. Clarke
**Secular and Christian Leadership in Corinth**
*A Socio-Historical and Exegetical Study of 1 Corinthians 1–6*
This volume is an investigation into the leadership structures and dynamics
of first-century Roman Corinth. These are compared with the practice of
leadership in the Corinthian Christian community which are reflected in 1
Corinthians 1–6, and contrasted with Paul's own principles of Christian
leadership.

*2004 / ISBN 1-84227-229-2 / xii + 188pp*

Stephen Finamore
**God, Order and Chaos**
*René Girard and the Apocalypse*
Readers are often disturbed by the images of destruction in the book of
Revelation and unsure why they are unleashed after the exaltation of Jesus.
This book examines past approaches to these texts and uses René Girard's
theories to revive some old ideas and propose some new ones.

*2004 / ISBN 1-84227-197-0 / approx. 344pp*

Scott J. Hafemann
**Suffering and Ministry in the Spirit**
*Paul's Defence of His Ministry in II Corinthians 2:14–3:3*
Shedding new light on the way Paul defended his apostleship, the author
offers a careful, detailed study of 2 Corinthians 2:14–3:3 linked with other
key passages throughout 1 and 2 Corinthians. Demonstrating the unity and
coherence of Paul's argument in this passage, the author shows that Paul's
suffering served as the vehicle for revealing God's power and glory
through the Spirit.

*2000 / ISBN 0-85364-967-7 / xiv + 262pp*

Douglas S. McComiskey
**Lukan Theology in the Light of the Gospel's Literary Structure**
Luke's Gospel was purposefully written with theology embedded in its
patterned literary structure. A critical analysis of this cyclical structure
provides new windows into Luke's interpretation of the individual
pericopes comprising the Gospel and illuminates several of his theological
interests.

*2004 / ISBN 1-84227-148-2 / approx. 400pp*

Stephen Motyer
**Your Father the Devil?**
*A New Approach to John and 'The Jews'*
Who are 'the Jews' in John's Gospel? Defending John against the charge
of anti-semitism, Motyer argues that, far from demonizing the Jews, the
Gospel seeks to present Jesus as 'Good News for Jews' in a late first
century setting.
*1997 / ISBN 0-85364-832-8 / xiv + 260pp*

Esther Ng
**Reconstructing Christian Origins?**
*The Feminist Theology of Elizabeth Schüssler Fiorenza: An Evaluation*
In a detailed evaluation, the author challenges Elizabeth Schüssler
Fiorenza's reconstruction of early Christian origins and her underlying
presuppositions. The author also presents her own views on women's roles
both then and now.
*2002 / ISBN 1-84227-055-9 / xxiv + 468pp*

Robin Parry
**Old Testament Story and Christian Ethics**
*The Rape of Dinah as a Case Study*
What is the role of story in ethics and, more particularly, what is the role of
Old Testament story in Christian ethics? This book, drawing on the work
of contemporary philosophers, argues that narrative is crucial in the ethical
shaping of people and, drawing on the work of contemporary Old
Testament scholars, that story plays a key role in Old Testament ethics.
Parry then argues that when situated in canonical context Old Testament
stories can be reappropriated by Christian readers in their own ethical
formation. The shocking story of the rape of Dinah and the massacre of the
Shechemites provides a fascinating case study for exploring the parameters
within which Christian ethical appropriations of Old Testament stories can
live.
*2004 / ISBN 1-84227-210-1 / approx. 350pp*

David Powys
**'Hell': A Hard Look at a Hard Question**
*The Fate of the Unrighteous in New Testament Thought*
This comprehensive treatment seeks to unlock the original meaning of
terms and phrases long thought to support the traditional doctrine of hell. It
concludes that there is an alternative – one which is more biblical, and
which can positively revive the rationale for Christian mission.
*1997 / ISBN 0-85364-831-X / xxii + 478pp*

May 2004

Rosalind Selby
**The Comical Doctrine**
*Can a Gospel Convey Truth?*
This book argues that the Gospel breaks through postmodernity's critique
of truth and the referential possibilities of textuality and its gift of grace.
With a rigorous, philosophical challenge to modernist and postmodernist
assumptions, it offers an alternative epistemology to all who would still
read with faith *and* with academic credibility.
*2004 / ISBN 1-84227-212-8 approx. 350pp*

Kevin Walton
**Thou Traveller Unknown**
*The Presence and Absence of God in the Jacob Narrative*
The author offers a fresh reading of the story of Jacob in the book of Genesis through the paradox of divine presence and absence. The work also
seeks to make a contribution to Pentateuchal studies by bringing together a
close reading of the final text with historical critical insights, doing justice
to the text's historical depth, final form and canonical status.
*2003 / ISBN 1-84227-059-1 / xvi + 238pp*

Alistair Wilson
**When Will These Things Happen?**
*A Study of Jesus as Judge in Matthew 21–25*
This study seeks to allow Matthew's carefully constructed presentation of
Jesus to be given full weight in the modern evaluation of Jesus'
eschatology. Careful analysis of the text of Matthew 21–25 reveals Jesus to
be standing firmly in the Jewish prophetic and wisdom traditions as he
proclaims and enacts imminent judgement on the Jewish authorities then
boldly claims the central role in the final and universal judgement.
*2004 / ISBN 1-84227-146-6 / xvi + 292pp*

Lindsay Wilson
**Joseph Wise and Otherwise**
*The Intersection of Covenant and Wisdom in Genesis 37–50*
This book offers a careful literary reading of Genesis 37–50 that argues
that the Joseph story contains both strong covenant themes and many
wisdom-like elements. The connections between the two helps to explore
how covenant and wisdom might intersect in an integrated biblical
theology.
*2004 / ISBN 1-84227-140-7 approx. 350pp*

Stephen I. Wright
**The Voice of Jesus**
*Studies in the Interpretation of Six Gospel Parables*
This literary study considers how the 'voice' of Jesus has been heard in different periods of parable interpretation, and how the categories of figure and trope may help us towards a sensitive reading of the parables today.
*2000 / ISBN 0-85364-975-8 / xiv + 280pp*

May 2004

# Paternoster Theological Monographs

*(All titles uniform with this volume)*

Emil Bartos
**Deification in Eastern Orthodox Theology**
*An Evaluation and Critique of the Theology of Dumitru Staniloae*
Bartos studies a fundamental yet neglected aspect of Orthodox theology: deification. By examining the doctrines of anthropology, christology, soteriology and ecclesiology as they relate to deification, he provides an important contribution to contemporary dialogue between Eastern and Western theologians.
*1999 / ISBN 0-85364-956-1 / xii + 370pp*

James Bruce
**Prophecy, Miracles, Angels *and* Heavenly Light?**
*The Eschatology, Pneumatology and Missiology of Adomnán's* Life of
Columba
This book surveys approaches to the marvellous in hagiography, providing the first critique of Plummer's hypothesis of Irish saga origin. It then analyses the uniquely systematized phenomena in the *Life of Columba* from Adomnán's seventh-century theological perspective, identifying the coming of the eschatological Kingdom as the key to understanding.
*2004 / ISBN 1-84227-227-6 / approx. 400pp*

Colin J. Bulley
**The Priesthood of Some Believers**
*Developments from the General to the Special Priesthood in the Christian
Literature of the First Three Centuries*
The first in-depth treatment of early Christian texts on the priesthood of all believers shows that the developing priesthood of the ordained related closely to the division between laity and clergy and had deleterious effects on the practice of the general priesthood.
*2000 / ISBN 1-84227-034-6 / xii + 336pp*

May 2004

Iain D. Campbell
**Fixing the Indemnity**
*The Life and Work of George Adam Smith*
When Old Testament scholar George Adam Smith (1856–1942) delivered the Lyman Beecher lectures at Yale University in 1899 he confidently declared that 'modern criticism has won its war against traditional theories. It only remains to fix the amount of the indemnity.' In this biography, Iain D. Campbell assesses Smith's critical approach to the Old Testament and evaluates its consequences, showing that Smith's life and work still raises questions about the relationship between biblical scholarship and evangelical faith.
*2004 / ISBN 1-84227-228-4 / approx. 276pp*

Sylvia W. Collinson
**Making Disciples**
*The Significance of Jesus' Educational Strategy for Today's Church*
This study examines the biblical practice of discipling, formulates a definition, and makes comparisons with modern models of education. A recommendation is made for greater attention to its practice today.
*2004 / ISBN 1-84227-116-4 / approx. 320pp*

Stephen M. Dunning
**The Crisis and the Quest**
*A Kierkegaardian Reading of Charles Williams*
Employing Kierkegaardian categories and analysis, this study investigates both the central crisis in Charles Williams's authorship between hermetism and Christianity (Kierkegaard's Religions A and B), and the quest to resolve this crisis, a quest that ultimately presses the bounds of orthodoxy.
*2000 / ISBN 0-85364-985-5 / xxiv + 254pp*

Keith Ferdinando
**The Triumph of Christ in African Perspective**
*A Study of Demonology and Redemption in the African Context*
The book explores the implications of the gospel for traditional African fears of occult aggression. It analyses such traditional approaches to suffering and biblical responses to fears of demonic evil, concluding with an evaluation of African beliefs from the perspective of the gospel.
*1999 / ISBN 0-85364-830-1 / xviii + 450pp*

Andrew Goddard
**Living the Word, Resisting the World**
*The Life and Thought of Jacques Ellul*
This work offers a definitive study of both the life and thought of the
French Reformed thinker Jacques Ellul (1912-1994). It will prove an
indispensable resource for those interested in this influential theologian
and sociologist and for Christian ethics and political thought generally.
*2002 / ISBN 1-84227-053-2 / xxiv + 378pp*

Ruth Gouldbourne
**The Flesh and the Feminine**
*Gender and Theology in the Writings of Caspar Schwenckfeld*
Caspar Schwenckfeld and his movement exemplify one of the radical
communities of the sixteenth century. Challenging theological and
liturgical norms, they also found themselves challenging social and
particularly gender assumptions. In this book, the issues of the relationship
between radical theology and the understanding of gender are considered.
*2004 / ISBN 1-84227-048-6 / approx. 304pp*

Roger Hitching
**The Church and Deaf People**
*A Study of Identity, Communication and Relationships with Special*
*Reference to the Ecclesiology of Jürgen Moltmann*
In *The Church and Deaf People* Roger Hitching sensitively examines the
history and present experience of deaf people and finds similarities
between aspects of sign language and Moltmann's theological method that
'open up' new ways of understanding theological concepts.
*2003 / ISBN 1-84227-222-5 / xxii + 236pp*

John G. Kelly
**One God, One People**
*The Differentiated Unity of the People of God in the Theology of*
*Jürgen Moltmann*
The author expounds and critiques Moltmann's doctrine of God and high-
lights the systematic connections between it and Moltmann's influential
discussion of Israel. He then proposes a fresh approach to Jewish-Christian
relations building on Moltmann's work using insights from Habermas and
Rawls.
*2004 / ISBN 0-85346-969-3 / approx. 350pp*

Mark F.W. Lovatt
**Confronting the Will-to-Power**
*A Reconsideration of the Theology of Reinhold Niebuhr*
Confronting the Will-to-Power is an analysis of the theology of Reinhold
Niebuhr, arguing that his work is an attempt to identify, and provide a
practical theological answer to, the existence and nature of human evil.
*2001 / ISBN 1-84227-054-0 / xviii + 216pp*

Neil B. MacDonald
**Karl Barth and the Strange New World within the Bible**
*Barth, Wittgenstein, and the Metadilemmas of the Enlightenment*
Barth's discovery of the strange new world within the Bible is examined in
the context of Kant, Hume, Overbeck, and, most importantly, Wittgenstein.
MacDonald covers some fundamental issues in theology today:
epistemology, the final form of the text and biblical truth-claims.
*2000 / ISBN 0-85364-970-7 / xxvi + 374pp*

Gillian McCulloch
**The Deconstruction of Dualism in Theology**
*With Reference to Ecofeminist Theology and New Age Spirituality*
This book challenges eco-theological anti-dualism in Christian theology,
arguing that dualism has a twofold function in Christian religious
discourse. Firstly, it enables us to express the discontinuities and divisions
that are part of the process of reality. Secondly, dualistic language allows
us to express the mysteries of divine transcendence/immanence and the
survival of the soul without collapsing into monism and materialism, both
of which are problematic for Christian epistemology.
*2002 / ISBN 1-84227-044-3 / xii + 282pp*

Leslie McCurdy
**Attributes and Atonement**
*The Holy Love of God in the Theology of P.T. Forsyth*
Attributes and Atonement is an intriguing full-length study of P.T.
Forsyth's doctrine of the cross as it relates particularly to God's holy love.
It includes an unparalleled bibliography of both primary and secondary
material relating to Forsyth.
*1999 / ISBN 0-85364-833-6 / xiv + 328pp*

Nozomu Miyahira
**Towards a Theology of the Concord of God**
*A Japanese Perspective on the Trinity*
This book introduces a new Japanese theology and a unique Trinitarian formula based on the Japanese intellectual climate: three betweennesses and one concord. It also presents a new interpretation of the Trinity, a co-subordinationism, which is in line with orthodox Trinitarianism; each single person of the Trinity is eternally and equally subordinate (or serviceable) to the other persons, so that they retain the mutual dynamic equality.
*2000 / ISBN 0-85364-863-8 / xiv + 256pp*

Eddy José Muskus
**The Origins and Early Development of Liberation Theology in Latin America**
*With Particular Reference to Gustavo Gutiérrez*
This work challenges the fundamental premise of Liberation Theology, 'opting for the poor', and its claim that Christ is found in them. It also argues that Liberation Theology emerged as a direct result of the failure of the Roman Catholic Church in Latin America.
*2002 / ISBN 0-85364-974-X / xiv + 296pp*

Anna Robbins
**Methods in the Madness**
*Diversity in Twentieth-Century Christian Social Ethics*
The author compares the ethical methods of Walter Rauschenbusch, Reinhold Niebuhr and others. She argues that unless Christians are clear about the ways that theology and philosophy are expressed practically they may lose the ability to discuss social ethics across contexts, let alone reach effective agreements.
*2004 / ISBN 1-84227-211-X / xvi + 320pp*

Ed Rybarczyk
**Beyond Salvation**
*Eastern Orthodoxy and Classical Pentecostalism on becoming like Christ*
At first glance eastern Orthodoxy and Classical Pentecostalism seem quite distinct. This groundbreaking study shows that they share much in common, especially as it concerns the experiential elements of following Christ. Both traditions assert that authentic Christianity transcends the wooden categories of modernism.
*2003 / ISBN 1-84227-144-X / xii + 356pp*

Signe Sandsmark
**Is World View Neutral Education Possible and Desirable?**
*A Christian Response to Liberal Arguments*
(Published jointly with The Stapleford Centre)
This book discusses reasons for belief in world view neutrality, and argues that 'neutral' education will have a hidden, but strong world view influence. It discusses the place for Christian education in the common school.
*2000 / ISBN 0-85364-973-1 / xiv + 182pp*

Hazel Sherman
**Reading Zechariah**
*The Allegorical Tradition of Biblical Interpretation through the Commentaries of Didymus the Blind and Theodore of Mopsuestia*
A close reading of the commentary on Zechariah by Didymus the Blind alongside that of Theodore of Mopsuestia suggests that popular categorising of Antiochene and Alexandrian biblical exegesis as 'historical' or 'allegorical' is inadequate and misleading.
*2004 / ISBN 1-84227-213-6 / approx. 280pp*

Andrew Sloane
**On Being a Christian in the Academy**
*Nicholas Wolterstorff and the Practice of Christian Scholarship*
An exposition and critical appraisal of Nicholas Wolterstorff's epistemology in the light of the philosophy of science, and an application of his thought to the practice of Christian scholarship.
*2003 / ISBN 1-84227-058-3 / xvi + 274pp*

Daniel Strange
**The Possibility of Salvation Among the Unevangelised**
*An Analysis of Inclusivism in Recent Evangelical Theology*
For evangelical theologians the 'fate of the unevangelised' impinges upon fundamental tenets of evangelical identity. The position known as 'inclusivism', defined by the belief that the unevangelised can be ontologically saved by Christ whilst being epistemologically unaware of him, has been defended most vigorously by the Canadian evangelical Clark H. Pinnock. Through a detailed analysis and critique of Pinnock's work, this book examines a cluster of issues surrounding the unevangelised and its implications for christology, soteriology and the doctrine of revelation.
*2002 / ISBN 1-84227-047-8 / xviii + 362pp*

G. Michael Thomas
**The Extent of the Atonement**
*A Dilemma for Reformed Theology from Calvin to the Consensus*
This is a study of the way Reformed theology addressed the question, 'Did
Christ die for all, or for the elect only?', commencing with John Calvin,
and including debates with Lutheranism, the Synod of Dort and the
teaching of Moïse Amyraut.
*1997 / ISBN 0-85364-828-X / x + 278pp*

Mark D. Thompson
**A Sure Ground on which to Stand**
*The Relation of Authority and Interpretive Method in
Luther's Approach to Scripture*
The best interpreter of Luther is Luther himself. Unfortunately many
modern studies have superimposed contemporary agendas upon this
sixteenth-century Reformer's writings. This fresh study examines Luther's
own words to find an explanation for his robust confidence in the
Scriptures, a confidence that generated the famous 'stand' at Worms in
1521.
*2004 / ISBN 1-84227-145-8 / xvi + 322pp*

Graham Tomlin
**The Power of the Cross**
*Theology and the Death of Christ in Paul, Luther and Pascal*
This book explores the theology of the cross in St Paul, Luther and Pascal.
It offers new perspectives on the theology of each, and some implications
for the nature of power, apologetics, theology and church life in a
postmodern context.
*1999 / ISBN 0-85364-984-7 / xiv + 344pp*

Graham J. Watts
**Revelation and the Spirit**
*A Comparative Study of the Relationship between the Doctrine of
Revelation and Pneumatology in the Theology of Eberhard Jüngel and of
Wolfhart Pannenberg*
The relationship between revelation and pneumatology is relatively unex-
plored. This approach offers a fresh angle on two important twentieth cen-
tury theologians and raises pneumatological questions which are theologi-
cally crucial and relevant to mission in a post modern culture.
*2004 / ISBN 1-84227-104-0 / xxii + 232pp*

Nigel G. Wright
**Disavowing Constantine**
*Mission, Church and the Social Order in the Theologies of*
*John Howard Yoder and Jürgen Moltmann*
This book is a timely restatement of a radical theology of church and state
in the Anabaptist and Baptist tradition. Dr Wright constructs his argument
in dialogue and debate with Yoder and Moltmann, major contributors to a
free church perspective.
*2000 / ISBN 0-85364-978-2 / xvi + 252pp*

**The Paternoster Press**
PO Box 300,
Carlisle,
Cumbria CA3 0QS,
United Kingdom
Web: www.paternoster-publishing.com

May 2004